Jonathan Edwards

A careful and strict enquiry into freedom of will

Jonathan Edwards

A careful and strict enquiry into freedom of will

ISBN/EAN: 9783742840677

Manufactured in Europe, USA, Canada, Australia, Japa

Cover: Foto ©Andreas Hilbeck / pixelio.de

Manufactured and distributed by brebook publishing software
(www.brebook.com)

Jonathan Edwards

A careful and strict enquiry into freedom of will

A
CAREFUL and STRICT
ENQUIRY
INTO THE
MODERN PREVAILING NOTIONS
OF THAT
FREEDOM of WILL,
WHICH IS SUPPOSED TO BE ESSENTIAL
TO
MORAL AGENCY, VIRTUE and VICE,
REWARD and PUNISHMENT, PRAISE
and BLAME.

By JONATHAN EDWARDS, A. M.

Rom. ix. 16. *It is not of him that willeth—*

The FIFTH EDITION.

LONDON:
Printed for J. MURGATROYD, No 72. Chiſwell-Street;
Sold alſo by M BINNS, Leeds.
MDCCXC.

THE

PREFACE.

MANY find much fault with the calling professing Christians, that differ one from another in some matters of opinion, by distinct *names*; especially calling them by the names of particular men, who have distinguished themselves as maintainers and promoters of those opinions; as the calling some professing Christians *Arminians*, from *Arminius*; others *Arians*, from *Arius*; others *Socinians*, from *Socinus*, and the like. They think it unjust in itself; as it seems to suppose and suggest, that the persons marked out by these names, received those doctrines which they entertain, out of regard *to*, and reliance *on* those men after whom they are named; as though they made them their rule; in the same manner, as the followers of CHRIST are called *Christians*, after his name, whom they regard and depend upon, as their great Head and Rule. Whereas, this is an unjust and groundless imputation on those that go under the fore-mentioned denominations. Thus (say they) there is not the least ground to ſuppoſe, that the chief Divines, who embrace the ſcheme of doctrine which is, by many, called *Arminianiſm*, believe it the more, becauſe *Arminius* believed it: and that there is no reaſon to think any other, than that they ſincerely and impartially ſtudy the holy Scriptures, and enquire after the mind of Chriſt, with as much judgment and ſincerity, as any of thoſe that call them by theſe names; that they ſeek after truth, and are not careful whether they think exactly as *Arminius* did; yea, that, in ſome things, they actually differ from him. This practice is alſo eſteemed actually injurious on this account, that it is ſuppoſed naturally to lead the multitude to imagine the difference between perſons thus named and others, to be greater than it is; yea, as tho' it were ſo great, that they muſt be, as it were, another ſpecies of beings. And they object againſt it as ariſing from an uncharitable, narrow, contracted ſpirit; which, they ſay, commonly inclines perſons to confine all that is good to themſelves, and their own party, and to make a wide diſtinction between themſelves and others, and ſtigmatize thoſe that differ from them with odious names. They ſay, moreover, that the keeping up ſuch a diſtinction of names has a direct tendency to uphold diſtance and diſaffection, and keep alive mutual hatred among Chriſtians, who ought all to be united in friendſhip and charity, however they cannot, in all things, think alike.

I CONFESS,

I CONFESS, these things are very plausible. And I will not deny, that there are some unhappy consequences of this distinction of names, and that men's infirmities and evil dispositions often make an ill improvement of it. But yet, I humbly conceive, these objections are carried far beyond reason. The generality of mankind are disposed enough, and a great deal too much, to uncharitableness, and to be censorious and bitter towards those that differ from them in religious opinions: which evil temper of mind will take occasion to exert itself from many things in themselves innocent, useful and necessary. But yet there is no necessity to suppose, that the thus distinguishing persons of different opinions by different names, arises mainly from an uncharitable spirit. It may arise from the disposition there is in mankind (whom God has distinguished with an ability and inclination for speech) to improve the benefit of language, in the proper use and design of names, given to things which they have often occasion to speak of, or signify their minds about; which is to enable them to express their ideas with ease and expedition, without being incumbered with an obscure and difficult circumlocution. And the thus distinguishing of persons of different opinions in religious matters may not imply, nor infer, any more than that there is a difference, and that the difference is such as we find we have often occasion to take notice of, and make mention of. That which we have frequent occaſion to ſpeak of (whatever it be, that gives the occaſion) this wants a name: and it is always a defect in language, in ſuch caſes, to be obliged to make uſe of a deſcription, inſtead of a name. Thus we have often occaſion to ſpeak of thoſe who are the deſcendants of the ancient inhabitants of *France*, who were ſubjects or heads of the government of that land, and ſpake the language peculiar to it; in diſtinction from the deſcendants of the inhabitants of *Spain*, who belonged to that community, and ſpake the language of that country. And therefore we find the great need of diſtinct names to ſignify theſe different ſorts of people, and the great convenience of thoſe diſtinguiſhing words, *French* and *Spaniards*; by which the ſignification of our minds is quick and eaſy, and our ſpeech is delivered from the burden of a continual reiteration of diffuſe deſcriptions, with which it muſt otherwiſe be embarraſſed.

THAT the difference of the opinions of thoſe, who in their general ſcheme of divinity agree with theſe two noted men, *Calvin* and *Arminius*, is a thing there is often occaſion to ſpeak of, is what the practice of the latter itſelf confeſſes; who are often, in their diſcourſes and writings, taking notice of the ſuppoſed abſurd and pernicious opinions of the former ſort. And therefore the making uſe of different names in this caſe cannot reaſonably be objected againſt, or

con-

condemned, as a thing which muſt come from ſo bad a cauſe as they aſſign. It is eaſy to be accounted for, without ſuppoſing it to ariſe from any other ſource, than the exigence and natural tendency of the ſtate of things; conſidering the faculty and diſpoſition God has given to mankind, to expreſs things which they have frequent occaſion to mention, by certain diſtinguiſhing names. It is an effect that is ſimilar to what we ſee ariſe, in innumerable caſes which are parallel, where the cauſe is not at all blame-worthy.

Nevertheless, at firſt, I had thoughts of carefully avoiding the uſe of the appellation, *Arminian*, in this Treatiſe. But I ſoon found I ſhould be put to great difficulty by it; and that my Diſcourſe would be ſo encumbered with an often repeated circumlocution, inſtead of a name, which would expreſs the thing intended, as well and better, that I altered my purpoſe. And therefore I muſt aſk the excuſe of ſuch as are apt to be offended with things of this nature, that I have ſo freely uſed the term *Arminian* in the following Diſcourſe. I profeſs it to be without any deſign, to ſtigmatize perſons of any ſort with a name of reproach, or at all to make them appear more odious. If, when I had occaſion to ſpeak of thoſe Divines who are commonly called by this name, I had, inſtead of ſtyling them *Arminians*, called them *theſe men*, as Dr. *Whitby* does *Calviniſtic* Divines; it probably would not have been taken any better, or thought to ſhew a better temper, or more good manners. I have done as I would be done by, in this matter. However the term *Calviniſtic* is, in theſe days, among moſt, a term of greater reproach than the term *Arminian*; yet I ſhould not take it at all amiſs, to be called a *Calviniſt*, for diſtinction's ſake: though I utterly diſclaim a dependence on *Calvin*, or believing the doctrines which I hold, becauſe he believed and taught them; and cannot juſtly be charged with believing in every thing juſt as he taught.

But, leſt I ſhould really be an occaſion of injury to ſome perſon, I would here give notice, that though I generally ſpeak of that doctrine, concerning Free-will and moral Agency, which I oppoſe, as an *Arminian* doctrine; yet I would not be underſtood, as aſſerting, that every Divine or Author, whom I have occaſion to mention as maintaining that doctrine, was properly an *Arminian*, or one of that ſort which is commonly called by that name. Some of them went far beyond the *Arminians*: and I would by no means charge *Arminians* in general with all the corrupt doctrine, which theſe maintained. Thus, for inſtance, it would be very injurious, if I ſhould rank *Arminian* Divines, in general, with ſuch Authors as Mr. *Chubb*. I doubt not, many of them have ſome of his doctrines in abhorrence: though he agrees, for the moſt part, with *Arminians*, in his notion of the Freedom

Freedom of the Will. And, on the other hand, though I suppose this notion to be a leading article in the *Arminian* scheme, that which, if pursued in its consequences, will truly infer, or naturally lead to all the rest; yet I do not charge all that have held this doctrine, with being *Arminians*. For whatever may be the consequences of the doctrine really, yet some that hold this doctrine, may not own nor see these consequences; and it would be unjust, in many instances, to charge every Author with believing and maintaining all the real consequences of his avowed doctrines. And I desire it may be particularly noted, that though I have occasion, in the following Discourse, often to mention the Author of the book, entitled, *An Essay on the Freedom of the Will, in God and the Creature*, as holding that notion of Freedom of Will, which I oppose; yet I do not mean to call him an *Arminian*: however, in that doctrine he agrees with *Arminians*, and departs from the current and general opinion of *Calvinists*. If the Author of that Essay be the same as it is commonly ascribed to, he, doubtless was not one that ought to bear that name. But however good a Divine he was in many respects, yet that particular *Arminian* doctrine which he maintained, is never the better for being held by such an one: nor is there less need of opposing it on that account; but rather is there the more need of it; as it will be likely to have the more pernicious influence, for being taught by a Divine a Divine of his name and character; supposing the doctrine to be wrong, and in itself to be of an ill tendency.

I HAVE nothing further to say by way of preface, but only to bespeak the Reader's candor, and calm attention to what I have written. The subject is of such importance, as to *demand* attention, and the most thorough consideration. Of all kinds of knowledge that we can ever obtain, the knowledge of God, and the knowledge of ourselves, are the most important. As religion is the great business, for which we are created, and on which our happiness depends; and as religion consists in an intercourse between ourselves and our Maker; and so has its foundation in God's nature and ours, and in the relation that God and we stand in to each other; therefore a true knowledge of both must be needful, in order to true religion. But the knowledge of ourselves consists chiefly in right apprehensions concerning those two chief faculties of our nature, the *understanding* and *will*. Both are very important: yet the science of the latter must be confessed to be of greatest moment; inasmuch as all virtue and religion have their seat more immediately in the will, consisting more especially in right acts and habits of this faculty. And the grand question about the Freedom of the Will, is the main point that belongs to the science of the Will. Therefore, I say, the importance of this subject greatly *demands* the attention

of

of Christians, and especially of Divines. But as to my manner of handling the subject, I will be far from presuming to say, that it is such as *demands* the attention of the Reader to what I have written. I am ready to own, that in this matter I depend on the Reader's *courtesy*. But only thus far I may have some colour for putting in a *claim*; that if the Reader be disposed to pass his censure on what I have written, I may be fully and patiently heard, and well attended to, before I am condemned. However, this is what I would humbly *ask* of my Readers; together with the prayers of all sincere lovers of truth, that I may have much of that spirit which Christ promised his disciples, which guides into all truth; and that the blessed and powerful influences of this Spirit would make truth victorious in the world.

A GENERAL

A

GENERAL TABLE

OF THE

CONTENTS.

PART I.

Wherein are explained various *Terms* and *Things* belonging to the ſubject of the enſuing diſcourſe.

PART

The CONTENTS.

PART II.

Wherein it is considered, whether there is, or can be, any such sort of FREEDOM OF WILL, as that wherein *Arminians* place the Essence of the Liberty of all moral Agents; and whether any such thing ever *was*, or *can be* conceived of.

And

PART III.

Wherein is enquired, whether any ſuch Liberty of Will as *Arminians* hold, be neceſſary to moral Agency, Virtue and Vice, Praiſe and Diſpraiſe, &c.

PART IV.

Wherein the chief *Grounds* of the Reaſonings of *Arminians*, in Support and Defence of their Notions of Liberty, moral Agency, &c. and againſt the oppoſite Doctrine, are conſidered.

SECT.

The

The CONCLUSION.

Just published, Price 2s. sewed,

AN

HUMBLE INQUIRY

INTO THE

RULES OF THE WORD OF GOD:

By the late JONATHAN EDWARDS, A. M.

May be had of J. MURGATROYD: and all the Author's other Works.

PART I.

WHEREIN ARE EXPLAINED AND STATED VARIOUS *TERMS* AND *THINGS* BELONGING TO THE SUBJECT OF THE ENSUING DISCOURSE.

SECTION I.

Concerning the Nature of the Will.

IT may possibly be thought, that there is no great need of going about to define or describe the *Will*; this word being generally as well understood as any other words we can use to explain it; and so perhaps it would be, had not philosophers, metaphysicians, and polemic divines brought the matter into obscurity by the things they have said of it. But since it is so, I think it may be of some use, and will tend to the greater clearness in the following discourse, to say a few things concerning it.

AND therefore I observe, that the *Will* (without any metaphysical refining) is plainly, *That by which the mind chuses any thing*. The faculty of the *Will* is that faculty, or power, or principle of mind by which it is capable of *chusing*: an act of the *Will* is the same as an act of *chusing* or *choice*.

If any think it is a more perfect definition of the Will, to ſay, that it is that by which the ſoul either *chuſes* or *refuſes*; I am content with it: though I think that it is enough to ſay, It is that by which the ſoul chuſes: for in every act of Will whatſoever, the mind chuſes one thing rather than another; it chuſes ſomething rather than the contrary, or rather than the want or non-exiſtence of that thing. So in every act of refuſal, the mind chuſes the abſence of the thing refuſed; the poſitive and the negative are ſet before the mind for its choice, and it chuſes the negative; and the mind's making its choice in that caſe is properly the act of the Will: the Will's determining between the two is a voluntary determining; but that is the ſame thing as making a choice. So that whatever names we call the act of the Will by *chuſing*, *refuſing*, *approving*, *diſapproving*, *liking*, *diſliking*, *embracing*, *rejecting*, *determining*, *directing*, *commanding*, *forbidding*, *inclining* or being *averſe*, a *being pleaſed* or *diſpleaſed with*; all may be reduced to this of *chuſing*. For the ſoul to act *voluntarily*, is evermore to act *electively*.

Mr. *Locke** ſays, "The Will ſignifies nothing but a power or ability to *prefer* or *chuſe*." And in the foregoing page ſays, "The word *preferring* ſeems beſt to expreſs the act of volition;" But adds, that "it does not preciſely; for (ſays he) though a man would prefer flying to walking, yet who can ſay he ever wills it?" But the inſtance he mentions does not prove that there is any thing elſe in *willing*, but merely *preferring*; for it ſhould be conſidered what is the next and immediate object of the Will, with reſpect to a man's walking, or any other external action; which is not being

* Human Underſtanding. Edit. 7. vol. i. p. 197.

being removed from one place to another; on the earth, or through the air; these are remoter objects of preference; but such or such an immediate exertion of himself. The thing nextly chosen or preferred when a man wills to walk, is not his being removed to such a place where he would be, but such an exertion and motion of his legs and feet, &c. in order to it. And his willing such an alteration in his body in the present moment, is nothing else but his chusing or preferring such an alteration in his body at such a moment, or his liking it better than the forbearance of it. And God has so made and established the human nature, the soul being united to a body in proper state, that the soul preferring or chusing such an immediate exertion or alteration of the body, such an alteration instantaneously follows. There is nothing else in the actions of my mind, that I am conscious of while I walk, but only my preferring or chusing, through successive moments, that there should be such alterations of my external sensations and motions; together with a concurring habitual expectation that it will be so; having ever found by experience, that on such an immediate preference, such sensations and motions do actually instantaneously, and constantly arise. But it is not so in the case of flying: though a man may be said remotely to chuse or prefer flying; yet he does not chuse or prefer, incline to or desire, under circumstances in view, any immediate exertion of the members of his body in order to it; because he has no expectation that he should obtain the desired end by any such exertion; and he does not prefer or incline to any bodily exertion or effort under this apprehended circumstance, of its being wholly in vain. So that if we carefully distinguish the proper objects of the several acts of the Will, it will not appear by this, and ſuch-like inſtances, that there is any difference between *volition* and *preference*; or that a man's chuſing, liking beſt, or being beſt pleaſed with a thing, are not the ſame with his willing that thing; as they ſeem to be according to thoſe general and more natural motions of men, according to which language is formed. Thus an act of the Will is commonly expreſſed by *its pleaſing a man* to do thus or thus; and a man doing as he *wills*, and doing as he *pleaſes*, are the ſame thing in common ſpeech.

Mr. *Locke** ſays, "The Will is perfectly diſtinguiſhed from Deſire; which in the very ſame action may have a quite contrary tendency from that which our Wills ſet us upon. A man (ſays he) whom I cannot deny, may oblige me to uſe perſuaſions to another, which, at the ſame time I am ſpeaking, I may wiſh may not prevail on him. In this caſe it is plain the Will and Deſire run counter." I do not ſuppoſe, that *Will* and *Deſire* are words of preciſely the ſame ſignification; *Will* ſeems to be a word of a more general ſignification, extending to things preſent and abſent. *Deſire* reſpects ſomething abſent. I may prefer my preſent ſituation and poſture, ſuppoſe ſitting ſtill, or having my eyes open, and ſo may will it. But yet I cannot think they are ſo entirely diſtinct, that they can ever be properly ſaid to run counter. A man never, in any inſtance, wills any thing contrary to his Deſires, or deſires any thing contrary to his Will. The forementioned inſtance, which Mr. *Locke* produces, does not prove that he ever does. He may, on ſome conſideration or other, will to utter ſpeeches which have a tendency to perſuade another, and ſtill may deſire that they may not perſuade him: but yet his Will and Deſire

* Hum. Und. vol. i. p. 203, 204.

Desire do not run counter at all: the thing which he wills, the very same he desires; and he does not will a thing, and desire the contrary in any particular. In this instance, it is not carefully observed, what is the thing willed, and what is the thing desired: if it were, it would be found that Will and Desire do not clash in the least. The thing willed, on some consideration, is to utter such words; and certainly, the same consideration so influences him, that he does not desire the contrary; all things considered, he chuses to utter such words, and does not desire not to utter them. And so as to the thing which Mr. *Locke* speaks of as desired, *viz.* That the words, though they tend to persuade, should not be effectual to that end, his Will is not contrary to this; he does not will that they should be effectual, but rather wills that they should not, as he desires. In order to prove that the will and desire may run counter, it should be shewn that they may be contrary one to the other in the same thing, or with respect to the very same object of Will or Desire: but here the objects are two; and in each, taken by themselves, the Will and Desire agree. And it is no wonder that they should not agree in different things, however little distinguished they are in their nature. The Will may not agree with the Will, nor Desire agree with Desire, in different things. As in this very instance which Mr. *Locke* mentions, a person may, on some consideration, desire to use persuasions, and at the same time may desire they may not prevail; but yet no body will say, that *Desire* runs counter to *Desire*; or that this proves that *Desire* is perfectly a distinct thing from *Desire*.—The like might be observed of the other instance Mr. *Locke* produces, of a man's desiring to be eased of pain, &c.

But not to dwell any longer on this, whether *Desire* and *Will*, and whether *Preference* and *Volition* be precisely the same things or no; yet, I trust it will be allowed by all, that in every act of Will there is an act of choice; that in every volition there is a preference, or a prevailing inclination of the soul, whereby the soul, at that instance, is out of a state of perfect indifference, with respect to the direct object of the volition. So that in every act, or going forth of the Will, there is some preponderation of the mind or inclination, one way rather than another; and the soul had rather *have* or *do* one thing than another, or than not to have or do that thing; and that there, where there is absolutely no preferring or chusing, but a perfect continuing equilibrium, there is no volition.

SECTION II.

Concerning the Determination *of the Will.*

By *determining the Will*, if the phrase be used with any meaning, must be intended, *causing that the Act of the Will or Choice should be thus, and not otherwise:* and the Will is said to be determined, when, in consequence of some action, or influence, its choice is directed to, and fixed upon a particular object. As when we speak of the Determination of motion, we mean causing the motion of the body to be such a way, or in such a direction, rather than another.

To talk of the Determination of the Will, supposes an effect, which must have a cause. If the Will be determined, there is a determiner. This must be supposed to be intended even by them that say, the Will determines itself. If it be so, the Will

Will is both Determiner and determined; it is a cause that acts and produces effects upon itself, and is the object of its own influence and action.

WITH respect to that grand inquiry, *What determines the Will*, it would be very tedious and unnecessary at present to enumerate and examine all the various opinions which have been advanced concerning this matter; nor is it needful that I should enter into a particular disquisition of all points debated in disputes on that question, *Whether the Will always follows the last dictate of the understanding*. It is sufficient to my present purpose to say,—*It is that motive, which, as it stands in the view of the mind, is the strongest that determines the Will*—but it may be necessary that I should a little explain my meaning in this.

BY *Motive*, I mean the whole of that which moves, excites or invites the mind to volition, whether that be one thing singly, or many things conjunctly. Many particular things may concur and unite their strength to induce the mind; and when it is so, all together are as it were one complex motive. And when I speak of the *strongest motive*, I have respect to the strength of the whole that operates to induce to a particular act of volition, whether that be the strength of one thing alone, or of many together.

WHATEVER is a motive, in this sense, must be something that is *extant in the view or apprehension of the understanding*, or perceiving faculty. Nothing can induce or invite the mind to will or act any thing, any further than it is perceived, or is some way or other in the mind's view; for what is wholly unperceived, and perfectly out of the mind's view, cannot effect the mind at all. It is most evident, that nothing is in the mind, or reaches it, or takes any hold of it, any otherwise than as it is perceived or thought of.

And I think it must also be allowed by all, that every thing that is properly called a motive, excitement or inducement to a perceiving willing agent, has some sort and degree of *tendency*, or *advantage* to move or excite the Will, previous to the effect, or to the act of the Will excited. This previous tendency of the motive is what I call *the strength of the motive.* That motive which has a less degree of previous advantage or tendency to move the Will, or that appears less inviting, as it stands in the view of the mind, is what I call a *weaker motive.* On the contrary, that which appears most inviting, and has, by what appears concerning it to the understanding or apprehension, the greatest degree of previous tendency to excite and induce the choice, is what I call the *strongest motive.* And in this sense, I suppose the Will is always determined by the strongest motive.

Things that exist in the view of the mind have their strength, tendency or advantage to move or excite its Will, from many things appertaining to the nature and circumstances of the *thing viewed*, the nature and circumstances of the *mind that views*, and the degree and manner of its *view*; which it would perhaps be hard to make a perfect enumeration of. But so much I think may be determined in general, without room for controversy, that whatever is perceived or apprehended by an intelligent and voluntary agent, which has the nature and influence of a motive to volition or choice, is considered or viewed *as good*; nor has it any tendency to invite or engage the election of the

the soul in any further degree than it appears such. For to say otherwise, would be to say, that things that appear have a tendency by the appearance they make, to engage the mind to elect them, some other way than by their appearing eligible to it; which is absurd. And therefore it must be true, in some sense, that *the Will always is as the greatest apparent good is.* But only, for the right understanding of this, two things must be well and distinctly observed.

1. It must be observed in what sense I use the term *good*; namely, as of the same import with *agreable*. To appear *good* to the mind, as I use the phrase, is the same as to *appear agreable*, or *seem pleasing* to the mind. Certainly, nothing appears inviting and eligible to the mind, or tending to engage its inclination and choice, considered as *evil* or *disagreable*; nor indeed, as *indifferent*, and neither agreable nor disagreable. But if it tends to draw the inclination, and move the Will, it must be under the notion of that which *suits* the mind. And therefore that must have the greatest tendency to attract and engage it, which, as it stands in the mind's view, suits it best, and pleases it most; and in that sense, is the greatest apparent good: to say otherwise, is little, if any thing, short of a direct and plain contradiction.

The word *good*, in this sense, includes in its signification, the removal or avoiding of evil, or of that which is disagreable and uneasy. It is agreable and pleasing, to avoid what is disagreable and displeasing, and to have uneasiness removed. So that here is included what Mr. *Locke* supposes determines the Will. For when he speaks of uneasiness as determining the Will, he must be understood as supposing that the end or aim which governs

governs in the volition or act of preference, is the avoiding or removal of that uneasiness; and that is the same thing as chusing and seeking what is more easy and agreable.

2. WHEN I say, the Will is as the greatest apparent good is, or (as I have explained it) that volition has always for its object the thing which appears most agreable; it must be carefully observed, to avoid confusion and needless objection, that I speak of the *direct* and *immediate* object of the act of volition; and not some object that the act of Will has not an immediate, but only an indirect and remote respect to. Many acts of volition have some remote relation to an object, that is different from the thing most immediately willed and chosen. Thus, when a drunkard has his liquor before him, and he has to chuse whether to drink it or no; the proper and immediate objects, about which his present volition is conversant, and between which his choice now decides, are his own acts, in drinking the liquor, or letting it alone; and this will certainly be done according to what, in the present view of his mind, taken in the whole of it, is most agreable to him. If he chuses or wills to drink it, and not to let it alone; then this action, as it stands in the view of his mind, with all that belongs to its appearance there, is more agreable and pleasing than letting it alone.

BUT the objects to which this act of volition may relate more remotely, and between which his choice may determine more indirectly, are the present pleasure the man expects by drinking, and the future misery which he judges will be the consequence of it: he may judge that this future misery, when it comes, will be more disagreable and

and unpleasant, than refraining from drinking now would be. But these two things are not the proper objects that the act of volition spoken of is nextly conversant about. For the act of Will spoken of is concerning present drinking or forbearing to drink. If he wills to drink, then drinking is the proper object of the act of his Will; and drinking, on some account or other, now appears most agreable to him, and suits him best. If he chuses to refrain, then refraining is the immediate object of his Will, and is most pleasing to him. If in the choice he makes in the case, he prefers a present pleasure to a future advantage, which he judges will be greater when it comes; then a lesser present pleasure appears more agreable to him than a greater advantage at a distance. If, on the contrary, a future advantage is preferred, then that appears most agreable, and suits him best. And so still the present volition is as the greatest apparent good at present is.

I HAVE rather chosen to express myself thus, *that the Will always is as the greatest apparent good*, or *as what appears most agreable, is*, than to say that the Will *is determined by* the greatest apparent good, or by what seems most agreable; because an appearing most agreable or pleasing to the mind, and the mind's preferring and chusing, seem hardly to be properly and perfectly distinct. If strict propriety of speech be insisted on, it may more properly be said, that the *voluntary action* which is the immediate consequence and fruit of the mind's volition or choice, is *determined* by that which appears most agreable, than the preference or choice itself; but that the act of volition itself is always determined by that in or about the mind's view of the object, which *causes it to appear* most agreable. I say,

I ſay, *in or about the mind's view* of the object, becauſe what has influence to render an object in view agreable, is not only what appears *in* the object viewed, but alſo *the manner* of the view, and *the ſtate and circumſtances* of the mind that views.—Particularly to enumerate all things pertaining to the mind's view of the objects of volition, which have influence in their appearing agreable to the mind, would be a matter of no ſmall difficulty, and might require a treatiſe by itſelf, and is not neceſſary to my preſent purpoſe. I ſhall therefore only mention ſome things in general.

I. ONE thing that makes an object propoſed to choice agreable, is the *apparent nature* and *circumſtances of the object.* And there are various things of this ſort, that have an hand in rendering the object more or leſs agreable; as,

1. THAT which appears in the object, which renders it *beautiful* and pleaſant, or *deformed* and irkſome to the mind; viewing it as it is *in itſelf.*

2. THE apparent degree of pleaſure or trouble *attending* the object, or the *conſequence* of it. Such concomitants and conſequents being viewed as circumſtances of the objects, are to be conſidered as belonging to it, and, as it were, parts of it; as it ſtands in the mind's view, as a propoſed object of choice.

3. THE *apparent ſtate* of the pleaſure or trouble that appears, with reſpect to *diſtance of time*; being either nearer or farther off. It is a thing in itſelf agreable to the mind, to have pleaſure ſpeedily; and diſagreable, to have it delayed: ſo that if there be two equal degrees of pleaſure ſet

in

in the mind's view, and all other things are equal, but only one is beheld as near, and the other far off; the nearer will appear most agreable, and so will be chosen. Because, though the agreableness of the objects be exactly equal, as viewed in themselves, yet not as viewed in their circumstances; one of them having the additional agreableness of the circumstance of nearness.

II. Another thing that contributes to the agreableness of an object of choice, as it stands in the mind's view, is the *manner of the view*. If the object be something which appears connected with future pleasure, not only will the degree of apparent pleasure have influence, but also the manner of the view, especially in two respects.

1. With respect to the degree of *judgment*, or firmness of *assent*, with which the mind judges the pleasure to be future. Because it is more agreable to have a *certain* happiness, than an *uncertain* one; and a pleasure viewed as more probable, all other things being equal, is more agreable to the mind, than that which is viewed as less probable.

2. With respect to the degree of the *idea* of the future pleasure. With regard to things which are the subject of our thoughts, either past, present, or future, we have much more of an idea or apprehension of some things than others; that is, our idea is much more clear, lively and strong. Thus the ideas we have of sensible things by immediate sensation, are usually much more lively than those we have by mere imagination, or by contemplation of them when absent. My idea of the sun, when I look upon it, is more vivid, than when I only think of it. Our idea of the sweet relish of a delicious

a delicious fruit is uſually ſtronger when we taſte it, that when we only imagine it. And ſometimes the idea we have of things by contemplation, are much ſtronger and clearer than at other times. Thus, a man at one time has a much ſtronger idea of the pleaſure which is to be enjoyed in eating ſome ſort of food that he loves, than at another. Now the degree, or ſtrength of the idea or ſenſe that men have of future good or evil, is one thing that has great influence on their minds to excite choice or volition. When of two kinds of future pleaſure, which the mind conſiders of, and are preſented for choice, both are ſuppoſed exactly equal by the judgment, and both equally certain, and all other things are equal but only one of them is what the mind has a far more lively ſenſe of, than of the other; this has the greateſt advantage by far to affect and attract the mind, and move the Will. It is now more agreable to the mind, to take the pleaſure it has a ſtrong and lively ſenſe of, than that which it has only a faint idea of. The view of the former is attended with the ſtrongeſt appetite, and the greateſt uneaſineſs attends the want of it; and it is agreable to the mind to have uneaſineſs removed, and its appetite gratified. And if ſeveral future enjoyments are preſented together, as competitors for the choice of the mind, ſome of them judged to be greater, and others leſs; the mind alſo having a greater ſenſe and more lively idea of the good of ſome of them, and of others a leſs; and ſome are viewed as of greater certainty or probability than others; and thoſe enjoyments that appear moſt agreable in one of theſe reſpects, appear leaſt ſo in others: in this caſe, all other things being equal, the agreableneſs of a propoſed object of choice will be in a degree ſome way compounded of the degree of good ſuppoſed by the judgment,

the

the degree of apparent probability or certainty of that good, and the degree of the view, or ſenſe, or livelineſs of the idea the mind has, of that good; becauſe all together concur to conſtitute the degree in which the object appears at preſent agreable; and accordingly volition will be determined.

I MIGHT further obſerve, the ſtate of the mind that views a propoſed object of choice, is another thing that contributes to the agreableneſs or diſagreableneſs of that object; the particular temper which the mind has by nature, or that has been introduced and eſtabliſhed by education, example, cuſtom, or ſome other means; or the frame or ſtate that the mind is in on a particular occaſion. That object which appears agreable to one, does not ſo to another. And the ſame object does not always appear alike agreable to the ſame perſon, at different times. It is moſt agreable to ſome men, to follow their reaſon; and to others, to follow their appetites: to ſome men it is more agreable to deny a vicious inclination, than to gratify it: others it ſuits beſt to gratify the vileſt appetites. It is more diſagreable to ſome men than others, to counteract a former reſolution. In theſe reſpects, and many others which might be mentioned, different things will be moſt agreable to different perſons; and not only ſo, but to the ſame perſons at different times.

BUT poſſibly it is needleſs and improper, to mention the frame and ſtate of the mind, as a diſtinct ground of the agreableneſs of objects from the other two mentioned before; *viz.* The apparent nature and circumſtances of the objects viewed, and the manner of the view: perhaps if we ſtrictly conſider the matter, the different temper and ſtate of of the mind makes no alteration as to the agreableneſs of objects, any other way, than as it makes the objects themſelves appear differently beautiful or deformed, having apparent pleaſure or pain attending them: and as it occaſions the manner of the view to be different, cauſes the idea of beauty or deformity, pleaſure or uneaſineſs to be more or leſs lively.

However, I think ſo much is certain, that volition, in no one inſtance that can be mentioned, is otherwiſe than the greateſt apparent good is, in the manner which has been explained. The choice of the mind never departs from that which, at that time, and with reſpect to the direct and immediate objects of that deciſion of the mind, appears moſt agreable and pleaſing, all things conſidered. If the immediate objects of the will are a man's own actions, then thoſe actions which appear moſt agreable to him he wills. If it be now moſt agreable to him, all things conſidered, to walk, then he now wills to walk. If it be now, upon the whole of what at preſent appears to him, moſt agreable to ſpeak, then he chuſes to ſpeak: if it ſuits him beſt to keep ſilence, then he chuſes to keep ſilence. There is ſcarcely a plainer and more univerſal dictate of the ſenſe and experience of mankind, than that, when men act voluntarily, and do what they pleaſe, then they do what ſuits them beſt, or what is moſt *agreable to them.* To ſay, that they do what they pleaſe, or what pleaſes them, but yet do not do what is *agreable* to them, is the ſame thing as to ſay, they do what they pleaſe, but do not act their pleaſure; and that is to ſay, that they do what they pleaſe, and yet do not do what they pleaſe.

IT

It appears from these things, that in some sense, *the Will always follows the last dictate of the understanding*. But then the *understanding* must be taken in a large sense, as including the whole faculty of perception or apprehension, and not meerly what is called *reason* or *judgment*. If by the dictate of the understanding is meant what reason declares to be best or most for the person's happiness, taking in the whole of its duration, it is not true, that the Will always follows the last dictate of the understanding. Such a dictate of reason is quite a different matter from things appearing now most *agreable*; all things being put together which pertain to the mind's present perceptions, apprehensions or ideas, in any respect. Altho' that dictate of reason when it takes place, is one thing that is put into the scales, and is to be considered as a thing that has concern in the compound influence which moves and induces the Will; and is one thing that is to be considered in estimating the degree of that appearance of good which the Will always follows; either as having its influence added to other things, or subducted from them. When it concurs with other things, then its weight is added to them, as put into the same scale; but when it is against them, it is as a weight in the opposite scale, where it resists the influence of other things: yet its resistance is often overcome by their greater weight, and so the act of the Will is determined in opposition to it.

The things which I have said, may, I hope, serve, in some measure to illustrate and confirm the position I laid down in the beginning of this section, *viz.* That *the Will is always determined by the strongest motive*, or by that view of the mind which has the greatest degree of *previous* tendency to excite volition. But whether I have been so happy as rightly to explain the thing wherein conſiſts the ſtrength of motives, or not, yet my failing in this will not overthrow the poſition itſelf; which carries much of its own evidence with it, and is the thing of chief importance to the purpoſe of the enſuing diſcourſe: And the truth of it, I hope, will appear with great clearneſs, before I have finiſhed what I have to ſay on the ſubject of human liberty.

SECTION III.

Concerning the Meaning of the Terms Neceſſity, Impoſſibility, Inability, &c. *and of* Contingence.

THE words *neceſſary*, *impoſſible*, &c. are abundantly uſed in controverſies about Free-Will and moral agency; and therefore the ſenſe in which they are uſed, ſhould be clearly underſtood.

HERE I might ſay, that a thing is then ſaid to be *neceſſary*, when it muſt be, and cannot be otherwiſe. But this would not properly be a definition of Neceſſity, or an explanation of the word, any more than if I explained the word *muſt*, by there being a Neceſſity. The words *muſt*, *can*, and *cannot*, need explication as much as the words *neceſſary*, and *impoſſible*; excepting that the former are words that children commonly uſe, and know ſomething of the meaning of earlier than the latter.

THE word *neceſſary*, as uſed in common ſpeech, is a relative term; and relates to ſome ſuppoſed oppoſition made to the exiſtence of the thing ſpoken of, which is overcome, or proves in vain to hinder or alter it. That is neceſſary, in the original and proper ſenſe of the word, which is, or will be, notwithſtanding all ſuppoſable oppoſition.

ſition. To ſay, that a thing is neceſſary, is the ſame thing as to ſay, that it is impoſſible, it ſhould not be: But the word *impoſſible* is manifeſtly a relative term, and has reference to ſuppoſed power exerted to bring a thing to paſs, which is inſufficient for the effect; as the word *unable* is relative, and has relation to ability or endeavour which is inſufficient; and as the word *irreſiſtible* is relative, and has always reference to reſiſtance which is made, or may be made to ſome force or power tending to an effect and is ſufficient to withſtand the power, or hinder the effect. The common notion of Neceſſity and impoſſibility implies ſomething that fruſtrates endeavour or deſire.

Here ſeveral things are to be noted.

1. Things are ſaid to be neceſſary in *general*, which are or will be notwithſtanding any ſuppoſable oppoſition *from us or others*, or from whatever quarter. But things are ſaid to be neceſſary *to us*, which are or will be notwithſtanding all oppoſition ſuppoſable in the caſe *from us*. The ſame may be obſerved of the word *impoſſible*, and other ſuch like terms.

2. These terms *neceſſary*, *impoſſible*, *irreſiſtible*, *&c.* do eſpecially belong to controverſy about liberty and moral agency, as uſed in the latter of the two ſenſes now mentioned, *viz.* as neceſſary or impoſſible *to us*, and with relation to any ſuppoſable oppoſition or endeavour *of ours*.

3. As the word *Neceſſity*, in its vulgar and common uſe, is relative, and has always reference to ſome ſuppoſable inſufficient oppoſition; ſo when we ſpeak of any thing as neceſſary *to us*, it is with relation to ſome ſuppoſable oppoſition of *our Wills*,

or ſome voluntary exertion or effort of ours to the contrary. For we do not properly make oppoſition to an event, any otherwiſe than as we *voluntarily* oppoſe it. Things are ſaid to be what muſt be, or *neceſſarily* are, *as to us*, when they are, or will be, though we deſire or endeavour the contrary, or try to prevent or remove their exiſtence: but ſuch oppoſition of ours always either conſiſts in, or implies oppoſition of our wills.

It is manifeſt that all ſuch like words and phraſes, as vulgarly uſed, are uſed and accepted in this manner. A thing is ſaid to be *neceſſary*, when we cannot help it, let us do what we will. So any thing is ſaid to be *impoſſible* to us, when we would do it, or would have it brought to paſs, and endeavour it; or at leaſt may be ſuppoſed to deſire and ſeek it; but all our deſires and endeavours are, or would be vain. And that is ſaid to be *irreſiſtible*, which overcomes all our oppoſition, reſiſtence, and endeavour to the contrary. And we are to be ſaid *unable* to do a thing, when our ſuppoſable deſires and endeavours to do it are inſufficient.

We are accuſtomed in the common uſe of language, to apply and underſtand theſe phraſes in this ſenſe: we grow up with ſuch a habit; which by the daily uſe of theſe terms, in ſuch a ſenſe, from our childhood, becomes fixed and ſettled; ſo that the idea of a relation to a ſuppoſed will, deſire and endeavour of ours, is ſtrongly connected with theſe terms, and naturally excited in our minds, whenever we hear the words uſed. Such ideas, and theſe words, are ſo united and aſſociated, that they unavoidably go together; one ſuggeſts the other, and carries the other with it, and never can be ſeparated as long as we

live;

live. And if we use the words, as terms of art, in another sense, yet, unless we are exceeding circumspect and wary, we shall insensibly slide into the vulgar use of them, and so apply the words in a very inconsistant manner: this habitual connection of ideas will deceive and confound us in our reasonings and discourses, wherein we pretend to use these terms in that manner, as terms of art.

4. It follows from what has been observed, that when these terms *necessary*, *impossible*,, *irresistible*, *unable*, &c. are used in cases wherein no opposition, or insufficient will or endeavour, is supposed, or can be supposed, but the very nature of the supposed case itself excludes, and denies any such opposition, will or endeavour, these terms are then not used in their proper signification, but quite beside their use in common speech. The reason is manifest; namely, that in such cases we cannot use the words with reference to a supposable opposition, will or endeavour. And therefore if any man uses these terms in such cases, he either uses them nonsensically, or in some new sense, diverse from their original and proper meaning. As for instance; if a man should affirm after this manner, That it is necessary for a man, and what must be, that a man should chuse virtue rather than vice, during the time that he prefers virtue to vice; and that it is a thing impossible and irresistible, that it should be otherwise than that he should have this choice, so long as this choice continues; such a man would use the terms *must*, *irresistible*, &c. with perfect insignificance and nonsense, or in some new sense, diverse from their common use; which is with reference, as has been observed, to supposable opposition, unwillingness and resistance; whereas, here, the very supposition excludes and denies any

ſuch thing: for the caſe ſuppoſed is that of being willing and chuſing.

5. IT appears from what has been ſaid, that theſe terms *neceſſary*, *impoſſible*, &c. are often uſed by philoſophers and metaphyſicians in a ſenſe quite diverſe from their common uſe and original ſignification: For they apply them to many caſes in which no oppoſition is ſuppoſed or ſuppoſable. Thus they uſe them with reſpect to God's exiſtence before the creation of the world, when there was no other being but He: ſo with regard to many of the diſpoſitions and acts of the divine Being, ſuch as his loving himſelf, his loving righteouſneſs, hating ſin, &c. So they apply theſe terms to many caſes of the inclinations and actions of created intelligent beings, angels and men; wherein all oppoſition of the Will is ſhut out and denied, in the very ſuppoſition of the caſe.

Metaphyſical or *Philoſophical* Neceſſity is nothing different from their certainty. I ſpeak not now of the certainty of knowledge, but the certainty that is in things themſelves, which is the foundation of the certainty of the knowledge of them; or that wherein lies the ground of the infallibility of the propoſition which affirms them.

WHAT is ſometimes given as the definition of philoſophical Neceſſity, namely, *That by which a thing cannot but be*, or *whereby it cannot be otherwiſe*, fails of being a proper explanation of it, on two accounts; *Firſt*, the words *can*, or *cannot*, need explanation as much as the word *Neceſſity*; and the former may as well be explained by the latter, as the latter by the former. Thus, if any one aſked us what we mean, when we ſay, a thing *cannot but be*, we might explain ourſelves by ſaying,

ing, we mean, it muſt neceſſarily be ſo; as well as explain Neceſſity, by ſaying, it is that by which a thing cannot but be. And *Secondly*, this definition is liable to the fore-mentioned great inconvenience: the words *cannot* or *unable*, are properly relative, and have relation to power exerted, or that may be exerted, in order to the thing ſpoken of; to which, as I have now obſerved, the word *Neceſſity*, as uſed by philoſophers has no reference.

Philosophical Neceſſity is really nothing elſe than the full and fixed connection between the things ſignified by the ſubject and predicate of a propoſition, which affirms ſomething to be true. When there is ſuch a connection, then the thing affirmed in the propoſition is neceſſary, in a philoſophical ſenſe; whether any oppoſition, or contrary effort be ſuppoſed, or ſuppoſable in the caſe, or no. When the ſubject and predicate of the propoſition, which affirms the exiſtence of any thing, either ſubſtance, quality, act or circumſtance, have a full and certain connection, then the exiſtence or being of that thing is ſaid to be neceſſary in a metaphiſical ſenſe. And in this ſenſe I uſe the word *Neceſſity*, in the following diſcourſe, when I endeavour to prove *that Neceſſity is not inconſiſtent with liberty*.

The ſubject and predicate of a propoſition, which affirms exiſtence of ſomething, may have a full, fixed, and certain connection ſeveral ways.

(1.) They may have a full and perfect connection *in and of themſelves*; becauſe it may imply a contradiction, or groſs abſurdity, to ſuppoſe them not connected. Thus many things are neceſſary in their own nature. So the eternal exiſtence of being generally conſidered, is neceſſary *in itſelf* becauſe it would be in itſelf the greateſt abſurdity to deny the exiſtence of being in general, or to ſay there was abſolute and univerſal nothing; and is as it were the ſum of all contradictions; as might be ſhewn, if this were a proper place for it. So God's infinity, and other attributes are neceſſary. So it is neceſſary *in its own nature*, that two and two ſhould be four; and it is neceſſary, that all right lines drawn from the centre of a circle to the circumference ſhould be equal. It is neceſſary, fit and ſuitable, that men ſhould do to others, as they would that they ſhould do to them. So innumerable metaphyſical and mathematical truths are neceſſary *in themſelves:* the ſubject and predicate of the propoſition which affirms them, are perfectly connected *of themſelves.*

(2.) The connection of the ſubject and predicate of a propoſition, which affirms the exiſtence of ſomething, may be fixed and made certain, becauſe the exiſtence of that thing is already come to paſs; and either now is, or has been; and ſo has as it were made ſure of exiſtence. And therefore, the propoſition which affirms preſent and paſt exiſtence of it, may by this means be made certain, and neceſſarily and unalterably true; the paſt event has fixed and decided the matter, as to its exiſtence; and has made it impoſſible but that exiſtence ſhould be truly predicated of it. Thus the exiſtence of whatever is already come to paſs, is now become neceſſary; it is become impoſſible it ſhould be otherwiſe than true, that ſuch a thing has been.

(3.) The ſubject and predicate of a propoſition which affirms ſomething to be, may have a real and certain connection *conſequentially*; and

ſo

ſo the exiſtence of the thing may be conſequentially neceſſary; as it may be ſurely and firmly connected with ſomething elſe, that is neceſſary in one of the former reſpects. As it is either fully and thoroughly connected with that which is abſolutely neceſſary in its own nature, or with ſomething which has already received and made ſure of exiſtence. This Neceſſity lies *in*, or may be explained *by* the connection of two or more propoſitions one with another. Things which are perfectly connected with other things that are neceſſary, are neceſſary themſelves, by a neceſſity of conſequence.

And here it may be obſerved, that all things which are future, or which will hereafter begin to be, which can be ſaid to be neceſſary, are neceſſary only in this laſt way. Their exiſtence is not neceſſary in itſelf; for if ſo, they always would have exiſted. Nor is their exiſtence become neceſſary by being made ſure, by being already come to paſs. Therefore, the only way that any thing that is to come to paſs hereafter, is or can be neceſſary, is by a connection with ſomething that is neceſſary in its own nature, or ſomething that already is, or has been; ſo that the one being ſuppoſed, the other certainly follows. And this alſo is the only way that all things paſt, excepting thoſe which were from eternity, could be neceſſary *before they came to paſs*, or could come to paſs neceſſarily; and therefore the only way in which any effect or event, or any thing whatſoever that ever has had, or will have a beginning, has come into being neceſſarily, or will hereafter neceſſarily exiſt. And therefore *this* is the Neceſſity which eſpecially belongs to controverſies about the acts of the will.

It may be of ſome uſe in theſe controverſies, further to obſerve concerning *metaphyſical* Neceſſity, that

that (agreable to the diſtinction before obſerved of Neceſſity, as *vulgarly* underſtood) things that exiſt may be ſaid to be neceſſary, either with a general or particular Neceſſity. The exiſtence of a thing may be ſaid to be neceſſary with a *general* Neceſſity, when all things whatſoever being conſidered, there is a foundation for certainty of their exiſtence; or when in the moſt general and univerſal view of things, the ſubject and predicate of the propoſition, which affirms its exiſtence, would appear with an infallible connection.

An event, or the exiſtence of a thing, may be ſaid to be neceſſary with a *particular* Neceſſity, or with regard to a particular perſon, thing or time, when nothing that can be taken into conſideration, in or about that perſon, thing or time, alters, the caſe at all, as to the certainty of that event, or the exiſtence of that thing; or can be of any account at all, in determining the infallibility of the connection of the ſubject and predicate in the propoſition which affirms the exiſtence of the thing; ſo that it is all one, as to that perſon, or thing, at leaſt, at that time, as if the exiſtence were neceſſary with a Neceſſity that is moſt *univerſal* and *abſolute*. Thus there are many things that happen to particular perſons, which they have no hand in, and in the exiſtence of which no will of theirs has any concern, at leaſt, at that time; which, whether they are neceſſary or not, with regard to things in general, yet are neceſſary to them, and with regard to any volition of theirs at that time; as they prevent all acts of the will about the affair.——I ſhall have occaſion to apply this obſervation to particular inſtances in the following diſcourſe.—Whether the ſame things that are neceſſary with a *particular* Neceſſity, be not alſo neceſſary with a *general* Neceſſity, may he a matter of of future conſideration. Let that be as it will, it alters not the caſe, as to the uſe of this diſtinction of the kinds of Neceſſity.

These things may be ſufficient for the explaining of the terms *neceſſary* and *Neceſſity*, as terms of art, and as often uſed by metaphyſicians, and controverſial writers in divinity, in a ſenſe diverſe from, and more extenſive than their original meaning in common language, which was before explained.

What has been ſaid to ſhew the meaning of the terms *neceſſary* and *Neceſſity*, my be ſufficient for the explaining of the oppoſite terms, *impoſſible* and *impoſſibility*. For there is no difference, but only the latter are negative, and the former poſitive. *Impoſſibility* is the ſame as *negative Neceſſity*, or a Neceſſity that a thing ſhould not be. And it is uſed as a term of art in a like diverſity from the original and vulgar meaning, with Neceſſity.

The ſame may be obſerved concerning the words *unable* and *Inability* It has been obſerved, that theſe terms, in their original and common uſe, have relation to will and endeavour, as ſuppoſable in the caſe, and as inſufficient for the bringing to paſs the thing willed and endeavoured. But as theſe terms are often uſed by philoſophers and divines, eſpecially writers on controverſies about Free Will, they are uſed in a quite different, and far more extenſive ſenſe, and are applied to many caſes wherein no will or endeavour for the bringing of the thing to paſs, is or can be ſuppoſed, but is actually denied and excluded in the nature of the caſe.

As the words *neceſſary*, *impoſſible*, *unable*, &c. are uſed by polemic writers, in a ſenſe diverſe from

from their common ſignification, the like has happened to the term *contingent.* Any thing is ſaid to be contingent, or to come to paſs by chance or accident, in the original meaning of ſuch words, when its connection with its cauſes or antecedents, according to the eſtabliſhed courſe of things, is not diſcerned; and ſo is what we have no means of the foreſight of. And eſpecially is any thing ſaid to be contingent or accidental with regard to us, when any thing comes to paſs that we are concerned in, as occaſions or ſubjects, without our foreknowledge, and beſide our deſign and ſcope.

But the word *contingent* is abundantly uſed in a very different ſenſe; not for that whoſe connection with the ſeries of things we cannot diſcern, ſo as to foreſee the event, but for ſomething which has abſolutely no previous ground or reaſon, with which its exiſtence has any fixed and certain connection.

SECTION IV.

Of the Diſtinction of natural *and* moral Neceſſity, *and* Inability.

THAT Neceſſity which has been explained, conſiſting in an infallible connection of the things ſignified by the ſubject and predicate of a propoſition, as intelligent beings are the ſubjects of it, is diſtinguiſhed into *moral* and *natural* Neceſſity.

I shall not now ſtand to enquire whether this diſtinction be a proper and perfect diſtinction; but ſhall only explain how theſe two ſorts of Neceſſity are underſtood, as the terms are ſometimes uſed,

uſed, and as they are uſed in the following diſcourſe.

The phraſe, *moral Neceſſity*, is uſed variouſly; ſometimes it is uſed for a Neceſſity of moral obligation. So we ſay, a man is under Neceſſity, when he is under bonds of duty and conſcience, which he cannot be diſcharged from. So the word *Neceſſity* is often uſed for great obligation in point of intereſt. Sometimes by moral Neceſſity is meant that apparent connection of things, which is the ground of *moral evidence*; and ſo is diſtinguiſhed from *abſolute Neceſſity*, or that ſure connection of things, that is a foundation for *infallible certainty*. In this ſenſe, moral Neceſſity ſignifies much the ſame as that high degree of probability, which is ordinarily ſufficient to ſatisfy, and be relied upon by mankind, in their conduct and behaviour in the world, as they would conſult their own ſafety and intereſt, and treat others properly as members of ſociety. And ſometimes by moral Neceſſity is meant that Neceſſity of connection and conſequence, which ariſes from ſuch *moral cauſes*, as the ſtrength of inclination, or motives, and the connection which there is in many caſes between theſe, and ſuch certain volitions and actions. And it is in this ſenſe, that I uſe the phraſe, *moral Neceſſity*, in the following diſcourſe.

By *natural Neceſſity*, as applied to men, I mean ſuch Neceſſity as men are under through the force of natural cauſes; as diſtinguiſhed from what are called moral cauſes, ſuch as habits and diſpoſitions of the heart, and moral motives and inducements. Thus men placed in certain circumſtances, are the ſubjects of particular ſenſations by Neceſſity; they feel pain when their bodies are wounded; they ſee the objects preſented before

them

them in a clear light, when their eyes are opened: ſo they aſſent to the truth of certain propoſitions, as ſoon as the terms are underſtood; as that two and two make four, that black is not white, that two parallel lines can never croſs one another; ſo by a natural Neceſſity mens' bodies move downwards, when there is nothing to ſupport them.

But here ſeveral things may be noted concerning theſe two kinds of Neceſſity.

1. Moral Neceſſity may be as abſolute, as natural Neceſſity. That is, the effect may be as perfectly connected with its moral cauſe, as a natural neceſſary effect is with its natural cauſe. Whether the Will in every caſe is neceſſarily determined by the ſtrongeſt motive, or whether the Will ever makes any reſiſtance to ſuch a motive, or can ever oppoſe the ſtrongeſt preſent inclination, or not; if that matter ſhould be controverted, yet I ſuppoſe none will deny, but that, in ſome caſes, a previous bias and inclination, or the motive preſented, may be ſo powerful, that the act of the Will may be certainly and indiſſolubly connected therewith. When motives or previous bias are very ſtrong, all will allow that there is ſome difficulty in going againſt them. And if they were yet ſtronger, the difficulty would be ſtill greater. And therefore, if more were ſtill added to their ſtrength, to a certain degree, it would make the difficulty ſo great, that it would be wholly impoſſible to ſurmount it; for this plain reaſon, becauſe whatever power men may be ſuppoſed to have to ſurmount difficulties, yet that power is not infinite; and ſo goes not beyond certain limits. If a man can ſurmount ten degrees of difficulty of this kind with twenty degrees of ſtrength, becauſe the degrees of ſtrength are beyond the degrees of difficulty: yet if the difficulty

difficulty be increaſed to thirty, or an hundred or a thouſand degrees, and his ſtrength not alſo increaſed, his ſtrength will be wholly inſufficient to ſurmount the difficulty. As therefore it muſt be allowed, that there may be ſuch a thing as a *ſure* and *perfect* connection between moral cauſes and effects; ſo this only is what I call by the name of *moral Neceſſity*.

2. When I uſe this diſtinction of *moral* and *natural Neceſſity*, I would not be underſtood to ſuppoſe, that if any thing comes to paſs by the former kind of Neceſſity, the *nature* of things is not concerned in it, as well as in the latter. I do not mean to determine, that when a *moral* habit or motive is ſo ſtrong, that the act of the Will infallibly follows, this is not owing to the *nature of things*. But theſe are the names that theſe two kinds of Neceſſity have uſually been called by; and they muſt be diſtinguiſhed by ſome names or other; for there is a diſtinction or difference between them, that is very important in its conſequences. Which difference does not lie ſo much in the nature of the *connection*, as in the two terms *connected*. The cauſe with which the effect is connected, is a particular kind; *viz.* that which is of a moral nature; either ſome previous habitual diſpoſition, or ſome motive exhibited to the underſtanding. And the effect is alſo of a particular kind; being likewiſe of a moral nature; conſiſting in ſome inclination or volition of the ſoul or voluntary action.

I suppose, that neceſſity which is called *natural* in diſtinction from *moral* neceſſity, is ſo called, becauſe *meer nature*, as the word is vulgarly uſed, is concerned, without any thing of *choice*. The word *nature* is often uſed in oppoſition to *choice*; not

not becauſe nature has indeed never any hand in our choice; but this probably comes to paſs by means that we firſt get our notion of nature from that diſcernible and obvious courſe of events, which we obſerve in many things that our choice has no concern in; and eſpecially in the material world; which, in very many parts of it, we eaſily perceive to be in a ſettled courſe; the ſtated order and manner of ſucceſſion being very apparent. But where we do not readily diſcern the rule and connection, (though there be a connection, according to an eſtabliſhed law, truly taking place) we ſignify the manner of event by ſome other name. Even in many things which are ſeen in the material and inanimate world, which do not diſcernibly and obviouſly come to paſs according to any ſettled courſe, men do not call the manner of the event by the name of *nature*, but by ſuch names as *accident*, *chance*, *contingent*, &c. So men make a diſtinction between nature and choice; as though they were compleatly and univerſally diſtinct. Whereas, I ſuppoſe none will deny but that choice, *in many caſes*, ariſes from nature, as truly as other events. But the dependence and connection between acts of volition or choice, and their cauſes; according to eſtabliſhed laws, is not ſo ſenſible and obvious. And we obſerve that choice is as it were a new principle of motion and action, different from that eſtabliſhed law and order of things which is moſt obvious, that is ſeen eſpecially in corporeal and ſenſible things; and alſo the choice often interpoſes, interrupts and alters the chain of events in theſe external objects, and cauſes them to proceed otherwiſe than they would do, if let alone, and left to go on according to the laws of motion among themſelves. Hence it is ſpoken of as if it were a principle of motion entirely diſtinct from nature, and properly ſet in op-

poſition

poſition to it. Names being commonly given to things, according to what is moſt obvious, and is ſuggeſted by what appears to the ſenſes without reflection and reſearch.

3. It muſt be obſerved, that in what has been explained, as ſignified by the name of *moral Neceſſity*, the word *Neceſſity* is not uſed according to the original deſign and meaning of the word: for, as as was obſerved before, ſuch terms, *neceſſary*, *impoſſible*, *irreſiſtible*, &c. in common ſpeech, and their moſt proper ſenſe, are always relative; having reference to ſome ſuppoſable voluntary oppoſition or endeavour, that is inſufficient. But no ſuch oppoſition, or contrary will and endeavour, is ſuppoſable in the caſe of moral Neceſſity; which is a certainty of the inclination and will itſelf; which does not admit of the ſuppoſition of a will to oppoſe and reſiſt it. For it is abſurd, to ſuppoſe the ſame individual will to oppoſe itſelf, in its preſent act; or the preſent choice to be oppoſite to, and reſiſting preſent choice: as abſurd as it is to talk of two contrary motions, in the ſame moving body, at the ſame time. And therefore the very caſe ſuppoſed never admits of any trial, whether an oppoſing or reſiſting will can overcome this Neceſſity.

What has been ſaid of natural and moral Neceſſity, may ſerve to explain what is intended by natural and moral *Inability*. We are ſaid to be *naturally* unable to do a thing, when we cannot do it if we will, becauſe what is moſt commonly called *nature* do not allow of it, or becauſe of ſome impeding defect or obſtacle that is extrinſic to the will; either in the faculty of underſtanding, conſtitution of body, or external objects. *Moral* Inability conſiſts not in any of theſe things; but either in the want of inclination; or the ſtrength of a contrary inclination; or the want of ſufficient motives in view, to induce and excite the act of the will, or the ſtrength of apparent motives to the contrary. Or both theſe may be reſolved into one; and it may be ſaid in one word, that moral Inability conſiſts in the oppoſition or want of inclination. For when a perſon is unable to will or chuſe ſuch a thing, through a defect of motives, or prevalence of contrary motives, it is the ſame thing as his being unable through the want of an inclination, or the prevalence of a contrary inclination, in ſuch circumſtances, and under the influence of ſuch views.

To give ſome inſtance of this *moral Inability.*—A woman of great honour and chaſtity may have a moral Inability to proſtitute herſelf to her ſlave. A child of great love and duty to his parents, may be unable to be willing to kill his father. A very laſcivious man, in caſe of certain opportunities and temptations, and in the abſence of ſuch and ſuch reſtraints, may be unable to forbear gratifying his luſt. A drunkard, under ſuch and ſuch circumſtances, may be unable to forbear taking of ſtrong drink. A very malicious man may be unable to exert benevolent acts to an enemy, or to deſire his proſperity: yea, ſome may be ſo under the power of a vile diſpoſition, that they may be unable to love thoſe who are moſt worthy of their eſteem and affection. A ſtrong habit of virtue, and great degree of holineſs may cauſe a moral Inability to love wickneſs in general, may render a man unable to take complacence in wicked perſons or things: or to chuſe a wicked life, and prefer it to a virtuous life. And on the other hand, a great degree of habitual wickedneſs may lay a man under an Inability to love and chuſe holineſs; and render him utterly

utterly unable to love an infinitely holy Being, or to chuſe and cleave to him as his chief good.

Here it may be of uſe to obſerve this diſtinction of moral Inability, *viz* of that which is *general and habitual*, and that which is *particular and occaſional*. By a *general and habitual* moral Inability, I mean an Inability in the heart to all exerciſes or acts of will of that nature or kind, through a fixed and habitual inclination, or an habitual and ſtated defect, or want of a certain kind of inclination. Thus a very ill-natured man may be unable to exert ſuch acts of benevolence, as another, who is full of good nature, commonly exerts; and a man, whoſe heart is habitually void of gratitude, may be unable to exert ſuch and ſuch grateful acts, through that ſtated defect of a grateful inclination. *By particular and occaſional* moral Inability, I mean an Inability of the will or heart to a particular act, through the ſtrength or defect of preſent motives, or of inducements preſented to the view of the underſtanding, *on this occaſion*.——If it be ſo, that the will is always determined by the ſtrongeſt motive, then it muſt always have an Inability, in this latter ſenſe, to act otherwiſe than it does; it not being poſſible, in any caſe, that the will ſhould, at preſent, go againſt the motive which has now, all things conſidered, the greateſt ſtrength and advantage to excite and induce it.——The former of theſe kinds of moral Inability, conſiſting in that which is ſtated, habitual and general, is moſt commonly called by the name of Inability; becauſe the word *Inability*, in its moſt proper and original ſignification, has reſpect to ſome *ſtated defect*. And this eſpecially obtains the name of *Inability* alſo upon another account:—I before obſerved, that the word Inability in its original

original and moſt common uſe, is a relative term; and has reſpect to will and endeavour, as ſuppoſable in the caſe, and as inſufficient to bring to paſs the thing deſired and endeavoured. Now there may be more of an appearance and ſhadow of this, with reſpect to the acts which ariſe from a fixed and ſtrong habit, than others that ariſe only from tranſient occaſions and cauſes. Indeed will and endeavour againſt, or diverſe from preſent acts of the will, are in no caſe ſuppoſable, whether thoſe acts be occaſional or habitual; for that would be to ſuppoſe the will, at preſent, to be otherwiſe than, at preſent, it is. But yet there may be will and endeavour againſt *future* acts of the will, or volitions that are likely to take place, as viewed at a diſtance. It is no contradiction, to ſuppoſe that the acts of the will at one time, may be againſt the acts of the will at another time; and there may be deſires and endeavours to prevent or excite future acts of the will; but ſuch deſires and endeavours are, in many caſes, rendered inſufficient and vain, through fixedneſs of habit; when the occaſion returns, the ſtrength of habit overcomes and baffles all ſuch oppoſition. In this reſpect, a man may be in miſerable ſlavery and bondage to a ſtrong habit. But it may be comparatively eaſy to make an alteration with reſpect to ſuch future acts, as are only occaſional and tranſient; becauſe the occaſion or tranſient cauſe, if foreſeen, may often eaſily be prevented or avoided. On this account, the moral Inability that attends fixed habits, eſpecially obtains the name of Inability. And then, as the will may remotely and indirectly reſiſt itſelf, and do it in vain, in the caſe of ſtrong habits; ſo reaſon may reſiſt preſent acts of the will, and its reſiſtance be inſufficient; and this is more commonly the caſe alſo, when the acts ariſe from ſtrong habit.

BUT

BUT it muſt be obſerved concerning moral Inability, in each kind of it, that the word *Inability* is uſed in a ſenſe very diverſe from its original import. The word ſignifies only a natural Inability, in the proper uſe of it; and is applied to ſuch caſes only wherein a preſent will or inclination to the thing, with reſpect to which a perſon is ſaid to be unable, is ſuppoſable. It cannot be truly ſaid, according to the ordinary uſe of language, that a malicious man, let him be never ſo malicious, cannot hold his hand from ſtriking, or that he is not able to ſhew his neighbour kindneſs; or that a drunkard, let his appetite be never ſo ſtrong, cannot keep the cup from his mouth. In the ſtricteſt propriety of ſpeech, a man has a thing in his power, if he has it in his choice, or at his election: and a man cannot be truly ſaid to be unable to do a thing, when he can do it if he will. It is improperly ſaid, that a perſon cannot perform thoſe external actions, which are dependent on the act of the will, and which would be eaſily performed, if the act of the will were preſent. And if it be improperly ſaid, that he cannot perform thoſe external voluntary actions, which depend on the will, it is in ſome reſpect more improperly ſaid, that he is unable to exert the acts of the will themſelves; becauſe it is more evidently falſe, with reſpect to theſe, that he cannot if he will: for to ſay ſo, is a downright contradiction: it is eaſy to ſay he *cannot* will, if he *does* will. And in this caſe, not only is it true, that it is eaſy for a man to do the thing if he will, but the very willing is the doing; when once he has willed, the thing is performed; and nothing elſe remains to be done. Therefore, in theſe things to aſcribe a non-performance to the want of power or ability, is not juſt; becauſe the thing wanting is not a being *able*, but a being *willing.* There are faculties of mind, and capacity of nature, and every thing elſe, ſufficient, but a diſpoſition: nothing is wanting but a will.

SECTION V.

Concerning the Notion of Liberty, *and of* moral Agency.

THE plain and obvious meaning of the words *Freedom* and *Liberty*, in common ſpeech, is *power, opportunity, or advantage, that any one has, to do as he pleaſes* Or in other words, his being free from hinderance or impediment in the way of doing, or conducting in any reſpect, as he wills. * And the contrary to liberty, whatever name we call that by, is a perſon's being hindred or unable to conduct as he will, or being neceſſitated to do otherwiſe.

If this which I have mentioned be the meaning of the word Liberty, in the ordinary uſe of language; as I truſt that none that has ever learned to talk, and is unprejudiced, will deny: then it will follow, that in propriety of ſpeech, neither Liberty, nor its contrary, can properly be aſcribed to any being or thing, but that which has ſuch a faculty, power or property, as is called will. For that which is poſſeſſed of no ſuch thing as *will*, cannot have any *power* or *opportunity* of doing *according to its will*, nor be neceſſitated to act *contrary to its will*, nor be reſtrained from acting agreably to it. And therefore to talk of

* I ſay not only *doing*, but *conducting*; becauſe a voluntary forbearing to do, ſitting ſtill, keeping ſilence, &c. are inſtances of perſons' *conduct*, about which Liberty is exerciſed; though they are not ſo properly called *doing*.

of Liberty, or the contrary, as belonging to the *very will itſelf*, is not to ſpeak good ſenſe; if we judge of ſenſe, and nonſenſe, by the original and proper ſignification of words. For the *will itſelf* is not an Agent that *has a will:* the power of chuſing, itſelf, has not a power of chuſing. That which has the power of volition or choice is the man or the ſoul, and not the power of volition itſelf. And he that has the liberty of doing according to his will, is the Agent or doer who is poſſeſſed of the will; and not the will which he is poſſeſſed of. We ſay with propriety, that a bird let looſe has power and liberty to fly; but not that the bird's power of flying has a power and Liberty of flying. To be free is the property of an Agent, who is poſſeſſed of powers and faculties, as much as to be cunning, valiant, bountiful, or zealous. But theſe qualities are the properties of men or perſons; and not the properties of properties.

There are two things that are contrary to this which is called Liberty in common ſpeech. One is *conſtraint*: the ſame is otherwiſe called *force*, *compulſion*, and *coaction*; which is a perſon's being neceſſitated to do a thing *contrary* to his will. The other is *reſtraint*; which is his being hindred, and not having power to do *according* to his will. But that which has no will, cannot be the ſubject of theſe things.—I need ſay the leſs on this head, Mr. *Locke* having ſet the ſame thing forth, with ſo great clearneſs, in his *Eſſay on the Human Underſtanding*.

But one thing more I would obſerve concerning what is vulgarly called *Liberty*; namely, that power and opportunity for one to do and conduct as he will, or according to his choice, is all that is meant by it; without taking into the meaning of the word, any thing of the cause or original of that choice; or at all considering how the person came to have such a volition; whether it was caused by some external motive, or internal habitual bias; whether it was determined by some internal antecedent volition, or whether it happened without a cause; whether it was necessarily connected with something foregoing, or not connected. Let the person come by his volition or choice how he will, yet, if he is able, and there is nothing in the way to hinder his pursuing and executing his will, the man is fully and perfectly free, according to the primary and common notion of freedom.

WHAT has been said may be sufficient to shew what is meant by *Liberty*, according to the common notions of mankind, and in the usual and primary acceptation of the word: but the word, as used by *Arminians*, *Pelagians* and others, who oppose the *Calvinists*, has an entirely different signification.—These several things belong to their notion of Liberty. 1. That it consists in a *self-determining power* in the will, or a certain sovereignty the will has over itself, and its own acts, whereby it determines its own volitions; so as not to be dependent in its determinations, on any cause without itself, nor determined by any thing prior to its own acts 2. *Indifference* belongs to Liberty in their notion of it, or that the mind, previous to the act of volition be, *in eqilibrio*. 3. *Contingence* is another thing that belongs and is essential to it; not in the common acceptation of the word, as that as been already explained, but as opposed to all *necessity*, or any fixed and certain connection with some previous ground or reason of its existence. They suppose the essence of Liberty so much to consist in in these things, that unless the will of man be free in this sense, he has no real freedom, how much soever he may be at Liberty to act according to his will.

A *moral Agent* is a being that is capable of those actions that have a moral quality, and which can properly be denominated good or evil in a moral sense, virtuous or vicious, commendable or faulty. To moral Agency belongs a *moral faculty*, or sense of moral good and evil, or of such a thing as desert or worthiness, of praise or blame, reward or punishment; and a capacity which an Agent has of being influenced in his actions by moral inducements or motives, exhibited to the view of understanding and reason, to engage to a conduct agreeable to the moral faculty.

THE sun is very excellent and beneficial in its action and influence on the earth, in warming it, and causing it to bring forth its fruits; but it is not a moral Agent: its action, though good, is not virtuous or meritorious. Fire that breaks out in a city, and consumes great part of it, is very mischievous in its operation; but is not a moral Agent: what it does is not faulty or sinful, or deserving of any punishment. The brute creatures are not moral Agents: the actions of some of them are very profitable and pleasant; others are very hurtful: yet, seeing they have no moral faculty, or sense of desert, and do not act from choice guided by understanding, or with a capacity of reasoning and reflecting, but only from instinct, and are not capable of being influenced by moral inducements, their actions are not properly sinful or virtuous; nor are they properly the subjects of any such moral treatment for what they do, as moral Agents are for their faults or good deeds.

Here it may be noted, that there is a circumstantial difference between the moral Agency of a *ruler* and a *ſubject*. I call it *circumſtantial*, becauſe it lies only in the difference of moral inducements they are capable of being influenced by, ariſing from the differrence of *circumſtances*. A *ruler* acting in that capacity only, is not capable of being influenced by a moral law, and its ſanctions of threatnings and promiſes, rewards and puniſhments, as the *ſubject* is; though both may be influenced by a knowledge of moral good and evil. And therefore the moral Agency of the ſupreme Being, who acts only in the capacity of a *ruler* towards his creatures, and never as a *ſubject*, differs in that reſpect from the moral Agency of created intelligent beings. God's actions, and particularly thoſe which he exerts as a moral governor, have moral qualifications, are morally good in the higheſt degree. They are moſt perfectly holy and righteous; and we muſt conceive of Him as influenced in the higheſt degree, by that which, above all others, is properly a moral inducement; *viz.* the moral good which He ſees in ſuch and ſuch things: and therefere He is, in the moſt proper ſenſe, a moral Agent, the ſource of all moral ablilty and Agency, the fountain and rule of all virtue and moral good; though by reaſon of his being ſupreme over all, it is not poſſible He ſhould be under the influence of law or command, promiſes or threatnings, rewards or puniſhments, counſels or warnings. The eſſential qualities of a moral Agent are in God, in the greateſt poſſible perfection; ſuch as underſtanding, to perceive the difference between moral good and evil; a capacity of diſcerning that moral worthineſs and demerit, by which ſome things are praiſe-worthy, others deſerving of blame and puniſhment; and alſo a capacity of choice, and choice guided by underſtanding,

ing, and power of acting according to his choice or pleasure, and being capable of doing those things which are in the highest sense praise-worthy. And herein does very much consist that image of God wherein he made man, (which we read of *Gen.* i. 26, 27. and *chap.* ix. 6.) by which God distinguished man from the beasts, *viz.* in those faculties and principles of nature, whereby He is capable of moral Agency. Herein very much consists the *natural* image of God; as his *spiritual* and *moral* image, wherein man was made at first, consisted in that moral excellency, that he was endowed with.

PART II.

Wherein it is considered whether there is or can be any ſuch Sort of FREEDOM OF WILL, as that wherein ARMINIANS place the Eſſence of the Liberty of all moral Agents; and whether any ſuch Thing ever *was* or *can be* conceived of.

SECTION I.

Shewing the manifeſt Inconſiſtence of the Arminian *Notion of* Liberty of Will, *conſiſting in the Will's* ſelf-determining Power.

HAVING taken notice of thoſe things which may be neceſſary to be obſerved, concerning the meaning of the principal terms and phraſes made uſe of in controverſies concerning human Liberty, and particularly obſerved what *Liberty* is according to the common language and general apprehenſion of mankind, and what it is as underſtood and maintained by *Arminians*; I proceed to conſider the *Arminian* notion of the *Freedom of the Will*, and the ſuppoſed neceſſity of it in order to moral agency, or in order to any one's being capable of virtue or vice, and properly the ſubject of command or counſel, praiſe or blame, promiſes or threatnings, rewards or puniſhments; or whether that which has been deſcribed, as the thing meant by liberty in common ſpeech, be not ſufficient and the only Liberty, which makes, or can

can make any one a moral agent, and so properly the subject of these things. In *this Part*, I shall consider whether any such thing be possible or conceivable, as that Freedom of Will which *Arminians* insist on; and shall enquire, whether any such sort of Liberty be necessary to moral agency, *&c.* in the *next* Part.

And first of all, I shall consider the notion of *a self-determining Power* in the Will: wherein, according to the *Arminians*, does most essentially consist the Will's Freedom; and shall particularly enquire, whether it be not plainly absurd, and a manifest inconsistence, to suppose that *the will itself determines all the free acts of the Will.*

Here I shall not insist on the great impropriety of such phrases, and ways of speaking, as *the Will's determining itself*; because actions are to be ascribed to agents, and not properly to the powers of agents; which improper way of speaking leads to many mistkaes, and much confusion, as Mr. *Locke* observes. But I shall suppose that the *Arminians*, when they speak of the Will's determining itself, do by the *Will* mean the *soul willing*. I shall take it for granted, that when they speak of the Will, as the determiner, they mean *the soul in the exercise of a power of willing*, or acting voluntarily. I shall suppose this to be their meaning, because nothing else can be meant, without the grossest and plainest absurdity. In all cases when we speak of the powers or principles of acting, as doing such things, we mean that the agents which have these Powers of acting, do them, in the exercise of those Powers So when we say, valour fights courageously, we mean, the man who is under the influence of valour fights courageously. When we say, love seeks the ob-

ject,

ject loved, we mean, the person loving, seeks that object. When we say, the understanding discerns, we mean the soul in the exercise of that faculty. So when it is said, the will decides or determines, the meaning must be, that the person in the exercise of a Power of willing and chusing, or the soul acting voluntarily, determines.

THEREFORE, if the Will determines all its own free acts, the soul determines all the free acts of the will in the exercise of a Power of willing and chusing; or, which is the same thing, it determines them of choice; it determines its own acts by chusing its own acts. If the Will determines the Will, then choice orders and determines the choice: and acts of choice are subject to the decision, and follow the conduct of other acts of choice. And therefore if the Will determines all its own free acts, then every free act of choice is determined by a preceding act of choice, chusing that act. And if that preceding act of the Will or choice be also a free act, then by these pinciples, in this act too, the Will is self-determined: that is, this, in like manner, is an act that the soul voluntary chuses; or, which is the same thing, it is an act determined still by a preceding act of the Will, chusing that. And the like may again be observed of the last mentioned act. Which brings us directly to a contradiction: for it supposes an act of the Will preceding the first act in the whole train, directing and determining the rest; or a free act of the Will, before the first free act of the Will. Or else we must come at last to an act of the Will, determining the consequent acts, wherein the Will is not self-determined, and so is not a free act, in this notion of freedom: but if the first act in the train, determining and fixing the rest, be not free, none of them all can be free;

as

as is manifest at first view, but shall be demonstrated presently.

If the Will, which we find governs the members of the body, and determines and commands their motions and actions, does also govern itself, and determine its own motions and actions, it doubtless determines them the same way, even by antecedent volitions. The Will determines which way the hands and feet shall move, by an act of volition or choice: and there is no other way of the Will's determining, directing or commanding any thing at all. Whatsoever the will commands, it commands by an act of the Will. And if it has itself under its command, and determines itself in its own actions, it doubtless does it the same way that it determines other things which are under its command. So that if the freedom of the Will consists in this, that it has itself and its own actions under its command and direction, and its own volitions are determined by itself, it will follow, that every free volition arises from another antecedent volition, directing and commanding that: and if that *directing* volition be also free, in that also the will is determined; that is to say, that directing volition is determined by another going before that; and so on till we come to the first volition in the whole series: and if that first volition be free, and the Will self-determined in it, then that is determined by another volition preceding that. Which is a contradiction; because by the supposition, it can have none before it, to direct or determine it, being the first in the train. But if that first volition is not determined by any preceding act of the Will, then that act is not determined by the Will, and so is not free in the *Arminian* notion of freedom, which consists in the Will's self-determinatermination. And if that first act of the Will, which determines and fixes the subsequent acts, be not free, none of the following acts, which are determined by it, can be free.—If we suppose there are five acts in the train, the fifth and last determined by the fourth, and the fourth by the third, the third by the second, and the second by the first; if the first is not determined by the Will, and so not free, then none of them are truly determined by the Will: that is, that each of them are as they are, and not otherwise, is not first owing to the Will, but to the determination of the first in the series, which is not dependent on the Will, and is that which the Will has no hand in the determination of. And this being that which decides what the rest shall be, and determines their existence; therefore the first determination of their existence is not from the Will. The case is just the same, if instead of a chain of five acts of the Will, we should suppose a succession of ten, or an hundred, or ten thousand. If the first act be not free, being determined by something out of the Will, and this determines the next to be agreable to itself, and that the next, and so on; they are none of them free, but all originally depend on, and are determined by some cause out of the Will: and so all freedom in the case is excluded, and no act of the Will can be free, according to this notion of freedom. If we should suppose a long chain of ten thousand links, so connected, that if the first link moves, it will move the next, and that the next; and so the whole chain must be determined to motion, and in the direction of its motion by the motion of the first link; and that is moved by something else: in this case, though all the links, but one, are moved by other parts of the same chain; yet it appears that the motion of no one

one, nor the direction of its motion, is from any self-moving or self-determining Power in the chain, any more than if every link were immediately moved by something that did not belong to the chain.—If the will be not free in the first act, which causes the next, then neither is it free in the next, which is caused by that first act: for though indeed the will caused it, yet it did not cause it freely; because the preceding act, by which it was caused, was not free. And again, if the will be not free in the second act, so neither can it be in the third, which is caused by that; because in like manner, that third was determined by an act of the will that was not free. And so we may go on to the next act, and from that to the next; and how long soever the succession of acts is, it is all one; if the first on which the whole chain depends, and which determines all the rest, be not a free act; the will is not free in causing or determining any one of those acts; because the act by which it determines them all, is not a free act; and therefore the will is no more free in determining them, than if it did not cause them at all.—Thus, this *Arminian* notion of Liberty of the Will, consisting in the Will's *Self-determination*, is repugnant to itself, and shuts itself wholly out of the world.

SECTION II.

Several supposed Ways of evading *the foregoing Reasoning, considered.*

IF to evade the force of what has been observed, it should be said, that when the *Arminians* speak of the will's determining its own acts, they do not mean that the will determines its acts by any preceding act, or that one act of the will determines another; but only that the faculty or power of will, or the soul in the use of that power, determines its own volitions; and that it does it without any act going before the act determined; such an evasion would be full of the most gross absurdity.——I confess, it is an Evasion of my own inventing; and I do not know but I should wrong the *Arminians*, in supposing that any of them would make use of it. But it being as good a one as I can invent, I would observe upon it a few things.

First, If the faculty or power of the will determines an act of volition, or the soul in the *use* or *exercise of that power*, determines it, that is the same thing as for the soul to determine volition *by an act of will.* For an *exercise* of the power of will, and an act of that power, are the same thing. Therefore to say, that the power of will, or the soul in the *use* or *exercise* of that power, determines volition, without an *act* of will preceding the volition determined, is a contradiction.

Secondly, If a power of will determines the act of the will, then a power of chusing determines it. For, as was before observed, in every act of will, there is choice, and a power of willing is a power of chusing. But if a power of chusing determines the act of volition, it determines it by chusing it. For it is most absurd to say, that a power of chusing determines one thing rather than another, without chusing any thing. But if a power of chusing determines volition by chusing it, then here is the act of volition determined by an antecedent choice, chusing that volition.

Thirdly,

THIRDLY, To say, the faculty, or the soul, determines its own volition, but not by any act, is a contradiction. Because for the soul to *direct*, *decide*, or *determine* any thing, is to act; and this is supposed; for the soul is here spoken of as being a cause in this affair, bringing something to pass, or doing something; or, which is the same thing, exerting itself in order to an effect, which effect is the determination of volition, or the particular kind and manner of an act of will. But certainly, this exertion or action is not the same with the effect, in order to the production of which it is exerted; but must be something prior to it.

AGAIN, The advocates for this notion of the freedom of the will, speak of a certain *sovereignty* in the will, whereby it has power to determine its own volitions. And therefore the determination of volition must itself be an act of the will; for otherwise it can be no exercise of that supposed power and sovereignty.

AGAIN, If the will determines itself, then either the will is *active* in determining its volitions, or it is not. If it be active in it, then the determination is an *act* of the will; and so there is one act of the will determining another. But if the will is not *active* in the determination, then how does it *exercise* any liberty in it? These gentlemen suppose that the thing wherein the will *exercises* liberty, is in its determining its own acts. but how can this be, if it be not *active* in determining? Certainly the will, or the soul, cannot *exercise any liberty* in that wherein it doth not *act*, or wherein it doth not *exercise itself*. So that if either part of this dilemma be taken, this scheme of liberty, consisting in self-determining power, is over-

 thrown.

thrown. If there be an act of the will in determining all its own free acts, then one free act of the will is determined by another; and ſo we have the abſurdity of every free act, even the very firſt, determined by a foregoing free act. But if there be no act or exerciſe of the will in determining its own acts, then no liberty is exerciſed in determining them. From whence it follows, that no liberty conſiſts in the will's power to determine its own acts; or, which is the ſame thing, that there is no ſuch thing as liberty conſiſting in a ſelf-determining power of the will.

If it ſhould be ſaid, That although it be true, if the ſoul determines its own volitions, it muſt be active in ſo doing, and the determination itſelf muſt be an act; yet there is no need of ſuppoſing this act to be prior to the volition determined: but the will or ſoul determines the act of the will *in willing*; it determines its own volition, *in* the very act of volition; it directs and limits the act of the will, cauſing it be ſo and not otherwiſe, *in* exerting the act, without any preceding act to exert that. If any ſhould ſay after this manner, they muſt mean one of theſe three things; Either, (1.) That the determining act, though it be before the act determined in the order of nature, yet it is not before it in order of time. Or, (2.) That the determining act is not before the act determined, either in the order of time or nature, nor is truly diſtinct from it; but that the ſoul's determining the act of volition is the ſame thing with its exerting the act of volition: the mind's exerting ſuch a particular act, is its cauſing and determining the act. Or, (3.) That volition has no cauſe, and is no effect; but comes into exiſtence, with ſuch a particular determination, without

out any ground or reason of its existence and determination. I shall consider these distinctly.

(1.) If all that is meant, be, that the determining act is not before the act determined in order of *time*, it will not help the case at all, though it should be allowed. If it be before the determined act in the order of nature, being the cause or ground of its existence, this as much proves it to be distinct from it, and independent on it, as if it were before in the order of time. As the cause of the particular motion of a natural body in a certain direction, may have no distance as to time, yet cannot be the same with the motion effected by it, but must be as distinct from it, as any other cause, that is before its effect in the order of time: as the architect is distinct from the house which he builds, or the father distinct from the son which he begets. And if the act of the will determining be distinct from the act determined, and before it in the order of nature, then we can go back from one to another, till we come to the first in the series, which has no act of the will before it in the order of nature, determining it; and consequently is an act not determined by the will, and so not a free act, in this notion of freedom. And this being the act which determines all the rest, none of them are free acts. As when there is a chain of many links, the first of which only is taken hold of and drawn by hand; all the rest may follow and be moved at the same instant, without any distance of time; but yet the motion of one link is before that of another in the order of nature; the last is moved by the next, and that by the next, and so till we come to the first; which not being moved by any other, but by something distinct from the whole chain, this as much proves that no part is moved

moved by any self-moving power in the chain, as if the motion of one link followed that of another in the order of time.

(2.) If any should say, that the determining act is not before the determined act, either in the order of time, or of nature, nor is distinct from it; but that the *exertion* of the act is the *determination* of the act; that for the soul to exert a particular volition, is for it to cause and determine that act of volition: I would on this observe, that the thing in question seems to be forgotten, or kept out of sight, in a darkness and unintelligibleness of speech; unless such an objector would mean to contradict himself.— The very act of volition itself is doubtless a determination of mind; *i. e.* it is the mind's drawing up a conclusion, or coming to a choice, between two things, or more, proposed to it. But determining among external *objects* of choice, is not the same with determining the *act* of choice itself, among various possible acts of choice.— The question is, What influences, directs, or determines the mind or will to come to such a conclusion or choice as it does? Or what is the cause, ground, or reason, why it concludes thus, and not otherwise? Now it must be answered, according to the *Arminian* notion of freedom, that the will influences, orders and determines itself thus to act. And if it does, I say, it must be by some antecedent act. To say, it is caused, influenced and determined by something, and yet not determined by any thing antecedent, either in order of time or nature, is a contradiction. For that is what is meant by a thing's being prior in the order of nature, that it is some way the cause or reason of the thing, with respect to which it is said to be prior.

If the particular act or exertion of will which comes into exiſtence, be any thing properly determined at all, then it has ſome cauſe of its exiſting, and of its exiſting in ſuch a particular determinate manner, and not another; ſome cauſe, whoſe influence *decides the matter:* which cauſe is diſtinct from the effect, and prior to it. But to ſay, that the will or mind orders, influences and determines itſelf to exert ſuch an act as it does, by the very exertion itſelf, is to make the exertion both cauſe and effect; or the exerting ſuch an act, to be a cauſe of the exertion of ſuch an act. For the queſtion is, What is the cauſe and reaſon of the ſoul's exerting ſuch an act? To which the anſwer is, The ſoul exerts ſuch an act, and that is the cauſe of it. And ſo, by this, the exertion muſt be prior in the order of nature to itſelf, and diſtinct from itſelf.

(3.) If the meaning be, that the ſoul's exertion of ſuch a particular act of will, is a thing that comes to paſs *of itſelf*, without any cauſe; and that there is abſolutely no ground or reaſon of the ſoul's being determined to exert ſuch a volition, and make ſuch a choice, rather than another, I ſay, if this be the meaning of *Arminians*, when they contend ſo earneſtly for the will's determining its own acts, and for liberty of will conſiſting in ſelf-determining power; they do nothing but confound themſelves and others with words without a meaning. In the queſtion, *What determines the will?* and in their anſwer, that *the will determines itſelf*, and in all the diſpute about it, it ſeems to be taken for granted, that ſomething determines the will; and the controverſy on this head is not, whether any thing at all determines it, or whether its determination has any cauſe or foundation at all: but where the foundation

dation of it is, whether in the will itself, or somewhere else. But if the thing intended be what is above-mentioned, then all comes to this, that nothing at all determines the will; volition having absolutely no cause or foundation of its existence, either within, or without. There is a great noise made about self-determining power, as the source of all free acts of the will: but when the matter comes to be explained, the meaning is, that no power at all is the source of these acts, neither self-determining power, nor any other, but they arise from nothing; no cause, no power, no influence, being at all concerned in the matter.

However, this very thing, even that the free acts of the will are events which come to pass without a cause, is certainly implied in the *Arminian* notion of liberty of will; though it be very inconsistent with many other things in their scheme, and repuguant to some things implied in their notion of liberty. Their opinion implies, that the particular determination of volition is without any cause; because they hold the free acts of the will to be *contingent* events; and contingence is essential to freedom in their notion of it. But certainly, those things which have a prior ground and reason of their particular existence, a cause which antecedently determines them to be, and determines them to be just as they are, do not happen contingently. If something foregoing, by a causal influence and connection, determines and fixes precisely their coming to pass, and the manner of it, then it does not remain a contingent thing whether they shall come to pass or no.

And because it is a question, in many respects, very important in this controversy about the freedom of will, *whether the free acts of the will are events*

events which come to paſs without a cauſe? I ſhall be particular in examining this point in the two following ſections.

SECTION III.

Whether any Event whatſoever, and Volition *in particular, can come to paſs* without *a* Cauſe *of its exiſtence.*

BEFORE I enter on any argument on this ſubject, I would explain how I would be underſtood, when I uſe the word *Cauſe* in this diſcourſe: ſince, for want of a better word, I ſhall have occaſion to uſe it in a ſenſe which is more extenſive, than that in which it is ſometimes uſed, The word is often uſed in ſo reſtrained a ſenſe as to ſignify only that which has a *poſitive efficiency* or influence *to produce* a thing, or bring it to paſs. But there are many things which have no ſuch poſitive productive influence; which yet are cauſes in that reſpect, that they have truly the nature of a ground or reaſon why ſome things are, rather than others; or why they are as they are, rather than otherwiſe. Thus the abſence of the ſun in the night, is not the Cauſe of the falling of the dew at that time, in the ſame manner as its beams are the Cauſe of the aſcending of the vapours in the day-time; and its withdrawment in the winter, is not in the ſame manner the Cauſe of the freezing of the waters, as its approach in the ſpring is the cauſe of their thawing. But yet the withdrawment or abſence of the ſun is an antecedent, with which theſe effects in the night and winter are connected, and on which they depend; and is one thing that belongs to the ground and reaſon why they come to paſs at that time, rather than at other times; though the abſence of the

the ſun is nothing poſitive, nor has any poſitive influence.

It may be further obſerved, that when I ſpeak of *connection of Cauſes and Effects*, I have reſpect to *moral* Cauſes, as well as thoſe that are called *natural* in diſtinction from them. Moral Cauſes may be Cauſes in as proper ſenſe, as any Cauſes whatſoever; may have as real an influence, and may as truly be the ground and reaſon of an Event's coming to paſs.

Therefore I ſometimes uſe the word *Cauſe*, in this enquiry, to ſignify any *antecedent*, either natural or moral, poſitive or negative, on which an Event, either a thing, or the manner and circumſtance of a thing, ſo depends, that it is the ground and reaſon, either in whole, or in part, why it is, rather than not; or why it is as it is, rather than otherwiſe; or, in other words, any antecedent with which a conſequent Event is ſo connected, that it truly belongs to the reaſon why the propoſition which affirms that Event, is true; whether it has any poſitive influence, or not. And in an agreeableneſs to this, I ſometimes uſe the word effect for the conſequence of another thing, which is perhaps rather an occaſion than a Cauſe, moſt properly ſpeaking.

I am the more careful thus to explain my meaning, that I may cut off occaſion, from any that might ſeek occaſion to cavil and object againſt ſome things which I may ſay concering the dependence of all things which come to paſs, on ſome Cauſe, and their connection with their Cauſe.

Having thus explained what I mean by *Cauſe*, I aſſert, that nothing ever comes to paſs without a Cauſe.

a Cause. What is self-existent must be from eternity, and must be unchangeable: but as to all things that *begin to be*, they are not self-existent, and therefore must have some foundation of their existence without themselves.——That whatsoever begins to be, which before was not, must have a Cause why it then begins to exist, seems to be the first dictate of the common and natural sense which God hath implanted in the minds of all mankind, and the main foundation of all our reasonings about the existence of things, past, present, or to come.

And this dictate of common sense equally respects substances and modes, or things and the manner and circumstances of things. Thus, if we see a body which has hitherto been at rest, start out of a state of rest, and begin to move, we do as naturally and necessarily suppose there is some Cause or reason of this new mode of existence, as of the existence of a body itself which had hitherto not existed. And so if a body, which had hitherto moved in a certain direction, should suddenly change the direction of its motion; or if it should put off its old figure, and take a new one; or change its colour: the beginning of these new modes is a new Event, and the mind of mankind necessarily supposes that there is some Cause or reason of them.

If this grand principle of common sense be taken away, all arguing from effects to Causes ceaseth, and so all knowledge of any existence, besides what we have by the most direct and immediate intuition. Particularly all our proof of the being of God ceases: we argue His being from our own being, and the being of other things, which we are sensible once were not, but have begun to be; and from the being of the world,

world, with all its constituent parts, and the manner of their existence; all which we see plainly are not necessary in their own nature, and so not self-existent, and therefore must have a Cause. But if things, not in themselves necessary, may begin to be without a Cause, all this arguing is vain.

INDEED, I will not affirm, that there is in the nature of things no foundation for the knowledge of the Being of God without any evidence of it from His works. I do suppose there is a great absurdity, in the nature of things simply considered, in supposing that there should be no God, or in denying Being in general, and supposing an eternal, absolute, universal nothing: and therefore that here would be foundation of intuitive evidence that it cannot be, and that eternal infinite most perfect Being must be; if we had strength and comprehension of mind sufficient, to have a clear idea of general and universal Being, or, which is the same thing, of the infinite, eternal, most perfect Divine Nature and Essence. But then we should not properly come to the knowledge of the Being of God by arguing; but our evidence would be intuitive: we should see it, as we see other things that are necessary in themselves, the contraries of which are in their own nature absurd and contradictory; as we see that twice two is four; and as we see that a circle has no angles. If we had as clear an idea of universal infinite entity, as we have of these other things, I suppose we should most intuitively see the absurdity of supposing such Being not to be; should immediately see there is no room for the question, whether it is possible that Being, in the most general abstracted notion of it, should not be. But we have not that strength and extent of of mind, to know this certainly in this intuitive independent manner: but the way that mankind come to the knowledge of the Being of God, is that which the apostle speaks of, Rom. i. 20. *The invisible things of Him, from the creation of the world, are clearly seen; being understood by the things that are made; even his eternal Power and Godhead.* We *first ascend*, and prove *à posteriori*,, or from effects, that there must be an eternal Cause; and then, *secondly*, prove by argumentation, not intuition, that this Being must be necessarily existent; and then, *thirdly*, from the proved necessity of his existence, we may *descend*, and prove many of his perfections *à priori*.

But if once this grand principle of common sense be given up, that *what is not necessary in itself, must have a Cause*; and we begin to maintain, that things may come into existence, and begin to be, which heretofore have not been, of themselves, without any cause; all our means of ascending in our arguing from the creature to the Creator, and all our evidence of the Being of God, is cut off at one blow. In this case, we cannot prove that there is a God, either from the Being of the world, and the creatures in it, or from the manner of their being, their order, beauty and use. For if things may come into existence without any Cause at all, then they doubtless may without any Cause answerable to the effect. Our minds do alike naturally suppose and determine both these things; namely, that what begins to be has a Cause, and also that it has a Cause proportionable and agreeable to the effect. The same principle which leads us to determine, that there cannot be any thing coming to pass without a Cause, leads us to determine that there cannot be more in the effect than in the Cause.

YEA,

Yea, if once it should be allowed, that things may come to pass without a Cause, we should not only have no proof of the Being of God, but we should be without evidence of the existence of any thing whatsoever, but our own immediately present ideas and consciousness. For we have no way to prove any thing else, but by arguing from effects to Causes: from the ideas now immediately in view, we argue other things not immediately in view: from sensations now excited in us, we infer the existence of things without us, as the Causes of these sensations: and from the existence of these things, we argue other things, which they depend on, as effects on Causes. We infer the past existence of ourselves, or any thing else, by memory; only as we argue, that the ideas, which are now in our minds, are the consequences of past ideas and sensations. We immediately perceive nothing else but the ideas which are this moment extant in our minds. We perceive or know other things only *by means* of these, as necessarily connected with others, and dependent on them. But if things may be without Causes, all this necessary connection and dependence is dissolved, and so all means of our knowledge is gone. If there be no absurdity or difficulty in supposing one thing to start out of non-existence, into being, of itself without a Cause; then there is no absurdity or difficulty in supposing the same of millions of millions. For nothing, or no difficuly multiplied, still is nothing, or no difficulty: nothing multiplied by nothing, does not increase the sum.

And indeed, according to the hypothesis I am opposing, of the acts of the will coming to pass without a Cause, it is the case in fact, that millions of millions of Events are continually coming

ing into existence *contingently* without any Cause or reason why they do so, all over the world, every day and hour, through all ages. So it is in a constant succession, in every moral agent. This contingency, this efficient nothing, this effectual No Cause, is always ready at hand, to produce this sort of effects, as long as the agent exists, and as often as he has occasion.

If it were so, that things only of one kind, *viz.* acts of the will, seemed to come to pass of themselves; but those of this sort in general came into being thus; and it were an event that was continual, and that happened in a course, wherever were capable subjects of such events; this very thing would demonstrate that there was some Cause of them, which made such a difference between this event and others, and that they did not really happen contingently. For contingence is blind, and does not pick and chuse for a particular sort of Events. Nothing has no choice. This No-Cause, which causes no existence, cannot cause the existence which comes to pass, to be of one particlar sort only, distinguished from all others. Thus, that only one sort of matter drops out of the heavens, even water, and that this comes so often, so constantly and plentifully, all over the world, in all ages, shows that there is some Cause or Reason of the falling of water out of the heavens; and that something besides mere contingence has a hand in the matter.

If we should suppose Non-entity to be about to bring forth; and things were coming into existence, without any Cause or Antecedent, on which the existence, or kind, or manner of existence depends; or which could at all determine whether the things should be; stones, or stars, or beasts,

or

or angels, or human bodies, or souls, or only some new motion or figure in natural bodies, or some new sensations in animals, or new ideas in the human understanding, or new volitions in the will; or any thing else of all the infinite number of possibles; then certainly it would not be expected, although many millions of millions of things are coming into existence in this manner, all over the face of the earth, that they should all be only of one particular kind, and that it should be thus in all ages, and that this sort of existences should never fail to come to pass where there is room for them, or a subject capable of them, and that constantly, whenever there is occasion for them.

If any should imagine, there is something in the sort of Event that renders it possible for it to come into existence without a Cause, and should say, that the free acts of the will are existences of an exceeding different nature from other things; by reason of which they may come into existence without any previous ground or reason of it, though other things cannot; if they make this objection in good earnest, it would be an evidence of their strangely forgetting themselves: for they would be giving an account of some ground of the existence of a thing, when at the same time they would maintain there is no ground of its existence. Therefore I would observe, that the particular nature of existence, be it never so diverse from others, can lay no foundation for that thing's coming into existence without a Cause; because to suppose this, would be to suppose the particular nature of existence to be a thing prior to the existence, and so a thing which makes way for existence, with such a circumstance, namely, without a cause or reason of exis-

existence. But that which in any respect makes way for a thing's coming into being, or for any manner or circumstance of its first existence, must be prior to the existence. The distinguished nature of the effect, which is something belonging to the effect, cannot have influence backward, to act before it is. The peculiar nature of that thing called volition, can do nothing, can have no influence, while it is not. And afterwards it is too late for its influence: for then the thing has made sure of existence already, without its help.

So that it is indeed as repugnant to reason, to suppose that an act of the will should come into existence without a cause, as to suppose the human soul, or an angel, or the globe of the earth, or the whole universe, should come into existence without a cause. And if once we allow, that such a sort of effect as a Volition may come to pass without a Cause, how do we know but that many other sorts of effects may do so too? It is not the particular kind of effect that makes the absurdity of supposing it has been without a Cause, but something which is common to all things that ever begin to be, *viz.* That they are not self-existent, or necessary in the nature of things.

SECTION IV.

Whether Volition *can arise without a Cause, through the* Activity *of the Nature of the Soul.*

THE author of the *Essay on the Freedom of the Will in God and the Creatures*, in answer to that objection against his doctrine of a self-determining power in the will, (p. 68, 69.) *That nothing is, or comes to paſs, without a ſufficient reaſon why it is, and why it is in this manner rather than another*, allows that it is thus in corporeal things, *which are properly and philoſophically ſpeaking, paſſive being*; but denies that it is thus in *ſpirits, which are beings of an active, nature, who have the ſpring of action within themſelves, and can determine themſelves.* By which it is plainly ſuppoſed, that ſuch an event as an act of the will, may come to paſs in a ſpirit, without a ſufficient reaſon why it comes to paſs, or why it is after this manner, rather than another; by reaſon of the activity of the nature of a ſpirit.——But certainly this author, in this matter, muſt be very unwary and inadvertent. For,

1. The objection or difficulty propoſed by this author, ſeems to be forgotten in his anſwer or ſolution. The very difficulty, as he himſelf propoſes it, is this; How an event can *come to paſs without a ſufficent reaſon why it is, or why it is in this manner rather than another?* Inſtead of ſolving this difficulty, or anſwering this queſtion with regard to Volition, as he propoſes, he forgets himſelf, and anſwers another queſtion quite diverſe, and wholly inconſiſtent with this, *viz.* What is a ſufficient reaſon why it is, and why it is in this manner rather than another? And he aſſigns the active being's own determination as the Cauſe, and a Cauſe ſufficient for the effect; and leaves all the difficulty unreſolved, and the queſtion unanſwered, which yet returns, even, How the ſoul's own determination, which he ſpeaks of, came to exiſt, and to be what it was without a Cauſe? The activity of the ſoul may enable it to be the Cauſe of effects; but it does not at all enable or help it to be the ſubject of effects which have

have no cause; which is the thing this author supposes concerning acts of the will. Activity of nature will no more enable a being to produce effects, and determine the manner of their existence, *within* itself, without a Cause, than *out of* itself, in some other being. But if an active being should, through its activity, produce and determine an effect in some external object, how absurd would it be to say, that the effect was produced without a Cause!

2. The question is not so much, How a spirit endowed with activity comes to act, as why it exerts such an act, and not another; or why it acts with such a particular determination? If activity of nature be the Cause why a spirit (the soul of man for instance) acts, and does not lie still; yet that alone is not the Cause why its action is thus and thus limited, directed and determined. Active nature is a *general* thing; it is an ability or tendency of nature to action, generally taken; which may be a Cause why the soul acts as occasion or reason is given; but this alone cannot be a sufficient Cause why the soul exerts such a *particular* act, at such a time, rather than others. In order to this, there must be something besides a *general* tendency to action; there must also be a *particular* tendency to that individual action.— If it should be asked, why the soul of man uses its activity in such a manner as it does; and it should be answered, that the soul uses its activity thus, rather than otherwise, because it has activity; would such an answer satisfy a rational man? Would it not rather be looked upon as a very impertinent one?

3. An active being can bring no effects to pass by his activity, but what are consequent upon his

acting: he produces nothing by his activity, any other way than by the exercise of his activity, and so nothing but the fruits of its exercise: he brings nothing to pass by a dormant activity. But the exercise of his activity is action; and so his action, or exercise of his activity, must be prior to the effects of his activity, If an active being produces an effect in another being, about which his activity is conversant, the effect being the fruit of his activity, his activity must be first exercised or exerted, and the effect of it must follow So it must be, with equal reason, if the active being is his own object, and his activity is conversant about himself, to produce and determine some effect in himself; still the exercise of his activity must go before the effect, which he brings to pass and determines by it. And therefore his activity cannot be the Cause of the determination of the first action, or exercise of activity itself, whence the effects of activity arise; for that would imply a contradiction; it would be to say, the first exercise of activity is before the first exercise of activity, and is the Cause of it.

4. That the soul, though an active substance, cannot *diversify* its own acts, but by first acting; or be a determining Cause of *different* acts, or any different effects, sometimes of one kind, and sometimes of another, any other way than in consequence of its own diverse acts, is manifest by this; that if so, then the *same* Cause, the *same* causal Power, Force or Influence, *without variation in any respect*, would produce *different* effects at different times. For the same substance of the soul before it acts, and the same active nature of the soul before it is exerted (*i. e.* before in the order of nature) would be the Cause of different

effects,

effects, *viz.* Different Volitions at different times. But the ſubſtance of the ſoul before it acts, and its active nature before it is exerted, are the ſame without variation. For it is ſome act that makes the firſt variation in the Cauſe, as to any cauſal exertion, force or influence; but if it be ſo, that the ſoul has no different cauſality, or diverſe cauſal force or influence, in producing theſe diverſe effects; then it is evident, that the ſoul has no influence, no hand in the diverſity of the effect; and that the difference of the effect cannot be owing to any thing in the ſoul; or which is the ſame thing, the ſoul does not determine the diverſity of the effect; which is contrary to the ſuppoſition.—It is true, the ſubſtance of the ſoul before it acts, and before there is any difference in that reſpect, may be in a different ſtate and circumſtances: but thoſe whom I oppoſe, will not allow the different circumſtances of the ſoul to be the determining Cauſes of the acts of the will; as being contrary to their notion of ſelf-determination and ſelf-motion.

5. Let us ſuppoſe, as theſe divines do, that there are no acts of the ſoul, ſtrictly ſpeaking, but free Volitions; then it will follow, that the ſoul is an active being in nothing further than it is a voluntary or elective being; and whenever it produces effects actively, it produces effects voluntarily and electively. But to produce effects thus, is the ſame thing as to produce effects *in conſequence of*, and *according to* its own choice. And if ſo, then ſurely the ſoul does not by its activity produce all its own acts of will or choice themſelves: for this, by the ſuppoſition, is to produce all its free acts of choice voluntarily and electively, or in conſequence of its own free acts of choice, which brings the matter directly to the

fore-mentioned contradiction, of a free act of choice before the first free act of choice.—According to these gentlemen's own notion of action, if there arises in the mind a Volition without a free act of the will or choice to determine and produce it, the mind is not the active voluntary Cause of that Volition; because it does not arise from, nor is regulated by choice or design. And therefore it cannot be, that the mind should be the active, voluntary, determining Cause of the first and leading Volition that relates to the affair. —The mind's being a *designing* Cause, only enables it to produce effects in consequence of its *design*; it will not enable it to be the designing Cause of all its own designs. The mind's being an *elective* Cause, will only enable it to produce effects in consequence of its *elections*, and according to them; but cannot enable it to be the elective Cause of all its own elections; because that supposes an election before the first election. So the mind's being an *active* Cause enables it to produce effects in consequence of its own *acts*, but cannot enable it to be the determining Cause of all its own *acts*; for that is still in the same manner a contradiction; as it supposes a determining act conversant about the first act, and prior to it, having a causal influence on its existence, and manner of existence.

I CAN conceive of nothing else that can be meant by the soul's having power to cause and determine its own Volitions, as a being to whom God has given a power of action, but this; that God has given power to the soul, sometimes at least, to excite Volitions at its pleasure, or according as it chuses. And this certainly supposes, in all such cases, a choice preceding all Volitions which are thus

thus caused, even the first of them. Which runs into the fore-mentioned great absurdity.

THEREFORE the activity of the nature of the soul affords no relief from the difficulties which the notion of a self-determining power in the will is attended with, nor will it help, in the least, its absurdities and inconsistences.

SECTION V.

Shewing, that if the things asserted in these Evasions should be supposed to be true, they are altogether impertinent, and cannot help the cause of Arminian *Liberty; and how (this being the state of the case)* Arminian *Writers are obliged to talk inconsistently.*

WHAT was last observed in the preceding section may shew, not only that the active nature of the soul cannot be a reason why an act of the will is, or why it is in this manner, rather than another; but also that if it could be so, and it could be proved that volitions are contingent events, in that sense, that their being and manner of being is not fixed or determined by any cause, or any thing antecedent; it would not at all serve the purpose of *Arminians*, to establish the Freedom of the Will, according to their notion of its freedom, as consisting in the will's *determination of itself*; which supposes every free act of the will to be determined by some act of the will going before to determine it; inasmuch as for the *will* to determine a thing, is the same as for the soul to determine a thing by *willing*; and there is no way that the *will* can determine an act of the will, than by willing that act of the will, or, which is the ſame thing, *chuſing* it. So that here muſt be two acts of the will in the caſe, one going before another, one converſant about the other, and the latter the object of the former, and choſen by the former. If the will does not cauſe and determine the act by choice, it does not cauſe or determine it at all; for that which is not determined by choice, is not determined voluntarily or *willingly:* and to ſay, that the will determines ſomething which the ſoul does not determine willingly, is as much as to ſay, that ſomething is done by the will, which the ſoul doth not with its will.

So that if *Arminian* liberty of will, conſiſting in the will's determining its own acts, be maintained, the old abſurdity and contradiction muſt be maintained, that every free act of will is cauſed and determined by a foregoing free act of will. Which doth not conſiſt with the free acts ariſing without any cauſe, and being ſo contingent, as not to be fixed by any thing foregoing. So that this evaſion muſt be given up, as not at all relieving, and as that which, inſtead of ſupporting this ſort of liberty, directly deſtroys it.

And if it ſhould be ſuppoſed, that the ſoul determines its own acts of will ſome other way, than by a foregoing act of will; ſtill it will not help the cauſe of their liberty of will. If it determines them by an act of the underſtanding, or ſome other power, then *the will* does not determine *itſelf*; and ſo the *ſelf-determining* power of the will is given up. And what liberty is there exerciſed according to their own opinion of liberty, by the ſoul's being determined by ſomething beſides *its own choice?* The acts of the will, it is true, may be directed, and effectually determined

mined and fixed; but it is not done by the soul's own will and pleasure: there is no exercise at all of choice or will in producing the effect: and if *will* and choice are not exercised in it, how is the *liberty of the will* exercised in it?

So that let *Arminians* turn which way they please with their notion of liberty, consisting in the will's determining its own acts, their notion destroys itself. If they hold every free act of will to be determined by the soul's own free choice, or foregoing free act of will; *foregoing*, either in the order of time, or nature; it implies that gross contradiction, that the first free act belonging to the affair, is determined by a free act which is before it. Or if they say that the free acts of the will are determined by some *other act* of the soul, and not an act of will or choice. This also destroys their notion of liberty consisting in the acts of the will being determined by the *will itself*; or if they hold that the acts of the will are determined by *nothing at all* that is prior to them, but that they are contingent in that sense, that they are determined and fixed by no cause at all; this also destroys their notion of liberty, consisting in the will's determining its own acts.

THIS being the true state of the *Arminian* notion of liberty, it hence comes to pass, that the writers that defend it are forced into gross inconsistences, in what they say upon this subject. To instance, in Dr. *Whitby*; he in his discourse on the freedom of the will *, opposes the opinion of the *Calvinists*, who place man's liberty *only in a power of doing what he will*, as that wherein they

* In his Book on the five Points, Second Edit. p. 350 351, 352.

plainly

plainly agree with Mr *Hobbes*. And yet ye himself mentions the very same notion of liberty, as the dictate of *the sense and common reason of mankind, and a rule laid down by the light of nature*; viz that *liberty is a power of acting from ourselves, or DOING WHAT WE WILL* †. This is indeed, as he says, a thing agreable to *the sense and common reason of mankind*; and therefore it is not so much to be wondered at, that he unawares acknowledges it against himself: for if liberty does not consist in this, what else can be devised that it should consist in? if it be said, as Dr. *Whitby* elsewhere insists, that it does not only consist in liberty of *doing what we will*, but also a liberty of willing without necessity; still the question returns, what does that liberty of willing without necessity consist in, but in a power of willing *as we please*, without being impeded by a contrary necessity? or in other words, a liberty for the soul in its willing to act *according to its own choice?* Yea, this very thing the same author seems to allow, and suppose again and again, in the use he makes of sayings of the Fathers, whom he quotes as his vouchers. Thus he cites the words of *Origen*, which he produces as a testimony on his side ‡; *The soul acts by HER OWN CHOICE, and it is free for her to incline to whatever part SHE WILL.* And those words of *Justin Martyr* §; *the Doctrine of the Christinas is this, that nothing is done or suffered according to fate, but that every man doth good or evil ACCORDING TO HIS OWN FREE CHOICE.* And from *Eusebius*, these words ¶; *If fate be established, philosophy and piety are overthrown.— All these things depending upon the necessity introduced by the stars, and not upon meditation and exercise*

† In his Books on the five Points, Second Edit. p. 325, 326. ‡ ibid. 342, § ibid. p. 360. ¶ ibid. 363.

PRO-

PROCEEDING FROM OUR OWN FREE CHOICE. And again, the words of *Maccarius*; † *God, to preserve the liberty of man's will, suffered their bodies to die, that it might be IN THEIR CHOICE to turn to good or evil.——They who are acted by the Holy Spirit, are not held under any necessity, but have liberty to turn themselves, and DO WHAT THEY WILL in this life.*

Thus, the Doctor in effect comes into that very notion of liberty, which the *Calvinists* have; which he at the same time condemns, as agreeing with the opinion of Mr. *Hobbes*, namely, *the soul's acting by its own choice, men's doing good or evil according to their own free choice, their being in that exercise which proceeds from their own free choice, having it in their choice to turn to good or evil, and doing what they will.* So that if men exercise this liberty in the acts of the will themselves, it must be in exerting acts of will as they will, or *according to their own* free *choice*; or exerting acts of will *that proceed from their choice.* And if it be so, then let every one judge whether this does not suppose a free choice going before the free act of will, or whether an act of choice does not go before that act of the will which *proceeds from it.* And if it be thus with all free acts of the will, then let every one judge whether it will not follow that there is a free choice or will going before the first free act of the will exerted in the case. And then let every one judge, whether this be not a contradiction. And finally, let every one judge whether in the scheme of these writers there be any possibilty of avoiding these absurdities.

† In his Book on the five Points, Second Edit. 369, 370.

If liberty conſiſts, as Dr. *Whitby* himſelf ſays, in a man's *doing what he will*; and a man exerciſes this liberty, not only in external actions, but in the acts of the will themſelves; then ſo far as liberty is exerciſed in the latter, it conſiſts in *willing what he wills:* and if any ſay ſo, one of theſe two things muſt be meant, either, 1. That a man has power to will, as he does will; becauſe what he wills, he wills; and therefore has power to will what he has power to will. If this be their meaning, then all this mighty controverſy about freedom of the will and ſelf-determining power, comes wholly to nothing; all that is contended for being no more than this, that the mind of man does what it does, and is the ſubject of what it is the ſubject of, or that what is, is; wherein none has any controverſy with them. Or, 2. The meaning muſt be, that a man has power to will as he pleaſes or chuſes to will: that is, he has power by one act of choice, to chuſe another; by an antecedent act of will to chuſe a conſequent act; and therein to execute his own choice. And if this be their meaning, it is nothing but ſhuffling with thoſe they diſpute with, and baffling their own reaſon. For ſtill the queſtion returns, wherein lies man's liberty in that antecedent act of will which choſe the conſequent act. The anſwer according to the ſame principles muſt be, that his liberty in this alſo lies in his willing as he would, or as he choſe, or agreable to another act of choice preceding that. And ſo the queſtion returns *in infinitum*, and the like anſwer muſt be made *in infinitum*: in order to ſupport their opinion, there muſt be no beginning, but free acts of will muſt have been choſen by foregoing free acts of will in the ſoul of every man, without beginning; and ſo before he had a being, from all eternity.

SEC-

SECTION VI.

Concerning the Will's determining in Things which are perfectly indifferent *in the View of the Mind.*

A Great argument for self determining power, is the supposed experience we universally have an ability to determine our Wills, in cases wherein no prevailing motive is presented: the Will (as is supposed) has its choice to make between two or more things, that are perfectly equal in the view of the mind; and the Will is apparently altogether indifferent; and yet we find no difficulty in coming to a choice; the Will can instantly determine itself to one, by a sovereign power which it has over itself, without being moved by any preponderating inducement.

Thus the fore-mentioned author of an *Essay on the Freedom of the Will*, &c. p. 25, 26, 27. supposes, "That there are many instances, wherein the Will is determined neither by present uneasiness, nor by the greatest apparent good, nor by the last dictate of the understanding, nor by any thing else, but merely by itself, as a sovereign self-determining power of the soul; and that the soul does not will this or that action, in some cases, by any other influence but because it will. Thus (says he) I can turn my face to the South, or the North; I can point with my finger upward or downward.— And thus, in some cases, the Will determines itself in a very sovereign manner, because it will, without a reason borrowed from the understanding: and hereby it discovers its own perfect power of choice, rising from within itself,

ſelf and free from all influence or reſtraint of any kind." And in pages 66, 70, and 73, 74. this author very expreſsly ſuppoſes the Will in many caſes to be determined by *no motive at all, and acts altogether without motive, or ground of preference.*— Here I would obſerve,

1. The very ſuppoſition which is here made, directly contradicts and overthrows itſelf. For the thing ſuppoſed, wherein this grand argument conſiſts, is, that among ſeveral things the Will actually chuſes one before another, at the ſame time that it is perfectly indifferent; which is the very ſame thing as to ſay, the mind has a preference, at the ſame time that it has no preference. What is meant cannot be, that the mind is indifferent before it comes to have a choice, or until it has a preference; or, which is the ſame thing, that the mind is indifferent until it comes to be not indifferent. For certainly this author did not ſuppoſe he had a controverſy with any perſon in ſuppoſing this. And then it is nothing to his purpoſe, that the mind which chuſes, was indifferent once; unleſs it chuſes, remaining indifferent; for otherwiſe, it does not chuſe at all in that caſe of indifference, concerning which is all the queſtion. Beſides, it appears in fact, that the thing which this author ſuppoſes, is not that the Will chuſes one thing before another, concerning which it is indifferent *before it chuſes*; but alſo is indifferent *when* it *chuſes*; and that its being otherwiſe than indifferent is not until afterwards, in conſequence of its choice; that the choſen thing's appearing preferable and more agreable than another, ariſes from its choice already made. His words are (p. 30.) " Where the objects which are propoſed, appear equally fit or good, the Will is left without a guide or director;

and

and therefore must take its own choice, by its own determination; it being properly a self-determining power. And in such cases the will does as it were make a good to itself by its own choice, *i. e.* creates its own pleasure or delight in this self-chosen good. Even as a man by seizing upon a spot of unoccupied land, in an uninhabited country, makes it his own possession and property, and as such rejoices in it. Where things were indifferent before, the will finds nothing to make them more agreable, considered merely in themselves; but the pleasure it feels ARISING FROM ITS OWN CHOICE, and its perseverance therein. We love many things which we have chosen, AND PURELY BECAUSE WE CHOSE THEM."

This is as much as to say, that we first begin to prefer many things, now ceasing any longer to be indifferent with respect to them, purely because we have prefered and chosen them before. —These things must needs be spoken inconsiderately by this author. Choice or preference cannot be before itself in the same instance, either in the order of time or nature · It cannot be the foundation of itself, or the fruit or consequence of itself. The very act of chusing one thing *rather than another*, is *preferring* that thing, and that is setting a higher value on that thing. But that the mind sets an higher value on one thing than another, is not, in the first place, the fruit of its setting a higher value on that thing.

This author says, p. 36. "The will may be perfectly indifferent, and yet the will may determine itself to chuse one or the other." And again in the same page, " I am entirely indifferent

different to either; and yet my Will may determine itſelf to chuſe." And again, "Which I ſhall chuſe muſt be determined by the mere act of my Will." If the choice is determined by a mere act of Will; then the choice is determined by a mere act of choice. And concerning this matter, *viz.* That the act of the Will itſelf is determined by an act of choice, this writer is expreſs, in page 72. Speaking of the caſe, where there is no ſuperior fitneſs in objects preſented, he has theſe words: "There it muſt act by its own CHOICE, and determine itſelf as it PLEASES." Where it is ſuppoſed that the very *determination*, which is the ground and ſpring of the Will's act, is an act of *choice* and *pleaſure*, wherein one act is more agreable, and the mind better pleaſed in it than another; and this *preference* and *ſuperior pleaſedneſs* is the ground of all it does in the caſe. And if ſo, the mind is not indifferent when it determines itſelf, but *had rather* do one thing than another, had rather determine itſelf one way than another. And therefore the Will does not act at all in indifference; not ſo much as in the firſt ſtep it takes, or the firſt riſe and beginning of its acting. If it be poſſible for the underſtanding to act in indifference, yet to be ſure the Will never does; becauſe the Will's beginning to act is the very ſame thing as its beginning to chuſe or prefer. And if in the very firſt act of the Will, the mind prefers ſomething, then the idea of that thing preferred, does at that time preponderate, or prevail in the mind: or, which is the ſame thing, the idea of it has a prevailing influence on the Will. So that this wholly deſtroys the thing ſuppoſed, *viz.* That the mind can by a ſovreign power chuſe one of two or more things, which in the view of the mind are, in every reſpect, perfectly equal,

equal, one of which does not at all preponderate, nor has any prevailing influence on the mind above another.

So that this author, in his grand argument for the ability of the Will to chuse one of two, or more things, concerning which it is perfectly indifferent, does at the same time, in effect, deny the thing he supposes, and allows and asserts the point he endeavours to overthrow; even that the Will, in chusing, is subject to no prevailing influence of the idea, or view of the thing chosen. And indeed it is impossible to offer this argument without overthrowing it; the thing supposed in it being inconsistent with itself, and that which denies itself. To suppose the Will to act at all in a state of perfect indifference, either to determine itself, or to do any thing else, is to assert that the mind chuses without chusing. To say that when it is indifferent, it can do as it pleases, is to say that it can follow its pleasure, when it has no pleasure to follow. And therefore if there be any difficulty in the instances of two cakes, or two eggs, &c. which are exactly alike, one as good as another; concerning which this author supposes the mind in fact has a *choice*, and so in effect supposes that it has a *preference*; it as much concerned himself to solve the difficulty, as it does those whom he opposes. For if these instances prove any thing to his purpose, they prove that a man chuses without choice. And yet this is not to his purpose; because if this is what he asserts, his own words are as much against him, and do as much contradict him, as the words of those he disputes against can do.

2. There is no great difficulty in shewing, in such instances as are alledged, not only *that it*

must needs be so, that the mind must be influenced in its choice by something that has a preponderating influence upon it, but also *how it is so*. A little attention to our own experience, and a distinct consideration of the acts of our own minds, in such cases, will be sufficient to clear up the matter.

Thus, supposing I have a chess-board before me; and because I am required by a superior, or desired by a friend, or to make some experiment concerning my own ability and liberty, or on some other consideration, I am determined to touch some one of the spots or squares on the board with my finger; not being limited or directed in the first proposal, or my own first purpose, which is general, to any one in particular; and there being nothing in the squares in themselves considered, that recommends any one of all the sixty-four, more than another: in this case, my mind determines to give itself up to what is vulgarly called *acccident**, by determining to touch that square which happens to be most in view, which my eye is especially upon at that moment, or which happens to be then most in my mind, or which I shall be directed to by some other such-like accident. Here are several steps of the mind's proceeding, (though all may be done as it were in a moment) the *first* step is its *general* determination that it will touch one of the squares. The *next* step is another *general* determination to give itself up to accident, in some certain way; as

* I have elsewhere observed what that is which is vulgarly called *accident*; that it is nothing akin to the *Arminian* metaphysical notion of *contingence*, something not connected with any thing foregoing; but that it is something that comes to pass in the course of things, in some affair that men are concerned in, unforeseen, and not owing to their design.

as to touch that which ſhall be moſt in the eye or mind at that time, or to ſome other ſuch-like accident. The *third* and laſt ſtep is a *particular* determination to touch a certain individual ſpot, even that ſquare, which, by that ſort of accident the mind has pitched upon, has actually offered itſelf beyond others. Now it is apparent that in none of theſe ſeveral ſteps does the mind proceed in abſolute indifference, but in each of them is influenced by a preponderating inducement. So it is in the *firſt* ſtep; the mind's general determination to touch one of the ſixty-four ſpots: the mind is not abſolutely indifferent whether it does ſo or no: it is induced to it, for the ſake of making ſome experiment, or by the deſire of a friend, or ſome other motive that prevails. So it is in the *ſecond* ſtep, the mind's determining to give itſelf up to accident, by touching that which ſhall be moſt in the eye, or the idea of which ſhall be moſt prevalent in the mind, &c. The mind is not abſolutely indifferent whether it proceeds by this rule or no; but chuſes it becauſe it appears at that time a convenient and requiſite expedient in order to fulfil the general purpoſe aforeſaid. And ſo it is in the *third* and laſt ſtep, it is determining to touch that individual ſpot which actually does prevail in the mind's view. The mind is not indifferent concerning this; but is influenced by a prevailing inducement and reaſon; which is, that this is a proſecution of the preceding determination, which appeared requiſite, and was fixed before in the ſecond ſtep.

Accident will ever ſerve a man, without hindering him a moment, in ſuch a caſe. It will always be ſo among a number of objects in view, one will prevail in the eye, or in idea beyond others: When we have our eyes open in the clear ſun-ſhine, many objects ſtrike the eye at once, and innumerable images may be at once painted in it by the rays of light; but the attention of the mind is not equal to ſeveral of them at once; or if it be, it does not continue ſo for any time. And ſo it is with reſpect to the ideas of the mind in general: ſeveral ideas are not in equal ſtrength in the mind's view and notice at once; or at leaſt, does not remain ſo for any ſenſible continuance. There is nothing in the world more conſtantly varying, than the ideas of the mind: they do not remain preciſely in the ſame ſtate for the leaſt perceivable ſpace of time: as is evident by this. That all perceivable time is judged and perceived by the mind only by the ſucceſſion or the ſucceſſive changes of its own ideas. Therefore while the views or perceptions of the mind remain preciſely in the ſame ſtate, there is no perceivable ſpace or length of time, becauſe no ſenſible ſucceſſion at all.

As the acts of the Will, in each ſtep of the fore-mentioned procedure, does not come to paſs without a particular cauſe, every act is owing to a prevailing inducement: ſo the accident, as I have called it, or that which happens in the unſearchable courſe of things, to which the mind yields itſelf, and by which it is guided, is not any thing that comes to paſs without a cauſe; and the mind in determining to be guided by it, is not determined by ſomething that has no cauſe; any more than if it determined to be guided by a lot, or the caſting of a die. For though the die's falling in ſuch a manner be accidental to him that caſts it, yet none will ſuppoſe that there is no cauſe why it falls as it does. The involuntary changes in the ſucceſſion of our ideas, though the

cauſe

cause may not be observed, have as much a cause as the changeable motions of the motes that float in the air, or the continual, infinitely various, successive changes of the unevennesses on the surface of the water.

THERE are two things especially, which are probably the occasions of confusion in the minds of them who insist upon it, that the will acts in a proper indifference, and without being moved by any inducement, in its determinations in such cases as have been mentioned.

1. THEY seem to mistake the point in question, or at least not to keep it distinctly in view. The question they dispute about, is, Whether the mind be indifferent about the *objects* presented, one of which is to be taken, touched, pointed to, &c. as two eggs, two cakes, which appear equally good. Whereas the question to be considered is, Whether the person be indifferent with respect to his own *actions*; whether he does not, on some consideration or other, prefer one act with respect to these objects before another. The mind in its determination and choice, in these cases, is not most immediately and directly conversant about the *objects presented*; but *the acts to be done* concerning these objects. The objects may appear equal, and the mind may never properly make any choice between them: but the next act of the Will being about the external actions to be performed, taking, touching, &c. these may not appear equal, and one action may properly be chosen before another. In each step of the mind's progress, the determination is not about the objects, unless indirectly and improperly, but about the actions, which it chuses for other reasons than any preference of the objects, and for reasons not taken at all from the objects.

There is no necessity of supposing, that the mind does ever at all properly chuse one of the objects before another; either before it has taken, or afterwards. Indeed the man chuses to *take* or *touch* one rather than another; but not because it chuses the *thing taken*, or *touched*; but from foreign considerations. The case may be so, that of two things offered, a man may, for certain reasons, chuse and prefer the taking of that which he *undervalues*, and chuse to neglect to take that which his mind *prefers*. In such a case, chusing the thing taken, and chusing to take, are diverse: and so they are in a case where the things presented are equal in the mind's esteem, and neither of them preferred. All that fact and experience makes evident, is, that the mind chuses one action rather than another. And therefore the arguments which they bring, in order to be to their purpose, ought to be to prove that the mind chuses the action in perfect indifference, with respect to *that action*; and not to prove that the mind chuses the action in perfect indifference with respect to the *object*; which is very possible, and yet the will not act at all without prevalent inducement, and proper preponderation.

2. Another reason of confusion and difficulty in this matter, seems to be, not distinguishing between a *general* indifference, or an indifference with respect to what is to be done in a more distant and general view of it, and a *particular* indifference, or an indifference with respect to the next immediate act, viewed with its particular and present circumstances. A man may be perfectly indifferent with respect to his own *actions*, in the former respect; and yet not in the latter. Thus, in the foregoing instance of touching one of the squares of a chess-board; when it is first proposed

posed that I should touch one of them, I may be perfectly indifferent which I touch; because as yet I view the matter remotely and generally, being but in the first step of the mind's progress in the affair. But yet, when I am actually come to the last step, and the very next thing to be determined is which is to be touched, having already determined that I will touch that which happens to be most in my eye or mind, and my mind being now fixed on a particular one, the act of touching that, considered thus immediately, and in these particular present circumstances, is not what my mind is absolutely indifferent about.

SECTION VII.

Concerning the notion of Liberty of Will, *consisting in* Indifference.

WHAT has been said in the foregoing section, has a tendency in some measure to evince the absurdity of the opinion of such as place Liberty in Indifference, or in that equilibrium whereby the Will is without all antecedent determination or bias, and left hitherto free from any prepossessing inclination to one side or the other; that the determination of the Will to either side may be entirely from itself, and that it may be owing only to its own power, and that sovereignty which it has over itself, that it goes this way rather than that.*

* Dr. *Whitby*, and some other *Arminians*, make a distinction of different kinds of freedom; one of God, and perfect spirits above; another of persons in a state of trial. The former Dr. *Whitby* allows to consist with necessity; the latter he holds to be without necessity: and this latter he supposes to be requisite

But in as much as this has been of ſuch long ſtanding, and has been ſo generally received, and ſo much inſiſted on by *Pelagians*, *Semi-Pelagians*, *Jeſuits*, *Socinians*, *Arminians*, and others, it may deſerve a more full conſideration. And therefore I ſhall now proceed to a more particular and thorough enquiry into this notion.

Now leſt ſome ſhould ſuppoſe that I do not underſtand thoſe that place Liberty in Indifference, or ſhould charge me with miſrepreſenting their opinion, I would ſignify, that I am ſenſible, there are ſome, who when they talk of the Liberty of the Will as conſiſting in Indifference, expreſs themſelves as though they would not be underſtood of the Indifference of the inclination or tendency of the will, but of, I know not what, Indifference of the ſoul's power of willing; or that the Will, with reſpect to its power or ability to chuſe, is indifferent, can go either way indifferently, either to the right hand or left, either act or forbear to act, one as well as the other. Though this ſeems to be a refining only of ſome particular writers, and newly invented, and which will by no means conſiſt

requiſite to our being the ſubjects of praiſe or diſpraiſe, rewards or puniſhments, precepts and prohibitions, promiſes and threats, exhortations and dehortations, and a covenant-treaty. And to this freedom he ſuppoſes *Indifference* to be requiſite. In his Diſcourſe on the five points, p. 299, 300, he ſays; "It is a freedom (ſpeaking of a freedom not only from co-action, but from neceſſity) requiſite, as we conceive, to render us capable of trial or probation, and to render our actions worthy of praiſe or diſpraiſe, and our perſons of rewards or puniſhments." And in the next page, ſpeaking of the ſame matter, he ſays, "Excellent to this purpoſe, are the words of Mr. *Thorndike: We ſay not, that Indifference is requiſite to all freedom, but to the freedom of man alone in this ſtate of travail and proficience: the ground of which is God's tender of a treaty, and conditions of peace and reconcilement to fallen man, together with thoſe precepts and prohibitions, thoſe promiſes and threats, thoſe exhortations and dehortations, it is enforced with.*"

confiſt with the manner of expreſſion uſed by the defenders of Liberty of Indifference in general. And I wiſh ſuch refiners would thoroughly conſider, whether they diſtinctly know their own meaning, when they make a diſtinction between Indifference of the ſoul as to its *power* or *ability* of willing or chuſing, and the ſoul's Indifference as to the preference or choice itſelf; and whether they do not deceive themſelves in imagining that they have any diſtinct meaning at all. The Indifference of the ſoul as to its ability or power to will, muſt be the ſame thing as the Indifference of the ſtate of the power or faculty of the Will, or the Indifference of the ſtate which the ſoul itſelf, which has that power or faculty, hitherto remains in, as to the exerciſe of that power, in the choice it ſhall by and by make.

But not to inſiſt any longer on the abſtruſeneſs and inexplicableneſs of this diſtinction; let what will be ſuppoſed concerning the meaning of them that make uſe of it, thus much muſt at leaſt be intended by *Arminians* when they talk of Indifference as eſſential to Liberty of Will, if they intend any thing, in any reſpect to their purpoſe, *viz.* That it is ſuch an Indifference as leaves the Will not determined already; but free from actual poſſeſſion, and vacant of predetermination, ſo far, that there may be room for the exerciſe of the *ſelf-determining power* of the Will; and that the Will's freedom conſiſts in, or depends upon this vacancy and opportunity that is left for the Will itſelf to be the determiner of the act that is to be the free act.

And here I would obſerve in the *firſt* place, that to make out this ſcheme of Liberty, the Indifference muſt be *perfect* and *abſolute*; there muſt be a per-a perfect freedom from all antecedent preponderation or inclination. Because if the Will be already inclined, before it exerts its own sovereign power on itself, then its inclination is not wholly owing to itself: if when two opposites are proposed to the soul for its choice, the proposal does not find the soul wholly in a state of Indifference, then it is not found in a state of Liberty for mere self determination.—The least degree of an antecedent bias must be inconsistent with their notion of Liberty. For so long as prior inclination possesses the Will, and is not removed, it binds the Will, so that it is utterly impossible that the Will should act otherwise than agreably to it. Surely the Will cannot act or chuse contrary to a remaining prevailing inclination of the Will. To suppose otherwise, would be the same thing as to suppose, that the Will is *inclined* contrary to its present prevailing *inclination*, or contrary to what it is *inclined* to. That which the Will chuses and prefers, that, all things considered, it preponderates and inclines to. It is equally impossible for the Will to chuse contrary to its own remaining and present preponderating inclination, as it is to *prefer* contrary to its own present *preference*, or *chuse* contrary to its own present *choice*. The Will, therefore, so long as it is under the influence of an old preponderating inclination, is not at Liberty for a new free act, or any act that shall now be an act of self-determination. The act which is a self-determined free act, must be an act which the will determines in the possession and use of such a Liberty, as consists in a freedom from every thing, which, if it were there, would make it impossible that the Will, at that time, should be otherwise than that way to which it tends.

If any one should say, there is no need that the Indifference should be perfect; but although a former inclination and preference still remains, yet, if it be not very strong and violent, possibly the strength of the Will may oppose and overcome it: This is grossly absurd; for the strength of the Will, let it be never so great, does not at all enable it to act one way, and not the contrary way, both at the same time. It gives it no such sovereignty and command, as to cause itself to prefer and not to prefer at the same time, or to chuse contrary to its own present choice.

Therefore, if there be the least degree of antecedent preponderation of the Will, it must be perfectly abolished, before the Will can be at liberty to determine itself the contrary way. And if the Will determines itself the same way, it was not a *free determination*, because the Will is not wholly at Liberty in so doing: its determination is not altogether *from itself*, but it was partly determined before, in its prior inclination: and all the freedom the Will exercises in the case, is in an increase of inclination, which it gives itself, over and above what it had by foregoing bias; so much is from itself, and so much is from perfect Indifference. For though the Will had a previous tendency that way, yet as to that additional degree of inclination, it had no tendency. Therefore the previous tendency is of no consideration, with respect to the act wherein the Will is free. So that it comes to the same thing which was said at first, that as to the act of the Will, wherein the Will is free, there must be *perfect Indifference* or *equilibrium*.

To illustrate this; if we should suppose a sovereign self-moving power in a natural body: but that

that the body is in motion already, by an antecedent bias; for inſtance, gravitation towards the center of the earth; and has one degree of motion already, by virtue of that previous tendency; but by its ſelf moving power it adds one degree more to its motion, and moves ſo much more ſwiftly towards the center of the earth than it would do by its gravity only: it is evident, that all that is owing to a ſelf-moving power in this caſe, is the additional degree of motion; and that the other degree of motion which it had from gravity, is of no conſideration in the caſe, does not help the effect of the free ſelf-moving power in the leaſt; the effect is juſt the ſame, as if the body had received from itſelf one degree of motion from a ſtate of perfect reſt. So if we ſhould ſuppoſe a ſelf moving power given to the ſcale of a balance, which has a weight of one degree beyond the oppoſite ſcale; and we aſcribe to it an ability to add to itſelf another degree of force the ſame way, by its ſelf-moving power; this is juſt the ſame thing as to aſcribe to it a power to give itſelf one degree of preponderation from a perfect equilibrium; and ſo much power as the ſcale has to give itſelf an over-balance from a perfect equipoiſe, ſo much ſelf-moving ſelf-preponderating power it has, and no more. So that its free power this way is always to be meaſured from perfect equilibrium.

I NEED ſay no more to prove, that if Indifference be eſſential to Liberty, it muſt be perfect Indifference; and that ſo far as the Will is deſtitute of this, ſo far it is deſtitute of that freedom by which it is its own maſter, and in a capacity of being its own determiner, without being at all paſſive, or ſubject to the power and ſway of

ſome-

ſomething elſe, in its motions and determinations.

HAVING obſerved theſe things, let us now try whether this notion of the Liberty of Will conſiſting in Indifierence and equilibrium, and the Will's ſelf-determination in ſuch a ſtate be not abſurd and inconſiſtent.

AND here I would lay down this as an axiom of undoubted truth; *that every free act is done in a ſtate of freedom, and not only after ſuch a ſtate.* If an act of the Will be an act wherein the ſoul is free, it muſt be exerted in a *ſtate of freedom*, and in the *time of freedom.* It will not ſuffice, that the act immediately follows a ſtate of Liberty; but Liberty muſt yet continue, and co-exiſt with the act; the ſoul remaining in poſſeſſion of Liberty. Becauſe that is the notion of a free act of the ſoul, even an act wherein the ſoul *uſes* or *exerciſes Liberty.* But if the ſoul is not, in the very time of the act, in the *poſſeſſion* of Liberty, it cannot at that time be in the *uſe* of it.

Now the queſtion is, whether ever the ſoul of man puts forth an act of Will, while it yet remains in a ſtate of Liberty, in that notion of a ſtate of Liberty, *viz.* as implying a ſtate of Indifference; or whether the ſoul ever exerts an act of choice or preference, while at that very time the Will is in a perfect equilibrium, not inclining one way more than another. The very putting of the queſtion is ſufficient to ſhew the abſurdity of the affirmative anſwer: for how ridiculous would it be for any body to inſiſt, that the ſoul chuſes one thing before another, when at the very ſame inſtant it is perfectly indifferent with reſpect to each! This is the ſame thing as to ſay, the ſoul

ſoul prefers one thing to another, at the very ſame time that it has no preference.——Choice and preference can no more be in a ſtate of Indifference, than motion can be in a ſtate of reſt, or than the preponderation of the ſcale of a balance can be in a ſtate of equilibrium. Motion may be the next moment after reſt; but cannot co-exiſt with it, in *any*, even the *leaſt* part of it. So choice may be immediately after a ſtate of Indifference, but has no co-exiſtence with it: even the very beginning of it is not in a ſtate of Indifference. And therefore if this be Liberty, no act of the Will, in any degree, is ever performed in a ſtate of Liberty, or in the time of Liberty. Volition and Liberty are ſo far from agreeing together, and being eſſential one to another, that they are contrary one to another, and one excludes and deſtroys the other, as much as motion and reſt, light and darkneſs, or life and death. So that the Will acts not at all, does not ſo much as begin to act in the time of ſuch Liberty: freedom is perfectly at an end, and has ceaſed to be, at the firſt moment of action; and therefore Liberty cannot reach the action, to affect, or qualify it, or give it a denomination, or any part of it, any more than if it had ceaſed to be twenty years before the action began. The moment that Liberty ceaſes to be, it ceaſes to be a qualification of any thing. If light and darkneſs ſucceed one another inſtantaneouſly, light qualifies nothing after it is gone out, to make any thing lightſome or bright, any more at the firſt moment of perfect darkneſs, than months or years after. Life denominates nothing *vital* at the firſt moment of perfect death. So freedom, if it conſiſts in, or implies Indifference, can denominate nothing free, at the firſt moment of preference or preponderation. Therefore it is manifeſt, that no Liberty

Liberty which the soul is possessed of, or ever uses, in any of its acts of volition, consists in Indifference; and that the opinion of such as suppose, that Indifference belongs to the very essence of Liberty, is to the highest degree absurd and contradictory.

If any one should imagine, that this manner of arguing is nothing but a trick and delusion; and to evade the reasoning, should say, that the thing wherein the Will exercises its Liberty, is not in the act of choice or preponderation itself, but in *determining* itself to a certain choice or preference; that the act of the Will wherein it is free, and uses its own sovereignty, consists in its *causing* or *determining* the *change* or *transition* from a state of Indifference to a certain preference, or determining to give a certain turn to the balance, which has hitherto been even; and that this act the Will exerts in a state of Liberty, or while the Will yet remains in equilibrium, and perfect master of itself.—I say, if any one chuses to express his notion of Liberty after this, or some such manner, let us see if he can make out his matters any better than before.

What is asserted is, that the Will, while it yet remains in perfect equilibrium, without preference, determines to change itself from that state, and excite in itself a certain choice or preference. Now let us see whether this does not come to the same absurdity we had before. If it be so, that the Will, while it yet remains perfectly indifferent, determines to put itself out of that state, and give itself a certain preponderation; then I would enquire, whether the soul does not determine this of choice; or whether the Will's coming to a determination to do so, be not the same thing

as

as the soul's coming to a choice to do so. If the soul does not determine this of choice, or in the exercise of choice, then it does not determine it voluntarily. And if the soul does not determine it voluntarily, or of its own *will*, then in what sense does its *will* determine it? And if the will does not determine it, then how is the *Liberty of the Will* exercised in the determination? What sort of Liberty is exercised by the soul in those determinations, wherein there is no exercise of choice, which are not voluntary, and wherein the will is not concerned? But if it be allowed, that this determination is an act of choice, and it be insisted on, that the soul, while it yet remains in a state of perfect Indifference, chuses to put itself out of that state, and to turn itself one way; then the soul is already come to a choice, and chuses that way. And so we have the very same absurdity which we had before. Here is the soul in a state of choice, and in a state of equilibrium, both at the same time: the soul already chusing one way, while it remains in a state of perfect Indifference, and has no choice of one way more than the other. And indeed this manner of talking, though it may a little hide the absurdity, in the obscurity of expression, is more nonsensical, and increases the inconsistence. To say, the free act of the will, or the act which the will exerts in a state of freedom and Indifference, does not imply preference in it, but is what the will does in order to causing or producing a preference, is as much as to say, the soul chuses (for to will and to chuse are the same thing) without choice, and prefers without preference, in order to cause or produce the beginning of a preference, or the first choice. And that is, that the first choice is exerted without choice, in order to produce itself.

If any, to evade theſe things, ſhould own, that a ſtate of Liberty, and a ſtate of indifference are not the ſame, and that the former may be without the latter; but ſhould ſay, that indifference is ſtill *eſſential to* the freedom of an act of will, in ſome ſort, namely, as it is neceſſary to go immediately *before it*; it being eſſential to the freedom of an act of will that it ſhould directly and immediately *ariſe out* of a ſtate of indifference: ſtill this will not help the cauſe of *Arminian* Liberty, or make it conſiſtent with itſelf. For if the act ſprings immediately out of a ſtate of Indifference, then it does not ariſe from *antecedent* choice or preference. But if the act ariſes directly out of a ſtate of Indifference, without any intervening choice to chuſe and determine it, then the act not being determined by choice, is not determined by the will; the mind exerciſes no free choice in the affair, and free choice and free will have no hand in the determination of the act. Which is entirely inconſiſtent with their notion of the freedom of Volition.

If any ſhould ſuppoſe, that theſe difficulties and abſurdities may be avoided, by ſaying, that the Liberty of the mind conſiſts in a power to *ſuſpend* the act of the will, and ſo to keep it in a ſtate of *Indifference*, until there has been opportunity for conſideration; and ſo ſhall ſay, that however Indifference is not eſſential to Liberty in ſuch a manner, that the mind muſt make its choice in a ſtate of Indifference, which is an inconſiſtency, or that the act of will muſt ſpring immediately out of Indifference; yet Indifference may be eſſential to the liberty of acts of the will in this reſpect; *viz.* That Liberty conſiſts in a Power of the mind to forbear or ſuſpend the act of Volition, and keep the mind in a ſtate of Indifference for the preſent, until there has been opportunity for proper deliberation: I ſay, if any one imagines that this helps the matter, it is a great miſtake: it reconciles no inconſiſtency, and relieves no difficulty which the affair is attended with.—For here the following things muſt be obſerved,

1. THAT this *ſuſpending* of Volition, if there be properly any ſuch thing, is itſelf an act of Volition. If the mind determines to ſuſpend its act, it determines it voluntarily; it chuſes, on ſome conſideration, to ſuſpend it. And this choice or determination, is an act of the will: And indeed it is ſuppoſed to be ſo in the very hypotheſis; for it is ſuppoſed that the Liberty *of the will* conſiſts in its Power to do this, and that its doing it is the very thing wherein *the will exerciſes its Liberty.* But how can the will exerciſe Liberty in it, if it be not an act of the will? The Liberty of the will is not exerciſed in any thing but what the will does.

2. THIS determining to ſuſpend acting is not only an act of the will, but it is ſuppoſed to be the only free act of the will; becauſe it is ſaid, that *this is the thing wherein the Liberty of the will conſiſts*—Now if this be ſo, then this is all the act of will that we have to conſider in this controverſy, about the Liberty of will, and in our enquiries, wherein the Liberty of man conſiſts. And now the forementioned difficulties remain: the former queſtion returns upon us; *viz.* Wherein conſiſts the freedom of the will *in thoſe acts* wherein it is free? And if this act of determining a ſuſpenſion be the only act in which the

will

will is free, then wherein conſiſts the will's freedom with reſpect to this act of ſuſpenſion? And how is indifference eſſential to this act? The anſwer muſt be, according to what is ſuppoſed in the evaſion under conſideration, that the Liberty of the will in this act of ſuſpenſion, conſiſts in a Power to ſuſpend even this act, until there has been opportunity for thorough deliberation. But this will be to plunge directly into the groſſeſt nonſenſe: for it is the act of ſuſpenſion itſelf that we are ſpeaking of; and there is no room for a ſpace of deliberation and ſuſpenſion in order to determine whether we will ſuſpend or no. For that ſuppoſes, that even ſuſpenſion itſelf may be deferred: which is abſurd; for the very deferring the determination of ſuſpenſion, to conſider whether we will ſuſpend or no, will be actually ſuſpending. For during the ſpace of ſuſpenſion, to conſider whether to ſuſpend, the act is *ipſo facto* ſuſpended. There is no medium between ſuſpending to act, and immediately acting; and therefore no poſſibility of avoiding either the one or the other one moment.

And beſides, this is attended with ridiculous abſurdity another way: for now it is come to that, that Liberty conſiſts wholly in the mind's having Power to ſuſpend its determination whether to ſuſpend or no; that there may be time for conſideration, whether it be beſt to ſuſpend. And if Liberty conſiſts in this only, then this is the Liberty under conſideration: we have to enquire now, how Liberty with reſpect to this act of ſuſpending a determination of ſuſpenſion, conſiſts in Indifference, or how Indifference is eſſential to it. The anſwer, according to the hypotheſis we are upon, muſt be, that it conſiſts in a Power of ſuſpending even this laſt-mentioned act, to have time to conſider whether to ſuſpend that. And then the ſame difficulties and enquiries return over again with reſpect to that; and ſo on for ever. Which, if it would ſhew any thing, would ſhew only that there is no ſuch thing as a free act It drives the exerciſe of freedom back *in infinitum*; and that is to drive it out of the world.

And beſides all this, there it a Deluſion, and a latent groſs contradiction in the affair another way; in as much as in explaining how, or in what reſpect the will is free with regard to a particular act of Volition, it is ſaid, that its Liberty conſiſts in a Power to determine to ſuſpend *that act*, which places Liberty not in *that act* of Volition which the enquiry is about, but altogether in another antecedent act. Which contradicts the thing ſuppoſed in both the queſtion and anſwer. The queſtion is, wherein conſiſts the mind's Liberty *in any particular act* of Volition? And the anſwer, in pretending to ſhew wherein lies the mind's Liberty *in that act*, in effect ſays, it does not lie in that act at all, but in another, *viz.* a Volition *to ſuſpend that act*. And therefore the anſwer is both contradictory, and altogether impertinent and beſide the purpoſe. For it does not ſhew wherein the Liberty of the will conſiſts in the act in queſtion; inſtead of that, it ſuppoſes it does not conſiſt in that act at all, but in another diſtinct from it, even a Volition to ſuſpend that act, and take time to conſider of it. And no account is pretended to be given wherein the mind is free with reſpect to that act, wherein this anſwer ſuppoſes the Liberty of the mind indeed

deed consists, *viz.* the act of suspension, or of determining the suspension.

On the whole, it is exceeding manifest, that the Liberty of the mind does not consist in Indifference, and that Indifference is not essential or necessary to it, or at all belonging to it, as the *Arminians* suppose; that opinion being full of nothing but absurdity and self-contradiction.

SECTION VIII.

Concerning the supposed Liberty of the Will, as opposite to all Necessity.

It is a thing chiefly insisted on by *Arminians*, in this controversy, as a thing most important and essential in human Liberty, that volitions, or the acts of the will, are *contingent* events; understanding contingence as opposite not only to constraint, but to all Necessity. Therefore I would particularly consider this matter. And,

1. I would enquire, whether there is, or can be any such thing, as a volition which is contingent in such a sense, as not only to come to pass without any necessity of constraint or co-action, but also without a *Necessity of consequence*, or an infallible connection with any thing foregoing.

2. Wether, if it were so, this would at all help the cause of Liberty.

I. I would consider whether volition is a thing that ever does, or can come to pass, in this manner, contingently.

And

And here it muſt be remembered, that it has been already ſhewn, that nothing can ever come to paſs without a cauſe, or reaſon why it exiſts in this manner rather than another; and the evidence of this has been particularly applied to the acts of the will. Now if this be ſo, it will demonſtrably follow, that the acts of the will are never contingent, or without neceſſity in the ſenſe ſpoken of; in as much as thoſe things which have a cauſe, or reaſon of their exiſtence, muſt be connected with their cauſe. This appears by the following conſiderations.

1. For an event to have a cauſe and ground of its exiſtence, and yet not to be connected with its cauſe, is an inconſiſtence. For if the event be not connected with the cauſe, it is not dependent on the cauſe; its exiſtence is as it were looſe from its influence, and may attend it, or may not; it being a mere contingence, whether it follows or attends the influence of the cauſe, or not: And that is the ſame thing as not to be dependent on it. And to ſay, the event is not dependent on its cauſe, is abſurd: It is the ſame thing as to ſay, it is not its cauſe, nor the event the effect of it: For dependence on the influence of a cauſe is the very notion of an effect. If there be no ſuch relation between one thing and another, conſiſting in the connection and dependence of one thing on the influence of another, then it is certain there is no ſuch relation between them as is ſignified by the terms *cauſe* and *effect*. So far as an event is dependent on a cauſe and connected with it, ſo much cauſality is there in the caſe, and no more. The cauſe does, or brings to paſs no more in any event, than is dependent on it. If we ſay, the connection

tion and dependence is not total, but partial, and that the effect, though it has ſome connection and dependence, yet is not entirely dependent on it; that is the ſame thing as to ſay, that not all that is in the event is an effect of that cauſe, but that only part of it ariſes from thence, and part ſome other way.

2. If there are ſome events which are not neceſſarily connected with their cauſes, then it will follow, that there are ſome things which come to paſs without any cauſe, contrary to the ſuppoſition. For if there be any event which was not neceſſarily connected with the influence of the cauſe under ſuch circumſtances, then it was contingent whether it would attend or follow the influence of the cauſe, or no; it might have followed, and it might not, when the cauſe was the ſame, its influence the ſame, and under the ſame circumſtances. And if ſo, why did it follow, rather than not follow? There is no cauſe or reaſon of this. Therefore here is ſomething without any cauſe or reaſon why it is, *viz.* the following of the effect on the influence of the cauſe, with which it was not neceſſarily connected. If there be a neceſſary connection of the effect on any thing antecedent, then we may ſuppoſe that ſometimes the event will follow the cauſe, and ſometimes not, when the cauſe is the ſame, and in every reſpect in the ſame ſtate and circumſtances. And what can be the cauſe and reaſon of this ſtrange phenomenon, even this diverſity, that in one inſtance, the effect ſhould follow, in another not? It is evident by the ſuppoſition, that this is wholly without any cauſe or ground. Here is ſomething in the preſent manner of the exiſtence of things, and ſtate of the world, that

is absolutely without a cause. Which is contrary to the supposition, and contrary to what has been before demonstrated.

3. To suppose there are some events which have a cause and ground of their existence, that yet are not necessarily connected with their cause is to suppose that they have a cause which is not their cause. Thus; if the effect be not necessarily connected with the cause, with its influence, and influential circumstance; then, as I observed before, it is a thing possible and supposable, that the cause may sometimes exert the same influence, under the same circumstances, and yet the effect not follow. And if this actually happens in any instance, this instance is a proof, in fact, that the influence of the cause is not sufficient to produce the effect. For if it had been sufficient, it would have done it. And yet, by the supposition, in another instance, the same cause, with perfectly the same influence, and when all circumstances which have any influence, are the same, it *was followed* with the effect. By which it is manifest, that the effect in this last instance was not owing to the influence of the cause, but must come to pass some other way. For it was proved before, that the influence of the cause was not sufficient to produce the effect.

And if it was not sufficient to produce it, then the production of it could not be owing to that influence, but must be owing to something else, or owing to nothing. And if the effect be not owing to the influence of the cause, then it is not the cause. Which brings us to the contradiction, of a cause, and no cause, that which is the ground and reason of the existence of a thing,

thing, and at the ſame time is not the ground and reaſon of its exiſtence, nor is ſufficient to be ſo.

If the matter be not already ſo plain as to render any further reaſoning upon it impertinent, I would ſay, that that which ſeems to be the cauſe in the ſuppoſed caſe, can be no cauſe; its power and influence having, on a full trial, proved inſufficient to produce ſuch an effect: and if it be not ſufficient to produce it, then it does not produce it. To ſay otherwiſe, is to ſay, there is power to do that which there is not power to do. If there be in a cauſe ſufficient power exerted, and in circumſtances ſufficient to produce an effect, and ſo the effect be actually produced at *one time*; theſe things all concurring, will produce the effect at *all times*. And ſo we may turn it the other way; that which proves not ſufficient at one time, cannot be ſufficient at another, with preciſely the ſame influential circumſtances. And therefore if the effect follows, it is not owing to that cauſe; unleſs the different time be a circumſtance which has influence: but that is contrary to the ſuppoſition; for it is ſuppoſed that all circumſtances that have influence, are the ſame. And beſides, this would be to ſuppoſe the time to be the cauſe; which is contrary to the ſuppoſition of the other thing's being the cauſe. But if merely diverſity of time has no influence, then it is evident that it is as much of an abſurdity to ſay, the cauſe was ſufficient to produce the effect at one time, and not at another; as to ſay, that it is ſufficient to produce the effect at a certain time, and yet not ſufficient to produce the ſame effect at the ſame time.

On

On the whole, it is clearly manifeſt, that every effect has a neceſſary connection with its cauſe, or with that which is the true ground and reaſon of its exiſtence. And therefore if there be no event without a cauſe, as was proved before, then no event whatſoever is contingent in the manner, that *Arminians* ſuppoſe the free acts of the will to be contingent.

SECTION IX.

Of the Connection *of the Acts of the Will with the Dictates of the* Underſtanding.

IT is manifeſt, that the Acts of the Will are none of them contingent in ſuch a ſenſe as to be without all neceſſity, or ſo as not to be neceſſary with a neceſſity of conſequence and Connection; becauſe every Act of the Will is ſome way connected with the Underſtanding, and is as the greateſt apparent good is, in the manner which has already been explained; namely, that the ſoul always wills or chuſes that which, in the preſent view of the mind, conſidered in the whole of that view, and all that belongs to it, appears moſt agreable. Becauſe, as was obſerved before, nothing is more evident than that, when men act voluntarily, and do what they pleaſe, then they do what appears moſt agreable to them; and to ſay otherwiſe, would be as much as to affirm, that men do not chuſe what appears to ſuit them beſt, or what ſeems moſt pleaſing to them; or that they do not chuſe what they prefer. Which brings the matter to a contradiction.

se Brt I Sect. II.

AND

And it is very evident in itſelf, that the Acts of the Will have ſome Connection with the dictates or views of the Underſtanding, ſo this is allowed by ſome of the chief of the *Arminian* writers: particularly by Dr. *Whitby* and Dr. *Samuel Clark.* Dr. *Turnbull,* though a great enemy to the doctrine of neceſſity, allows the ſame thing. In his *Chriſtian Philoſophy,* (p. 196.) he with much approbation cites another philoſopher, as of the ſame mind, in theſe words: "No man, (ſays an excellent philoſopher) ſets himſelf about any thing, but upon ſome view or other, which ſerves him for a reaſon for what he does; and whatſoever faculties he employs, the Underſtanding, with ſuch light as it has, well or ill formed, conſtantly leads; and by that light, true or falſe, all her operative powers are directed. The Will itſelf, how abſolute and incontroulable ſoever it may be thought, never fails in its obedience to the dictates of the Underſtanding. Temples have their ſacred images: and we ſee what influence they have always had over a great part of mankind; but in truth, the ideas and images in men's minds are the inviſible powers that conſtantly govern them; and to theſe they all pay univerſally a ready ſubmiſſion."

But whether this be in a juſt conſiſtence with themſelves, and their own notions of liberty, I deſire may now be impartially conſidered.

Dr. *Whitby* plainly ſuppoſes, that the Acts and Determinations of the Will always follow the Underſtanding's apprehenſion or view of the greateſt good to be obtained, or evil to be avoided, or, in other words, that the Determinations of the

Will

Will conſtantly and infallibly follow theſe two things in the Underſtanding; 1. The *degree of good* to be obtained, and evil to be avoided, propoſed to the Underſtanding, and apprehended, viewed, and taken notice of by it. 2. The *degree of the underſtanding's view*, notice or apprehenſion of that good or evil; which is increaſed by attention and conſideration. That this is an opinion he is exceeding peremptory in (as he is in every opinion which he maintains in his controverſy with the *Calviniſts*) with diſdain of the contrary opinion, as abſurd and ſelf-contradictory, will appear by the following words of his, in his Diſcourſe on the Five Points*.

" Now, it is certain, that what naturally makes the Underſtanding to perceive, is evidence propoſed, and apprehended, conſidered or adverted to: for nothing elſe can be requiſite to make us come to the knowledge of the truth. Again, what makes the will chuſe, is ſomething approved by the Underſtanding; and conſequently appearing to the ſoul as good. And whatſoever it refuſeth, is ſomething repreſented by the Underſtanding, and ſo appearing to the Will, as evil. Whence all that God requires of us is and can be only this; to refuſe the evil, and chuſe the good. Wherefore, to ſay that evidence propoſed, apprehended and conſidered, is not ſufficient to make the Underſtanding approve; or that the greateſt good propoſed, the greateſt evil threatened, when equally believed and reflected on, is not ſufficient to engage the Will to chuſe the good and refuſe the evil, is in effect to ſay, *that which alone doth*

* Second Edit. p. 211, 212, 213.

doth move the Will, to chuſe or to refuſe, is not ſufficient to engage it ſo to do; which being contradictory to itſelf, muſt of neceſſity be falſe. Be it then ſo, that we naturally have an averſion to the truths propoſed to us in the Goſpel; that only can make us indiſpoſed to attend to them, but cannot hinder our conviction, when we do apprehend them, and attend to them—Be it, that there is in us alſo a renitency to the good we are to chuſe; that only can indiſpoſe us to believe it is, and to approve it as our chiefeſt good. Be it, that we are prone to the evil that we ſhould decline; that only can render it the more difficult for us to believe it is the worſt of evils. But yet, *what we do really believe to be our chiefeſt good, will ſtill be choſen; and what we apprehend to be the worſt of evils, will, whilſt we do continue under that conviction, be refuſed by us.* It therefore can be only requiſite, in order to theſe ends, that the Good Spirit ſhould ſo illuminate our Underſtandings, that we attending to, and conſidering what lies before us, ſhould apprehend and be convinced of our duty; and that the bleſſings of the goſpel ſhould be ſo propounded to us, as that we may diſcern them to be our chiefeſt good; and the miſeries it threateneth, ſo as we may be convinced that they are the worſt of evils; that we may chuſe the one, and refuſe the other."

Here let it be obſerved, how plainly and peremptorily it is aſſerted, *that the greateſt good propoſed, and the greateſt evil threatened, when equally believed and reflected on, is ſufficient to engage the Will to chuſe the good, and refuſe the evil, and is that alone which doth move the Will to chuſe or to refuſe; and that it is is contradictory to itself, to suppose otherwise; and therefore must of necessity be false; and then what we do really believe to be our chiefest good will still be chosen, aad what we apprehend to be the worst of evils, will, whilst we continue under that conviction, be refused by us.* Nothing could have been said more to the purpose, fully to signify and declare, that the determinations of the Will must evermore follow the illumination, conviction and notice of the Understanding, with regard to the greatest good and evil proposed, reckoning both the degree of good and evil understood, and the degree of Understanding, notice and conviction of that proposed good and evil; and that it is thus necessarily, and can be otherwise in no instance: because it is asserted, that it implies a contradiction, to suppose it ever to be otherwise.

I AM sensible, the Doctor's aim in these assertions is against the *Calvinists*; to shew, in opposition to them, that there is no need of any physical operation of the Spirit of God on the Will, to change and determine that to a good choice, but that God's operation and assistance is only moral, suggesting ideas to the Understanding; which he supposes to be enough, if those ideas are attended to, infallibly to obtain the end. But whatever his design was, nothing can more directly and fully prove, that every determination of the Will, in chusing and refusing, *is necessary*; directly contrary to his own notion of the liberty of the Will. For if the determination of the Will, evermore, in this manner, follows the light, conviction and view of the Understanding, concerning the greatest good and evil, and this be that alone which moves the Will, and it be a contradiction to suppose otherwise; then it is *necessarily*

ſarily ſo, the Will neceſſarily follows this light or view of the Underſtanding, not only in ſome of its acts, but in every act of chuſing and refuſing. So that the Will does not determine itſelf in any one of its own acts; but all its acts, every act of choice and refuſal depends on, and is neceſſarily connected with ſome antecedent cauſe; which cauſe is not the Will itſelf, nor any act of its own, nor any thing pertaining to that faculty, but ſomething belonging to another faculty, whoſe acts go before the will, in all its acts, and govern and determine them every one.

Here, if it ſhould be replied, that although it be true, that according to the Doctor, the final determination of the Will always depends upon, and is infallibly connected with the Uuderſtanding's conviction, and notice of the greateſt good; yet the acts of the Will are not neceſſary; becauſe that conviction and notice of the Underſtanding is firſt dependent on a preceding Act of the Will, in determining to attend to, and take notice of the evidence exhibited; by which means the mind obtains that degree of conviction, which is ſufficient and effectual to determine the conſequent and ultimate choice of the Will; and that the Will with regard to that preceding act, whereby it determines whether to attend or no, is not neceſſary; and that in this, the liberty of the Will conſiſts, that when God holds forth ſufficient objective light, the Will is at liberty whether to command the attention of the mind to it.

Nothing can be more weak and inconſiderate than ſuch a reply as this. For that preceding Act of the Will, in determining to attend and conſider, ſtill is an *Act of the Will* (it is ſo to be

ſure

ſure, if the *liberty of the Will* conſiſts in it, as is ſuppoſed) and if it be an act of the Will, it is an act of *choice* or *refuſal*. And therefore, if what the Doctor aſſerts be true, it is determined by ſome antecedent light in the Underſtanding concerning the greateſt apparent good or evil. For he aſſerts, it is that light *which alone doth move the Will to chuſe or refuſe*. And therefore the Will muſt be moved by that in chuſing to attend to the objective light offered, in order to another conſequent act of choice: ſo that this act is no leſs neceſſary than the other. And if we ſuppoſe another Act of the Will, ſtill preceding both theſe mentioned, to determine both, ſtill that alſo muſt be an Act of the Will, and an Act of choice; and ſo muſt, by the ſame principles, be infallibly determined by ſome certain degree of light in the Underſtanding concerning the greateſt good. And let us ſuppoſe as many Acts of the Will, one preceding another, as we pleaſe, yet they are every one of them neceſſarily determined by a certain degree of light in the Underſtanding, concerning the greateſt and moſt eligible good in that caſe; and ſo, not one of them free according to Dr. *Whitby*'s notion of freedom. And if it be ſaid, the reaſon, why men do not attend to light held forth, is becauſe of ill habits contracted by evil acts committed before, whereby their minds are indiſpoſed to attend to, and conſider of the truth held forth to them by God, the difficulty is not at all avoided: ſtill the queſtion returns, What determined the Will in thoſe preceding evil acts? It muſt, by Dr. *Whitby*'s principles, ſtill be the view of the Underſtanding concerning the greateſt good and evil. If this view of the Underſtanding be *that alone which doth move the Will to chuſe or refuſe*, as the Doctor aſſerts, then every act of *choice or refuſal*, from a man's man's firſt exiſtence, is moved and determined by this view; and this view of the underſtanding exciting and governing the act, muſt be before the act: And therefore the Will is neceſſarily determined, in every one of its acts, from a man's firſt exiſtence, by a cauſe beſide the Will, and a cauſe that does not proceed from, or depend on any act of the Will at all. Which at once utterly aboliſhes the Doctor's whole ſcheme of Liberty of Will; and he, at one ſtroke, has cut the ſinews of all his arguments from the goodneſs, righteouſneſs, faithfulneſs and ſincerity of God, in his commands, promiſes, threatenings, calls, invitations, expoſtulations; which he makes uſe of, under the heads of reprobation, election, univerſal redemption, ſufficient and effectual grace, and the freedom of the Will of man; and has enervated and made vain all thoſe exclamations againſt the doctrine of the *Calviniſts*, as charging God with manifeſt unrighteouſneſs, unfaithfulneſs, hypocriſy, fallaciouſneſs, aud cruelty; which he has over, and over, and over again, numberleſs times in his book.

Dr. *Samuel Clark*, in his Demonſtration of the Being and Attributes of God*, to evade the argument to prove the neceſſity of volition, from its neceſſary Connection with the laſt dictate of the Underſtanding, ſuppoſes the latter not to be diverſe from the Act of the Will itſelf. But if it be ſo, it will not alter the caſe as to the evidence of the neceſſity of the Act of the Will. If the dictate of the Underſtanding be the very ſame with the determination of the Will or Choice, as Dr. *Clark* ſuppoſes, then this determination is no *fruit* or *effect of choice*: and if ſo, no liberty of choice has any hand in it: as to volition or

 choice,

* Edit. VI. p. 93.

choice, it is necessary; that is, choice cannot prevent it. If the last dictate of the Understanding be the same with the determination of volition itself, then the existence of that determination must be necessary as to volition; in as much as volition can have no opportunity to determine whether it shall exist or no, it having existence already before volition has opportunity to determine any thing. It is itself the very rise and existence of volition. But a thing, after it exists, has no opportunity to determine as to its own existence; it is too late for that.

If liberty consists in that which *Arminians* suppose, *viz.* in the Will's determining its own acts, having free opportunity, and being without all necessity; this is the same as to say, that liberty consists in the soul's having power and opportunity to have what determinations of the Will it pleases or chuses. And if the determinations of the Will, and the last dictates of the Understanding be the same thing, then Liberty consists in the mind's having power to have, what dictates of the Understanding it pleases, having opportunity to chuse its own dictates of Understanding. But this is absurd; for it is to make the determination of choice prior to the dictate of Understanding, and the ground of it; which cannot consist with the dictate of Understanding's being the determination of choice itself.

Here is no way to do in this case, but only to recur to the old absurdity of one determination before another, and the cause of it; and another before that, determining that; and so on *in infinitum*. If the last dictate of the Understanding be the determination of the Will itself, and the soul be free with regard to that dictate, in the

Arminian

Arminian notion of freedom; then the ſoul, before that dictate of its Underſtanding exiſts, voluntarily, and according to its own choice determines, in every caſe, what that dictate of the Underſtanding ſhall be; otherwiſe that dictate, as to the Will, is neceſſary; and the acts determined by it muſt alſo be neceſſary. So that here is a determination of the mind prior to that dictate of the Underſtanding, an act of choice going before it, chuſing and determining what that dictate of the Underſtanding ſhall be: and this preceding act of choice, being a free act of Will, muſt alſo be the ſame with another laſt dictate of the Underſtanding: And if the mind alſo be free in that dictate of Underſtanding, that muſt be determined ſtill by another; and ſo on for ever.

Besides, if the dictate of the Underſtanding, and determination of the Will be the ſame, this confounds the Underſtanding and Will, and makes them the ſame. Whether they be the ſame or no, I will not now diſpute; but only would obſerve, that if it be ſo, and the *Arminian* notion of liberty conſiſts in a ſelf-determining power in the Underſtanding, free of all neceſſity; being independent, undetermined by any thing prior to its own acts and determinations; and the more the Underſtanding is thus independent, and ſovereign over its own determinations the more free. By this therefore the freedom of the ſoul, as a moral agent, muſt conſiſt in the independence of the underſtanding on any evidence or appearance of things, or any thing whatſoever, that ſtands forth to the view of the mind, prior to the Underſtanding's determination. And what a ſort of liberty is this! conſiſting in an ability, freedom and eaſineſs of judging, either according to evidence, or againſt it; having a ſovereign command over itſelf at all times, to judge, either agreably or diſagreably to what is plainly exhibited to its own view, Certainly, it is no liberty that renders perſons the proper ſubjects of perſuaſive reaſoning, arguments, expoſtulations, and ſuch-like moral means and inducements. The uſe of which with mankind is a main argument of the *Arminians*, to defend their notion of liberty without all neceſſity. For according to this, the more free men are, the leſs they are under the government of ſuch means, leſs ſubject to the power of evidence and reaſon, and more independent on their influence, in their determinations.

And whether the Underſtanding and Will are the ſame or no, as Dr. *Clark* ſeems to ſuppoſe, yet in order to maintain the *Arminian* notion of liberty without neceſſity, the Free Will is not determined by the Underſtanding, nor neceſſarily connected with the Underſtanding; and the further from ſuch Connection, the greater the freedom. And when the liberty is full and compleat, the determinations of the Will have no Connection at all with the dictates of the Underſtanding. And if ſo, in vain are all the applications to the Underſtanding, in order to induce to any free virtuous act; and ſo in vain are all inſtructions, counſels, invitations, expoſtulations, and all arguments and perſuaſives whatſoever: for theſe are but applications to the Underſtanding, and a clear and lively exhibition of the objects of choice to the mind's view. But if, after all, the Will muſt be ſelf-determined, and independent on the Underſtanding, to what purpoſe are things thus repreſented to the Underſtanding, in order to determine the choice?

SECTION X.

Volition neceſſarily connected with the Influence of Motives; *with particular Obſervations on the great Inconſiſtence of Mr.* Chubb's *Aſſertions and Reaſonings, about the Freedom of the Will.*

THAT every act of the will has ſome cauſe, and conſequently (by what has been already proved) has a neceſſary connection with its cauſe, and ſo is neceſſary by a neceſſity of connection and conſequence, is evident by this, that every act of the will whatſoever is excited by ſome motive: which is manifeſt, becauſe, if the will or mind, in willing and chuſing after the manner that it does, is excited ſo to do by no motive or inducement, then it has no end which it propoſes to itſelf, or purſues in ſo doing; it aims at nothing, and ſeeks nothing. And if it ſeeks nothing, then it does not go after any thing, or exert any inclination or preference towards any thing. Which brings the matter to a contradiction; becauſe for the mind to will ſomething, and for it to go after ſomething by an act of preference and inclination, are the ſame thing.

BUT if every act of the will is excited by a Motive, then that Motive is the cauſe of the act of the will. If the acts of the will are excited by Motives, then Motives are the cauſes of their being excited; or which is the ſame thing, the cauſe of their being put forth into act and exiſtence. And if ſo, the exiſtence of the acts of the will is properly the effect of their Motives. Motives do nothing as Motives or inducements, but by their influence; and ſo much as is done by their influence is the effect of them. For that is the notion of an effect, ſomething that is brought to paſs by the influence of another thing.

And if volitions are properly the effects of their Motives, then they are neceſſarily connected with their Motives. Every effect and event being as was proved before, neceſſarily connected with that, which is the proper ground and reaſon of its exiſtence. Thus it is manifeſt, that volition is neceſſary, and is not from any ſelf-determining power in the will: the volition, which is cauſed by previous Motive and inducement, is not cauſed by the will exerciſing a ſovereign power over itſelf, to determine, cauſe and excite volitions in itſelf. This is not conſiſtent with the will's acting in a ſtate of indifference and equilibrium, to determine itſelf to a preference; for the way in which motives operate, is by biaſſing the will, and giving it a certain inclination or preponderation one way.

Here it may be proper to obſerve, that Mr. *Chubb*, in his Collection of Tracts on various Subjects, has advanced a ſcheme of liberty, which is greatly divided againſt itſelf, and thoroughly ſubverſive of itſelf; and that many ways.

I. He is abundant in aſſerting, that the will, in all its acts, is influenced by Motive and excitement; and that this is the *previous ground and reaſon* of all its acts, and that it is never otherwiſe in any inſtance. He ſays, (p. 202.) *No action can take place without ſome Motive to excite it.* And in p. 263. *Volition cannot take place without ſome PREVIOUS reaſon or Motive to induce it.* And in p. 310. *Action would not take place without ſome reaſon or Motive to induce it; it being abſurd to ſuppoſe*

pose that the active faculty would be exerted without some PREVIOUS reason to dispose the mind to action. So also p. 257. And he speaks of these things, as what we may be absolutely certain of, and which are the foundation, the only foundation we have of a certainty of the moral perfections of God, p. 252, 253, 254, 255, 261, 262, 263, 264.

And yet at the same time, by his scheme, the influence of Motives upon us to excite to action, and to be actually a ground of volition, is *consequent* on the volition or choice of the mind. For he very greatly insists upon it, that in all free actions, before the mind is the subject of those volitions, which Motives excite, it chuses to be so. It chuses, whether it will comply with the Motive, which presents itself in view, or not; and when various Motives are presented, it chuses, which it will yield to, and which it will reject. So p. 256. *Every man has power to act, or to refrain from acting agreable with, or contrary to, any Motive that presents.* P. 257. *Every Man is at liberty to act, or refrain from acting agreably with, or contrary to, what each of these Motives, considered singly, would excite him to.—Man has power, and is as much at liberty to reject the motive, that does prevail, as he has power, and is at liberty to reject those Motives that do not.* And so p. 310, 311. *In order to constitute a moral agent, it is necessary, that he should have power to act, or to refrain from acting, upon such moral motives as he pleases.* And to the like purpose in many other places. According to these things, the will acts first, and chuses or refuses to comply with the Motive, that is presented, before it falls under its prevailing influence: and it is first determined by the mind's pleasure or choice, what Motives it will be induced by, before it is induced by them.

Now, how can these things hang together? How can the mind first act, and by its act of *volition* and *choice* determine, what Motives shall be the ground and reason of its *volition* and *choice?* For this supposes the choice is already made, before the Motive has its effect; and that the volition is already exerted, before the Motive prevails, so as actually to be the ground of the volition; and makes the prevailing of the motive, the consequence of the volition, which yet it is the ground of. If the mind has already chosen to comply with a Motive, and to yield to its excitement, it does not need to yield to it after this: for the thing is effected already, that the Motive would excite to, and the will is beforehand with the excitement; and the excitement comes in too late, and is needless and in vain afterwards. If the mind has already chosen to yield to a Motive which *invites* to a thing, that implies, and in fact is a chusing the thing *invited to*; and the very act of choice is before the influence of the Motive which induces, and is the ground of the choice; the son is beforehand with the father that begets him: the choice is supposed to be the ground of that influence of the Motive, which very influence is supposed to be the ground of the choice. And so *vice versa*, the choice is supposed to be the consequence of the influence of the Motive, which influence of the Motive is the consequence of that very choice.

And besides, if the will acts first towards the Motive before it falls under its influence, and the prevailing of the motive upon it to induce it to act and chuse, be the fruit and consequence of its act and choice, then how is the Motive *a PREVIOUS ground and reason of the act and choice, so* that *in the nature of the things, volition cannot take place without some* PREVIOUS *reason and Motive to induce it*; and that this act is consequent upon, and follows the Motive? Which things Mr. *Chubb* often asserts, as of certain and undoubted truth. So that the very same Motive is both *previous* and *consequent*, both before and after, both the ground and fruit of the very same thing!

II. Agreable to the fore-mentioned inconsistent notion of the will's first acting towards the Motive, chusing whether it will comply with it, in order to its becoming a ground of the will's acting, before any act of volition can take place, Mr. *Chubb* frequently calls Motives and excitements to the action of the will, *the passive ground or reason of that action.* Which is a remarkable phrase; than which I presume there is none more unintelligible, and void of distinct and consistent meaning, in all the writings of *Duns Scotus*, or *Thomas Aquinas.* When he represents the Motive to action or volition as passive, he must mean—passive in that affair, or passive with respect to that action, which he speaks of; otherwise it is nothing to his purpose, or relating to the design of his argument: he must mean, (if that can be called a meaning) that the motive to volition is first acted *upon* or *towards* by the volition, chusing to yield to it, making it a ground of action, or determining to fetch its influence from thence; and so to make it a previous ground of its own excitation and existence. Which is the same absurdity, as if one should say, that the soul of man, or any other thing should, previous to its existing, chuse what cause it would come into existence

existence by, and should act upon its cause, to fetch influence from thence, to bring it into being; and so its cause should be a passive ground of its existence!

Mr. *Chubb* does very plainly suppose Motive or excitement to be the *ground of the being* of volition. He speaks of it as the ground or reason of the EXERTION of an act of the will, p. 391, and 392. and expresly says, that *volition cannot TAKE PLACE without some previous ground or Motive to induce it*, p. 363. And he speaks of the act as *FROM the Motive*, and *FROM THE INFLUENCE of the Motive*, p. 352, and from *the influence that the Motive has on the man, for the PRODUCTION of an action*, p. 317. Certainly there is no need of multiplying words about this; it is easily judged, whether Motive can be the ground of volition's being exerted and taking place, so that the very production of it is from the influence of the Motive, and yet the Motive, before it becomes the ground of the volition, is passive or acted upon by the volition. But this I will say, that a man, who insists so much on clearness of meaning in others, and is so much in blaming their confusion and inconsistence, ought, if he was able, to have explained his meaning in this phrase of *passive ground of action*, so as to shew it not to be confused and inconsistent.

If any man should suppose, that Mr. *Chubb*, when he speaks of Motive as a *passive ground of action*, does not mean passive with regard to that volition which it is the ground of, but some other antecedent volition (though his purpose and argument, and whole discourse, will by no means allow of such a supposition) yet it would not help the matter

matter in the leaſt. For, (1.) If we ſuppoſe there to be an act of volition or choice, by which the ſoul chuſes to yield to the invitation of a Motive to another volition, by which the ſoul chuſes ſomething elſe; both theſe ſuppoſed volitions are in effect the very ſame. A volition, or chuſing to yield to the force of a Motive inviting to chuſe ſomething, comes to juſt the ſame thing as chuſing the thing, which the Motive invites to, as I obſerved before. So that here can be no room to help the matter, by a diſtinction of two volitions. (2.) If the Motive be paſſive with reſpect, not to the ſame volition, that the Motive excites to, but one truly diſtinct and prior; yet, by Mr. *Chubb*, that prior volition cannot take place, without a Motive or excitement, as a *previous ground* of its exiſtence. For he inſiſts, that *it is abſurd to ſuppoſe any volition ſhould take place without ſome previous Motive to induce it.* So that at laſt it comes to juſt the ſame abſurdity: for if *every* volition muſt have a previous Motive, then the very *firſt* in the whole ſeries muſt be excited by a previous Motive; and yet the Motive to that firſt volition is paſſive; but cannot be paſſive with regard to another antecedent volition, becauſe, by the ſuppoſition, it is the very firſt: therefore if it be paſſive with reſpect to any volition, it muſt be ſo with regard to that very volition that it is the ground of, and that is excited by it.

III. Though Mr. *Chubb* aſſerts, as above, that every volition has ſome Motive, and that *in the nature of the thing, no volition can take place without ſome Motive to induce it*; yet he aſſerts, that volition does not always follow the ſtrongeſt Motive; or, in other words, is not governed by any ſuperior ſtrength of the Motive that is followed, beyond Motives to the contrary, previous to the volition

volition itself. His own words, p. 258, are as follow: "Though with regard to physical causes, that which is strongest always prevails, yet it is otherwise with regard to moral causes. Of these, sometimes the stronger, sometimes the weaker prevails. And the ground of this difference is evident, namely, that what we call moral causes, strictly speaking are no causes at all, but barely passive reasons of, or excitements to the action, or to the refraining from acting: which excitements we have power, or are at liberty to comply with or reject, as I have shewed above." And so throughout the paragraph, he, in a variety of phrases insists, that the will is not always determined by the strongest Motive, unless by strongest we preposteriously mean actually prevailing in the event; which is not in the Motive, but in the will; but that the will is not always determined by the Motive, which is strongest, by any strength previous to the volition itself. And he elsewhere does abundantly assert, that the will is determined by no superior strength or advantage, that Motives have, from any constitution or state of things, or any circumstances whatsoever, previous to the actual determination of the will. And indeed his whole discourse on human liberty implies it, his whole scheme is founded upon it.

But these things cannot stand together.—— There is such a thing as a diversity of strength in Motives to choice, previous to the choice itself. Mr. *Chubb* himself supposes, that they do *previously invite*, *induce*, *excite* and *dispose the mind to action*. This implies, that they have something in themselves that is *inviting*, some tendency to *induce* and *dispose* to volition, previous to volition itself. And if they have in themselves this nature

ture and tendency, doubtleſs they have it in certain limited degrees, which are capable of diverſity; and ſome have it in greater degrees, others in leſs; and they that have moſt of this tendency, conſidered with all their nature and circumſtances, previous to volition, they are the ſtrongeſt motives; and thoſe that have leaſt, are the weakeſt Motives.

Now if volition ſometimes does not follow the Motive which is ſtrongeſt, or has moſt previous tendency or advantage, all things conſidered, to induce or excite it, but follows the weakeſt, or that which as it ſtands previouſly in the mind's view, has leaſt tendency to induce it; herein the will apparently acts wholly without Motive, without any previous reaſon to diſpoſe the mind to it, contrary to what the ſame author ſuppoſes. The act, wherein the will muſt proceed without a previous motive to induce it, is the act of preferring the weakeſt motive. For how abſurd is it to ſay, the mind ſees previous reaſon in the motive, to prefer that motive before the other; and at the ſame time to ſuppoſe, that there is nothing in the Motive, in its nature, ſtate or any circumſtance of it whatſoever, as it ſtands in the previous view of the mind, that gives it any preference; but on the contrary, the other Motive that ſtands in competition with it, in all theſe reſpects, has moſt belonging to it, that is inviting and moving, and has moſt of a tendency to choice and preference. This is certainly as much as to ſay, there is previous ground and reaſon in the Motive for the act of preference, and yet no previous reaſon for it. By the ſuppoſition, as to all that is in the two rival Motives, which tends to preference, previous to the act of preference, it is not in that which is preferred, but wholly in the other!

other: because appearing superior strength, and all appearing preferableness is in that; and yet Mr. *Chubb* supposes, that the act of preference is from *previous ground and reason* in the motive which is preferred. But are these things consistent? Can there be previous ground in a thing for an event that takes place, and yet no previous tendency in it to that event? If one thing follows another, without any previous tendency to it following, then I should think it very plain, that it follows it without any manner of previous reason, why it should follow.

Yea, in this case, Mr. *Chubb* supposes, that the event follows an antecedent or a previous thing, as the ground of its existence, not only that has *no existence* to it, but *a contrary tendency.* The event is the preference, which the mind gives to that Motive, which is weaker as it stands in the previous view of the mind; the immediate antecedent is the view the mind has of the two rival Motives conjunctly; in which previous view of the mind, all the preferableness, or previous tendency to preference, is supposed to be on the other side, or in the contrary Motive; and all the unworthiness of preference, and so previous tendency to comparative neglect, rejection or undervaluing, is on that side which is preferred: and yet in this view of the mind is supposed to be the *previous ground or reason* of this act of preference, *exciting it, and disposing the mind to it.* Which, I leave the reader to judge, whether it be absurd or not. If it be not, then it is not absurd to say, that the previous tendency of an antecedent to a consequent, is the ground and reason why that consequent does not follow; and the want of a previous tendency to an event, yea, a tendency to the contrary, is the true

true ground and reaſon why that event does follow.

An act of choice or preference is a comparative act, wherein the mind acts with reference to two or more things that are compared, and ſtand in competition in the mind's view. If the mind, in this comparative act, prefers that which appears inferior in the compariſon, then the mind herein acts abſolutely without Motive, or inducement, or any temptation whatſoever. Then, if a hungry man has the offer of two ſorts of food, both which he finds an appetite to, but has a ſtronger appetite to one than the other; and there be no circumſtances or excitements whatſoever in the caſe to induce him to take either the one or the other, but merely his appetite: if in the choice he makes between them, he chuſes that, which he has leaſt appetite to, and refuſes that, to which he has the ſtrongeſt appetite, this is a choice made abſolutely without previous Motive, Excitement, Reaſon, or Temptation, as much as if he were perfectly without all appetite to either: becauſe his volition in this caſe is a comparative act, attending and following a comparative view of the food, which he chuſes, viewing it as related to, and compared with the other ſort of food, in which view his preference has abſolutely no previous ground, yea, is againſt all previous ground and Motive. And if there be any principle in man, from whence an act of choice may ariſe after this manner, from the ſame principle volition may ariſe wholly without Motive on either ſide. If the mind in its volition can go beyond Motive, then it can go without Motive: for when it is beyond the Motive, it is out of the reach of the Motive, out of the limits of its influence, and ſo so without Motive. If volition goes beyond the strength and tendency of Motive, and especially if it goes against its tendency, this demonstrates the independence of volition or Motive. And if so, no reason can be given for what Mr. *Chubb* so often asserts, even that *in the nature of things volition cannot take place without a Motive to induce it.*

If the Most High should endow a ballance with agency or activity of nature, in such a manner, that when unequal weights are put into the scales, its agency could enable it to cause that scale to descend, which has the least weight, and so to raise the greater weight; this would clearly demonstrate, that the motion of the ballance does not depend on weights in the scales, at least as much as if the ballance should move itself, when there is no weight in either scale. And the activity of the ballance which is sufficient to move itself against the greater weight, must certainly be more than sufficient to move it when there is no weight at all.

Mr. *Chubb* supposes, that the will cannot stir at all without some Motive; and also supposes, that if there be a Motive to one thing, and none to the contrary, volition will infallibly follow that Motive. This is virtually to suppose an entire dependence of the will on Motives: if it were not wholly dependent on them, it could surely help itself a little without them, or help itself a little against a Motive, without help from the strength and weight of a contrary Motive. And yet his supposing that the will, when it has before it various opposite Motives, can use them as it pleases, and chuse its own influence from them, and neglect

lect the strongest, and follow the weakest, supposes it to be wholly independent on Motives.

It further appears, on Mr. *Chubb's* supposition, that volition must be without any previous ground in any Motive, thus: if it be, as he supposes, that the will is not determined by any previous superiour strength of the Motive, but determines and chuses its own Motive, then, when the rival Motives are exactly equal in strength and tendency to induce, in all respects, it may follow either; and may in such a case, sometimes follow one, sometimes the other. And if so, this diversity which appears between the acts of the will, is plainly without previous ground in either of the Motives; for all that is previously in the Motives, is supposed precisely and perfectly the same, without any diversity whatsoever. Now perfect identity, as to all that is previous in the antecedent, cannot be the ground and reason of diversity in the consequent. Perfect identity in the ground cannot be a reason why it is not followed with the same consequence. And therefore the source of this diversity of consequence must be sought for elsewhere.

And lastly, it may be observed, that however Mr. *Chubb* does much insist that no volition can take place without some Motive to induce it, which previously disposes the mind to it; yet, as he also insists that the mind, without reference to any superior strength of Motives, picks and chuses for its Motive to follow; he himself herein plainly supposes, that with regard to the mind's preference of one Motive before another, it is not the Motive that disposes the will, but the will disposes itself to follow the Motive.

IV. Mr. *Chubb* supposes necessity to be utterly inconsistent with *agency*: and that to suppose a being to be an agent in that which is necessary, is a plain contradiction. P. 311, and throughout his discourses on the subject of Liberty, he supposes, that necessity cannot consist with agency or freedom; and that to suppose otherwise, is to make Liberty and necessity, Action and Passion, the same thing. And so he seems to suppose, that there is no action, strictly speaking, but volition; and that as to the effects of volition in body or mind, in themselves considered, being necessary, they are said to be free, only as they are the effects of an act that is not necessary.

And yet, according to him, volition itself is the *effect of volition*; yea, every act of free volition: and therefore every act of free volition must, by what has now been observed from him, be necessary. That every act of free volition is itself the effect of volition, is abundantly supposed by him. In p. 341, he says, "If a man is such a creature as I have proved him to be, that is, if he has in him a power or Liberty of doing either good or evil, and either of these is the subject of his own free choice, so that he might, IF HE HAD PLEASED, have CHOSEN and done the contrary."—— Here he supposes, all that is good or evil in man is the effect of his choice; and so that his good or evil choice itself is the effect of his pleasure or choice, in these words, *he might, if he had PLEASED, have CHOSEN the contrary.* So in p. 356, "Though it be highly reasonable, that a man should always chuse the greater good,—yet he may, if he PLEASE, CHUSE otherwise." Which is the same thing as if he had said, *he may, if he chuses, chuse otherwise.* And then

then he goes on,—"that is, he may, *if he pleases*, *chuse* what is good for himself, &c." And again in the same page, "The will is not confined by the understanding, to any particular sort of good, whether greater or less; but is at liberty *to chuse* what kind of good it *pleases*." —If there be any meaning in the last words, the meaning must be this, that *the Will is at liberty to chuse what kind of good it chuses to chuse*; supposing the act of choice itself determined by an antecedent choice. The Liberty Mr. *Chubb* speaks of, is not only a man's having power to move his body agreably to an antecedent act of choice, but to use, or exert the faculties of his soul. Thus, in p. 379, speaking of the faculties of his mind, he says, "Man has power, and is at liberty to neglect these faculties, to use them aright, or to abuse them, *as he pleases*." And that he supposes an act of choice, or exercise of pleasure, properly distinct *from*, and antecedent *to*, those acts thus chosen, directing, commanding and producing the chosen acts, and even the acts of choice themselves, is very plain in p. 283. "He can *command his actions*; and herein consists his liberty; he can give or deny himself that pleasure, *as he pleases*." And p. 377. If the actions of men—are not the *produce of a free choice*, or election, but spring from a necessity of nature,——he cannot in reason be the object of reward or punishment on their account. Whereas, if action in man, whether good or evil is *the produce of will or free choice*; so that a man in either case, had it in his power, and was at liberty to have CHOSEN the contrary, he is the proper object of reward or punishment, according as he CHUSES to behave himself." Here, in these last words, he speaks of *Liberty of CHUSING according as he CHUSES.*

CHUSES. So that the behaviour which he speaks of as subject to his choice, is his *chusing* itself, as well as his external conduct consequent upon it. And therefore it is evident, he means not only external actions, but the acts of choice themselves, when he speaks of *all free actions as the PRODUCE of free choice.* And this is abundantly evident in what he says in p. 372, 373.

Now these things imply a twofold great absurdity and inconsistence.

1. To suppose, as Mr. *Chubb* plainly does, that every free act of choice is *commanded by*, and is the *produce of free choice*, is to suppose the first free act of choice belonging to the case, yea, the first free act of choice that ever man exerted, to be *the produce* of an antecedent act of choice. But I hope I need not labour at all to convince my readers, that it is an absurdity to say, the very *first* act is the produce of another act that went *before* it.

2. If it were both possible and real, as Mr. *Chubb* insists, that every free act of choice were the produce or the effect of a free act of choice; yet even then, according to his principles, no one act of choice would be free, but every one necessary; because, every act of choice being the effect of a foregoing act, every act would be necessarily connected with that foregoing cause. For Mr. *Chubb* himself says, p. 389, "When the self-moving power is exerted, it becomes the necessary cause of its effects."——So that his notion of a free act, that is rewardable or punishable, is a heap of contradictions. It is a free act, and yet, by his own notion of freedom, is necessary; and therefore by him it is a contradiction, to

to ſuppoſe it to be free. According to him, every free act is the produce of a free act; ſo that there muſt be an infinite number of free acts in ſucceſſion, without any beginning, in an agent that has a beginning. And therefore here is an infinite number of free acts, every one of them free; and yet not any one of them free, but every act in the whole infinite chain a neceſſary effect. All the acts are rewardable or puniſhable, and yet the agent cannot, in reaſon, be the object of reward or puniſhment, on account of any one of theſe actions. He is active in them all, and paſſive in none; yet active in none, but paſſive in all, *&c.*

V. Mr. *Chubb* does moſt ſtrenuouſly deny, that Motives are *cauſes* of the acts of the will; or that the moving principle in man is *moved* or *cauſed to be exerted* by Motives. His words, p. 388 and 389, are, " If the moving principle in man is MOVED, or CAUSED TO BE EXERTED, by ſomething external to man, *which all Motives are*, then it would not be a ſelf-moving principle, ſeeing it would be moved by a principle external to itſelf. And to ſay, that a ſelf-moving principle is MOVED, or CAUSED TO BE EXERTED, by a cauſe external to itſelf, is abſurd and a contradiction, &c.—And in the next page, it is particularly and largely inſiſted, that Motives are cauſes in no caſe, that *they are merely paſſive in the production of action, and have no cauſality in the production of it,—no cauſality, to be the cauſe of the exertion of the will.*

Now I deſire it may be conſidered, how this can poſſibly conſiſt with what he ſays in other places. Let it be noted here,

1. Mr. *Chubb* abundantly speaks of Motives as *excitements of the acts of the will*; and says, that *Motives do excite volition, and induce it*, and that they are necessary to this end; that *in the reason and nature of things, volition cannot take place without Motives to excite it.* But now, if Motives *excite* the will, they *move* it; and yet he says, it is absurd to say, the will is moved by Motives. And again, if language is of any significancy at all) if Motives excite volition, then they are the *cause* of its being excited; and to cause volition to be excited, is to cause it to be put forth or *exerted.* Yea, Mr. *Chubb* says himself, p. 317, Motive is necessary to the *exertion* of the active faculty. To excite, is positively to *do* something; and certainly that which does something, is the cause of the thing *done* by it. To create, is to cause to be created; to make, is to cause to be made; to kill, is to cause to be killed; to quicken, is to cause to be quickened; and *to excite*, is *to cause to be excited.* To excite, is to be a cause, in the most proper sense, not merely a negative occasion, but a ground of existence by positive influence. The notion of *exciting*, is exerting influence to cause the effect to arise or come forth into existence.

2. Mr. *Chubb* himself, p. 317, speaks of Motives as the ground and reason of action BY INFLUENCE, and BY PREVAILING INFLUENCE. Now, what can be meant by a cause, but something that is the ground and reason of a thing by its influence, an influence that is *prevalent* and so effectual?

3. This author not only speaks of Motives as the ground and reason of action, by prevailing influence; but expresly of their *influence as prevailing*

ing FOR THE PRODUCTION of an action, in the same p. 317: which makes the inconsistency still more palpable and notorious. The production of an effect is certainly the *causing* of an effect; and *productive influence* is *causal influence*, if any thing is; and that which has this influence prevalently, so as thereby to become the ground of another thing, is a cause of that thing, if there be any such thing as a cause. This influence, Mr. *Chubb* says, Motives have to produce an action; and yet, he says, it is absurd and a contradiction, to say they are causes.

4. In the same page, he once and again speaks of Motives as *disposing* the Agent to action, *by their influence*. His words are these: "As Motive, which takes place in the understanding, and is the product of intelligence, is NECESSARY to action, that is, to the EXERTION of the active faculty, because that faculty would not be exerted without some PREVIOUS REASON to DISPOSE the mind to action; so from hence it plainly appears, that when a man is said to be *disposed* to one action rather than another, this properly signifies the PREVAILING INFLUENCE that one Motive has upon a man FOR THE PRODUCTION of an action, or for the being at rest, before all other Motives, for the *production* of the contrary. For as Motive is the ground and reason of any action, so the Motive that *prevails*, DISPOSES the agent to the performance of that action."

Now, if Motives dispose the mind to action, then they *cause* the mind to be disposed; and to cause the mind to be disposed is to cause it to be willing; and to cause it to be willing is to cause it to will; and that is the same thing as to be the cause of an act of the will. And yet this same Mr *Chubb* holds it to be absurd, to suppose Motive to be a cause of the act of the will.

And if we compare these things together, we have here again a whole heap of inconsistences. *Motives are the previous ground and reason* of the acts of the will; yea, the *necessary* ground and reason of *their exertion, without which they will not be exerted, and cannot, in the nature of things, take place*; and they do *excite* these acts of the will, and do this by *a prevailing influence*; yea, *an influence which prevails for the production of the act* of the will, and for *the disposing of the mind to it*; and yet it is *absurd*, to suppose *Motive to be a cause* of an act of the will, or that *a principle of will is moved or caused to be exerted by it*, or that it has *any causality in the production of it*, or *any causality to be the cause of the exertion of the will.*

A due consideration of these things which Mr. *Chubb* has advanced, the strange inconsistences which the notion of Liberty, consisting in the will's power of self-determination void of all necessity, united with that dictate of common sense, that there can be no volition without a Motive, drove him into, may be sufficient to convince us, that it is utterly impossible ever to make that notion of Liberty consistent with the influence of Motives in volition. And as it is in a manner self-evident, that there can be no act of will, choice, or preference of the mind, without some Motive or inducement, something in the mind's view, which it aims at, seeks, inclines to, and goes after; so it is most manifest, there is no such Liberty in the universe as *Arminians* insist on; nor any such thing possible, or conceivable.

SEC-

SECTION XI.

The Evidence of GOD's certain Foreknowledge *of the Volitions of moral Agents.*

THAT the acts of the wills of moral Agents are not contingent events, in that ſenſe, as to be without all neceſſity, appears by God's certain Foreknowledge of ſuch events.

In handling this argument, I would in the *firſt* place prove, that God has a certain Foreknowledge of the voluntary acts of moral Agents; and *ſecondly*, ſhew the conſequence, or how it follows from hence, that the Volitions of moral Agents are not contingent, ſo as to be without neceſſity of connection and conſequence.

First, I am to prove, that God has an abſolute and certain Foreknowledge of the free actions of moral Agents.

One would think, it ſhould be wholly needleſs to enter on ſuch an argument with any that profeſs themſelves Chriſtians: but ſo it is; God's certain Foreknowledge of the free acts of moral Agents, is denied by ſome that pretend to believe the ſcriptures to be the Word of God; and eſpecially of late. I therefore ſhall conſider the evidence of ſuch a preſcience in the Moſt High, as fully as the deſigned limits of this eſſay will admit of; ſuppoſing myſelf herein to have to do with ſuch as own the truth of the Bible.

Arg. I. My *firſt* argument ſhall be taken from God's *prediction* of ſuch events. Here I would,

in

in the firſt place, lay down theſe two things as axioms.

(1.) If God does not foreknow, He cannot foretell ſuch events; that is, He cannot peremptorily and certainly foretell them. If God has no more than an uncertain gueſs concerning events of this kind, then He can declare no more than an uncertain gueſs. Poſitively to foretell, is to profeſs to foreknow, or declare poſitive Foreknowledge.

(2.) If God does not certainly foreknow the future Volitions of moral Agents, then neither can He certainly foreknow thoſe events which are conſequent and dependent on theſe Volitions. The exiſtence of the one depending on the exiſtence of the other, the knowledge of the exiſtence of the one depends on the knowledge of the exiſtence of the other; and the one cannot be more certain than the other.

Therefore, how many, how great, and how extenſive ſoever the conſequences of the Volitions of moral Agents may be; though they ſhould extend to an alteration of the ſtate of things through the univerſe, and ſhould be continued in a ſeries of ſucceſſive events to all eternity, and ſhould in the progreſs of things branch forth into an infinite number of ſeries, each of them going on in an endleſs line or chain of events; God muſt be as ignorant of all theſe conſequences, as He is of the Volition whence they firſt take their riſe: all theſe events, and the whole ſtate of things depending on them, how important, extenſive and vaſt ſoever, muſt be hid from him.

These poſitions being ſuch as, I ſuppoſe, none will deny, I now proceed to obſerve the following things.

1. MEN's moral conduct and qualities, their virtues and vices, their wickedness and good practice, things rewardable and punishable, have often been foretold by God.—*Pharaoh*'s moral conduct, in refusing to obey God's command, in letting his people go, was foretold. God says to *Moses*, Exod. iii. 19. *I am sure that the King of* Egypt *will not let you go.* Here God professes not only to guess at, but to know *Pharaoh*'s future disobedience. In chap. vii. 4. God says, *but* Pharaoh *shall not hearken unto you*; *that I may lay mine hand upon* Egypt, &c. And chap. ix. 30. *Moses* says to *Pharaoh*, *as for thee, and thy servants, I KNOW that ye will not fear the Lord.* See also chap. xi. 9.—The moral conduct of *Josiah*, by name, in his zealously exerting himself in opposition to idolatry, in particular acts of his, was foretold above three hundred years before he was born, and the prophecy sealed by a miracle, and renewed and confirmed by the words of a second prophet, as what surely would not fail, 1 *Kings* xiii. 1——6, 32. This prophecy was also in effect a prediction of the moral conduct of the people, in upholding their schismatical and idolatrous worship until that time, and the idolatry of those priests of the high places, which it is foretold *Josiah* should offer upon that altar of *Bethel.*——*Micaiah* foretold the foolish and sinful conduct of *Ahab*, in refusing to hearken to the word of the Lord by him, and chusing rather to hearken to the false prophets, in going to *Ramoth-Gilead* to his ruin, 1 *Kings* xxi. 20—22.—The moral conduct of *Hazael* was foretold, in that cruelty he should be guilty of; on which *Hazael* says, *What, is thy servant a dog, that he should do this thing!* The prophet speaks of the event as what he knew, and not what he conjectured, 2 Kings viii. 12. *I know the evil that thou wilt do unto the children of* Israel: *Thou wilt dash their children, and rip up their women with child.*—The moral

moral conduct of *Cyrus* is foretold, long before he had a being, in his mercy to God's people, and regard to the true God, in turning the captivity of the *Jews*, and promoting the building of the Temple, Isa. xliv. 28. and lxv. 13. Compare 2 *Chron.* xxxvi. 22, 23. and *Ezra* i. 1—4.—How many instances of the moral conduct of the *Kings of the North and South*, particular instances of the wicked behaviour of the Kings of *Syria* and *Egypt*, are foretold in the xith chapter of *Daniel?* Their corruption, violence, robbery, treachery, and lies. And particularly, how much is foretold of the horrid wickedness of *Antiochus Epiphanes*, called there a *vile person*, instead of *Epiphanes*, or illustrious. In that chapter, and also in chap. viii. ver. 9, 14, 23, to the end, are foretold his flattery, deceit and lies, his having *his heart set to do mischief*, and set *against the holy covenant*, his *destroying and treading under foot the holy people*, in a marvellous manner, his *having indignation against the holy covenant*, *setting his heart against it*, and *conspiring against it*, his *polluting the sanctuary of strength*, *treading it under foot*, *taking away the daily sacrifice*, *and placing the abomination that maketh desolate*; his great pride, *magnifying himself against God*, and *uttering marvellous blasphemies against Him*, until God in *indignation should destroy him*. Withal, the moral conduct of the *Jews*, on occasion of his persecution, is predicted. It is foretold, that *he should corrupt many by flatteries*, chap. xi. 32—34. But that others should behave with a glorious constancy and fortitude, in opposition to him, ver. 32. And that some good men should fall and repent, ver. 35. Christ foretold *Peter*'s sin, in denying his Lord, with its circumstances, in a peremptory manner. And so, that great sin of *Judas*, in betraying his Master, and its dreadful and eternal punishment in hell, was fore-

told

told in the like positive manner, *Matt.* xxvi. 21—25. and parallel places in the other evangelists.

2. Many events have been foretold by God, which are consequent and dependent on the moral conduct of particular persons, and were accomplished, either by their virtuous or vicious actions. —Thus, the children of *Israel*'s going down into *Egypt* to dwell there, was foretold to *Abraham*, Gen. xv. which was brought about by the wickedness of *Joseph*'s brethren in selling him, and the wickedness of *Joseph*'s mistress, and his own signal virtue in resisting her temptation. The accomplishment of the thing prefigured in *Joseph*'s dream, depended on the same moral conduct. *Jotham's* parable and prophecy, *Judges* ix. 15—20. was accomplished by the wicked conduct of *Abimelech*, and the men of *Shechem*. The prophecies against the house of *Eli*, 1 *Sam.* chap. ii. and iii. were accomplished by the wickedness of *Doeg* the *Edomite*, in accusing the priests; and the great impiety, and extreme cruelty of *Saul* in destroying the priests at *Nob*. 1 *Sam.* xxii. —*Nathan*'s prophecy against *David*, 2 *Sam.* xii. 11, 12. was fulfilled by the horrible wickedness of *Absalom*, in rebelling against his father, seeking his life, and lying with his concubines in the sight of the sun. The prophecy against *Solomon*, 1 *Kings* xi. 11—13. was fulfilled by *Jeroboam*'s rebellion and usurpation, which are spoken of as his wickedness, 2 *Chron.* xiii. 5, 6. compare ver. 18. The prophecy against *Jeroboam*'s family, 1 *Kings* xiv. was fulfilled by the conspiracy, treason, and cruel murders of *Baasha*, 2 *Kings* xv. 27, &c. The predictions of the prophet *Jehu* against the house of *Baasha*, 1 *Kings* xvi. at the beginning, were fulfilled by the treason and parricide of *Zimri*, 1 *Kings* xvi. 9—13, 20.

3. How often has God foretold the future moral conduct of nations and people, of numbers, bodies, and successions of men: with God's judicial proceedings, and many other events consequent and dependent on their virtues and vices; which could not be foreknown, if the Volitions of men, wherein they acted as *moral Agents*, had not been foreseen? The future cruelty of the *Egyptians* in oppressing *Israel*, and God's judging and punishing them for it, was foretold long before it came to pass, *Gen.* xv. 13, 14. The continuance of the iniquity of the *Amorites*, and the increase of it until it *should be full*, and they ripe for destruction, was foretold above four hundred years before-hand, *Gen.* xv. 16. *Acts* vii. 6, 7. The prophecies of the destruction of *Jerusalem*, and the land of *Judah*, were absolute; 2 *Kings* xx. 17—19. chap. xxii. 15, to the end. It was foretold in *Hezekiah*'s time, and was abundantly insisted on in the book of the prophet *Isaiah*, who wrote nothing after *Hezekiah*'s days. It was foretold in *Josiah*'s time, in the beginning of a great reformation, 2 *Kings* xxii. And it is manifest by innumerable things in the prediction of the prophets, relating to this event, its time, its circumstances, its continuance and end; the return from the captivity, the restoration of the temple, city and land, and many circumstances, and consequences of *that*; I say, these shew plainly, that the prophecies of this great event were *absolute*. And yet this event was connected with, and dependent on two things in men's moral conduct: first, the injurious rapine and violence of the king of *Babylon* and his people, as the efficient cause; which God often speaks of as what he highly resented, and would severely punish; and 2dly, the final obstinacy of the *Jews*. That great event is often spoken of as suspended on this, *Jer.* iv. 1. and v. 1. vii. 1—7. xi. 1—6. xvii. 24, to the

the end. xxv, 1—7. xxvi. 1—8, 13. and xxxviii. 17, 18. Therefore this destruction and captivity could not be foreknown, unless such a moral conduct of the *Chaldeans* and *Jews* had been foreknown. And then it was foretold, that the people *should be finally obstinate*, to the destruction and utter desolation of the city and land. *Isa.* vi. 9—11. *Jer.* i. 18, 19. vii. 27—29. *Ezek.* iii. 7. and xxiv. 13, 14.

The final obstinacy of those *Jews* who were left in the land of *Israel*, in their idolatry and rejection of the true God, was foretold by God, and the prediction confirmed with an oath, *Jer.* xliv. 26, 27. And God tells the people, *Isa.* xlviii. 3, 4—8. that he had predicted those things which should be consequent on their treachery and obstinacy, because he knew they would be obstinate; and that he had declared these things before-hand, for their conviction of his being the only true God, &c.

The destruction of *Babylon*, with many of the circumstances of it, was foretold, as the judgment of God for the exceeding pride and haughtiness of the heads of that monarchy, *Nebuchadnezzar*, and his successors, and their wickedly destroying other nations, and particularly for their exalting themselves against the true God and his people, before any of these monarchs had a being; *Isa.* chap. xiii. xiv. xlvii. compare *Hab.* ii. 5. to the end, and *Jer.* chap. l. and li. That *Babylon*'s destruction was to be a *recompence, according to the works of their own hands*, appears by *Jer.* xxv. 14.——The immorality with which the people of *Babylon*, and particularly her princes and great men, were guilty of, that very night that the city was destroyed, their revelling

revelling and drunkenneſs at *Balſhazzar's* idolatrous feaſt, was foretold, *Jer.* li. 39, 57.

The return of the Jews from the *Babyloniſh* captivity is often very particularly foretold, with many circumſtances, and the promiſes of it are very peremptory; *Jer.* xxxi. 35—40, and xxxii. 6—15, 41—44. and xxxiii. 24—26. And the very time of their return was prefixed; *Jer.* xxv. 11, 12. and xxix. 10, 11. 2 *Chron.* xxxvi. 21. *Ezek.* iv. 6. and *Dan.* ix. 2. And yet the prophecies repreſent their return as conſequent on their repentance. And their repentance itſelf is very expreſsly and particularly foretold, *Jer.* xxix. 12, 13, 14. xxxi. 8, 9, 18—31. xxxiii. 8. l. 4, 5. *Ezek.* vi. 8, 9, 10. vii. 16. xiv. 22, 23. and xx. 43, 44.

It was foretold under the Old Teſtament, that the Meſſiah ſhould ſuffer greatly through the malice and cruelty of men; as is largely and fully ſet forth, *Pſalm* xxii. applied to Chriſt in the New Teſtament, *Matt.* xxvii. 35, 43. *Luke* xxiii. 34. *John* xix. 24. *Heb.* ii. 12. And likewiſe in *Pſalm* lxix, which, it is alſo evident by the New Teſtament, is ſpoken of Chriſt; *John* xv. 25. vii. 5, &c. and ii. 17. *Rom.* xv. 3. *Matt.* xxvii. 34, 48. *Mark* xv. 23. *John* xix. 29. The ſame thing is alſo foretold, *Iſa.* liii. and l. 6. and *Mic.* v. 1. This cruelty of men was their ſin, and what they acted as moral Agents. It was foretold, that there ſhould be an union of Heathen and *Jewiſh* rulers againſt Chriſt, *Pſalm* ii. 1, 2. compared with *Acts* iv. 25—28. It was foretold, that the *Jews* ſhould generally reject and deſpiſe the Meſſiah, *Iſa.* xlix. 5, 6, 7. and liii. 1—3. *Pſalm* xxii. 6, 7. and lxix. 4, 8, 19, 20. And it was foretold, that the body of that nation ſhould be rejected in the Meſſiah's days,

days, from being God's people, for their obstinacy in sin; *Isa.* xlix. 4—7. and viii. 14, 15, 16. compared with *Rom.* x. 19. and *Isa.* lxv. at the beginning, compared with *Rom.* x. 20, 21. It was foretold, that Christ should be rejected by the chief priests and rulers among the *Jews*; *Psalm* cxviii. 22. compared with *Matt.* xxi. 42. *Acts* iv. 11. 1 *Pet.* ii. 4, 7.

Christ himself foretold his being delivered into the hands of the elders, chief priests and scribes, and his being cruelly treated by them, and condemned to death; and that he by them should be *delivered to the Gentiles:* and that He should be *mocked*, and *scourged*, and *crucified*, (*Matt.* xvi. 21. and xx. 17—19. *Luke* ix. 22. *John* viii. 28.) and that the people should be concerned in and consenting to his death, (*Luke* xx. 13—18.) especially the inhabitants of *Jerusalem*; Luke xiii. 33—35. He foretold, that the disciples should all be offended because of Him that night that he was betrayed, and should forsake him; *Matt.* xxvi. 31. *John* xvi. 32. He foretold, that He should be rejected of that generation, even the body of the people, and that they should continue obstinate, to their ruin; *Matt.* xii. 45. xxi. 33—42. and xxii. 1—7. *Luke* xiii. 16, 21, 24. xvii. 25. xix. 14, 27, 41—44. xx. 13—18. and xxiii. 34—39.

As it was foretold in both Old Testament and New, that the *Jews* should reject the Messiah, so it was foretold that the *Gentiles* should receive Him, and so be admitted to the privileges of God's people; in places too many to be now particularly mentioned. It was foretold in the Old Testament, that the *Jews* should envy the *Gentiles* on this account; *Deut.* xxxii. 21. compared with

 Rom.

Rom. x. 19. Christ himself often foretold; that the *Gentiles* would embrace the true religion; and become his followers and people; *Matt.* viii. 10, 11, 12. xxi. 41—43. and xxii. 8—10. *Luke* xiii. 28. xiv 16—24. and xx. 16. *John* x. 16. He also foretold the *Jews* envy of the *Gentiles* on this occasion; *Matt.* xx. 12—16. *Luke* xv. 26. to the end. He foretold, that they should continue in this opposition and envy, and should manifest it in the cruel persecutions of his followers, to their utter destruction; *Matt.* xxi. 33—42. xxii 6. and xxiii. 34—39. *Luke* xi. 49—51. The *Jews* obstinacy is also foretold, Acts xxii. 18. Christ often foretold the great persecutions his followers should meet with, both from *Jews* and *Gentiles*; *Matt.* x. 16—18, 21, 22, 34—36. and xxiv. 9. *Mark* xiii. 9. *Luke* x. 3. xii. 11, 49—53. and xxi. 12, 16, 17. *John* xv. 18—21. and xvi. 1—4, 20—22, 23. He foretold the martyrdom of particular persons; *Matt.* xx. 23. *John* xiii. 36. and xxi. 18, 19, 22. He foretold the great success of the Gospel in the city of *Samaria*, as near approaching; which afterwards was fulfilled by the preaching of *Philip*, John iv. 35—38. He foretold the rising of many deceivers after his departure, *Matt.* xxiv. 4, 5, 11. and the apostacy of many of his professed followers; *Matt.* xxiv. 10—12.

The persecutions which the apostle *Paul* was to meet with in the world, were foretold; *Acts* ix. 16. xx. 23, and xxi. 11. The apostle says to the Christian *Ephesians*, Acts xx. 29, 30. *I know, that after my departure shall grievous wolves enter in among you, not sparing the flock: also of your own selves shall men arise, speaking perverse things, to draw away disciples after them.* The apostle says, *He knew this*: but

but he did not know it, if God did not know the future actions of moral Agents.

4. Unless God foreknows the future acts of moral Agents, all the prophecies we have in Scripture concerning the great *Antichristian* apostacy: the rise, reign, wicked qualities, and deeds of the *man of sin*, and his instruments and adherents; the extent and long continuance of his dominion, his influence on the minds of princes and others, to corrupt them, and draw them away to idolatry, and other foul vices; his great and cruel persecutions; the behaviour of the saints under these great temptations, &c. &c. I say, unless the Volitions of moral Agents are foreseen, all these prophecies are uttered without knowing the things foretold.

The predictions relating to this great apostacy are all of a moral nature, relating to men's virtues and vices, and their exercises, fruits and consequences, and events depending on them; and are very particular; and most of them often repeated, with many precise characteristics, descriptions, and limitations of qualities, conduct, influence, effects, extent, duration, periods, circumstances, final issue, &c. which it would be very long to mention particularly. And to suppose, all these are predicted by God without any certain knowledge of the future moral behaviour of free Agents, would be to the utmost degree absurd.

5. Unless God foreknows the future acts of men's wills, and their behaviour as moral Agents, all those great things which are foretold in both Old Testament and New concerning the erection, establishment, and universal extent of the *Kingdom*

of the *Messiah*, were predicted and promised while God was in ignorance whether any of these things would come to pass or no, and did but guess at them. For that kingdom is not of this world, it does not consist in things external, but is within men, and consists in the dominion of virtue in their hearts, in righteousness, and peace, and joy in the Holy Ghost; and in these things made manifest in practice, to the praise and glory of God. The Messiah came to *save men from their sins*, and deliver them *from their* spiritual *enemies*; *that they might serve him in righteousness and holiness before him: he gave himself for us, that he might redeem us from all iniquity, and purify unto himself a peculiar people, zealous of good works.* And therefore his success consists in gaining men's hearts to virtue, in their being made *God's willing people in the day of his power.* His conquest of his enemies consists in his victory over men's corruptions and vices. And such success, such victory, and such a reign and dominion is often expressly foretold: that his kingdom *shall fill the earth*; *that all people, nations and languages should serve and obey him:* and so that *all nations should go up to the mountain of the House of the Lord, that he might teach them his ways, and that they might walk in his paths: and* that *all men should be drawn to Christ, and the earth be full of the knowledge of the Lord* (by which, in the style of Scripture, is meant true virtue and religion) *as the waters cover the seas*; that *God's law should be put into men's inward parts, and written in their hearts*; and that *God's people should be all righteous*, &c. &c.

A VERY great part of the prophecies of the Old Testament is taken up in such predictions as these.—And here I would observe, that the prophecies of the universal prevalence of the kingdom of the Messiah, and true religion of Jesus Christ, are

are delivered in the moſt peremptory manner, and confirmed by the oath of God, *Iſa.* xlv. 22, to the end, *Look to me, and be ye ſaved, all the ends of the earth; for I am God, and there is none elſe. I have SWORN by my Self, the word is gone out of my mouth in righteouſneſs, and ſhall not return, that unto me every knee ſhall bow; and every tongue ſhall ſwear. SURELY, ſhall one ſay, in the Lord have I righteouſneſs and ſtrength: even to him ſhall men come,* &c. But here this peremptory declaration, and great oath of the Moſt High, are delivered with ſuch mighty ſolemnity, to things which God did not know, if he did not certainly foreſee the Volitions of moral Agents.

AND all the predictions of Chriſt and his apoſtles, to the like purpoſe, muſt be without knowledge: as thoſe of our Saviour comparing the kingdom of God to a grain of muſtard-ſeed, growing exceeding great, from a ſmall beginning; and to leaven hid in three meaſures of meal, until the whole was leavened, &c.——And the prophecies in the epiſtles concerning the reſtoration of the nation of the *Jews* to the true church of God, and the bringing in the fulneſs of the *Gentiles*; and the prophecies in all the *Revelation* concerning the glorious change in the moral ſtate of the world of mankind, attending the deſtruction of Antichriſt, *the kingdoms of the world becoming the kingdoms of our Lord and of his Chriſt*; and *its being granted to the church to be arrayed in that fine linen, white and clean, which is the righteouſneſs of ſaints,* &c.

Corol. 1. Hence that great promiſe and oath of God to *Abraham*, *Iſaac* and *Jacob*, ſo much celebrated in Scripture, both in the Old Teſtament and New, namely, *That in their ſeed all the nations and families of the earth ſhould be bleſſed,* muſt be made on uncertainties, if God does not certainly foreknow the Volitions of moral Agents. For the fulfilment of this promise consists in that success of Christ in the work of redemption, and that setting up of his spiritual kingdom, over the nations of the world, which has been spoken of. Men are *blessed in Christ* no otherwise than as they are brought to acknowledge Him, trust in Him, love and serve Him, as is represented and predicted in *Psalm* lxxii. 11. *All Kings shall fall down before Him; all nations shall serve Him.* With ver. 17. *Men shall be blessed in Him; all nations shall call Him blessed.* This oath to *Jacob* and *Abraham* is fulfilled in subduing men's iniquities; as is implied in that of the prophet *Micah*, chap. vii. 19, 20.

Corol. 2. Hence also it appears, that first gospel promise that ever was made to mankind, that great prediction of the salvation of the Messiah, and his victory over *Satan*, made to our first parents, *Gen.* iii. 15. if there be no certain prescience of the Volitions of moral Agents, must have no better foundation than conjecture. For Christ's victory over *Satan* consists in men's being saved from sin, and in the victory of virtue and holiness, over that vice and wickedness, which *Satan*, by his temptation has introduced, and wherein his kingdom consists.

6. If it be so, that God has not a prescience of the future actions of moral Agents, it will follow, that the prophecies of Scripture in *general* are without Foreknowledge. For Scripture-prophecies, almost all of them, if not universally without any exception, are either predictions of the actings and behaviours of moral Agents, or of events depending on them, or some way connected with them; judicial dispensations, judgments on men for their wickedness;

wickedneſs, or rewards of virtue and righteouſneſs, remarkable manifeſtations of favour to the righteous, or manifeſtations of ſovereign mercy to ſinners, forgiving their iniquities, and magnifying the riches of divine Grace; or diſpenſations of Providence, in ſome reſpect or other, relating to the conduct of the ſubjects of God's moral government, wiſely adapted thereto; either providing for what ſhould be in a future ſtate of things, through the Volitions and voluntary actions of moral Agents, or conſequent upon them, and regulated and ordered according to them. So that all events that are foretold, are either moral events, or other events which are connected with, and accommodated to moral events.

That the predictions of Scripture in general muſt be without knowledge, if God does not foreſee the Volitions of men, will further appear, if it be conſidered, that almoſt all events belonging to the future ſtate of the world of mankind, the changes and revolutions which come to paſs in empires, kingdoms, and nations, and all ſocieties, depend innumerable ways on the acts of men's wills; yea, on an innumerable multitude of millions of millions of Volitions of mankind. Such is the ſtate and courſe of things in the world of mankind, that one ſingle event, which appears in itſelf exceeding inconſiderable, may, in the progreſs and ſeries of things, occaſion a ſucceſſion of the greateſt and moſt important and extenſive events; cauſing the ſtate of mankind to be vaſtly different from what it would otherwiſe have been, for all ſucceeding generations.

For inſtance, the coming into exiſtence of thoſe particular men, who have been the great conquerors of the world, which, under God, have had the main hand in all the consequent state of the world, in all after-ages; such as *Nebuchadnezzar*, *Cyrus*, *Alexander*, *Pompey*, *Julius Cæsar*, &c. undoubtedly depended on many millions of acts of the will, which followed, and were occasioned one by another, in their parents. And perhaps most of these Volitions depended on millions of Volitions of hundreds and thousands of others, their contemporaries of the same generation; and most of these on millions of millions of Volitions of others in preceding generations. As we go back, still the number of Volitions, which were some way the occasion of the event, multiply as the branches of a river, until they come at last, as it were, to an infinite number. This will not seem strange, to any one who well considers the matter; if we recollect what philosophers tell us of the innumerable multitudes of those things which are, as it were, the *principia*, or *stamina vitæ*, concerned in generation; the *animalcula* in *semen masculo*, and the *ova* in the womb of the female; the impregnation or animating of one of these, in distinction from all the rest, must depend on things infinitely minute, relating to the time and circumstances of the act of the parents, the state of their bodies, &c. which must depend on innumerable foregoing circumstances and occurrences; which must depend, infinite ways, on foregoing acts of their wills; which are occasioned by innumerable things that happen in the course of their lives, in which their own, and their neighbour's behaviour, must have a hand, an infinite number of ways. And as the Volitions of others must be so many ways concerned in the conception and birth of such men; so, no less, in their preservation, and circumstances of life, their particular determinations and actions, on which the great revolutions they were the occasions of, depended. As, for instance, when the conspirators

in

in *Persia*, against the *Magi*, were consulting about a succession to the empire, it came into the mind of one of them, to propose, that he whose horse neighed first, when they came together the next morning, should be king. Now such a thing's coming into his mind, might depend on innumerable incidents, wherein the Volitions of mankind had been concerned. But, in consequence of this accident, *Darius*, the son of *Hystaspes*, was king. And if this had not been, probably his successor would not have been the same, and all the circumstances of the *Persian* empire might have been far otherwise. And then perhaps *Alexander* might never have conquered that empire. And then probably the circumstances of the world in all succeeding ages, might have been vastly otherwise. I might further instance in many other occurrences; such as those on which depended *Alexander*'s preservation, in the many critical junctures of his life, wherein a small trifle would have turned the scale against him; and the preservation and success of the *Roman* people, in the infancy of their kingdom and common-wealth, and afterwards; which all the succeeding changes in their state, and the mighty revolutions that afterwards came to pass in the habitable world, depended upon. But these hints may be sufficient for every discerning considerate person, to convince him, that the whole state of the world of mankind, in all ages, and the very being of every person who has ever lived in it, in every age, since the times of the ancient prophets, has depended on more Volitions, or acts of the wills of men, than there are sands on the sea-shore.

And therefore, unless God does most exactly and perfectly foresee the future acts of men's wills, all the predictions which he ever uttered concerning

cerning *David*, *Hezekiah*, *Josiah*, *Nebuchadnezzar*, *Cyrus*, *Alexander*; concerning the four monarchies, and the revolutions in them; and concerning all the wars, commotions, victories, prosperities and calamities, of any of the kingdoms, nations or communities of the world, have all been without knowledge.

So that, according to this notion of God's not foreseeing the Volitions and free actions of men, God could foresee nothing appertaining to the state of the world of mankind in future ages; not so much as the being of one person that should live in it; and could foreknow no events, but only such as He would bring to pass Himself, by the extraordinary interposition of his immediate power; or things which should come to pass in the natural material world, by the laws of motion, and course of nature, wherein that is independent on the actions or works of mankind: that is, as he might, like a very able mathematician and astronomer, with great exactness calculate the revolutions of the heavenly bodies, and the greater wheels of the machine of the external creation.

And if we closely consider the matter, there will appear reason to convince us, that he could not, with any absolute certainty, foresee even these. As to the *first*, namely, things done by the immediate and extraordinary interposition of God's power, these cannot be foreseen, unless it can be foreseen when there shall be occasion for such extraordinary interposition. And that cannot be foreseen, unless the state of the moral world can be foreseen. For whenever God thus interposes, it is with regard to the state of the moral world, requiring such divine interposition. Thus God could

could not certainly foresee the universal deluge, the calling of *Abraham*, the destruction of *Sodom* and *Gomorrah*, the plagues on *Egypt*, and *Israel's* redemption out of it, the expelling the seven nations of *Canaan*, and the bringing *Israel* into that land; for these all are represented as connected with things belonging to the state of the moral world. Nor can God foreknow the most proper and convenient time of the day of judgment and general conflagration; for that chiefly depends on the course and state of things in the moral world.

Nor, *Secondly*, can we on this supposition reasonably think, that God can certainly foresee what things shall come to pass, in the course of things, in the natural and material world, even those which in an ordinary state of things might be calculated by a good astronomer. For the moral world is the end of the natural world; and the course of things in the former, is undoubtedly subordinate to God's designs with respect to the latter. Therefore he has seen cause, from regard to the state of things in the moral world, extraordinarily to interpose, to interrupt and lay an arrest on the course of things in the natural world; and even in the greater wheels of its motion; even so as to stop the sun in its course. And unless he can foresee the Volitions of men, and so know something of the future state of the moral world, He cannot know but that he may still have as great occasion to interpose in this manner, as ever he had: nor can He foresee how, or when, He shall have occasion thus to interpose.

Corol. 1. It appears from the things which have been observed, that unless God foresees the

Volitions

Volitions of moral Agents, that cannot be true which is obſerved by the apoſtle *James*, Acts xv. 18. *Known unto God are all his works from the beginning of the world.*

Corol. 2. It appears from what has been obſerved, that unleſs God foreknows the Volitions of moral Agents, all the prophecies of Scripture have no better foundation than mere conjecture; and *That*, in moſt inſtances, a conjecture which muſt have the utmoſt uncertainty; depending on an innumerable, and, as it were, infinite multitude of Volitions, which are all, even to God, uncertain events; however, theſe prophecies are delivered as abſolute predictions, and very many of them in the moſt poſitive manner, with aſſeverations; and ſome of them with the moſt ſolemn oaths.

Corol. 3. It alſo follows, from what has been obſerved, that if this notion of God's ignorance of future Volitions be true, in vain did Chriſt ſay (after uttering many great and important predictions, concerning God's moral kingdom, and things depending on men's moral actions) *Matt.* xxiv. 35. *Heaven and earth ſhall paſs away, but my words ſhall not paſs away.*

Corol. 4. From the ſame notion of God's ignorance, it would follow, that in vain has God Himſelf often ſpoken of the predictions of his word, as evidences of Foreknowledge; and ſo as evidences of that which is his prerogative as GOD, and his peculiar glory, greatly diſtinguiſhing Him from all other beings; as in *Iſa.* xli. 22—26. xliii. 9, 10. xliv. 8. xlv. 21. xlvi. 10. and xlviii. 14.

Arg. II. If God does not foreknow the Volitions of moral Agents, then he did not foreknow the *fall* of man, nor of angels, and so could not foreknow the great things which are *consequent* on these events; such as his sending his Son into the world to die for sinners, and all things pertaining to the great work of redemption; all the things which were done for four thousand years before Christ came, to prepare the way for it; and the incarnation, life, death, resurrection and ascension of Christ; and the setting Him at the head of the universe, as King of heaven and earth, angels and men; and the setting up His church and kingdom in this world, and appointing Him the Judge of the world; and all that Satan should do in the world in opposition to the kingdom of Christ: and the great transactions of the day of judgment, that men and devils shall be the subjects of, and angels concerned in; they are all what God was ignorant of before the fall. And if so, the following Scriptures, and others like them, must be without any meaning, or contrary to truth. Eph. i. 4. *According as he hath chosen us in Him before the foundation of the world.* 1 Pet. i. 20. *Who verily was fore ordained before the foundation of the world.* 2 Tim. i. 9. *Who hath saved us, and called us with an holy calling; not according to our works, but according to his own purpose and grace, which was given us in Christ Jesus before the world began.* So, Eph iii. 11. (speaking of the wisdom of God in the work of redemption) *according to the eternal purpose which he purposed in Christ Jesus.* Tit. i. 2. *In hope of eternal life, which God that cannot lie, promised before the world began.* Rom. viii. 29. *Whom he did foreknow, them he also did predestinate,* &c. 1 Pet. i. 2. *Elect, according to the Foreknowledge of God the Father.*

If God did not foreknow the fall of man, nor the redemption by Jesus Christ, nor the Volitions of man since the fall; then he did not foreknow the saints in any sense; neither as particular persons, nor as societies or nations; either by election, or mere foresight of their virtue or good works; or any foresight of any thing about them relating to their salvation; or any benefit they have by Christ, or any manner of concern of their's with a Redeemer.

Arg. III. On the supposition of God's ignorance of the future Volitions of free Agents, it will follow, that God must in many cases truly *repent* what He has done, so as properly to wish He had done otherwise: by reason that the event of things, in those affairs which are most important, viz. the affairs of his moral kingdom, being uncertain and contingent, often happens quite otherwise than he was aware before-hand. And there would be reason to understand, that in the most literal sense, in *Gen.* vi. 6. *It repented the Lord, that he had made man on the earth, and it grieved him at his heart.* And that 1 *Sam.* xv. 11. contrary to that, *Num.* xxiii. 19. *God is not the Son of Man, that He should repent.* And 1 *Sam.* xv. 15, 29. *Also the Strength of Israel will not lie, nor repent; for He is not a man, that He should repent.* Yea, from this notion it would follow, that God is liable to repent and be grieved at His heart, in a literal sense, continually; and is always exposed to an infinite number of real disappointments in his governing the world; and to manifold, constant, great perplexity and vexation: but this is not very consistent with his title of *God over all, blessed for evermore*; which represents Him as possessed of perfect, constant, and uninterrupted tranquility and felicity, as God over the universe, and in his management of the affairs of the world,

as

as ſupreme and univerſal Ruler. See *Rom.* i. 25. ix. 5. 2 *Cor.* xi. 31. 1 *Tim.* vi. 15.

Arg. IV. It will alſo follow from this notion, that as God is liable to be continually repenting what He has done; ſo He muſt be expoſed to be conſtantly *changing* his mind and intentions, as to his future conduct; altering his meaſures, relinquiſhing his old deſigns, and forming new ſchemes and projections. For his purpoſes, even as to the main parts of his ſcheme, namely, ſuch as belong to the ſtate of his moral kingdom, muſt be always liable to be broken, through want of foreſight; and he muſt be continually putting his ſyſtem to rights, as it gets out of order, through the contingence of the actions of moral Agents: He muſt be a Being, who, inſtead of being abſolutely immutable, muſt neceſſarily be the ſubject of infinitely the moſt numerous acts of repentance, and changes of intention, of any being whatſoever; for this plain reaſon, that his vaſtly extenſive charge comprehends an infinitely greater number of thoſe things which are to him contingent and uncertain. In ſuch a ſituation, He muſt have little elſe to do, but to mend broken links as well as he can, and be rectifying his disjointed frame and diſordered movements, in the beſt manner the caſe will allow. The Supreme Lord of all things muſt needs be under great and miſerable diſadvantages, in governing the world which He has made, and has the care of, through his being utterly unable to find out things of chief importance, which hereafter ſhall befall his ſyſtem; which if He did but know, He might make ſeaſonable proviſion for. In many caſes, there may be very great neceſſity that He ſhould make proviſion, in the manner of his ordering and diſpoſing things, for ſome great events which are to happen, of vaſt and extenſive influence, and endleſs conſequence to the univerſe; which He may ſee afterwards, when it is too late, and may wiſh in vain that He had known before-hand, that He might have ordered his affairs accordingly. And it is in the power of man, on theſe principles, by his devices, purpoſes and actions, thus to diſappoint God, break his meaſures, make Him continually to change his mind, ſubject Him to vexation, and bring Him into confuſion.

But how do theſe things conſiſt with reaſon, or with the Word of God? Which repreſents, that *all God's works*, all that He has ever to do, the whole ſcheme and ſeries of his operations, are *from the beginning* perfectly in his view; and declares, that *whatever devices* and deſigns *are in the hearts of men, the counſel of the Lord is that which ſhall ſtand, and the thoughts of his heart to all generations*, Prov. xix. 21. Pſalm xxxiii. 10. 11. *And that which the Lord of Hoſts hath purpoſed, none ſhall diſannul*, Iſa. xiv. 27. And that he cannot be fruſtrated *in one deſign or thought*, Job xlii. 2. *And that which God doth, it ſhall be for ever, that nothing can be put to it, or taken from it*, Eccleſ. iii. 14. The ſtability and perpetuity of God's counſels are expreſsly ſpoken of as connected with the Foreknowledge of God, *Iſa*. xlvi. 10. *Declaring the end from the beginning, and from ancient times the things that are not yet done; ſaying, My counſel ſhall ſtand, and I will do all my pleaſure.*—And how are theſe things conſiſtent with what the Scripture ſays of God's immutability, which repreſents Him as *without variableneſs*, or *ſhadow of turning*; and ſpeaks of Him particularly as unchangeable with regard to his purpoſes, *Mal*. iii. 6. *I am the Lord; I change not; therefore ye ſons of* Jacob *are not conſumed*. Exod. iii. 14. *I AM THAT I AM*. Job. xxiii. 13, 14. He

He is in one mind; and who can turn Him? And what his soul desireth, even that he doth: for he performeth the thing that is appointed for me.

Arg. V. If this notion of God's ignorance of future Volitions of moral Agents be thoroughly considered in its consequences, it will appear to follow from it, that God, after he had made the world, was liable to be wholly *frustrated of his end* in the creation of it; and so has been, in like manner, liable to be frustrated of his end in all the great works, He hath wrought. It is manifest, the moral world is the end of the natural: the rest of the creation is but an house which God hath built, with furniture, for moral Agents: and the good or bad state of the moral world depends on the improvement they make of their natural Agency, and so depends on their Volitions. And therefore, if these cannot be foreseen by God, because they are contingent, and subject to no kind of necessity, then the affairs of the moral world are liable to go wrong, to any assignable degree; yea, liable to be utterly ruined. As on this scheme, it may well be supposed to be literally said, when mankind, by the abuse of their moral Agency, became very corrupt before the flood, *that the Lord repented that he had made man on the earth, and it grieved Him at his heart*; so, when He made the universe, He did not know but that he might be so disappointed in it, that it might grieve Him at his heart that he had made it. It actually proved, that all mankind become sinful, and a very great part of the angels apostatised: and how could God know before-hand, that all of them would not? And how could God know but that all mankind, notwithstanding means used to reclaim them, being still left to the freedom of their own will, would continue in their apostacy, and grow

 worse

worſe and worſe, as they of the old world before the flood did?

ACCORDING to the ſcheme I am endeavouring to confute, neither the fall of men nor angels, could be foreſeen, and God muſt be greatly diſappointed in theſe events; and ſo the grand ſcheme and contrivance for our redemption, and deſtroying the works of the devil, by the Meſſiah, and all the great things God has done in the proſecution of theſe deſigns, muſt be only the fruits of his own diſappointment, and contrivances of his to mend and patch up, as well as he could, his ſyſtem, which originally was all very good, and perfectly beautiful; but was marred, broken and confounded by the free will of angels and men. And ſtill he muſt be liable to be totally diſappointed a ſecond time: He could not know, that He ſhould have his deſired ſucceſs, in the incarnation, life, death, reſurrection and exaltation of his only begotten Son, and other great works accompliſhed to reſtore the ſtate of things: he could not know, after all, whether there would actually be any tolerable meaſure of reſtoration; for this depended on the free will of man. There has been a general great apoſtacy of almoſt all the Chriſtian World, to that which was worſe than Heatheniſm; which continued for many ages. And how could God, without foreſeeing men's Volitions, know whether ever Chriſtendom would return from this apoſtacy? And which way could he tell before hand how ſoon it would begin? The apoſtle ſays, it began to work in his time; and how could it be known how far it would proceed in that age? Yea, how could it be known that the Goſpel which was not effectual for the reformation of the *Jews*, would ever be effectual for the turning of the heathen

nations

nations from their heathen apostacy, which they had been confirmed in for so many ages?

It is represented often in Scripture, that God, who made the world for Himself, and created it for his pleasure, would infallibly obtain his end in the creation, and in all his works; that as all things are *of* Him, so they would all be *to* Him; and that in the final issue of things, it would appear that He is *the first, and the last.* Rev. xxi. 6. *And he said unto me, It is done. I am Alpha and Omega, the beginning and the end, the first and the last.* But these things are not consistent with God's being so liable to be disappointed in all his works, nor indeed with his failing of his end in any thing that he has undertaken, or done.

SECTION XII.

GOD's certain Foreknowledge *of the future volitions of moral agents inconsistent with such a* Contingence *of those volitions, as is without all* Necessity.

HAVING proved, that GOD has a certain and infallible Prescience of the act of the will of moral agents, I come now, in the *second* place, to shew the consequence; to shew how it follows from hence, that these events are *necessary*, with a Necessity of connection or consequence.

The chief *Arminian* divines, so far as I have had opportunity to observe, deny this consequence; and affirm, that if such Foreknowledge be allowed, it is no evidence of any Necessity of the event foreknown. Now I desire, that this matter may be particularly and thoroughly enquired into. I cannot but think, that on particular and full consideration, it may be perfectly determined, whether it be indeed ſo, or not.

In order to a proper conſideration of this matter, I would obſerve the following things.

I. It is very evident, with regard to a thing whoſe exiſtence is infallibly and indiſſolubly connected with ſomething which already hath, or has had exiſtence, the exiſtence of that thing is neceſſary. Here may be noted,

1. I obſerved before, in explaining the nature of Neceſſity, that in things which are paſt, their paſt exiſtence is now neceſſary: having already made ſure of exiſtence, it is too late for any poſſibility of alteration in that reſpect: it is now impoſſible that it ſhould be otherwiſe than true, that that thing has exiſted.

2. If there be any ſuch thing as a divine Foreknowledge of the volitions of free agents, that Foreknowledge, by the ſuppoſition, is a thing which already *has*, and long ago *had* exiſtence; and ſo, now its exiſtence is neceſſary; it is now utterly impoſſible to be otherwiſe, than that this Foreknowledge ſhould be, or ſhould have been.

3. It is alſo very manifeſt, that thoſe things which are indiſſolubly connected with other things that are neceſſary, are themſelves neceſſary. As that propoſition whoſe truth is neceſſarily connected with another propoſition, which is neceſſarily true, is itſelf neceſſarily true. To ſay otherwiſe, would be a contradiction: it would be in effect to ſay, that the connection was indiſſoluble, and yet was not ſo, but might be broken. If That, whoſe exiſtence

existence is indissolubly connected with something whose existence is now necessary, is itself not necessary, then it may *possibly not exist*, notwithstanding that indissoluble connection of its existence.—Whether the absurdity be not glaring, let the reader judge.

4. It is no less evident, that if there be a full, certain and infallible Foreknowledge of the future existence of the volitions of moral agents, then there is a certain infallible and indissoluble connection between those events and that Foreknowledge; and that therefore, by the preceding observations, those events are necessary events; being infallibly and indissolubly connected with that, whose existence already is, and so is now necessary, and cannot but have been.

To say, the Foreknowledge is certain and infallible, and yet the connection of the event with that Foreknowledge is not indissoluble, but dissoluble and fallible, is very absurd. To affirm it, would be the same thing as to affirm, that there is no necessary connection between a proposition's being infallibly known to be true, and its being true indeed. So that it is perfectly demonstrable, that if there be any infallible knowledge of future volitions, the event is *necessary*; or, in other words, that it is *impossible* but the event should come to pass. For if it be not impossible, but that it may be otherwise, then it is not impossible, but that the proposition which affirms its future coming to pass, may not now be true. But how absurd is that, on the supposition that there is now an infallible knowledge (*i. e.* knowledge which it is impossible should fail) that it is true. There is this absurdity in it, that it is not impossible, but that there now should be no truth in that proposition, which is now infallibly known to be true.

II. That no future event can be certainly foreknown, whose existence is contingent, and without all Necessity, may be proved thus; It is impossible for a thing to be certainly known to any intellect without *evidence*. To suppose otherwise, implies a contradiction: because for a thing to be certainly known to any understanding, is for it to be *evident* to that understanding: and for a thing to be *evident* to any understanding is the same thing as for that understanding to *see evidence* of it: but no understanding, created or increated, can *see evidence* where there is none: for that is the same thing, as to see that to be, which is not. And therefore, if there be any truth which is absolutely without evidence, that truth is absolutely unknowable, insomuch that it implies a contradiction to suppose that it is known.

But if there be any future event, whose existence is contingent, without all Necessity, the future existence of the event is absolutely *without evidence*. If there be any evidence of it, it must be one of these two sorts, either *self-evidence*, or *proof*; for there can be no other sort of evidence, but one of these two; an evident thing must be either evident *in itself*, or evident *in something else*; that is, evident by connection with something else. But a future thing, whose existence is without all Necessity, can have neither of these sorts of evidence. It cannot be *self-evident*: for if it be, it may be now known, by what is now to be seen in the thing itself; either its present existence, or the Necessity of its nature: but both these are contrary to the supposition. It is supposed, both that the thing has no present existence to be seen; and also that it is not of such a nature

nature as to be necessarily existent for the future: so that its future existence is not self-evident. And, *secondly*, neither is there any *proof*, or evidence *in any thing else*, or evidence of connection with something else that is evident; for this is also contrary to the supposition. It is supposed, that there is now nothing existent, with which the future existence of the *contingent* event is connected. For such a connection destroys its *Contingence*, and supposes Necessity. Thus it is demonstrated, that there is in the nature of things absolutely no evidence at all of the future existence of that event, which is contingent, without all Necessity (if any such event there be) neither self evidence nor proof. And therefore the thing in reality is not evident; and so cannot be seen to be evident, or, which is the same thing, cannot be known.

Let us consider this in an example. Suppose that five thousand seven hundred and sixty years ago, there was no other being but the Divine Being; and then this world, or some particular body or spirit, all at once starts out of nothing into being, and takes on itself a particular nature and form; all in *absolute Contingence* without any concern of God, or any other cause, in the matter; without any manner of ground or reason of its existence; or any dependence upon, or connection at all with any thing foregoing: I say, that if this be supposed, there was no evidence of that event before hand. There was no evidence of it to be seen *in the thing itself*; for the thing itself as yet, was not. And there was no evidence of it to be seen in *any thing else*; for *evidence in* something else is *connection with* something else: but such connection is contrary to the supposition. There was no evidence before, that this thing *would happen*; for by the supposition, there was no reason why *it should happen*, rather than ſomething elſe, or rather than nothing. And if ſo, then all things before were exactly equal, and the ſame, with reſpect to that and other poſſible things; there was no preponderation, no ſuperior weight or value; and therefore, nothing that could be of any weight or value to determine any underſtanding. The thing was abſolutely without evidence, and abſolutely unknowable. An increaſe of underſtanding, or of the capacity of diſcerning, has no tendency, and makes no advance, to a diſcerning any ſigns or evidences of it, let it be increaſed never ſo much; yea, if it be increaſed infinitely. The increaſe of the ſtrength of ſight may have a tendency to enable to diſcern the evidence which is far off, and very much hid, and deeply involved in clouds and darkneſs; but it has no tendency to enable to diſcern evidence where there is none. If the ſight be infinitely ſtrong, and the capacity of diſcerning infinitely great, it will enable to ſee all that there is, and to ſee it perfectly, and with eaſe; yet it has no tendency at all to enable a being to diſcern that evidence which is not; but, on the contrary, it has a tendency to enable to diſcern with great certainty that there is none.

III. To ſuppoſe the future volitions of moral agents not to be neceſſary events; or, which is the ſame thing, events which it is not impoſſible but that they may not come to paſs; and yet to ſuppoſe that God certainly foreknows them, and knows all things; is to ſuppoſe God's Knowledge to be inconſiſtent with itſelf. For to ſay, that God certainly, and without all conjecture, knows that a thing will infallibly be, which at the ſame time he knows to be ſo *contingent*, that it may poſſibly not be, is to ſuppoſe his knowledge inconſiſtent with itſelf; or that one thing, that he knows, is utterly inconsistent with another thing, that he knows. It is the same thing as to say, he now knows a proposition to be of certain infallible truth, which he knows to be of contingent uncertain truth. If a future volition is so without all Necessity, that there is nothing hinders, but that it may not be, then the proposition, which asserts its future existence, is so uncertain, that there is nothing hinders, but that the truth of it may entirely fail. And if God knows all things, he knows this proposition to be thus uncertain. And that is inconsistent with his knowing that it is infallibly true; and so inconsistent with his infallibly knowing that it is true. If the thing be indeed contingent, God views it so, and judges it to be contingent, if he views things as they are. If the event be not necessary, then it is possible it may never be: and if it be possible it may never be, God knows it may possibly never be; and that is to know that the proposition, which affirms its existence, may possibly not be true; and that is to know that the truth of it is uncertain; which surely is inconsistent with his knowing it as a certain truth. If volitions are in themselves contingent events, without all Necessity, then it is no argument of perfection of Knowledge in any being to determine peremptorily that they will be; but on the contrary, an argument of ignorance and mistake: because it would argue, that he supposes that proposition to be certain, which in its own nature, and all things considered, is uncertain and contingent. To say, in such a case, that God may have ways of knowing contingent events which we cannot conceive of, is ridiculous; as much so, as to say, that God may know contradictions to be true, for aught we know, or that he may know a thing to be certain, and at the same time know it not to be certain, though we cannot conceive how; because

cause he has ways of knowing, which we cannot comprehend.

Corol. 1. FROM what has been observed it is evident, that the absolute *decrees* of God are no more inconsistent with human liberty, on account of any Necessity of the event, which follows from such decrees, than the absolute *Foreknowledge* of God. Because the connection between the event and certain Foreknowledge, is as infallible and indissoluble, as between the event and an absolute decree. That is, it is no more impossible, that the event and decree should not agree together, than that the event and absolute Knowledge should disagree. The connection between the event and Foreknowledge is absolutely perfect, by the supposition: because it is supposed, that the certainty and infallibility of the Knowledge is absolutely perfect. And it being so, the certainty cannot be increased; and therefore the connection, between the Knowledge and thing known, cannot be increased; so that if a decree be added to the Foreknowledge, it does not at all increase the connection, or make it more infallible or indissoluble. If it were not so, the certainty of Knowledge might be increased by the addition of a decree; which is contrary to the supposition, which is, that the Knowledge is absolutely perfect, or perfect to the highest possible degree.

THERE is as much of an impossibility but that the things which are infallibly foreknown, should be, or (which is the same thing) as great a Necessity of their future existence, as if the event were already written down, and was known and read by all mankind, through all preceding ages, and there was the most indissoluble and perfect connection possible, between the writing, and the thing written. In

In such a case, it would be as impossible the event should fail of existence, as if it had existed already; and a decree cannot make an event surer or more necessary than this.

And therefore, if there be any such foreknowledge, as it has been proved there is, then Necessity of connection and consequence, is not at all inconsistent with any liberty which man, or any other creature enjoys. And from hence it may be inferred, that absolute decrees of God, which does not at all increase the Necessity, are not at all inconsistent with the liberty which man enjoys, on any such account, as that they make the event decreed necessary, and render it utterly impossible but that it should come to pass. Therefore, if absolute decrees are inconsistent with man's liberty as a moral agent, or his liberty in a state of probation, or any liberty whatsoever that he enjoys, it is not on account of any Necessity which absolute decrees infer.

Dr *Whitby* supposes, there is a great difference between God's Foreknowledge, and his decrees, with regard to Necessity of future events. In his Discourse on the five Points, p 474, &c he says, "God's Prescience has no influence at all on our actions. ——Should God (says he), by immediate Revelation, give me the knowledge of the event of any man's state or actions, would my knowledge of them have any influence upon his actions? Surely none at all. — Our knowledge doth not affect the things we know, to make them more certain, or more future, than they would be without it. Now, Foreknowledge in God is knowledge. As therefore knowledge has no influence on things that are, so neither has Foreknowledge on things that shall be. And

con-

consequently, the Foreknowledge of any action that would be otherwise free, cannot alter or diminish that freedom. Whereas God's decree of election is powerful and active, and comprehends the preparation and exhibition of such means, as shall unfrustrably produce the end.—— Hence God's Prescience renders no actions necessary." And to this purpose, p. 473. he cites *Origin*, where he says, *God's Prescience is not the cause of things future, but their being future is the cause of God's Prescience that they will be:* and *Le Blanc*, where he says, *This is the truest resolution of this difficulty, that Prescience is not the cause that things are future; but their being future is the cause they are foreseen.* In like manner, Dr *Clark*, in his Demonstration of the Being and Attributes of God, p. 95—99. And the Author of *the Freedom of the Will, in God and the Creature*, speaking to the like purpose with Dr. *Whitby*, represents *Foreknowledge as having no more influence on things known, to make them necessary*, than *After-knowledge*, or to that purpose.

To all which I would say; that what is said about Knowledge, its not having influence on the thing known to make it necessary, is nothing to the purpose, nor does in the least affect the foregoing reason. Whether Prescience be the thing that *makes* the event necessary or no, it alters not the case. Infallible Foreknowledge may *prove* the Necessity of the event foreknown, and yet not be the thing which *causes* the Necessity. If the Foreknowledge be absolute, this *proves* the event known to be necessary, or proves that it is impossible but that the event should be, by some means or other, either by a decree, or some other way, if there be any other way: because, as was said before, it is absurd to say, that a proposition is is known to be certainly and infallibly true, which yet may possibly prove not true.

The whole of the seeming force of this evasion lies in this; that, in as much as certain Foreknowledge does not *cause* an event to be necessary, as a decree does; therefore it does not *prove* it to be necessary, as a decree does. But there is no force in this arguing: for it is built wholly on this supposition, that nothing can *prove*, or *be an evidence* of a thing's being necessary, but that which has *a causal influence to make it so.* But this can never be maintained. If certain Foreknowledge of the future existing of an event, be not the thing, which first *makes* it impossible that it should fail of existence; yet it may, and certainly does *demonstrate*, that it is impossible it should fail of it, however that impossibility comes. If Foreknowledge be not the cause, but the effect of this impossibility, it may prove that there is such an impossibility, as much as if it were the cause. It is as strong arguing from the effect to the cause, as from the cause to the effect. It is enough, that an existence, which is infallibly foreknown, cannot fail, whether that impossibility arises from the Foreknowledge, or is prior to it. It is as evident, as it is possible any thing should be, that it is impossible a thing, which is infallibly known to be true, should prove not to be true: therefore there is a *Necessity* that it should be otherwise: whether the Knowledge be the cause of this Necessity, or the Necessity the cause of the Knowledge.

All certain Knowledge, whether it be Foreknowledge or After-knowledge, or concomitant Knowledge, proves the thing known now to be necessary, by some means or other; or proves that it is is impossible it should now be otherwise than true. —I freely allow, that Foreknowledge does not prove a thing to be necessary any more than After-knowledge: but then After-knowledge, which is certain and infallible, proves that it is now become impossible but that the proposition known should be true. Certain After-knowledge proves that it is now, in the time of the Knowledge, by some means or other, become impossible but that the proposition, which predicates *past* existence on the event, should be true. And so does certain Foreknowledge prove, that now, in the time of the Knowledge, it is by some means or other, become impossible but that the proposition, which predicates *future* existence on the event, should be true. The Necessity of the truth of the propositions consisting in the present impossibility of the non-existence of the event affirmed, in both cases, is the immediate ground of the certainty of the Knowledge; there can be no certainty of Knowledge without it.

There must be a certainty in things themselves, before they are certainly known, or (which is the same thing) known to be certain. For certainty of Knowledge is nothing else but knowing or discerning the certainty there is in the things themselves, which are known. Therefore there must be a certainty in things to be a ground of certainty of Knowledge, and to render things capable of being known to be certain. And this is nothing but the necessity of the truth known, or its being impossible but that it should be true; or, in other words, the firm and infallible connection between the subject and predicate of the proposition that contains that truth. All certainty of Knowledge consists in the view of the firmness of that connection. So God's certain Foreknowledge

ledge of the future existence of any event, is his view of the firm and indissoluble connection of the subject and predicate of the proposition that affirms its future existence. The subject is that possible event; the predicate is its future existing: but if future existence be firmly and indissolubly connected with that event, then the future existence of that event is necessary. If God certainly knows the future existence of an event which is wholly contingent, and may possibly never be, then He sees a firm connection between a subject and predicate that are not firmly connected; which is a contradiction.

I ALLOW what Dr. *Whitby* says to be true, *That mere Knowledge does not affect the thing known, to make it more certain or more future.* But yet, I say, it *supposes* and *proves* the thing to be *already*, both *future*, and *certain*; i. e. necessarily future. Knowledge of *futurity*, supposes *futurity*; and a *certain Knowledge* of futurity, supposes *certain futurity*, antecedent to that certain Knowledge. But there is no other certain futurity of a thing, antecedent to certainty of Knowledge, than a prior impossibility but that the thing should prove true; or (which is the same thing) the Necessity of the event.

I WOULD observe one thing further concerning this Matter, it is this; that if it be as those forementioned writers suppose, that God's Foreknowledge is not the cause, but the effect of the existence of the event foreknown; this is so far from shewing that this Foreknowledge doth not infer the Necessity of the existence of that event, that it rather shews the contrary the more plainly. Because it shews the existence of the event to be so settled and firm, that it is as if it had already been; in as much as *in effect* it actually exists already; its future existence has already had actual *influence* and *efficacy*, and has *produced an effect*, viz. Prescience: the effect exists already; and as the effect supposes the cause, is connected with the cause, and depends entirely upon it, therefore it is as if the future event, which is the cause, had existed already. The effect is firm as possible, it having already the possession of existence, and has made sure of it. But the effect cannot be more firm and stable than its cause, ground and reason. The building cannot be firmer than the foundation.

To illustrate this matter, let us suppose the appearances and images of things in a glass; for instance, a reflecting telescope, to be the real effects of heavenly bodies (at a distance, and out of sight) which they resemble: if it be so, then, as these images in the telescope have had a past actual existence, and it is become utterly impossible now that it should be otherwise than that they have existed; so they being the true effects of the heavenly bodies they resemble, this proves the existing of those heavenly bodies to be as real, infallible, firm and necessary, as the existing of these effects; the one being connected with, and wholly depending on the other.—Now let us suppose future existences some way or other to have influence back, to produce effects before-hand, and cause exact and perfect images of themselves in a glass, a thousand years before they exist, yea, in all preceding ages; but yet that these images are real effects of these future existences, perfectly dependent on, and connected with their cause; these effects and images, having already had actual existence, rendering that matter of their existing perfectly firm and stable, and utterly impossible

possible to be otherwise: this proves in like manner, as in the other instance, that the existence of the things, which are their causes, is also equally sure, firm and necessary; and that it is alike impossible but that they should be, as if they had been already, as their effects have. And if instead of images in a glass, we suppose the antecedent effects to be perfect ideas of them in the Divine Mind, which have existed there from all eternity, which are as properly effects, as truly and properly connected with their cause, the case is not altered.

ANOTHER thing which has been said by some *Arminians*, to take off the force of what is urged from God's Prescience, against the Contingence of the volitions of moral agents, is to this purpose; "That when we talk of Foreknowledge in God, there is no strict propriety in our so speaking; and that although it be true, that there is in God the most perfect Knowledge of all events from eternity to eternity, yet there is no such thing as *before* and *after* in God, but he sees all things by one perfect unchangeable view, without any succession."—To this I answer;

1. IT has been already shewn, that all certain Knowledge proves the Necessity of the truth known; whether it be *before*, *after*, or *at the same time*.—Though it be true, that there is no succession in God's Knowledge, and the manner of his Knowledge is to us inconceivable, yet thus much we know concerning it, that there is no event, past, present, or to come, that God is ever uncertain of; He never is, never was, and never will be without infallible Knowledge of it; He always sees the existence of it to be certain and infallible. And as he always sees things just as they

are in truth; hence there never is in reality any thing contingent in ſuch a ſenſe, as that poſſibly it may happen never to exiſt. If ſtrictly ſpeaking, there is no Foreknowledge in God, it is becauſe thoſe things, which are future to us, are as preſent to God, as if they already had exiſtence: and that is as much as to ſay, that future events are always in God's view as evident, clear, ſure and neceſſary, as if they already were. If there never is a time wherein the exiſtence of the event is not preſent with God, then there never is a time wherein it is not as much impoſſible for it to fail of exiſtence, as if its exiſtence were preſent, and were already come to paſs.

God's viewing things ſo perfectly and unchangeably as that there is no ſucceſſion in his ideas or judgment, do not hinder, but that there is properly now, in the mind of God, a certain and perfect Knowledge of moral actions of men, which to us are an hundred years hence: yea the objection ſuppoſes this; and therefore it certainly does not hinder but that, by the foregoing arguments, it is now impoſſible theſe moral actions ſhould not come to paſs.

We know, that God knows the future voluntary actions of men in ſuch a ſenſe before-hand, as that he is able particularly to declare, and foretell them, and write them, or cauſe them to be written down in a book, as he often has done; and that therefore the neceſſary connection which there is between God's Knowledge and the event known, does as much prove the event to be neceſſary before-hand, as if the Divine Knowledge were in the ſame ſenſe before the event, as the prediction or writing is. If the knowledge be infallible, then the expreſſion of it in the written pre-

prediction is infallible; that is, there is an infallible connection between that written prediction and the event. And if ſo, then it is impoſſible it ſhould ever be otherwiſe, than that that prediction and the event ſhould agree: and this is the ſame thing as to ſay, it is impoſſible but that the event ſhould come to paſs: and this is the ſame as to ſay that its coming to paſs is neceſſary.—So that it is manifeſt, that there being no proper ſucceſſion in God's mind, makes no alteration as to the Neceſſity of the exiſtence of the events which God knows. Yea,

2. THIS is ſo far from weakening the proof, which has been given of the impoſſibility of the not coming to paſs of future events known, as that it eſtabliſhes that, wherein the ſtrength of the foregoing arguments conſiſts, and ſhews the clearneſs of the evidence. For,

(1.) THE very reaſon, why God's Knowledge is without ſucceſſion, is, becauſe it is abſolutely perfect, to the higheſt poſſible degree of clearneſs and certainty: all things, whether paſt, preſent, or to come, being viewed with equal evidence and fulneſs; future things being ſeen with as much clearneſs, as if they were preſent; the view is always in abſolute perfection: and abſolute conſtant perfection admits of no alteration, and ſo no ſucceſſion; the actual exiſtence of the thing known, does not at all increaſe, or add to the clearneſs or certainty of the thing known: God calls the things that are not, as though they were; they are all one to him as if they had already exiſted. But herein conſiſts the ſtrength of the demonſtration before given, of the impoſſibility of the not exiſting of thoſe things, whoſe exiſtence God knows; that it is as impoſſible they ſhould fail of existence, as if they existed already. This objection, instead of weakening this argument, sets it in the clearest and strongest light; for it supposes it to be so indeed, that the existence of future events is in God's view so much as if it already had been, that when they come actually to exist, it makes not the least alteration or variation in his view or Knowledge of them.

(2.) The objection is founded on the *immutability* of God's Knowledge; for it is the immutability of Knowledge makes his Knowledge to be without succession. But this most directly and plainly demonstrates the thing I insist on, *viz.* that it is utterly impossible the known events should fail of existence. For if that were possible, then it would be possible for there to be a change in God's Knowledge and view of things. For if the known event should fail of existence, and not come into being, as God expected, then God would see it, and so would change his mind, and see his former mistake; and thus there would be change and succession in his Knowledge. But as God is immutable, and so it is utterly infinitely impossible that his view should be changed; so it is, for the same reason, just so impossible that the fore-known event should not exist: and that is to be impossible, in the highest degree: and therefore the contrary is necessary. Nothing is more impossible than that the immutable God should be changed, by the succession of time; who comprehends all things, from eternity to eternity, in one, most perfect, and unalterable view; so that his whole eternal duration is *vitæ interminabilis, tota, simul, & perfecta possessio.*

On the whole, I need not fear to say, that there is no geometrical theorem or proposition whatsoever

ſoever, more capable of ſtrict demonſtration, than that God's certain Preſcience of the volitions of moral agents is inconſiſtent with ſuch a Contingence of theſe events, as is without all Neceſſity; and ſo is inconſiſtent with the *Arminian* notion of liberty.

Corol. 2. HENCE the doctrine of the *Calviniſts*, concerning the abſolute decrees of God, does not at all infer any more *fatality* in things, than will demonſtrably follow from the doctrine of moſt *Arminian* divines, who acknowledge God's omniſcience, and univerſal Preſcience. Therefore all objections they make againſt the doctrine of the *Calviniſts*, as implying *Hobbes*'s doctrine of Neceſſity, or the *ſtoical* doctrine of *fate*, lie no more againſt the doctrine of *Calviniſts*, than their own doctrine: and therefore it doth not become thoſe divines, to raiſe ſuch an outcry againſt the *Calviniſts*, on this account.

Corol. 3. HENCE all arguing from Neceſſity, againſt the doctrine of the inability of unregenerate men to perform the conditions of ſalvation, and the commands of God requiring ſpiritual duties, and againſt the *Calviniſtic* doctrine of efficacious grace; I ſay, all arguings of *Arminians* (ſuch of them as own God's omniſcience) againſt theſe things, on this ground, that theſe doctrines, though they do not ſuppoſe men to be under any conſtraint or coaction, yet ſuppoſe them under Neceſſity, with reſpect to their moral actions, and thoſe things which are required of them in order to their acceptance with God; and their arguing againſt the Neceſſity of men's volitions, taken from the reaſonableneſs of God's commands, promiſes, and threatenings, and the ſincerity of his counſels and invitations; and all objections againſt any doctrines of the *Calvinists* as being inconsistent with human liberty, because they infer Necessity; I say, all these arguments and objections must fall to the ground, and be justly esteemed vain and frivolous, as coming from them; being maintained in an inconsistence with themselves, and in like manner levelled against their own doctrine, as against the doctrine of the *Calvinists.*

SECTION XIII.

Whether we suppose the volitions of moral agents to be connected with any thing antecedent, or not, yet they must be necessary in such a sense as to overthrow Arminian *Liberty.*

EVERY act of the will has a cause, or it has not. If it has a cause, then, according to what has already been demonstrated, it is not contingent, but necessary; the effect being necessarily dependent and consequent on its cause; and that, let the cause be what it will. If the cause is the will itself, by antecedent acts chusing and determining; still the *determined* and *caused* act must be a necessary effect. The act, that is the determined effect of the foregoing act which is its cause, cannot prevent the efficiency of its cause; but must be wholly subject to its determination and command, as much as the motions of the hands and feet. The consequent commanded acts of the will are as passive and as necessary, with respect to the antecedent determining acts, as the parts of the body are to the volitions which determine and command them. And therefore, if all the free acts of the will are thus, if they are all determined effects, determined by the will itself, that is, determined by antecedent choice, then they are all necessary; they

they are all subject to, and decisively fixed by the foregoing act, which is their cause: yea, even the determining act itself; for that must be determined and fixed by another act, preceding that, if it be a free and voluntary act; and so must be necessary. So that by this all the free acts of the will are necessary, and cannot be free unless they are necessary: because they cannot be free, according to the *Arminian* notion of freedom, unless they are determined by the will; which is to be determined by antecedent choice; which being their cause, proves them necessary. And yet they say, Necessity is utterly inconsistent with Liberty. So that, by their scheme, the acts of the will cannot be free unless they are necessary, and yet cannot be free if they be not necessary!

But if the other part of the dilemma be taken, and it be affirmed that the free acts of the will have no cause, and are connected with nothing whatsoever that goes before them and determines them, in order to maintain their proper and absolute Contingence, and this should be allowed to be possible; still it will not serve their turn. For if the volition come to pass by perfect Contingence, and without any cause at all, then it is certain, no act of the will, no prior act of the soul was the cause, no determination or choice of the soul, had any hand in it. The will, or the soul, was indeed the subject of what happened to it accidentally, but was not the cause. The will is not active in causing or determining, but purely the passive subject; at least, according to their notion of action and passion. In this case, Contingence does as much prevent the determination of the will, as a proper cause; and as to the will, it was necessary, and could be no otherwise. For to suppose that it could have been otherwise, if the will or soul

 had

had pleased, is to suppose that the act is dependent on some prior act of choice or pleasure; contrary to what now is supposed: it is to suppose that it might have been otherwise, if its cause had made it or ordered it otherwise. But this does not agree to its having no cause or order at all. That must be necessary as to the soul, which is dependent on no free act of the soul: but that which is without a cause, is dependent on no free act of the soul: because, by the supposition, it is dependent on nothing, and is connected with nothing. In such a case, the soul is necessarily subjected to what accident brings to pass, from time to time, as much as the earth, that is inactive, is necessarily subjected to what falls upon it. But this does not consist with the *Arminian* notion of liberty, which is the will's power of determining itself in its own acts, and being wholly active in it, without passiveness, and without being subject to Necessity.——Thus, Contingence belongs to the *Arminian* notion of Liberty, and yet is inconsistent with it.

I WOULD here observe, that the author of the *Essay on the Freedom of the Will, in God and the Creature*, page 76, 77, says as follows: "The word *Chance* always means something done without design. Chance and design stand in direct opposition to each other: and Chance can never be properly applied to acts of the will, which is the spring of all design, and which designs to chuse whatsoever it doth chuse, whether there be any superior fitness in the thing which it chuses, or no; and it designs to determine itself to one thing, where two things, perfectly equal, are proposed, merely because it will." But herein appears a very great inadvantage in this author. For if *the will be the spring of all design*, as he says, then certainly it is not always the *effect* of design; and the acts of the will themselves must

must sometimes come to pass, when they do not *spring from* design; and consequently come to pass by Chance, according to his own definition of Chance. And *if the will designs to chuse whatever it does chuse*, and *designs to determine itself*, as he says, then it designs to determine all its designs. Which carries us back from one design to a foregoing design determining that, and to another determining that; and so on *in infinitum*. The very first design must be the effect of foregoing design, or else it must be by Chance, in his notion of it.

Here another alternative may be proposed, relating to the connection of the acts of the will with something foregoing that is their cause, not much unlike to the other; which is this: either human liberty is such, that it may well stand with volitions being necessarily connected with the views of the understanding, and so is consistent with Necessity; or it is inconsistent with, and contrary to such a connection and Necessity. The former is directly subversive of the *Arminian* notion of liberty, consisting in freedom from all Necessity. And if the latter be chosen, and it be said, that liberty is inconsistent with any such necessary connection of volition with foregoing views of the understanding, it consisting in freedom from any such Necessity of the will as that would imply; then the liberty of the soul consists (in part at least) in the freedom from restraint, limitation and government, in its actings, by the understanding, and in liberty and liableness to act contrary, to the understanding's views and dictates: and consequently the more the soul has of this disengagedness, in its acting, the more liberty. Now let it be considered what this brings the noble principle of human liberty to, particularly when it is possessed and enjoyed in its perfection, *viz.* a full and perfect freedom and liableness to act altogether

altogether at random, without the least connection with, or restraint or government by, any dictate of reason, or any thing whatsoever apprehended, considered or viewed by the understanding; as being inconsistent with the full and perfect sovereignty of the will over its own determinations.—-The notion mankind have conceived of liberty, is some dignity or privilege, something worth claiming. But what dignity or privilege is there, in being given up to such a wild Contingence as this, to be perfectly and constantly liable to act unintelligently and unreasonably, and as much without the guidance of understanding, as if we had none, or were as destitute of perception, as the smoke that is driven by the wind!

PART

PART III.

Wherein is enquired, whether any ſuch Liberty of Will as ARMINIANS *hold, be neceſſary to* MORAL AGENCY, VIRTUE *and* VICE, PRAISE *and* DISPRAISE, *&c.*

SECTION I.

GOD's moral Excellency *neceſſary, yet virtuous and praiſe-worthy.*

HAVING conſidered the firſt thing that was propoſed to be enquired into, relating to that freedom of will which *Arminians* maintain; namely, Whether any ſuch thing does, ever did, or ever can exiſt, or be conceived of; I come now to the *ſecond* thing propoſed to be the ſubject of enquiry, *viz.* Whether any ſuch kind of liberty be requiſite to moral agency, virtue and vice, praiſe and blame, reward and puniſhment, &c.

I SHALL

I SHALL begin with some consideration of the virtue and agency of the Supreme moral Agent, and Fountain of all Agency and Virtue.

DR. *Whitby*, in his Discourse on the five Points, p. 14, says, "If all human actions are necessary, virtue and vice must be empty names; we being capable of nothing that is blame worthy, or deserveth praise; for who can blame a person for doing only what he could not help, or judge that he deserveth praise only for what he could not avoid?" To the like purpose he speaks in places innumerable; especially in his Discourse on the *Freedom of the Will*; constantly maintaining, that a *freedom not only from coaction, but necessity*, is absolutely requisite, in order to actions being either worthy of blame, or deserving of praise. And to this agrees, as is well known, the current doctrine of *Arminian* writers, who, in general, hold, that there is no virtue or vice, reward or punishment, nothing to be commended or blamed, without this freedom. And yet Dr. *Whitby*, p. 300, allows, that God is without this freedom; and *Arminians*, so far as I have had opportunity to observe, generally acknowledge, that God is necessarily holy, and his will necessarily determined to that which is good.

So that, putting these things together, the infinitely holy God, who always used to be esteemed by God's people not only virtuous, but a Being in whom is all possible virtue, and every virtue in the most absolute purity and perfection, and in infinitely greater brightness and amiableness than in any creature; the most perfect pattern of virtue, and the fountain from whom all other virtue is but as beams from the sun; and who has been supposed to be, on the account of his virtue

tue and holiness, infinitely more worthy to be esteemed, loved, honoured, admired, commended, extolled and praised, than any creature: and He, who is thus every where represented in scripture; I say, this Being, according to this notion of Dr. *Whitby*, and other *Arminians*, has no virtue at all; virtue, when ascribed to Him, is but *an empty name*; and he is deserving of no commendation or praise; because he is under necessity, He cannot avoid being holy and good as he is; therefore no thanks to him for it. It seems, the holiness, justness, faithfulness, &c. of the Most High, must not be accounted to be of the nature of that which is virtuous and praise worthy. They will not deny, that these things in God are good; but then we must understand them, that they are no more virtuous, or of the nature of any thing commendable, than the good that is in any other being that is not a moral agent; as the brightness of the sun, and the fertility of the earth, are good, but not virtuous, because these properties are necessary to these bodies, and not the fruit of self-determining power.

There needs no other confutation of this notion of God's not being virtuous or praise-worthy, to Christians acquainted with their Bible, but only stating and particularly representing of it. To bring texts of Scripture, wherein God is represented as in every respect, in the highest manner virtuous, and supremely praise-worthy, would be endless, and is altogether needless to such as have been bought up in the light of the Gospel.

It were to be wished, that Dr. *Whitby*, and other divines of the same sort, had explained themselves, when they have asserted, that *that* which is is necessary, is *not deserving of praise*; at the same time that they have owned God's perfection to be necessary, and so in effect represented God as not deserving praise. Certainly, if their words have any meaning at all, by *praise*, they must mean the exercise or testimony of some sorts of esteem, respect or honourable regard. And will they then say, that men are worthy of that esteem, respect and honour for their virtue, small and imperfect as it is, which yet God is not worthy of, for his infinite righteousness, holiness and goodness? If so, it must be, because of some sort of peculiar Excellency in the virtuous man, which is his prerogative, wherein he really has the preference; some dignity, that is entirely distinguished from any Excellency, amiableness or honourableness in God; not in imperfection and dependence, but in pre-eminence; which therefore he does not receive from God, nor is God the fountain or pattern of it; nor can God, in that respect, stand in competition with him, as the object of honour and regard; but man may claim a peculiar esteem, commendation and glory, that God can have no pretension to. Yea, God has no right, by virtue of his necessary holiness, to intermeddle with that grateful respect and praise, due to the virtuous man, who chuses virtue, in the exercise of a freedom *ad utrumque*; any more than a precious stone, which cannot avoid being hard and beautiful.

And if it be so, let it be explained what that peculiar respect is, that is due to the virtuous man, which differs in nature and kind, in some way of pre-eminence, from all that is due to God. What is the name or description of that peculiar affection? Is it esteem, love, admiration, honour, praise,

praise, or gratitude? The Scripture every where represents God as the highest object of all these: there we read of the *soul's magnifying the Lord*, of *loving Him with all the heart, with all the soul, with all the mind, and with all the strength*; *admiring* him and *his righteous acts*, or greatly regarding them, as *marvellous and wonderful*; *honouring, glorifying, exalting, extolling, blessing, thanking* and *praising* Him, *giving unto Him all the glory* of the good which is done or received, rather than unto men; *that no flesh should glory in his presence*; but that He should be regarded as the Being to whom all glory is due. What then is that respect? What passion, affection, or exercise is it, that *Arminians* call *praise*, diverse from all these things, which men are worthy of for their virtue, and which God is not worthy of, in any degree?

If that necessity which attends God's moral perfections and actions, be as inconsistent with a Being worthy of praise, as a necessity of co-action; as is plainly implied in, or inferred from Dr. *Whitby*'s discourse; then why should we thank God for his goodness, any more than if He were forced to be good, or any more than we should thank one of our fellow-creatures who did us good, not freely, and of good will, or from any kindness of heart, but from mere compulsion, or extrinsical Necessity? *Arminians* suppose, that God is necessarily a good and gracious Being: for this they make the ground of some of their main arguments against many doctrines maintained by *Calvinists*; they say, these are *certainly* false, and it is *impossible* they should be true, because they are not consistent with the goodness of God. This supposes, that it is *impossible* but that God should be good: for if it be possible that He

He ſhould be otherwiſe, then that impoſſibility of the truth of theſe doctrines ceaſes, according to their own argument.

THAT virtue in God is not, in the moſt proper ſenſe, *rewardable*, is not for want of merit in his moral perfections and actions, ſufficient to deſerve rewards from his creatures; but becauſe He is infinitely above all capacity of receiving any reward or benefit from the creature. He is already infinitely and unchangeably happy, and we cannot be profitable unto Him. But ſtill he is worthy of our ſupreme benevolence for his virtue; and would be worthy of our beneficence, which is the fruit and expreſſion of benevolence, if our goodneſs could extend to Him. If God deſerves to be thanked and praiſed for his goodneſs, He would, for the ſame reaſon, deſerve that we ſhould alſo *requite* his kindneſs, if that were poſſible. *What ſhall I render to the Lord for all his benefits?* is the natural language of thankfulneſs: and ſo far as in us lies, it is our duty to recompenſe God's goodneſs, and *render again according to benefits received.* And that we might have opportunity for ſo natural an expreſſion of our gratitude to God, as beneficence, notwithſtanding his being infinitely above our reach; He has appointed others to be his receivers, and to ſtand in his ſtead, as the objects of our beneficence; ſuch are eſpecially our indigent brethren.

SEC-

SECTION II.

The Acts of the Will of the human Soul of Jesus Christ necessarily holy; *yet truly virtuous, praise-worthy, rewardable;* &c.

I HAVE already considered how Dr. *Whitby* insists upon it, that a freedom, not only from coaction, but necessity, is *requisite either to virtue, vice, praise or dispraise, reward or punishment.* He also insists on the same freedom as absolutely requisite to a person's being the subject of a *law, of precepts* or *prohibitions*; in the book before-mentioned, (p. 301, 314, 328, 339, 340, 341, 342, 347, 361, 373, 410.) And of *promises* and *threatenings*, (p. 298, 301, 305, 311, 339, 340, 363.) And as requisite to *a state of trial*, (p. 297, &c.)

Now therefore, with an eye to these things, I would enquire into the moral conduct and practices of our Lord Jesus Christ, which he exhibited in his human nature here, in his state of humiliation. And *first*, I would shew, that his holy behaviour was *necessary*; or that it was *impossible* it should be otherwise, than that He should behave himself holily, and that he should be perfectly holy in each individual act of his life. And *secondly*, that his holy behaviour was properly the nature of *virtue*, and was *worthy of praise*; and that he was the subject of *law precepts* or *commands, promises and rewards*; and that he was *in a state of trial.*

I. It was *impossible*, that the Acts of the Will of the human soul of Christ should, in any instance, degree or circumstance, be otherwise than holy, and agreeable to God's nature and will. The following things make this evident.

1. God had promised so effectually to preserve and uphold Him by his Spirit, under all his temptations, that he could not fail of reaching the end for which He came into the world;—which he would have failed of, had he fallen into sin. We have such a promise, Isa. xliii. 1, 2, 3, 4. *Behold my Servant, whom I uphold; mine Elect, in whom my soul delighteth: I have put my Spirit upon him: He shall bring forth judgment to the Gentiles: He shall not cry, nor lift up, nor cause his voice to be heard in the street.—He shall bring forth judgment unto truth. He shall not fail, nor be discouraged, till He have set judgment in the earth; and the isles shall wait his law.* This promise of Christ's having God's Spirit put upon Him, and his not crying and lifting up his voice, &c. relates to the time of Christ's appearance on earth; as is manifest from the nature of the promise, and also the application of it in the New Testament, *Matthew* xii. 18. And the words imply a promise of his being so upheld by God's Spirit, that he should be preserved from sin; particularly from pride and vain-glory, and from being overcome by any of the temptations, he should be under to affect the glory of this world, the pomp of an earthly prince, or the applause and praise of men: and that he should be so upheld, that he should by no means fail of obtaining the end of his coming into the world, of bringing forth judgment unto victory, and establishing his kingdom of grace in the earth.—And in the following verses, this promise is confirmed, with the greatest imaginable solemnity. *Thus saith the LORD, HE that created the heavens, and*

and stretched them out; He that spread forth the earth, and that which cometh out of it; He that giveth breath unto the people upon it, and spirit to them that walk therein: I the Lord have called Thee in righteousness, and will hold thine hand; and will keep Thee; and give Thee for a Covenant of the people, for a Light of the Gentiles, to open the blind eyes, to bring out the prisoners from the prison, and them that sit in darkness out of the prison-house. I am JEHOVAH; that is my name, &c.

VERY parallel with these promises is that, *Isa.* xlix. 7, 8, 9. which also has an apparent respect to the time of Christ's humiliation on earth. —— *Thus saith the Lord, the Redeemer of* Israel, *and his Holy One, to Him whom man despiseth, to Him whom the nation abhorreth, to a Servant of the rulers; kings shall see and arise, princes also shall worship; because of the Lord that is faithful, and the Holy One of* Israel, *and he shall choose Thee. Thus saith the Lord, In an acceptable time have I heard Thee. In a day of salvation have I helped Thee; and I will preserve Thee, and give Thee for a covenant of the people, to establish the earth;* &c.

AND in *Isa.* l. 5—6. we have the Messiah expressing his assurance, that God would help Him, by so opening his ear, or inclining his heart to God's commandments that He should not be rebellious, but should persevere, and not apostatise, or turn his back: that through God's help, He should be immoveable, in a way of obedience, under the great trials of reproach and suffering he should meet with; setting his face like a flint: so that He knew, He should not be ashamed, or frustrated in his design; and finally should be approved and justified, as having done his work faithfully. *The Lord hath opened mine ear;*

so that I was not rebellious, neither turned away my back: I gave my back to the smiters, and my cheeks to them that plucked off the hair; I hid not my face from shame and spitting. For the Lord God will help me; therefore shall I not be confounded: therefore have I set my face as a flint, and I know that I shall not be ashamed. He is near that justifieth me: who will contend with me? Let us stand together. Who is mine adversary? Let him come near to me. Behold the Lord God will help me: who is he that shall condemn me? Lo, they shall all wax old as a garment, the moth shall eat them up.

2. The same thing is evident from all the promises which God made to the Messiah, of his future glory, kingdom and success, in his office and character of a Mediator: which glory could not have been obtained, if his holiness had failed, and he had been guilty of sin. God's absolute promise of any things makes the things promised *necessary*, and their failing to take place absolutely *impossible:* and, in like manner, it makes those things necessary, on which the thing promised depends, and without which it cannot take effect. Therefore it appears, that it was utterly impossible that Christ's holiness should fail, from such absolute promises as those, *Psalm* cx. 4. *The Lord hath sworn, and will not repent, Thou art a Priest forever, after the order of* Melchizedek. And from every other promise in that Psalm, contained in each verse of it. And *Psal.* ii. 6, 7. *I will declare the decree: The Lord hath said unto me, Thou art my Son, this day have I begotten Thee: Ask of me, and I will give Thee the Heathen for thine inheritance*, &c. Psalm xlv. 3, 4, &c. *Gird thy sword on thy thigh, O most Mighty, with thy Glory and thy Majesty; and in thy Majesty ride prosperously.* And so every thing that is said from thence to the

the end of the Pſalm. And thoſe promiſes, *Iſa.* iii. 13, 14, 15. liii. and 10, 11, 12. And all thoſe promiſes which God makes to the Meſſiah, of ſucceſs, dominion and glory in the character of a Redeemer, in *Iſa.* xlix.

3. It was often promiſed to the Church of God of old, for their comfort, that God would give them a righteous, ſinleſs Saviour. Jer. xxiii. 5, 6. *Behold, the days come, ſaith the Lord, that I will raiſe up unto* David *a righteous Branch; and a King ſhall reign and proſper, and ſhall execute judgment and juſtice in the earth. In his days ſhall* Judah *be ſaved, and* Iſrael *ſhall dwell ſafely. And this is the name whereby He ſhall be called, The Lord our Righteouſneſs.* So Jer. xxxiii. 15.——*I will cauſe the Branch of Righteouſneſs to grow up unto* David; *and he ſhall execute judgment and righteouſneſs in the land.* Iſa. xi. 6, 7. *For unto us a child is born;—upon the throne of* David *and of his kingdom, to order it, and to eſtabliſh it with judgment and juſtice, from henceforth, even for ever: the Zeal of the Lord of Hoſts will do this.* Chap. ix. at the beginning. *There ſhall come forth a Rod out of the Stem of* Jeſſe, *and a Branch ſhall grow out of his Roots; and the Spirit of the Lord ſhall reſt upon Him,—the Spirit of Knowledge, and the Fear of the Lord:—with righteouſneſs ſhall He judge the poor, and reprove with equity:—Righteouſneſs ſhall be the girdle of his loins, and faithfulneſs the girdle of his reins.* Chap. lii. 13. *My Servant ſhall deal prudently.* Chap. liii. 9. *Becauſe He had done no violence, neither was guile found in his mouth.* If it be impoſſible, that theſe promiſes ſhould fail, and it be eaſier for heaven and earth to paſs away, than for one jot or tittle of theſe promiſes of God to paſs away, then it was impoſſible that God ſhould commit any ſin. Chriſt himſelf ſignified, that it was impoſſible

but that the things which were spoken concerning Him, should be fulfilled. Luke xxiv. 44.—*That all things must be fulfilled, which were written in the law of* Moses, *and in the Prophets, and in the Psalms concerning Me.* Matt. xxvi. 53, 54. *But how then shall the Scripture be fulfilled, that thus it must be?* Mark xiv. 49. *But the Scriptures must be fulfilled.* And so the Apostle, Acts i. 16, 17.—*This Scripture must needs have been fulfilled.*

4. All the promises, which were made to the Church of old, of the Messiah as a future Saviour, from that made to our first parents in Paradise, to that which was delivered by the prophet *Malachi*, shew it to be impossible that Christ should not have persevered in perfect holiness. The antient predictions given to God's Church, of the Messiah as a Saviour, were of the nature of promises; as is evident by the predictions themselves, and the manner of delivering them. But they are expressly, and very often called *promises* in the New Testament; as in *Luke* i. 54, 55, 72, 73. *Acts* xiii. 32, 33. *Rom.* i. 1, 2, 3. and chap. xv. 8. *Heb.* vi. 13, &c. These promises were often made with great solemnity, and confirmed with an oath; as in *Gen.* xxii. 16, 17. *By myself have I sworn, saith the Lord, that in blessing, I will bless thee, and in multiplying, I will multiply thy seed, as the stars of heaven, and as the sand which is upon the sea-shore:—— And in thy seed shall all the nations of the earth be blessed.* Compare *Luke* i. 72, 73. and *Gal.* iii. 8, 5, 16. The Apostle in *Heb.* vi. 17, 18. speaking of this promise to *Abraham*, says, *Wherein God willing more abundantly to shew to the heirs of promise the immutability of his counsel, confirmed it by an oath; that by two IMMUTABLE things, in which it was IMPOSSIBLE for God to lie, we might have strong consolation.*—In which words, the *necessity*

cessity of the accomplishment, or (which is the same thing) the *impossibility* of the contrary, is fully declared. So God confirmed the promise of the great salvation of the Messiah, made to *David*, by an oath; Psalm lxxxix. 3, 4. *I have made a covenant with my chosen, I have sworn unto* David *my servant; thy seed will I establish forever, and build up thy throne to all generations.* There is nothing that is so absolutely set forth in Scripture, as sure and irrefragable, as this promise and oath of *David.* See *Psalm* lxxxix. 34, 35, 36. 2 *Sam.* xxiii. 5. *Isa.* lv. 4. *Acts* ii. 29, 30, and xiii. 34. The Scripture expresly speaks of it as utterly *impossible* that this promise and oath to *David*, concerning the everlasting dominion of the Messiah of his seed, should fail. Jer. xxxiii. 15, &c. *In those days, and at that time, I will cause the Branch of Righteousness to grow up unto* David.—*For thus saith the Lord,* David *shall never want a Man to set upon the throne of the House of* Israel.—Ver. 20, 21. *If you can break my covenant of the day, and my covenant of the night, and that there should not be day and night in their season; then may also my covenant be broken with* David *my servant, that He should not have a son to reign upon his throne.* So in ver. 25, 26.—Thus abundant is the Scripture in representing how *impossible* it was, that the promises made of old concerning the great salvation and kingdom of the Messiah should fail: which implies, that it was impossible that this Messiah, the second *Adam*, the promised seed of *Abraham*, and of *David*, should fall from his integrity, as the first *Adam* did.

5. All the promises that were made to the Church of God under the Old Testament, of the great enlargement of the Church, and advancement of her glory, in the days of the Gospel,

after the coming of the Messiah; the increase of her light, liberty, holiness, joy, triumph over her enemies, *&c.* of which so great a part of the Old Testament consists; which are repeated so often, are so variously exhibited, so frequently introduced with great pomp and solemnity, and are so abundantly sealed with typical and symbolitical representations; I say, all these promises imply, that the Messiah should perfect the work of redemption; and this implies, that he should persevere in the work, which the Father had appointed Him, being in all things conformed to his Will. These promises were often confirmed by an oath. See *Isa* liv. 9. with the context; *chap.* lxii. 18.) And it is represented as utterly impossible that these promises should fail. (*Isa.* xlix. 15. with the context, *chap.* liv. 10. with the context; *chap.* li. 4—8. *chap.* xl. 8. with the context.) And therefore it was *impossible*, that the Messiah should fail, or commit sin.

6. It was *impossible*, that the Messiah should fail of persevering in integrity and holiness, as the first *Adam* did, because this would have been inconsistent with the promises, which God made to the blessed Virgin, his mother, and to her husband; implying, that *He should save his people from their sins*, that *God would give Him the throne of his Father* David, that *He should reign over the house of* Jacob *for ever*; and that *of his kingdom there shall be no end.* These promises were sure, and it was *impossible* they should fail. And therefore the Virgin *Mary*, in trusting fully to them, acted reasonably, having an immoveable foundation of her faith; as *Elizabeth* observes, ver. 45. *And blessed is she that believeth; for there shall be a performance of those things, which were told her from the Lord.*

7. That

7. THAT it ſhould have been poſſible that Chriſt ſhould ſin, and ſo fail in the work of our redemption, does not conſiſt with the eternal purpoſe and decree of God, revealed in the Scriptures, that he would provide ſalvation for fallen man in and by Jeſus Chriſt; and that ſalvation ſhould be offered to ſinners through the preaching of the Goſpel. Such an abſolute decree as this *Arminians* do not deny. Thus much at leaſt (out of all controverſy) is implied in ſuch Scriptures, as 1 *Cor.* ii. 7. *Eph.* i. 4, 5. and chap. iii 9, 10, 11. 1 *Pet.* i. 19, 20, Such an abſolute decree as this, *Arminians* allow to be ſignified in theſe texts. And the *Arminians* election of nations and ſocieties, and general election of the Chriſtian Church, and conditional election of particular Perſons, imply this. God could not decree before the foundation of the world, to ſave all that ſhould believe in, and obey Chriſt, unleſs he had abſolutely decreed, that ſalvation ſhould be provided, and effectually wrought out by Chriſt. And ſince (as the *Arminians* themſelves ſtrenuouſly maintain) a decree of God infers *neceſſity*; hence it became *neceſſary*, that Chriſt ſhould perſevere, and actually work out ſalvation for us, and that he ſhould not fail by the commiſſion of ſin.

8. THAT it ſhould have been poſſible for Chriſt's Holineſs to fail, is not conſiſtent with what God promiſed to his Son, before all ages. For, that ſalvation ſhould be offered to men, through Chriſt, and beſtowed on all his faithful followers, is what is at leaſt implied in that certain and infallible promiſe ſpoken of by the apoſtle, Tit. i. 2. *In hope of eternal life; which God, that cannot lie, promiſed before the world began.* This does not ſeem to be controverted by *Arminians**.

* See Dr. *Whitby* on the five Points, p. 48, 49, 50.

9. THAT

9. That it ſhould be poſſible for Chriſt to fail of doing his Father's Will, is inconſiſtent with the promiſe made to the Father by the Son, by the *Logos* that was with the Father from the beginning, before he took the human nature: as may be ſeen in *Pſalm* xl. 6, 7, 8. (compared with the apoſtle's interpretation, *Heb.* x. 5—9.) *Sacrifice and offering thou didſt not deſire: mine ears haſt thou opened,* (or bored;) *burnt-offering and ſin-offering Thou haſt not required. Then ſaid I, Lo, I come: in the volume of the book it is written of me, I delight to do thy Will, O my God, and thy law is within my heart.* Where is a manifeſt alluſion to the covenant, which the willing ſervant, who loved his maſter's ſervice, made with his maſter, to be his ſervant for ever, on the day wherein he had his ear bored; which covenant was probably inſerted in the public records, called the *Volume of the Book*, by the judges, who were called to take cognizance of the tranſaction; *Exod.* xxi. If the *Logos*, who was with the Father before the world, and who made the world, thus engaged in covenant to do the Will of the Father in the human nature, and the promiſe, was as it were recorded, that it might be made ſure, doubtleſs it was *impoſſible* that it ſhould fail; and ſo it was *impoſſible* that Chriſt ſhould fail of doing the Will of the Father in the human nature.

10. If it was poſſible for Chriſt to have failed of doing the Will of his Father, and ſo to have failed of effectually working out redemption for ſinners, then the ſalvation of all the ſaints, who were ſaved from the beginning of the world, to the death of Chriſt, was not built on a firm foundation. The Meſſiah, and the redemption, which He was to work out by his obedience unto death, was the foundation of the ſalva-

tion

tion of all the poſterity of fallen man, that ever were ſaved. Therefore, if when the Old Teſtament ſaints had the pardon of their ſins, and the favour of God promiſed them, and ſalvation beſtowed upon them, ſtill it was poſſible that the Meſſiah, when he came, might commit ſin, then all this was on a foundation that was not firm and ſtable, but liable to fail; ſomething which it was poſſible might never be. God did as it were truſt to what his Son had engaged and promiſed to do in future time; and depended ſo much upon it, that He proceeded actually to ſure men on the account of it, as though it had been already done. But this truſt and dependence of God, on the ſuppoſition of Chriſt's being liable to fail of doing his Will, was leaning on a ſtaff that was weak, and might poſſibly break. The ſaints of old truſted on the promiſes of a future redemption to be wrought out and compleated by the Meſſiah, and built their comfort upon it: *Abraham* ſaw Chriſt's Day, and rejoiced; and he and the other Patriarchs died in the faith of the promiſe of it. (*Heb.* xi. 13.) But on this ſuppoſition, their faith and their comfort, and their ſalvation, was built on a moveable fallible foundation; Chriſt was not to them a tried ſtone, a ſure foundation; as in *Iſa.* xxviii. 16. *David* entirely reſted on the covenant of God with him, concerning the future glorious dominion and ſalvation of the Meſſiah, of his Seed; ſays, it was *all his ſalvation, and all his deſire*; and comforts himſelf that this covenant was an *everlaſting covenant, ordered in all things and ſure*, 2 Sam. xxiii. 5. But if Chriſt's virtue might fail, he was miſtaken: his great comfort was not built ſo ſure, as he thought it was, being founded entirely on the determinations of the Free-Will of Chriſt's human Soul; which was ſubject to no neceſſity, and might be deter-

mined

mined either one way or the other. Also the dependence of those, who looked for redemption in *Jerusalem*, and waited for the consolation of *Israel*, (*Luke* ii. 25, and 38.) and the confidence of the disciples of Jesus, who forsook all and followed Him, that they might enjoy the benefits of his future kingdom, was built on a sandy foundation.

II. The Man Christ Jesus, before he had finished his course of obedience, and while in the midst of temptations and trials, was abundant in positively predicting his own future glory in his kingdom, and the enlargement of his Church, the salvation of the Gentiles through Him, &c. and in promises of blessings he would bestow on his true disciples in his future kingdom; on which promises he required the full dependence of his disciples. (*John* xiv.) But the disciples would have no ground for such dependence, if Christ had been liable to fail in his work: and Christ Himself would have been guilty of presumption, in so abounding in peremptory promises of great things, which depend on a mere contingence; *viz.* the determinations of his Free Will, consisting in a freedom *ad utrumque*, to either sin or holiness, standing in indifference, and incident, in thousands of future instances, to go either one way or the other.

Thus it is evident, that it was *impossible* that the Acts of the Will of the human soul of Christ should be otherwise than holy, and conformed to the Will of the Father; or, in other words, they were necessarily so conformed.

I have been the longer in the proof of this matter, it being a thing denied by some of the greatest

greatest *Arminians*, by *Episcopius* in particular; and because I look upon it as a point clearly and absolutely determining the controversy between *Calvinists* and *Arminians*, concerning the necessity of such a freedom of will as is insisted on by the latter, in order to moral agency, virtue, command or prohibition, promise or threatening, reward or punishment, praise or dispraise, merit or demerit. I now therefore proceed,

II. To consider whether CHRIST, in his holy behaviour on earth, was not thus a *moral agent*, subject to *commands*, *promises*, &c.

DR. *Whitby* very often speaks of what he calls a freedom *ad utrumlibet*, without necessity, as requisite to *law and commands*; and speaks of necessity as entirely inconsistent with *injunctions and prohibitions*. But yet we read of Christ's being the subject of the commands of his Father, *Job* x. 18. and xv. 10. And Christ tells us, that every thing that he *said*, or *did*, was in compliance with *commandments he had received of the Father*; John xii. 49, 50. and xiv. 31. And we often read of Christ's *obedience* to his Father's commands, *Rom.* v. 19. *Phil.* ii. 18. *Heb.* v. 8.

THE forementioned writer represents *promises offered as motives* to persons to do their duty, or *a being moved and induced by promises*, as utterly inconsistent with a state wherein persons have not a liberty *ad utrumlibet*, but are necessarily determined to one. (See particularly, p. 298, and 311.) But the thing which this writer asserts, is demonstrably false, if the Christian religion be true. If there be any truth in Christianity or the holy Scriptures, the Man Christ Jesus had his Will infallibly, unalterably and unfrustrably determined

to

to good, and that alone; but yet he had promises of glorious rewards made to Him, on condition of his persevering in, and perfecting the work which God hath appointed Him; *Isa.* liii. 10, 11, 12. *Psalm* ii. and cx. *Isa.* xlix. 7, 8, 9.— In *Luke* xxii. 28, 29. Christ says to his disciples, *Ye are they which have continued with me in my temptations; and I appoint unto you a kingdom, as my Father hath appointed unto me.* The word most properly signifies to appoint by covenant, or promise. The plain meaning of Christ's words is this: "As you have partook of my temptations and trials, and have been stedfast, and have overcome; I promise to make you partakers of my reward, and to give you a kingdom; as the Father hath promised me a kingdom for continuing stedfast, and overcoming those trials." And the words are well explained by those in Rev. iii. 21. *To him that overcometh, will I grant to sit with me on my throne; even as I also overcame, and am set down with my Father in his throne.* And Christ had not only promises of glorious success and rewards made to his obedience and sufferings, but the Scriptures plainly represent Him as using these promises for motives and inducements to obey and suffer; and particularly that promise of a kingdom which the Father hath appointed Him, or sitting with the Father on his throne; as in Heb. xii. 1, 2. *Let us lay aside every weight, and the sin which doth easily beset us, and let us run with patience the race that is set before us, looking unto Jesus the Author and Finisher of our faith; who for the joy that was set before Him, endured the cross, despising the shame, and is set down on the right hand of the throne of God.*

AND how strange would it be to hear any Christian assert, that the holy and excellent temper

anp

and behaviour of Jesus Christ, and that obedience, which he performed under such great trials, was not *virtuous* or *praise-worthy*; because his Will was not free *ad utrumque*, to either holiness or sin, but was unalterably determined to one; that upon this account, there is no virtue at all, in all Christ's humility, meekness, patience, charity, forgiveness of enemies, contempt of the world, heavenly mindedness, submission to the Will of God, perfect obedience to his commands, (though He was obedient unto death, even the death of the cross) his great compassion to the afflicted, his unparallelled love to mankind, his faithfulness to God and man, under such great trials; his praying for his enemies, even when nailing Him to the cross; that *virtue*, when applied to these things, *is but an empty name*; that there was no merit in any of these things; that is, that Christ was *worthy* of nothing at all on the account of them, worthy of no reward, no praise, no honour or respect from God or Man; because his Will was not indifferent, and free either to these things, or the contrary; but under such a strong inclination or bias to the things that were excellent, as made it *impossible* that he should chuse the contrary; that upon this account (to use Dr. *Whitby*'s language) *it would be sensibly unreasonable* that the human nature should be rewarded for any of these things.

According to this doctrine, that creature who is evidently set forth in Scripture as the *first-born of every creature*, as having *in all things the preeminence*, and as the highest of all creatures in virtue, honour, and worthiness of esteem, praise and glory, on the account of his virtue, is less worthy of reward or praise, than the very least of saints; yea, no more worthy than a clock or mere

mere machine, that is purely passive, and moved by natural necessity.

IF we judge by scriptural representations of things, we have reason to suppose, that Christ took on him our nature, and dwelt with us in this world, in a suffering state, not only to satisfy for our sins; but that He, being in our nature and circumstances, and under our trials, might be our most fit and proper example, leader and captain, in the exercise of glorious and victorious virtue, and might be a visible instance of the glorious end and reward of it: that we might see in Him the beauty, amiableness, and true honour and glory, and exceeding benefit, of that virtue, which it is proper for us human beings to practice; and might thereby learn, and be animated, to seek the like glory and honour, and to obtain the like glorious reward. See *Heb.* ii. 9—14 with v. 8, 9. and xii. 1, 2, 3. *John* xv. 10. *Rom.* viii. 17. 2 Tim. ii. 11, 12. 1 *Pet* ii. 19, 20. and iv. 13. But if there was nothing of any virtue or merit, or worthiness of any reward, glory, praise or commendation at all, in all that He did, because it was all necessary, and He could not help it; then how is here any thing so proper to animate and incite us, free creatures, by patient continuance in well-doing, to seek for honour, glory, and virtue?

GOD speaks of Himself as peculiarly well-pleased with the Righteousness of this servant of his. Isa. xlii. 21. *The Lord is well-pleased for his Righteousness sake.* The sacrifices of old are spoken of as a sweet savour to God, but the obedience of Christ as far more acceptable than they. Psam xl. 6. 7. *Sacrifice and offering Thou didst not desire:— Mine ear hast Thou opened* [as thy servant performing

forming willing obedence;] *burnt-offering and sin offering hast thou not required: then, said I, Lo, I come* [as a servant that chearfully answers the calls of his master:] *I delight to do thy will, O my God, and thy law is within mine heart.* Matt. xvii. 5. *This is my beloved Son, in whom I am well-pleased.* And Christ tells us expresly, that the Father loves Him for that wonderful instance of his obedience, his voluntary yielding himself to death, in compliance with his Father's command; John x. 17, 18. *Therefore doth my Father love me, because I lay down my life:—No man taketh it from me; but I lay it down of myself:—This commandment received I of my Father.*

And if there was no merit in Christ's obedience unto death, if it was not worthy of praise, and of the most glorious rewards, the heavenly hosts were exceedingly mistaken, by the account that is given of them, in *Rev.* v. 8—12. *The four beasts, and the four and twenty elders fell down before the Lamb, having every one of them harps, and golden vials full of odours;—and they sung a new song, saying, Thou art WORTHY to take the book, and to open the seals thereof; for thou wast slain.—And I beheld, and I heard the voice of many angels round about the throne, and the beasts, and the elders, and the number of them was ten thousand times ten thousand, and thousands of thousands, saying with a loud voice, WORTHY is the Lamb that was slain, to receive power, and riches, and wisdom, and strength, and honour, and glory, and blessing.*

Christ speaks of the eternal life which He was to receive, as the reward of his obedience to the Father's commandments. John xii. 49, 50. *I have not spoken of myself; but the Father which sent me, He gave me a commandment what I should say, and what I should speak: and I know that his commandment is life everlasting: whatsoever I speak therefore, even as the Father said unto me, so I speak.*—God promises to divide him a portion with the great, &c. for his being his righteous Servant, for his glorious virtue under such great trials and afflictions, Isa. liii. 11, 12. *He shall see the travel of his soul and be satisfied: by his knowledge shall my righteous Servant justify many; for he shall bear their iniquities. Therefore will I divide him a portion with the great, and he shall divide the spoil with the strong, because he hath poured out his soul unto death.*—The Scriptures represent God as rewarding Him far above all his other Servants, Phil. ii. 7, 8, 9. *He took on Him the form of a servant, and was made in the likeness of men: and being found in fashion as a man, He humbled himself, and became obedient unto death, even the death of the cross: wherefore GOD also hath highly exalted Him, and given Him a Name above every Name,* Psalm xlv. 7. *Thou lovest Righteousness, and hatest wickedness; therefore God, thy God, hath anointed Thee with the oil of gladness above thy fellows.*

THERE is no room to pretend, that the glorious benefits bestowed in consequence of Christ's obedience, are not properly of the nature of a reward. What is a reward, in the most proper sense, but a benefit bestowed in consequence of something morally excellent in quality or behaviour, in testimony of well-pleasedness in that moral excellency, and respect and favour on that account? If we consider the nature of a reward most strictly, and make the utmost of it, and add to the things contained in this description, proper merit or worthiness, and the bestowment of the benefit in consequence of a promise; still it will be found, there is nothing belonging

longing to it, but that the Scripture is most express as to its belonging to the glory bestowed on Christ after his sufferings; as appears from what has been already observed: there was a glorious benefit bestowed in consequence of something morally excellent, being called *Righteousness* and *Obedience*; there was great favour, love and well-pleasedness, for this righteousness and obedience, in the Bestower; there was proper merit, or worthiness of the benefit, in the obedience; it was bestowed in fulfilment of promises, made to that obedience; and was bestowed *therefore*, or *because* he had performed that obedience.

I MAY add to all these things, that Jesus Christ, while here in the flesh, was manifestly in a state of trial. The last *Adam*, as Christ is called, 1 *Cor*. xv. 45. Rom. v. 14. taking on Him the human nature, and so the form of a servant, and being under the law, to stand and act for us, was put into a state of trial, as the first *Adam* was.—Dr. *Whitby* mentions these three things as evidences of persons being in a state of trial (on the five Points, p. 298, 299) namely, their afflictions being spoken of as their trials or temptations, their being the subjects of promises, and their being exposed to satan's temptations. But Christ was apparently the subject of each of these. Concerning promises made to Him, I have spoken already. The difficulties and *afflictions*, He met with in the course of his obedience, are called his *temptations* or *trials*, Luke xxii. 28. *Ye are they which have continued with me in my* temptations, *or* trials. Heb. ii. 18. *For in that he Himself hath suffered, being* tempted or tried] *He is able to succour them that are tempted.* And chap. iv. 15. *We have not an high priest, which cannot be touched with the feeling of our infirmities; but was in all points* tempted *like as we are, yet without sin.* And as to his being tempted by satan it is what none will dispute.

SECTION III.

The Case of such as are given up of God to Sin, *and of* fallen Man *in general, proves moral Necessity and Inability to be consistent with Blameworthiness.*

DR. *Whitby* asserts freedom, not only from co-action, but Necessity, to be essential to any thing deserving the name of sin, and to an action's being *culpable:* in these words (Discourse on five Points, edit. 3. p. 348.) "If they be thus necessitated, then neither their sins of omission, or commission could deserve that name; it being essential to the nature of Sin, according to St. *Austin*'s definition, that it be an action *à quo liberum est abstinere.* Three things seem plainly necessary to make an action or omission culpable; 1. That it be in our power to perform or forbear it: for, as *Origin*, and all the fathers say, no man is blame-worthy for not doing what he could not do." And elsewhere the Doctor insists, that "when any do evil of Necessity, what they do is novice, that they are guilty of no fault*, are worthy of no blame, dispraise†, or dishonour‡, but are unblameable§.

* Discourse on five Points, p. 347, 360, 361, 377.—— † 303, 326, 329, and many other places.——‡ 371.—— § 304, 361.

If

If these things are true, in Dr. *Whitby*'s sense of Necessity, they will prove all such to be blameless, who are given up of God to Sin, in what they commit after they are thus given up.—That there is such a thing as men's being judicially given up to sin, is certain, if the scripture rightly informs us; such a thing being often there spoken of: as in Psalm lxxxi. 12. *So I gave them up to their own hearts lust, and they walked in their own counsels.* Acts vii. 42. *Then God turned, and gave them up to worship the host of heaven.* Rom. i. 24. *Wherefore, God also gave them up to uncleanness, through the lusts of their own hearts, to dishonour their own bodies between themselves.* Ver. 26. *For this cause God gave them up to vile affections.* Ver. 28. *And even as they did not like to retain God in their knowledge, God gave them over to a reprobate mind, to do those things that are not convenient.*

It is needless to stand particularly to inquire, what God's *giving men up to their own hearts lusts* signifies: it is sufficient to observe, that hereby is certainly meant God's so ordering or disposing things, in some respect or other, either by doing or forbearing to do, as that the consequence should be men's continuing in their Sins. So much as men are given up *to*, so much is the consequence of their being given up, whether that be less or more. If God does not order things so, by action or permission, that Sin will be the consequence, then the event proves that they are not given up to that consequence. If good be the consequence, instead of evil, then God's mercy is to be acknowledged in that good; which mercy must be contrary to God's judgment in giving up to evil. If the event must prove, that they are given up to evil as the consequence, then the persons, who are the subjects of this judgment, must be the subjects of such an event, and so the event is necessary.

If not only *co-action*, but *all Necessity*, will prove men blameless, then *Judas* was blameless, after Christ had given him over, and had already declared his certain damnation, and that he should *verily* betray Him. He was guilty of no Sin in betraying his Master, on this supposition; though his so doing is spoken of by Christ as the most aggravated Sin, more heinous than the Sin of *Pilate* in crucifying Him. And the *Jews* in *Egypt*, in *Jeremiah's* time, were guilty of no Sin, in their not worshipping the true God, after God had *sworn by his great Name, that his Name should be no more named in the mouth of any man of* Judah, *in all the land of* Egypt. *Jer.* xliv. 26.

Dr. *Whitby* (Disc. on five Points, p. 302, 303.) denies, that men, in this world, are ever so given up by God to Sin, that their wills should be necessarily determined to evil; though he owns, that hereby it may become *exceeding difficult* for men to do good, having a strong bent, and powerful inclination, to what is evil.—But if we should allow the case to be just as he represents, the judgment of giving up to Sin will no better agree with his notions of that liberty, which is essential to praise or blame, than if we should suppose it to render the avoiding of Sin *impossible*. For if an *impossibility* of avoiding Sin wholly excuses a man; then, for the same reason, its being difficult to avoid it, excuses him in part; and this just in proportion to the degree of difficulty. —If the influence of *moral* impossibility or Inability be the same, to excuse persons in not doing, or not avoiding any thing, as that of *natural* Inability, (which is supposed) then undoubtedly

edly, in like manner, *moral difficulty* has the ſame influence to excuſe with *natural difficulty*. But all allow, that natural impoſſibility wholly excuſes, and alſo that *natural difficulty* excuſes in part, and makes the act or omiſſion leſs blameable in proportion to the difficulty. All *natural difficulty*, according to the plaineſt dictates of the light of nature, excuſes in ſome degree, ſo that the neglect is not ſo blameable, as if there had been no difficulty in the caſe: and ſo the greater the difficulty is, ſtill the more excuſeable, in proportion to the increaſe of the difficulty. And as *natural* impoſſibility wholly excuſes and excludes all blame, ſo the nearer the difficulty approaches to impoſſibility, ſtill the nearer a perſon is to blameleſſneſs in proportion to that approach. And if the caſe of moral impoſſibility or Neceſſity, be juſt the ſame with natural Neceſſity or co-action, as to influence to excuſe a neglect, then alſo, for the ſame reaſon, the caſe of natural difficulty, does not differ in influence, to excuſe a neglect, from moral difficulty, ariſing from a ſtrong bias or bent to evil, ſuch as Dr. *Whitby* owns in the caſe of thoſe that are given up to their own hearts luſts. So that the fault of ſuch perſons muſt be leſſened, in proportion to the difficulty, and approach to impoſſibility. If ten degrees of moral difficulty make the action quite impoſſible, and ſo wholly excuſe, then if there be nine degrees of difficulty, the perſon is in great part excuſed, and is nine degrees in ten, leſs blame-worthy, than if there had been no difficulty at all; and he has but one degree of blame-worthineſs. The reaſon is plain, on *Arminian* principles; *viz.* becauſe as difficulty, by antecedent bent and bias on the will, is increaſed, liberty of indifference, and ſelf-determination in the will, is diminiſhed: ſo much hindrance and impediment is there, in the

the way of the will's acting freely, by mere self-determination. And if ten degrees of such hindrance take away all such liberty, then nine degrees take away nine parts in ten, and leave but one degree of liberty. And therefore there is but one degree of blameableness, *cæteris paribus*, in the neglect; the man being no further blameable in what he does, or neglects, than he has liberty in that affair: for blame or praise (say they) arises wholly from a good use or abuse of liberty.

From all which it follows, that a strong bent and bias one way, and difficulty of going the contrary, never causes a person to be at all more exposed to sin, or any thing blameable: because, as the difficulty is increased, so much the less is required and expected. Though in one respect, exposedness to Sin or fault is increased, *viz.* by an increase of exposedness to the evil action or omission; yet it is diminished in another respect, to balance it; namely, as the sinfulness or blameableness of the action or omission is diminished in the same proposition. So that, on the whole, the affair, as to exposedness to guilt or blame, is left just as it was.

To illustrate this, let us suppose a scale of a balance to be intelligent, and a free agent, and indued with a self-moving power, by virtue of which it could act and produce effects to a certain degree, *ex. gr.* to move itself up or down with a force equal to a weight of ten pounds; and that it might therefore be required of it, in ordinary circumstance, to move itself down with that force; for which it has power and full liberty, and therefore would be blame-worthy if it failed of it. But then let us suppose a weight of ten

ten pounds to be put in the oppoſite ſcale, which in force entirely counter-balances its ſelf moving power, and ſo renders it impoſſible for it to move down at all; and therefore wholly excuſes it from any ſuch motion. But if we ſuppoſe there to be only nine pounds in the oppoſite ſcale, this renders its motion not impoſſible, but yet more difficult; ſo that it can now only move down with the force of one pound: but however this is all that is required of it under theſe circumſtances; it is wholly excuſed from nine parts of its motion: and if the ſcale under theſe circumſtances, neglects to move, and remains at reſt, all that it will be blamed for, will be its neglect of that one tenth part of its motion; which it had as much liberty and advantage for, as in uſual circumſtances, it has for the greater motion, which in ſuch a caſe would be required. So that this new difficulty, does not at all increaſe its expoſedneſs to any thing blame-worthy.

And thus the very ſuppoſition of difficulty in the way of a man's *duty*, or proclivity to Sin, through a being given up to hardneſs of heart, or indeed by any other means whatſoever, is an inconſiſtence, according to Dr. *Whitby's* notions of liberty, virtue and vice, blame and praiſe. The avoiding Sin and blame, and the doing what is virtuous and praiſe-worthy, muſt be always equally eaſy.

Dr. *Whitby's* notion of liberty, obligation, virtue, Sin, *&c.* led him into another great inconſiſtence. He abundantly inſiſts, that neceſſity is inconſiſtent with the nature of Sin, or fault. He ſays, in the fore mentioned treatiſe, p. 14. *Who can blame a perſon for doing what he could not help?* And p. 15. *It being ſenſibly unjuſt*

to

to punish any man for doing that which was never in his power to avoid. And in p. 341. to confirm his opinion, he quotes one of the Fathers, saying, *Why doth God command, if man hath not free-will and power to obey?* And again, in the same and the next page, *Who will not cry out, that it is folly to command him, that hath not liberty to do what is commanded; and that it is unjust to condemn him, that has it not in his power to do what is required?* And in p. 373. he cites another saying, *A law is given to him that can turn to both parts;* i. e. *obey or transgress it: but no law can be against him who is bound by nature.*

And yet the same Dr. *Whitby* asserts, that fallen Man is not able to perform perfect obedience. In p. 165, he has these words: "The nature of *Adam* had power to continue innocent, and without Sin; whereas, it is certain our nature never had so." But if we have not power to continue innocent and without Sin, then Sin is consistent with Necessity, and we may be sinful in that which we have not power to avoid; and those things cannot be true, which he asserts elsewhere, namely, "That if we be necessitated, "neither Sins of omission nor commission, would deserve that name," (p. 348.) If we have it not in our power to be innocent, then we have it not in our power to be blameless: and if so, we are under a Necessity of being blame-worthy. And how does this consist with what he so often asserts, that Necessity is inconsistent with blame or praise? If we have it not in our power to perform perfect obedience to all the commands of God, then we are under a Necessity of breaking some commands, in some degree; having no power to perform so much as is commanded. And if so, why does he cry out of the unreasonableness

ableneſs and folly of commanding beyond what men have power to do?

And *Arminians* in general are very inconſiſtent with themſelves in what they ſay of the Inability of fallen Man in this reſpect. They ſtrenuouſly maintain, that it would be unjuſt in God, to require any thing of us beyond our preſent power and ability to perform; and alſo hold, that we are now unable to perform perfect obedience, and that Chriſt died to ſatisfy for the *imperfections of our obedience*, and has made way, that our imperfect obedience might be accepted inſtead of perfect: wherein they ſeem inſenſibly to run themſelves into the groſſeſt inconſiſtence. For, (as I have obſerved elſewhere) "they hold, that God, in mercy to mankind, has aboliſhed that rigorous conſtitution or law, that they were under originally; and inſtead of it, has introduced a more mild conſtitution, and put us under a new law, which requires no more than imperfect ſincere obedience, in compliance with our poor infirm impotent circumſtances ſince the fall."

Now, how can theſe things be made conſiſtent? I would aſk, what law theſe imperfections of our obedience are a breach of? If they are a breach of no law, that we were ever under, then they are not Sins. And if they be not Sins, what need of Chriſt's dying to ſatisfy for them? But if they are Sins, and the breach of ſome law, what law is it? They cannot be a breach of their new law; for that requires no other than imperfect obedience, or obedience with imperfections: and therefore to have obedience attended with imperfections, is no breach of it; for it is as much as it requires. And they cannot be a breach

breach of their old law; for that, they say, is entirely abolished; and we never were under it.— They say, it would not be just in God to require of us perfect obedience, because it would not be just to require more than we can perform, or to punish us for failing of it. And, therefore, by their own scheme, the imperfections of our obedience do not deserve to be punished. What need therefore of Christ's dying, to satisfy for them? What need of his *suffering*, to satisfy for that which is no fault, and in its own nature deserves no *suffering*? What need of Christ's dying, to purchase, that our *imperfect* obedience should be accepted, when, according to their scheme, it would be unjust in itself, that any other obedience than *imperfect* should be required? What need of Christ's dying to make way for God's accepting such an obedience, as it would be unjust in Him not to accept? Is there any need of Christ's dying, to prevail with God not to do unrighteously?—If it be said, that Christ died to satisfy that old law for us, that so we might not be under it, but that there might be room for our being under a more mild law, still I would inquire, what need of Christ's dying, that we might not be under a law, which (by their principles) it would be in itself unjust that we should be under, whether Christ had died or no, because, in our present state, we are not able to keep it?

So the *Arminians* are inconsistent with themselves, not only in what they say of the need of Christ's satisfaction to atone for those imperfections, which we cannot avoid, but also in what they say of the grace of God, granted to enable men to perform the sincere obedience of the new law.

law. "I grant (says Dr. *Stebbing**) indeed, that by reason of original Sin, we are utterly disabled for the performance of the condition, without new grace from God. But I say then, that he gives such a grace to all of us, by which the performance of the condition is truly possible: and upon this ground he may, and doth most righteously require it." If Dr. *Stebbing* intends to speak properly, by *grace* he must mean, that assistance which is of grace, or of free favour and kindness. But yet in the same place he speaks of it as very *unreasonable*, *unjust* and *cruel*, for God to require that, as the condition of pardon, that is become impossible by original Sin. If it be so, what *grace* is there in giving assistance and ability to perform the condition of pardon? Or why is that called by the name of grace, that is an absolute debt, which God is bound to bestow, and which it would be unjust and cruel in Him to with-hold, seeing he requires that, *as the condition of pardon*, which he cannot perform without it?

SECTION IV.

Command *and* Obligation *to* Obedience, *consistent with moral Inability to obey.*

IT being so much insisted on by *Arminian* writers, that necessity is inconsistent with Law or Command, and particularly, that it is absurd to suppose God by his Command should require that of men which they are unable to do; not allowing in this case for any difference that there is between

* Treatise on the Operations of the Spirit. Second Edit, p. 112, 113.

between natural and moral Inability; I would therefore now particularly consider this matter.

And, for the greater clearness, I would distinctly lay down the following things.

I. The will itself, and not only those actions which are the effects of the will, is the proper object of Precept or Command. This is, such or such a state or acts of men's wills, is in many cases, properly required of them by Commands; and not only those alterations in the state of their bodies or minds that are the consequences of volition. This is most manifest; for it is the soul only that is properly and directly the subject of Precepts or Commands; that only being capable of receiving or perceiving Commands. The motions or state of the body are matter of Command, only as they are subject to the soul, and connected with its acts. But now the soul has no other faculty whereby it can, in the most direct and proper sense, consent, yield to, or comply with any Command, but the faculty of the will; and it is by this faculty only, that the soul can directly disobey, or refuse compliance: for the very notions of *consenting*, *yielding*, *accepting*, *complying*, *refusing*, *rejecting*, &c. are, according to the meaning of the terms, nothing but certain acts of the will. Obedience, in the primary nature of it, is the submitting and yielding of the will of one to the will of another. Disobedience is the not consenting, not complying of the will of the commanded to the manifested will of the commander. Other acts that are not the acts of the will, as certain motions of the body and alterations in the soul, are Obedience or Disobedience only indirectly, as they are connected with the state or actions of the will, according

according to an established law of nature. So that it is manifest, the will itself may be required: and the being of a good will is the most proper, direct and immediate subject of Command; and if this cannot be prescribed or required by Command or Precept, nothing can; for other things can be required no otherwise than as they depend upon, and are the fruits of a good will.

Corol. 1. If there be several acts of the will, or a series of acts, one following another, and one the effect of another, the *first and determining act* is properly the subject of Command, and not only the consequent acts, which are dependent upon it. Yea, it is this more especially, which is that, which Command or Precept has a proper respect to; because it is this act that determines the whole affair: in this act the Obedience or Disobedience lies, in a peculiar manner; the consequent acts being all subject to it, and governed and determined by it. This determining governing act must be the proper object of Precept, or none.

Corol. 2. It also follows, from what has been observed, that if there be any sort of act, or exertion of the soul, prior to all free acts of the will, or acts of choice in the case, directing and determining what the acts of the will shall be; that act or exertion of the soul cannot properly be subject to any Command or Precept, in any respect whatsoever, either directly or indirectly, immediately or remotely. Such acts cannot be subject to commands *directly*, because they are no acts of the will; being by the supposition prior to all acts of the will, determining and giving rise to all its acts: they not being acts of the will,

will, there can be in them no consent to, or compliance with any command. Neither can they be subject to Command or Precept *indirectly* or *remotely*; for they are not so much as the *effects* or *consequences* of the will, being prior to all its acts. So that if there be any Obedience in that original act of the soul, determining all volitions, it is an act of Obedience wherein the will has no concern at all; it preceding every act of will. And therefore, if the soul either obeys or disobeys in this act, it is wholly involuntarily; there is no willing Obedience or rebellion, no compliance or opposition of the will in the affair: and what sort of Obedience or rebellion is this?

And thus the *Arminian* notion of the freedom of the will consisting in the soul's determining its own acts of will, instead of being essential to moral agency, and to men's being the subjects of moral government, is utterly inconsistent with it. For if the soul determines *all* its acts of will, it is therein subject to no Command or moral government, as has been now observed; because its original determining act is no act of will or choice, it being prior, by the supposition, to *every act* of will. And the soul cannot be the subject of Command in the act of the will itself, which depends on the foregoing determining act, and is determined by it; in as much as this is necessary, being the necessary consequence and effect of that prior determining act, which is not voluntarily. Nor can the man be the subject of Command or government in his external actions; because these are all necessary, being the necessary effects of the acts of the will themselves. So that mankind, according to this scheme, are subjects of Command or moral

moral government in nothing at all; and all their moral agency is entirely excluded, and no room for virtue or vice in the world.

So that it is the *Arminian* ſcheme, and not the ſcheme of the *Calviniſts*, that is utterly inconſiſtent with moral government, and with all uſe of laws, precepts, prohibitions, promiſes or threatenings. Neither is there any way whatſoever to make their principles conſiſt with theſe things. For if it be ſaid, that there is no prior determining act of the ſoul, preceding the acts of the will, but that volitions are events that come to paſs by pure accident, without any determining cauſe, this is moſt palpably inconſiſtent with all uſe of laws and precepts; for nothing is more plain than that laws can be of no uſe to direct and regulate perfect accident: which, by the ſuppoſition of its being pure accident, is in no caſe regulated by any thing preceding; but happens, this way or that, perfectly by chance, without any cauſe or rule. The perfect uſeleſſneſs of laws and precepts alſo follows from the *Arminian* notion of indifference, as eſſential to that liberty, which is requiſite to virtue or vice. For the end of laws is to *bind to one ſide*; and the end of Commands is to turn the will one way: and therefore they are of no uſe, unleſs they turn or bias the will that way. But if liberty conſiſts in indifference, then their biaſſing the will one way only, deſtroys liberty; as it puts the will out of equilibrium. So that the will, having a bias, through the influence of binding law, laid upon it, is not wholly left to itſelf, to determine itſelf which way it will, without influence from without.

II. Having shewn that the will itself, especially in those acts, which are original, leading and determining in any case, is the proper subject of Precept and Command, and not only those alterations in the body, *&c.* which are the effects of the will; I now proceed, in the *second* place, to observe that the very opposition or defect of the will itself, in that act, which is its *original and determining act* in the case; I say, the will's opposition *in this act* to a thing proposed or commanded, or its failing of compliance, implies a moral inability to that thing: or, in other words, whenever a Command requires a certain state or act of the will, and the person commanded notwithstanding the command and the circumstances under which it is exhibited, still finds his will opposite or wanting, in *that*, belonging to its state or acts, *which is original and determining in the affair*, that man is morally unable to obey that Command.

This is manifest from what was observed in the first part, concerning the nature of *moral* Inability, as distinguished from *natural:* where it was observed, that a man may then be said to be morally unable to do a thing, when he is under the influence or prevalence of a contrary inclination, or has a want of inclination, under such circumstances and views. It is also evident, from what has been before proved, that the will is always, and in every individual act, necessarily determined by the strongest motive; and so is always unable to go against the motive, which, all things considered, has now the greatest strength and advantage to move the will.—But not further to insist on these things, the truth of the position now laid down, *viz.* that when the will is opposite *to*, or failing of a compliance with a thing

thing *in its original determining inclination or act*, it is not able to comply, appears by the consideration of these two things.

1. The will in the time of that diverse or opposite leading act or inclination, and when actually under the influence of it, is not able to exert itself to the contrary, to make an alteration, in order to a compliance. The inclination is unable to change itself; and that for this plain reason, that it is unable to incline to change itself. Present choice cannot at present chuse to be otherwise: for that would be *at present* to chuse something diverse from what is *at present* chosen. If the will, all things now considered, inclines or chuses to go that way, then it cannot chuse, all things now considered, to go the other way, and so cannot chuse to be made to go the other way. To suppose that the mind is now sincerely inclined to change itself to a different inclination, is to suppose the mind is now truly inclined otherwise than it is now inclined. The will may oppose some future remote act that it is exposed to, but not its own present act.

2. As it is impossible that the will should comply with the thing commanded, with respect to its *leading act*, by any act of its own, in the time of that diverse or opposite *leading and original act*, or after it has actually come under the influence of that *determining choice or inclination*; so it is impossible it should be determined to a compliance by any foregoing act; for, by the very supposition, there is no foregoing act; the opposite or non-complying act being that act which is *original* and *determining* in the case. Therefore it must be so, that if this *first determining act* be

 found

found non-complying, on the proposal of the Command, the mind is morally unable to obey. For to suppose it to be able to obey, is to suppose it to be able to determine and cause its *first determining act* to be otherwise, and that it has power better to govern and regulate its *first governing and regulating act*, which is absurd; for it is to suppose a prior act of the will, determining its first determining act; that is, an act prior to the first, and leading and governing the original and governing act of all; which is a contradiction.

Here if it should be said, that although the mind has not any ability to will contrary to what it does will, in the original and leading act of the will, because there is supposed to be no prior act to determine and order it otherwise, and the will cannot immediately change itself, because it cannot at present incline to a change; yet the mind has an ability for the present to *forbear* to proceed to action, and taking time for deliberation; which may be an occasion of the change of the inclination.

I answer, (1.) In this objection that seems to be forgotten, which was observed before, *viz.* that the determining to take the matter into consideration, is itself an act of the will: and if this be all the act wherein the mind exercises ability and freedom, then this, by the supposition, must be all that can be commanded or required by Precept. And if this act be the commanding act, then all that has been observed concerning the commanding act of the will remains true, that the very want of it is a moral Inability to exert it, *&c.* (2.) We are speaking concerning the first and leading act of the will in the case, or about the affair; and if a determining to deliberate, or, on the contrary, to proceed immediately without deliberating, be the firſt and leading act; or whether it be or no, if there be another act before it, which determines that; or whatever be the original and leading act; ſtill the foregoing proof ſtands good, that the non-compliance of the leading act implies moral Inability to comply.

If it ſhould be objected, that theſe things make all moral Inability equal, and ſuppoſe men morally unable to will otherwiſe than they actually do will, in all caſes, and equally ſo in every Inſtance.

In anſwer to this objection, I deſire two things may be obſerved. *Firſt*, That if by being *equally* unable be meant as *really* unable; then, ſo far as the Inability is merely moral, it is true, the will, in every inſtance, acts by moral neceſſity, and is morally unable to act otherwiſe, as truly and properly in one caſe as another; as I humbly conceive, has been perfectly and abundantly demonſtrated by what has been ſaid in the preceding part of this Eſſay. But yet, in ſome reſpect, the inability may be ſaid to be greater in ſome inſtances than others: though the man may be truly unable, (if moral inability can truly be called Inability,) yet he may be further from being able to do ſome things than others. As it is in things, which men are naturally unable to do. A perſon, whoſe ſtrength is no more than ſufficient to lift the weight of one hundred pounds, is as truly and really unable to lift one hundred and one pounds, as ten thouſand pounds; but yet he is further from being able to lift the latter weight than the former; and ſo, according to common uſe of ſpeech, has a greater Inability for it. So it is in moral Inability. A man is truly morally unable to chuse contrary to a present inclination, which in the least degree prevails; or, contrary to that motive, which, all things considered, has strength and advantage now to move the will, in the least degree, superior to all other motives in view: but yet he is further from ability to resist a very strong habit, and a violent and deeply rooted inclination, or a motive vastly exceeding all others in strength. And again, the Inability may, in some respects, be called greater in some instances than others, as it may be *more general* and *extensive to all acts of that kind*. So men may be said to be unable in a different sense, and to be further from moral ability, who have that moral Inability which is *general* and *habitual*, than they who have only that Inability which is *occasional* and *particular**. Thus in cases of natural Inability; he that is born blind may be said to be unable to see, in a different manner, and is, in some respects, further from being able to see, than he whose sight is hindered by a transient cloud or mist.

And besides, that which was observed in the first part of this discourse, concerning the Inability which attends a *strong and settled habit* should be here remembered; *viz.* that fixed habit is attended with this peculiar moral Inability, by which it is distinguished from *occasional volition*, namely, that endeavours to avoid future volitions of that kind, which are agreeable to such a habit, much more frequently and commonly prove vain and insufficient. For though it is impossible there should be any true sincere desires and endeavours against a pre-

* See this distinction of moral Inability explained in Part I. Sect. IV.

a preſent volition or choice, yet there may be againſt volitions of that kind, when viewed at a diſtance. A perſon may deſire and uſe means to prevent future exerciſes of a certain inclination; and, in order to it, may wiſh the habit might be removed; but his deſires and endeavours may be ineffectual. The man may be ſaid in ſome ſenſe to be unable; yea, even as the word *unable* is a *relative term*, and has relation to ineffectual endeavours; yet not with regard to preſent, but remote endeavours.

Secondly, It muſt be borne in mind, according to what was obſerved before, that indeed no Inability whatſoever, which is merely moral, is properly called by the name of *Inability*; and that in the ſtricteſt propriety of ſpeech, a man may be ſaid to have a thing in his power, if he has it at his election; and he cannot be ſaid to be unable to do a thing, when he can, if he now pleaſes, or whenever he has a proper, direct and immediate deſire for it. As to thoſe deſires and endeavours, that may be againſt the exerciſes of a ſtrong habit, with regard to which men may be ſaid to be unable to avoid thoſe exerciſes, they are remote deſires and endeavours in two reſpects. *Firſt*, as to *time*; they are never againſt preſent volitions, but only againſt volitions of ſuch a kind, when viewed at a diſtance. *Secondly*, as to their *nature*; theſe oppoſite deſires are not directly and properly againſt the habit and inclination itſelf, or the volitions in which it is exerciſed; for theſe, in themſelves conſidered, are agreeable: but againſt ſomething elſe, that attends them, or is their conſequence; the oppoſition of the mind is levelled entirely againſt this; the inclination or volitions themſelves are not at all oppoſed directly, and for their own ſake; but only indirectly

indirectly and remotely on the account of something alien and foreign.

III. Though the opposition of the will itself, or the very want of will to a thing commanded, implies a moral Inability to that thing; yet, if it be, as has been already shewn, that the being of a good state or act of will, is a thing most properly required by Command; then, in some cases, such a state or act of will may properly be required, which at present is not, and which may also be wanting after it is commanded. And therefore those things may properly be commanded, which men have a moral Inability for.

Such a state, or act of the will, may be required by Command, as does not already exist. For if that volition only may be commanded to be which already is, there could be no use of Precept; Commands in all cases would be perfectly vain and impertinent. And not only may such a will be required, as is wanting before the Command is given, but also such as may possibly be wanting afterwards; such as the exhibition of the Command may not be effectual to produce or excite. Otherwise, no such thing as disobedience to a proper and rightful Command is possible in any case; and there is no case supposable or possible, wherein there can be an inexcusable or faulty disobedience. Which *Arminians* cannot affirm, consistently with their principles: for this makes Obedience to just and proper Commands always *necessary*, and disobedience impossible. And so the *Arminian* would overthrow himself, yielding the very point we are upon, which he so strenuously denies, *viz.* that law and Command are consistent with necessity.

If

If merely that Inability will excuſe diſobedience, which is implied in the oppoſition or defect of inclination, remaining after the Command is exhibited, then wickedneſs always carries that in it which excuſes it. It is evermore ſo, that by how much the more wickedneſs there is in a man's heart, by ſo much is his inclination to evil the ſtronger, and by ſo much the more, therefore, has he of moral Inability to the good required. His moral Inability, conſiſting in the ſtrength of his evil inclination, is the very thing wherein his wickedneſs conſiſts; and yet, according to *Arminian* principles, it muſt be a thing inconſiſtent with wickedneſs; and by how much the more he has of it, by ſo much is he the further from wickedneſs.

Therefore, on the whole, it is manifeſt, that moral Inability alone (which conſiſts in diſinclination) never renders any thing improperly the ſubject matter of Precept or Command, and never can excuſe any perſon in diſobedience, or want of conformity to a command.

Natural Inability, ariſing from the want of natural capacity, or external hindrance (which alone is properly called Inability) without doubt wholly excuſes, or makes a thing improperly the matter of Command. If men are excuſed from doing or acting any good thing, ſuppoſed to be commanded, it muſt be through ſome defect or obſtacle that is not in the will itſelf, but intrinſic to it; either in the capacity of underſtanding, or body, or outward circumſtances.

Here two or three things may be obſerved,

1. As

1. As to ſpiritual duties or acts, or any good thing in the ſtate or imminent acts of the will itſelf, or of the affections (which are only certain modes of the exerciſe of the will) if perſons are juſtly excuſed, it muſt be through want of capacity in the natural faculty of underſtanding. Thus the ſame ſpiritual duties, or holy affections and exerciſes of heart, cannot be required of men, as may be of angels; the capacity of underſtanding being ſo much inferior. So men cannot be required to love thoſe amiable perſons, whom they have had no opportunity to ſee, or hear of, or come to the knowledge of, in any way agreable to the natural ſtate and capacity of the human underſtanding. But the inſufficiency of motives will not excuſe; unleſs their being inſufficient ariſes not from the moral ſtate of the will or inclination itſelf, but from the ſtate of the natural underſtanding. The great kindneſs and generoſity of another may be a motive inſufficient to excite gratitude in the perſon, that receives the kindneſs, through his vile and ungrateful temper: in this caſe, the inſufficiency of the motive ariſes from the ſtate of the will or inclination of heart, and does not at all excuſe. But if this generoſity is not ſufficient to excite gratitude, being unknown, there being no means of information adequate to the ſtate and meaſure of the perſon's faculties, this inſufficiency is attended with a natural Inability, which entirely excuſes.

2. As to ſuch motions of body, or exerciſes and alterations of mind, which does not conſiſt in the imminent acts or ſtate of the will itſelf, but are ſuppoſed to be required as effects of the will; I ſay, in ſuch ſuppoſed effects of the will, in caſes wherein there is no want of a capacity of underſtanding; that Inability, and that only excuſes

cuses, which consists in want of connection between them and the will. If the will fully complies, and the proposed effect does not prove, according to the laws of nature, to be connected, with his volition, the man is perfectly excused; he has a natural Inability to the thing required. For the will itself, as has been observed, is all that can be directly and immediately required by Command; and other things only indirectly, as connected with the will. If therefore there be a full compliance of will, the person has done his duty; and if other things do not prove to be connected with his volition, that is not owing to him.

3. Both these kinds of natural Inability that have been mentioned, and so all Inability that excuses, may be resolved into one thing; namely, want of natural capacity or strength: either capacity of understanding, or external strength. For when there are external defects and obstacles, they would be no obstacles, were it not for the imperfection and limitations of understanding and strength.

Corol. If things for which men have a moral Inability, may properly be the matter of Precept or Command, then they may also of invitation and counsel. Commands and invitations come very much to the same thing; the difference is only circumstantial: Commands are as much a manifestation of the will of him that speaks, as invitations, and as much testimonies of expectation of compliance. The difference between them lies in nothing that touches the affair in hand. The main difference between Command and invitation consists in the inforcement of the will of him who commands or invites. In the latter it is his *kindness*, the goodness which his will arises from; in in the former it is his *authority*. But whatever be the ground of the will of him that fpeaks, or the enforcement of what he fays, yet feeing neither his will nor expectation is any more teftified in the one cafe than the other; therefore a perfon's being directed *by invitation*, is no more an evidence of infincerity in him that directs, in manifefting either a will, or expectation which he has not, than his being known to be morally unable to do what he is directed to *by command*.—So that all this grand objection of *Arminians* againft the Inability of fallen men to exert faith in Chrift, or to perform other fpiritual gofpel-duties, from the fincerity of God's counfels and invitations, muft be without force.

SECTION V.

That Sincerity of Defires and Endeavours, *which is fuppofed to* excufe *in the Non-performance of things in themfelves good, particularly confidered.*

IT is what is much infifted on by many, that fome men, though they are not able to perform fpiritual duties, fuch as repentance of fin, love to God, a cordial acceptance of Chrift as exhibited and offered in the gofpel, &c. yet they may fincerely defire and endeavour thefe things, and therefore muft be excufed; it being unreafonable to blame them for the omiffion of thofe things; which they fincerely defire and endeavour to do, but cannot do.

Concerning this matter, the following things may be obferved.

1. What

1. What is here supposed, is a great mistake, and gross absurdity; even that men may sincerely chuse and desire those spiritual duties of love, acceptance, choice, rejection, &c. consisting in the exercise of the will itself, or in the disposition and inclination of the heart; and yet not be able to perform or exert them. This is absurd, because it is absurd to suppose that a man should directly, properly and sincerely incline to have an inclination, which at the same time is contrary to his inclination: for that is to suppose him not to be inclined to that, which he is inclined to. If a man, in the state and acts of his will and inclination, does properly and directly fall in with those duties, he therein performs them: for the duties themselves consist in that very thing; they consist in the state and acts of the will being so formed and directed. If the soul properly and sincerely falls in with a certain proposed act of will or choice, the soul therein makes that choice its own. Even as when a moving body falls in with a proposed direction of its motion, that is the same thing as to move in that direction.

2. That which is called a *desire* and *willingness* for those inward duties, in such as do not perform, has respect to these duties only indirectly and remotely, and is improperly represented as a willingness for them; not only because (as was observed before) it respects those good volitions only in a distant view, and with respect to future time; but also because evermore, not these things themselves, but something else, that is alien and foreign, is the object that terminates these volitions and desires.

A drunkard, who continues in his drunkenness, being under the power of a love, and violent

lent appetite to ſtrong drink, and without any love to virtue; but being alſo extremely covetous and cloſe, and very much exerciſed and grieved at the diminution of his eſtate, and proſpect of poverty, may in a ſort *deſire* the virtue of temperance; and though his preſent will is to gratify his extravagant appetite, yet he may wiſh he had a heart to forbear future acts of intemperance, and forſake his exceſſes, through an unwillingneſs to part with his money: but ſtill he goes on with his drunkenneſs; his wiſhes and endeavours are inſufficient and ineffectual: ſuch a man has no proper, direct, ſincere willingneſs to forſake this vice, and the vicious deeds which belong to it: for he acts voluntarily in continuing to drink to exceſs: his deſire is very improperly called a willingneſs to be temperate; it is no true deſire of that virtue; for it is not that virtue, that terminates his wiſhes; nor have they any direct reſpect at all to it. It is only *the ſaving his money*, and avoiding poverty, that terminates, and exhauſts the whole ſtrength of his deſire. The virtue of temperance is regarded only very indirectly and improperly, even as a neceſſary means of gratifying the vice of covetouſneſs.

So, a man of an exceeding corrupt and wicked heart, who has no love to God and Jeſus Chriſt, but, on the contrary, being very profanely and carnally inclined, has the greateſt diſtaſte of the things of religion, and enmity againſt them; yet being of a family, that from one generation to another, have moſt of them died, in youth, of an hereditary conſumption; and ſo havnig little hope of living long; and having been inſtructed in the neceſſity of a ſupreme love to Chriſt, and gratitude for his death and ſufferings, in order to his salvation from eternal misery; if under these circumstances he should, through fear of eternal torments, wish he had such a disposition: but his profane and carnal heart remaining, he continues still in his habitual distaste *of*, and enmity *to* God and religion, and wholly without any exercise of that love and gratitude, (as doubtless the very devils themselves, notwithstanding all the devilishness of their temper, would wish for a holy heart, if by that means they could get out of hell:) in this case, there is no sincere Willingness to love Christ and chuse him as his chief good: these holy dispositions and exercises are not at all the direct object of the will: they truly share no part of the inclination, or desire of the soul; but all is terminated on deliverance from torment: and these graces and pious volitions, notwithstanding this forced consent, are looked upon undesirable; as when a sick man desires a dose he greatly abhors, to save his life.— From these things it appears,

3. That this indirect Willingness which has been spoken of, is not that exercise of the will which the command requires; but is entirely a different one; being a volition of a different nature, and terminated altogether on different objects; wholly falling short of that virtue of will, which the command has respect to.

4. This other volition, which has only some indirect concern with the duty required, cannot excuse for the want of that good will itself, which is commanded; being not the thing which answers and fulfils the command, and being wholly destitute of the virtue which the command seeks.

Further

Further to illustrate this matter.—If a child has a most excellent father, that has ever treated him with fatherly kindness and tenderness, and has every way, in the highest degree, merited his love and dutiful regard, being withal very wealthy; but the son is of so vile a disposition, that he inveterately hates his father; and yet, apprehending that his hatred of him is like to prove his ruin, by bringing him finally to poverty and abject circumstances, through his father's disinheriting him, or otherwise; which is exceeding cross to his avarice and ambition; he, therefore, wishes it were otherwise: but remaining under the invisible power of his vile and malignant disposition, he continues still in his settled hatred of his father. Now, if such a son's indirect willingness to have love and honour towards his father, at all acquits or excuses before God, for his failing of actually exercising these dispositions towards him, which God requires, it must be on one of these accounts. (1.) Either that it answers and fulfils the command. But this it does not, by the supposition; because the thing commanded is love and honour to his worthy parent. If the command be proper and just, as is supposed, then it obliges to the thing commanded: and so nothing else but that can answer the obligation. Or, (2.) It must be at least, because there is that virtue or goodness in his indirect willingness, that is equivalent to the virtue required; and so balances or countervails it, and makes up for the want of it. But that also is contrary to the supposition. The willingness the son has merely from a regard to money and honour, has no goodness in it, to countervail the want of the pious filial respect required.

Sincerity and reality, in that indirect willingness, which has been spoken of, does not make it the better. That which is real and hearty is often called sincere; whether it be in virtue or vice. Some persons are sincerely *bad*; others are sincerely *good*; and others may be sincere and hearty; in things, which are in their own nature *indifferent*; as a man may be sincerely desirous of eating when he is hungry. But a being sincere, hearty and in good earnest, is no virtue, unless it be in a thing that is virtuous. A man may be sincere and hearty in joining a crew of pirates, or a gang of robbers. When the devils cried out, and besought Christ not to torment them, it was no mere pretence; they were very hearty in their desires not to be tormented: but this did not make their will or desires virtuous. And if men have sincere desires, which are in their kind and nature no better, it can be no excuse for the want of any required virtue.

And as a man's being sincere in such an indirect desire or *willingness* to do his duty, as has been mentioned, cannot excuse for the want of performance; so it is with *Endeavours* arising from such a willingness. The endeavours can have no more goodness in them, than the will which they are the effect and expression of. And, therefore, however sincere and real, and however great a person's Endeavours are; yea, though they should be to the utmost of his ability; unless the will which they proceed from be truly good and virtuous, they can be of no avail, influence or weight to any purpose whatsoever, in a moral sense or respect. That which is not truly virtuous in God's sight, is looked upon, by Him, as good for nothing: and so can be of no value, weight or influence in his account, to recommend, ſatisfy, excuſe or make up for any moral defect. For nothing can counter-ballance evil, but good. If evil be in one ſcale, and we put a great deal into the other, ſincere and earneſt Deſires, and many and great Endeavours; yet, if there be no real goodneſs in all, there is no weight in it; and ſo it does nothing towards balancing the real weight, which is in the oppoſite ſcale. It is only like the ſubſtracting a thouſand noughts from before a real number, which leaves the ſum juſt as it was.

Indeed ſuch endeavours may have a *negatively* good influence. Thoſe things, which have no poſitive virtue, have no poſſitive moral influence; yet they may be an occaſion of perſons avoiding ſome poſſitive evils. As if a man were in the water with a neighbour, that he had ill will to, who could not ſwim, holding him by his hand; which neighbour was much in debt to him; and ſhould be tempted to let him ſink and drown; but ſhould refuſe to comply with the temptation; not from love to his neighbour, but from the love of money, and becauſe by his drowning he ſhould loſe his debt; that which he does in preſerving his neighbour from drowning, is nothing good in the ſight of God: yet hereby he avoids the greater guilt that would have been contracted, if he had deſignedly let his neighbour ſink and periſh. But when *Arminians*, in their diſputes with *Calviniſts*, inſiſt ſo much on ſincere Deſires and Endeavours, as what muſt excuſe men, muſt be accepted of God, &c. it is manifeſt they have reſpect to ſome poſſitive moral weight or influence of thoſe Deſires and Endeavours. Accepting, juſtifying or excuſing on the account of ſincere honeſt endeavours (as they are called) and men's doing what they can, &c. has relation

to

to ſome moral value, ſomething that is accepted as good, and as ſuch, countervailing ſome defect.

But there is a great and unknown deceit, ariſing from the ambiguity of the phraſe, *ſincere Endeavours.* Indeed there is a vaſt indiſtinctneſs and unfixedneſs in moſt, or at leaſt very many of the terms uſed to expreſs things pertaining to moral and ſpiritual matters. Whence ariſe innumerable miſtakes, ſtrong prejudices, inextircable confuſion, and endleſs controverſy.

The word *ſincere* is moſt commonly uſed to ſignify ſomething that is good: men are habituated to underſtand by it the ſame as *honeſt* and *upright*; which terms excite an idea of ſomething good in the ſtricteſt and higheſt ſenſe; good in the ſight of Him, who ſees not only the outward appearance, but the heart. And, therefore, men think that if a perſon be *ſincere*, he will certainly be accepted. If it be ſaid that any one is ſincere in his Endeavours, this ſuggeſts to men's minds as much, as that his heart and will is good, that there is no defect of duty, as to virtuous inclination; he *honeſtly* and *uprightly* deſires and endeavours to do as he is required; and this leads them to ſuppoſe, that it would be very hard and unreaſonable to puniſh him, only becauſe he is unſucceſsful in his Endeavours, the thing endeavoured being beyond his power.—Whereas it ought to be obſerved, that the word *ſincere* has theſe different ſignifications.

1. Sincerity, as the word is ſometimes uſed, ſignifies no more than *reality of Will and Endeavour*, with reſpect to any thing that is profeſſed or pretended; without any conſideration of the

nature of the principle or aim, whence this real Will and true Endeavour arifes. If a man has fome real defire to obtain a thing, either direct or indirect, or does really endeavour after a thing, he is faid fincerely to defire or endeavour it; without any confideration of the goodnefs or virtuoufnefs of the principle he acts from, or any excellency or worthinefs of the end he acts for. Thus a man, who is kind to his neighbour's wife, who is fick and languifhing, and very helpful in her cafe, makes a fhew of defiring and endeavouring her reftoration to health and vigour; and not only makes fuch a fhew, but there is a reality in his pretence, he does heartily and earneftly defire to have her health reftored, and ufes his true and utmoft Endeavours for it; he is faid fincerely to defire and endeavour it, becaufe he does fo truly or really; though perhaps the principle he acts from, is no other than a vile and fcandalous paffion; having lived in adultery with her, he earneftly defires to have her health and vigour reftored, that he may return to his criminal pleafures with her. Or,

2. By *fincerity* is meant, not merely a *reality* of Will and Endeavour of fome fort or other, and from fome confideration or other, but a *virtuous fincerity*. That is, that in the performance of thofe particular acts, that are the matter of virtue or duty, there be not only the matter, but the form and effence of virtue, confifting in the aim that governs the act, and the principle exercifed in it. There is not only the reality of the act, that is as it were the *body* of the duty; but alfo the *foul*, which fhould properly belong to fuch a body. In this fenfe, a man is faid to be fincere, when he acts with a *pure intention*; not from finifter views, or bye-ends: he not only

in

in reality desires and seeks the thing to be done, or qualification to be obtained, for some end or other; but he wills the thing directly and properly, as neither forced nor bribed; the virtue of the thing is properly the object of the will.

In the former sense, a man is said to be sincere, in opposition to a mere pretence, and *shew of the particular thing to be done or exhibited*, without any real Desire or Endeavour at all. In the latter sense, a man is said to be sincere, in opposition to that *shew of virtue there is in merely doing the matter of duty*, without the reality of the virtue itself in the soul, and the essence of it, which there is a shew of. A man may be sincere in the former sense, and yet in the latter be in the sight of God, who searches the heart, a vile hypocrite.

In the latter kind of sincerity, only, is there any thing truly valuable or acceptable in the sight of God. And this is the thing, which in Scripture is called *sincerity*, *uprightness*, *integrity*, *truth in the inward parts*, and a *being of a perfect heart*. And if there be such a sincerity, and such a degree of it as there ought to be, and there be any thing further that the man is not able to perform, or which does not prove to be connected with his sincere Desires and Endeavours, the man is wholly excused and acquitted in the sight of God; his will shall surely be accepted for his deed: and such a sincere Will and Endeavour is all that in strictness is required of him, by any command of God. But as to the other kind of sincerity of Desires and Endeavours, it having no virtue in it, (as was observed before) can be of no avail before God, in any case, to recommend, satisfy, or excuse, and has no positive moral weight or influence whatsoever.

Corol. 1. Hence it may be inferred, that nothing in the reason and nature of things appears, from the consideration of any moral weight of that former kind of sincerity, which has been spoken of, at all obliging us to believe, or leading us to suppose, that God has made any positive Promises of salvation, or grace, or any saving assistance, or any spiritual benefit whatsoever, to any Desires, Prayers, Endeavours, Striving, or Obedience of those, who hitherto have no true virtue or holiness in their hearts; though we should suppose all the Sincerity, and the utmost degree of Endeavour, that is possible to be in a person without holiness.

Some object against God's requiring, as the condition of salvation, those holy exercises, which are the result of a supernatural renovation; such as a supreme respect to Christ, love to God, loving holiness for its own sake, &c. that these inward dispositions and exercises are above men's power, as they are by nature; and therefore that we may conclude, that when men are brought to be sincere in their Endeavours, and do as well as they can, they are accepted; and that this must be all that God requires, in order to men's being received as the objects of his favour, and must be what God has appointed as the condition of salvation. concerning which, I would observe, that in such a manner of speaking of *men's being accepted, because they are sincere, and do as well as they can,* there is evidently a supposition of some virtue, some degree of that which is truly good; though it does not go so far as were to be wished. For if men

men *do what they can*, unless their so doing be from some good principle, disposition, or exercise of heart, some virtuous inclination or act of the will; their so doing what they can, is in some respects not a whit better than if they did nothing at all. In such a case, there is no more positive moral goodness in a man's doing what he can, than in a wind-mill's doing what it can; because the action does not more proceed from virtue; and there is nothing in such sincerity of Endeavour, or doing what we can, that should render it any more a proper or fit recommendation to positive favour and acceptance, or the condition of any reward or actual benefit, than doing nothing; for both the one and the other are alike nothing, as to any true moral weight or value.

Corol. 2. Hence also it follows, there is nothing that appears in the reason and nature of things, which can justly lead us to determine, that God will certainly give the necessary means of salvation, or some way or other bestow true holiness and eternal life on those *Heathen*, who are sincere, (in the sense above explained) in their Endeavours to find out the will of the Deity, and to please him, according to their light, that they may escape his future displeasure and wrath, and obtain happiness in the future state, through his favour.

SECTION VI.

Liberty of Indifference, *not only not neceſſary to* Virtue, *but utterly inconſiſtent with it; and all, either virtuous or vicious* Habits or Inclinations, *inconſiſtent with* Arminian *Notions of Liberty and moral Agency.*

TO ſuppoſe ſuch a freedom of will, as *Arminians* talk of, to be requiſite to Virtue and Vice, is many ways contrary to common ſenſe.

IF Indifference belongs to Liberty of Will, as *Arminians* ſuppoſe, and it be eſſential to a virtuous action, that it be performed in a ſtate of Liberty, as they alſo ſuppoſe; it will follow, that it is eſſential to a virtuous action, that it be performed in a ſtate of indifference: and if it be performed in a *ſtate* of Indifference, then doubtleſs it muſt be performed in the *time* of Indifference. And ſo it will follow, that in order to the virtuouſneſs of an act, the heart muſt be indifferent in the time of the performance of that act, and the more indifferent and cold the heart is with relation to the act, which is performed, ſo much the better; becauſe the act is performed with ſo much the greater Liberty. But is this agreable to the light of nature? Is it agreable to the notions, which mankind, in all ages, have of Virtue, that it lies in that which is contrary to Indifference, even in the *Tendency* and *Inclination* of the heart to virtuous action; and that the ſtronger the Inclination, and ſo the further from Indifference, the more virtuous the *heart*, and ſo much

much the more praise-worthy the *act* which proceeds from it?

If we should suppose (contrary to what has been before demonstrated) that there may be an act of will in a state of indifference; for instance, this act, *viz.* The will's determining to put itself out of a state of Indifference, and give itself a preponderation one way, then it would follow, on *Arminian* principles, that this act or determination of the will is that alone wherein Virtue consists, because this only is performed, while the mind remains in a state of Indifference, and so in a state of Liberty: for when once the mind is put out of its equilibrium, it is no longer in such a state; and therefore all the acts, which follow afterwards, proceeding from bias, can have the nature neither of Virtue nor Vice. Or if the thing, which the will can do, while yet in a state of Indifference, and so of Liberty, be only to suspend acting, and determine to take the matter into consideration, then this determination is that alone wherein Virtue consists, and not proceeding to action after the scale is turned by consideration. So that it will follow, from these principles, all that is done after the mind, by any means, is once out of its equilibrium and already possessed by an Inclination, and arising from that Inclination, has nothing of the nature of Virtue or Vice, and is worthy of neither blame nor praise. But how plainly contrary is this to the universal sense of mankind, and to the notion they have of sincerely virtuous actions? Which is, that they are actions, which proceed from a heart *well disposed* and *inclined*; and the *stronger*, and the more *fixed* and *determined* the good disposition of the heart, the greater the sincerity of Virtue, and so the more of the truth and reality of of it. But if there be any acts, which are done in a state of equilibrium, or spring immediately from perfect Indifference and coldness of heart, they cannot arise from any good principle or disposition in the heart; and, consequently, according to common sense, have no sincere goodness in them, having no Virtue of heart in them. To have a virtuous heart, is to have a heart that favours Virtue, and is friendly to it, and not one perfectly cold and indifferent about it.

And besides, the actions that are done in a state of Indifference, or that arise immediately out of such a state, cannot be virtuous, because, by the supposition, they are not determined by any preceding choice. For if there be preceding choice, then choice intervenes between the act and the state of Indifference; which is contrary to the supposition of the act's arising immediately out of Indifference. But those acts which are not determined by preceding choice, cannot be virtuous or vicious by *Arminian* principles, because they are not determined by the will. So that neither one way, nor the other, can any actions be virtuous or vicious, according to *Arminian* principles. If the action *be determined* by a preceding act of choice, it cannot be virtuous; because the action is not done in a state of Indifference, nor does immediately arise from such a state; and so is not done in a state of Liberty. If the action be *not determined* by a preceding act of choice, then it cannot be virtuous; because then the will is not self-determined in it. So that it is made certain, that neither Virtue nor Vice can ever find any place in the universe.

Moreover, that it is necessary to a virtuous action that it be performed in a state of Indifference,

ference, under a notion of that being a ſtate of Liberty, is contrary to common ſenſe; as it is a dictate of common ſenſe, that Indifference itſelf, in many caſes, is vicious, and ſo to a high degree. As if when I ſee my neighbour or near friend, and one who has in the higheſt degree merited of me, in extreme diſtreſs, and ready to periſh, I find an Indifference in my heart with reſpect to any thing propoſed to be done, which I can eaſily do, for his relief. So if it ſhould be propoſed to me to blaſpheme God, or kill my father, or do numberleſs other things, which might be mentioned; the being indifferent, for a moment, would be highly vicious and vile.

And it may be further obſerved, that to ſuppoſe this Liberty of Indifference is eſſential to Virtue and Vice, deſtroys the great difference of degrees of the guilt of different crimes, and takes away the heinouſneſs of the moſt flagitious horrid iniquities; ſuch as adultery, beſtiality, murder, perjury, blaſphemy, &c. For, according to theſe principles, there is no harm at all in having the mind in a ſtate of perfect Indifference with reſpect to theſe crimes; nay, it is abſolutely neceſſary in order to any Virtue in avoiding them, or Vice in doing them. But for the mind to be in a ſtate of Indifference with reſpect to them, is to be next door to doing them: it is then infinitely near to chuſing, and ſo committing the fact: for equilibrium is the next ſtep to a degree of preponderation; and one, even the leaſt degree of preponderation (all things conſidered) is choice. And not only ſo, but for the will to be in a ſtate of perfect equilibrium with reſpect to ſuch crimes, is for the mind to be in ſuch a ſtate, as to be full as likely to chuſe them as to refuſe them, to do them as to omit them. And

if

if our minds must be in such a state, wherein it is as near to chusing as refusing, and wherein it must of necessity, according to the nature of things, be as likely to commit them, as to refrain from them; where is the exceeding heinousness of chusing and committing them? If there be no harm in often being in such a state, wherein the probability of doing and forbearing are exactly equal, there being an equilibrium, and no more tendency to one than the other; then, according to the nature and laws of such a contingence, it may be expected, as an *inevitable* consequence of such a disposition of things, that we should chuse them as often as reject them: that it should generally so fall out is necessary, as equality in the effect is the natural consequence of the equal tendency of the cause, or of the antecedent state of things from which the effect arises. Why then should we be so exceedingly to blame, if it does so fall out?

It is many ways apparent, that the *Arminians* scheme of Liberty is utterly inconsistent with the being of any such things as either virtuous or vicious Habits or Dispositions. If Liberty of *Indifference* be essential to moral agency, then there can be no Virtue in any habitual Inclinations of the heart; which are contrary to Indifference, and imply in their nature the very destruction and exclusion of it. They suppose nothing can be virtuous, in which no Liberty is exercised; but how absurd is it to talk of exercising Indifference under bias and preponderation!

And if *self determining power* in the will be necessary to moral agency, praise, blame, &c. then nothing done by the will can be any further praise or blame-worthy, than so far as the will

will is moved, swayed and determined by itself, and the scales turned by the sovreign power the will has over itself And therefore the will must not be put out of its balance already, the preponderation must not be determined and effected before-hand; and so the self-determining act anticipated. Thus it appears another way, that habitual bias is inconsistent with that Liberty, which *Arminians* suppose to be necessary to Virtue or Vice; and so it follows, that habitual bias itself cannot be either virtuous or vicious.

The same thing follows from their doctrine concerning the Inconsistence of *Necessity* with Liberty, Praise, Dispraise, &c. None will deny, that Bias and Inclination may be so strong as to be invincible, and leave no possibility of the will's determining contrary to it; and so be attended with Necessity. This Dr. *Whitby* allows concerning the will of God, Angels, and glorified Saints, with respect to good; and the will of Devils, with respect to evil. Therefore, if Necessity be inconsistent with Liberty; then, when fixed Inclination is to such a degree of strength, it utterly excludes all Virtue, Vice, Praise or Blame. And, if so, then the nearer habits are to this strength, the more do they impede Liberty, and so diminish Praise and Blame. If very strong Habits destroy Liberty, the lesser ones proportionably hinder it, according to their degree of strength. And therefore it will follow, that then is the act most virtuous or vicious, when performed without any Inclination or habitual Bias at all; because it is then performed with most liberty.

Every prepossessing fixed Bias on the mind brings a degree of moral Inability for the contrary;

trary; becaufe fo far as the mind is biaffed and prepoffeffed, fo much *hinderance* is there of the contrary. And therefore if moral Inability be confiftent with moral agency, or the nature of Virtue and Vice, then, fo far as there is any fuch thing as evil difpofition of heart, or habitual depravity of Inclination; whether covetoufnefs, pride, malice, cruelty, or whatever elfe; fo much the more excufeable perfons are; fo much the lefs have their evil acts of this kind the nature of Vice. And, on the contrary, whatever excellent Difpofitions and Inclinations they have, fo much are they the lefs virtuous.

It is evident, that no habitual difpofition of heart, whether it be to a greater or lefs degree, can be in *any degree* virtuous or vicious, or the actions which proceed from them *at all* praife or blame-worthy. Becaufe, though we fhould fuppofe the Habit not to be of fuch ftrength, as wholly to take away all moral ability and felf-determining power; or hinder but that, although the act be partly from Bias, yet it may be in part from felf determination; yet in this cafe, all that is from antecedent Bias muft be fet afide, as of no confideration; and in eftimating the degree of Virtue or Vice, no more muft be confidered than what arifes from felf-determining power, without any influence of that Bias, becaufe Liberty is exercifed in no more: fo that all that is the exercife of habitual Inclination, is thrown away, as not belonging to the morality of the action. by which it appears, that no exercife of thefe Habits, let them be ftronger or weaker, can ever have any thing of the nature of either Virtue or Vice.

HERE

Here if any one should say, that notwithstanding all these things, there may be the nature of Virtue and Vice in the Habits of the mind; because these Habits may be the effects of those acts, wherein the mind exercised Liberty; that however the forementioned reasons will prove that no Habits, which are natural, or that are born or created with us, can be either virtuous or vicious; yet they will not prove this of Habits, which have been acquired and established by repeated free acts.

To such an objector I would say, that this evasion will not at all help the matter. For if freedom of will be essential to the very *nature* of Virtue and Vice, then there is no Virtue or Vice but only in that very thing, wherein this Liberty is exercised. If a man in one or more things, that he does, exercises Liberty, and then by those acts is brought into such circumstances, that his Liberty ceases, and there follows a long series of acts or events that come to pass necessarily; those consequent acts are not virtuous or vicious, rewardable or punishable; but only the free acts that established this necessity; for in them alone was the man free. The following effects, that are necessary, have no more of the nature of Virtue or Vice, than health or sickness of body have properly the nature of Virtue or Vice, being the effects of a course of free acts of temperance or intemperance; or than the good qualities of a clock are of the nature of Virtue, which are the effects of free acts of the artificer; or the goodness and sweetness of the fruits of a garden are moral Virtues, being the effects of the free and faithful acts of the gardener. If Liberty be absolutely requisite to the morality of actions, and necessity wholly inconsistent with it, as as *Arminians* greatly inſiſt; then no *neceſſary effects* whatſoever, let the cauſe be never ſo good or bad, can be virtuous or vicious; but the virtue or vice muſt be only in the *free cauſe.* Agreably to this, Dr. *Whitby* ſuppoſes, the neceſſity that attends the good and evil Habits of the ſaints in heaven, and damned in hell, which are the conſequence of their free acts in their ſtate of probation, are not rewardable or puniſhable.

On the whole, it appears, that if the notions of *Arminians* concerning liberty and moral agency be true, it will follow, that there is no virtue in any ſuch Habits or qualities as humility, meekneſs, patience, mercy, gratitude, generoſity, heavenly-mindedneſs; nothing at all praiſeworthy in loving Chriſt above father and mother, wife and children, or our own lives; or in delight in holineſs, hungering and thirſting after righteouſneſs, love to enemies, univerſal benevolence to mankind: and, on the other hand, there is nothing at all vicious, or worthy of diſpraiſe, in the moſt ſordid, beaſtly, malignant, deviliſh diſpoſitions; in being ungrateful, profane, habitually hating God, and things ſacred and holy; or in being moſt treacherous, envious and cruel towards men. For all theſe things are *Diſpoſitions* and *Inclinations* of the heart. And in ſhort, there is no ſuch thing as any virtuous or vicious *quality of mind*; no ſuch thing as inherent virtue and holineſs, or vice and ſin: and the ſtronger thoſe Habits or Diſpoſitions are, which uſed to be called virtuous and vicious, the further they are from being ſo indeed; the more violent men's luſts are, the more fixed their pride, envy, ingratitude and maliciouſneſs, ſtill the further are they from being blame-worthy. If there be a man that by his own repeated acts, or by by any other means, is come to be of the moſt helliſh Diſpoſition, deſperately inclined to treat his neighbours with injurioúſneſs, contempt and malignity; the further they ſhould be from any Diſpoſition to be angry with him, or in the leaſt to blame him. So, on the other hand, if there be a perſon who is of a moſt excellent ſpirit, ſtrongly inclining him to the moſt amiable actions, admirably meek, benevolent, &c. ſo much is he further from any thing rewardable or commendable. On which principles, the man Jeſus Chriſt was very far from being praiſe-worthy for thoſe acts of holineſs and kindneſs, which He performed, theſe propenſities being ſtrong in his heart. And above all, the infinitely holy and gracious God is infinitely remote from any thing commendable, his good Inclinations being infinitely ſtrong, and He, therefore, at the utmoſt poſſible diſtance from being at liberty. And in all caſes, the ſtronger the Inclinations of any are to Virtue, and the more they love it, the leſs virtuous they are; and the more they love wickedneſs, the leſs vicious.——Whether theſe things are agreeable to Scripture, let every Chriſtian, and every man who has read the Bible, judge: and whether they are agreeable to common ſenſe, let every one judge, that has human underſtanding in exerciſe.

And, if we purſue theſe principles, we ſhall find that Virtue and Vice are wholly excluded out of the world; and that there never was, nor ever can be any ſuch thing as one or the other; either in God, angels or men. No Propenſity, Diſpoſition or Habit can be virtuous or vicious, as has been ſhewn; becauſe they, ſo far as they take place, deſtroy the freedom of the will, the foundation of all moral agency, and exclude all capacity of either Virtue or Vice.——And if Habits and Diſpoſitions themſelves be not virtuous nor vicious, neither can the exerciſe of theſe Diſpoſitions be ſo: for the exerciſe of *Bias* is not the exerciſe of *free ſelf-determining will*, and ſo there is no exerciſe of liberty in it. Conſequently, no man is virtuous or vicious, either in being well or ill-diſpoſed, nor in acting from a good or bad Diſpoſition. And whether this Bias or Diſpoſition, be habitual or not, if it exiſts but a moment before the act of will, which is the effect of it, it alters not the caſe, as to the neceſſity of the effect. Or if there be no previous Diſpoſition at all, either habitual or occaſional, that determines the act, then it is not choice that determines it: it is therefore a contingence, that happens to the man, ariſing from nothing in him; and is neceſſary, as to any Inclination or Choice of his; and therefore, cannot make him either the better or worſe, any more than a tree is better than other trees, becauſe it oftener happens to be lit upon by a ſwan or nightingale: or a rock more vicious than other rocks, becauſe rattle-ſnakes have happened oftener to crawl over it. So, that there is no Virtue nor Vice in good or bad Diſpoſitions, either fixed or tranſient; nor any Virtue or Vice in acting from any good or bad previous Inclination; nor yet any virtue or vice, in acting wholly without any previous Inclination. Where then ſhall we find room for Virtue or Vice?

SEC-

SECTION VII.

Arminian Notions of moral Agency consistent with all Influence of Motive *and* Inducement, *in either virtuous or vicious Actions.*

AS *Arminian* notions of that liberty, which is essential to virtue or vice, are inconsistent with common sense, in their being inconsistent with all virtuous or vicious habits and dispositions; so they are no less so in their inconsistency with all influence of Motives in moral actions.

IT is equally against those notions of liberty of will, whether there be, previous to the act of choice, a preponderancy of the inclination, or a preponderancy of those circumstances, which have a tendency to move the inclination. And, indeed, it comes to just the same thing: to say, the circumstances of the mind are such as tend to sway and turn its inclination one way, is the same thing as to say, the inclination of the mind, as under such circumstances, tends that way.

OR if any think it most proper to say, that Motives do alter the inclination, and give a new bias to the mind, it will not alter the case, as to the present argument. For if Motives operate by giving the mind an inclination, then they operate by destroying the mind's indifference, and laying it under a bias. But to do this, is to destroy the *Arminian* freedom: it is not to leave the will to its own self-determination, but to bring it into subjection to the power of something extrinſic, which operates upon it, ſways and determines it, previous to its own determination. So that what is done from Motive, cannot be either virtuous or vicious.—And beſides, if the acts of the will are excited by Motives, thoſe Motives are the *cauſes* of thoſe acts of the will; which makes the acts of the will neceſſary; as effects neceſſarily follow the efficiency of the cauſe. And if the influence and power of the Motive cauſes the volition, then the influence of the Motive determines volition, and volition does not determine itſelf; and ſo is not free, in the ſenſe of *Arminians* (as has been largely ſhewn already) and conſequently can be neither virtuous nor vicious.

The ſuppoſition, which has already been taken notice of as an inſufficient evaſion in other caſes, would be, in like manner, impertinently alledged in this caſe; namely, the ſuppoſition that liberty conſiſts in a power of ſuſpending action for the preſent, in order to deliberation. If it ſhould be ſaid, Though it be true, that the will is under a neceſſity of finally following the ſtrongeſt Motive; yet it may, for the preſent, forbear to act upon the Motive preſented, till there has been opportunity thoroughly to conſider it, and compare its real weight with the merit of other Motives. I anſwer as follows:

Here again, it muſt be remembered, that if determining thus to ſuſpend and conſider, be that act of the will, wherein alone liberty is exerciſed, then in this all virtue and vice muſt conſiſt; and the acts that follow this conſideration, and are the effects of it, being neceſſary, are no more virtuous or vicious than ſome good or bad events, which happen when they are faſt aſleep, and

and are the consequences of what they did when they were awake. Therefore, I would here observe two things:

1. To suppose, that all virtue and vice in every case, consists in determining, whether to take time for consideration or not, is not agreeable to common sense. For, according to such a supposition, the most horrid crimes, adultery, murder, sodomy, blasphemy, *&c.* do not at all consist in the horrid nature of the things themselves, but only in the neglect of thorough consideration before they were perpetrated, which brings their viciousness to a small matter, and makes all crimes equal. If it be said, that neglect of consideration, when such heinous evils are proposed to choice, is worse than in other cases: I answer, this is inconsistent, as it supposes the very thing to be, which, at the same time, is supposed not to be; it supposes all moral evil, all viciousness and heinousness, does not consist merely in the want of consideration. It supposes some crimes *in themselves*, in their *own nature*, to be more heinous than others, antecedent to consideration or inconsideration, which lays the person under a previous obligation to consider in some cases more than others.

2. If it were so, that all virtue and vice, in every case, consisted only in the act of the will, whereby it determines whether to consider or no, it would not alter the case in the least, as to the present argument. For still in this act of the will on this determination, it is induced by some Motive, and necessarily follows the strongest Motive; and so is necessarily, even in that act wherein alone it is either virtuous or vicious.

ONE

One thing more I would observe, concerning the inconsistence of *Arminian* notions of moral agency with the influence of Motives.—I suppose none will deny, that it is possible for Motives to be set before the mind so powerful, and exhibited in so strong a light, and under so advantageous circumstances, as to be invincible; and such as the mind cannot but yield to. In this case, *Arminians* will doubtless say, liberty is destroyed. And if so, then if Motives are exhibited with half so much power, they hinder liberty in proportion to their strength, and go half way towards destroying it. If a thousand degrees of Motives abolish all liberty, then five hundred take it half away. If one degree of the influence of Motive does not at all infringe or diminish liberty then no more do two degrees; for nothing doubled, is still nothing. And if two degrees do not diminish the will's liberty, no more do four, eight, sixteen, or six thousand. For nothing multiplied never so much comes to but nothing. If there be nothing in the nature of motive or moral suasion, that is at all opposite to liberty, then the greatest degree of it cannot hurt liberty. But if there be any thing in the nature of the thing, that is against liberty, then the least degree of it hurts it in some degree; and consequently hurts and diminishes virtue. If invincible Motives, to that action which is good, take away all the freedom of the act, and so all the virtue of it; then the more forceable the Motives are, so much the worse, so much the less virtue; and the weaker the Motives are, the better for the cause of virtue; and none is best of all.

Now let it be considered, whether these things are agreable to common sense. If it should be allowed,

allowed, that there are ſome inſtances wherein the ſoul chuſes without any Motive, what virtue can there be in ſuch a choice? I am ſure, there is no prudence or wiſdom in it. Such a choice is made for no good end; for it is for no end at all. If it were for any end, the view of the end would be the Motive exciting to the act; and if the act be for no good end, and ſo from no good aim, then there is no good intention in it: and, therefore, according to all our natural notions of virtue, no more virtue in it than in the motion of the ſmoak, which is driven too and fro by the wind, without any aim or end in the thing moved; and which knows not whither, nor why and wherefore, it is moved.

Corol. 1. By theſe things it appears, that the argument againſt the *Calviniſts*, taken from the uſe of counſels, exhortations, invitations, expoſtulations, *&c.* ſo much inſiſted on by *Arminians*, is truly againſt themſelves. For theſe things can operate no other way to any good effect, than as in them is exhibited Motive and Inducement, tending to excite and determine the acts of the will. But it follows, on their principles, that the acts of will excited by ſuch cauſes, cannot be virtuous; becauſe, ſo far as they are from theſe, they are not from the will's ſelf-determining power. Hence it will follow, that it is not worth the while to offer any arguments to perſuade men to any virtuous volition or voluntary action; it is in vain to ſet before them the wiſdom and aimiableneſs of ways of virtue, or the odiouſneſs and folly of ways of vice. This notion of liberty and moral agency fruſtrates all endeavours to draw men to virtue by inſtruction or perſuaſion, precept or example: for though theſe things may induce men to what is *materially* virtuous, yet at the same time they take away the *form* of Virtue, because they destroy Liberty; as they, by their own power, put the will out of its equilibrium, determine and turn the scale, and take the work of self-determining power out of its hands. And the clearer the instructions that are given, the more powerful the arguments that are used, and the more moving the persuasions or examples, the more likely they are to frustrate their own design; because they have so much the greater tendency to put the will out of its balance, to hinder its freedom of self-determination; and so to exclude the very form of virtue, and the essence of whatsoever is praise-worthy.

So it clearly follows, from these principles, that God has no hand in any man's virtue, nor does at all promote it, either by a physical or moral influence; that none of the moral methods, He uses with men to promote virtue in the world, have tendency to the attainment of that end; that all the instructions, which he has given to men, from the beginning of the world to this day, by Prophets or Apostles, or by His Son Jesus Christ; that all his counsels, invitations, promises, threatenings, warnings and expostulations; that all means, He has used with men, in ordinances, or providences; yea, all influences of his Spirit, ordinary and extraordinary, have had no tendency at all to excite any one virtuous act of the mind, or to promote any thing morally good and commendable, in any respect.—For there is no way that these or any other means can promote virtue, but one of these three. Either (1.) By a physical operation on the heart. But all effects that are wrought in men in this way, have no Virtue in them, by the

the concurring voice of all *Arminians*. Or, (2.) Morally, by exhibiting Motives to the understanding, to excite good acts in the will. But it has been demonstrated, that volitions, which are excited by Motives, are necessary, and not excited by a self-moving power; and therefore, by their principles, there is no Virtue in them. Or, (3.) By merely giving the will an opportunity to determine itself concerning the objects proposed, either to chuse or reject, by its own uncaused, unmoved, uninfluenced self-determination. And if this be all, then all those means do no more to promote virtue than vice: for they do nothing but give the will opportunity to determine itself *either way*, either to good or bad, without laying it under any bias to either; and so there is really as much of an opportunity given to determine in favour of evil, as of good.

Thus that horrid blasphemous consequence will certainly follow from the *Arminian* doctrine, which they charge on others; namely, that God acts an inconsistent part in using so many counsels, warnings, invitations, intreaties, *&c.* with sinners, to induce them to forsake sin, and turn to the ways of virtue; and that all are insincere and fallacious. It will follow, from their doctrine, that God does these things when He knows, at the same time, that they have no manner of tendency to promote the effect, He seems to aim at; yea, knows that if they have any influence, this very influence will be inconsistent with such an effect, and will prevent it. But what an imputation of insincerity would this fix on Him, who is infinitely holy and true!—So that their's is the doctrine which, if pursued in its consequences, does horribly reflect on the most High,

and

and fix on Him the charge of hypocrisy; and not the doctrine of the *Calvinist*; according to their frequent, and vehement exclamations and invectives.

Corol. 2. From what has been observed in this section, it again appears, that *Arminian* principles and notions, when fairly examined and pursued in their demonstrable consequences, do evidently shut all virtue out of the world, and make it impossible that there should ever be any such thing, in any case; or that any such thing should ever be conceived of. For, by these principles, the very notion of virtue or vice implies absurdity and contradiction. For it is absurd in itself, and contrary to common sense, to suppose a virtuous act of mind without any good intention or aim; and, by their principles, it is absurd to suppose a virtuous act with a good intention or aim; for to act for an end, is to act from a Motive. So that if we rely on these principles, there can be no virtuous act with a good design and end; and it is self-evident, there can be none without: consequently there can be no virtuous act at all.

Corol. 3. It is manifest, that *Arminian* notions of moral agency, and *the being* of a faculty of will, cannot consist together; and that if there be any such thing as either a virtuous or vicious act, it cannot be an act of the will; no will can be at all concerned in it. For that act which is performed without inclination, without Motive, without end, must be performed without any concern of the will. To suppose an act of the will without these, implies a contradiction. If the soul in its act has no motive or end; then, in that act (as was observed before) it seeks nothing,

thing, goes after nothing, exerts no inclination to any thing; and this implies, that in that act it desires nothing, and chuses nothing; so that there is no act of choice in the case: and that is as much as to say, there is no act of will in the case. Which very effectually shuts all vicious and virtuous acts out of the universe; in as much as, according to this, there can be no vicious or virtuous act wherein the will is concerned; and according to the plainest dictates of reason, and the light of nature, and also the principles of *Arminians* themselves, there can be no virtuous or vicious act wherein the will is not concerned. And therefore there is no room for any virtuous or vicious acts at all.

Corol. 4. If none of the moral actions of intelligent beings are influenced by either previous Inclination or Motive, another strange thing will follow; and this is, that God not only cannot fore know any of the future moral actions of his creatures, but he can make no conjecture, can give no probable guess concerning them. For, all conjecture in things of this nature, must depend on some discerning or apprehension of these two things, *previous Disposition*, and *Motive*, which, as has been observed, *Arminian* notions of moral agency, in their real consequence, altogether exclude.

PART

PART IV.

Wherein the chief Grounds of the Reaſonings of ARMINIANS, in Support and Defence of the forementioned Notions of LIBERTY, MORAL AGENCY, &c. and againſt the Oppoſite Doctrine, are conſidered.

SECTION I.

The Eſſence *of the Virtue and Vice of Diſpoſitions of the Heart, and Acts of the Will, lies not in their* Cauſe, *but their* Nature.

ONE main foundation of the reaſons, which are brought to eſtabliſh the forementioned notions of liberty, virtue, vice, *&c.* is a ſuppoſition, that the virtuouſneſs of the diſpoſitions, or acts of the will, conſiſts not in the nature of theſe diſpoſitions or acts, but wholly in the Origin or Cauſe of them: ſo that if the diſpoſition of the mind, or acts of the will, be never ſo good, yet if the Cauſe of the diſpoſition or act be not our virtue,

tue, there is nothing virtuous or praise-worthy in it, and, on the contrary, if the will, in its inclination or acts, be never so bad, yet, unless it arises from something that is our vice or fault, there is nothing vicious or blame-worthy in it. Hence their grand objection and pretended demonstration, or self-evidence, against any virtue and commendableness, or vice and blame-worthiness, of those habits or acts of the will, which are not from some virtuous or vicious determination of the will itself.

Now, if this matter be well considered, it will appear to be altogether a mistake, yea, a gross absurdity; and that it is most certain, that if there be any such things, as a virtuous or vicious disposition, or volition of mind, the virtuousness or viciousness of them consists not in the Origin or Cause of these things, but in the Nature of them.

If the Essence of virtuousness or commendableness, and of viciousness or fault, does not lie in the Nature of the dispositions or acts of mind, which are said to be our virtue or our fault, but in their Cause, then it is certain it lies no where at all. Thus, for instance, if the vice of a *vicious* act of will, lies not in the Nature of the act, but the Cause; so that its being of a bad Nature will not make it at all our fault, unless it arises from some faulty determination of our's, as its Cause, or something in us that is our fault; then, for the same reason, neither can the viciousness of that Cause lie in the Nature of the thing itself, but in *its* Cause: that evil determination of our's is not our fault, merely because it is of a bad Nature, unless it arises from some Cause in us that is our fault. And when we are come to this

this higher Cause, still the reason of the thing holds good; though this Cause be of a bad Nature, yet we are not at all to blame on that account, unless it arises from something faulty in us. Nor yet can blame-worthiness lie in the Nature of *this Cause*, but in the Cause of *that*. And thus we must drive faultiness back from step to step, from a lower Cause to a higher, *in infinitum*: and that is, thoroughly to banish it from the world, and to allow it no possibility of existence any where in the universality of things. On these principles, vice, or moral evil, cannot consist in any thing that is an *effect*; because *fault* does not consist in the Nature of things, but in their Cause; as well as because effects are necessary, being unavoidably connected with their Cause: therefore the Cause only is to blame. And so it follows, that faultiness can lie *only in that Cause*, which is a *Cause only*, and no effect of any thing. Nor yet can it lie in this; for then it must lie in the Nature of the thing itself; not in its being from any determination of our's, nor any thing faulty in us which is the Cause, nor indeed from any Cause at all; for, by the supposition, it is no effect, and *has no Cause*. And thus he that will maintain, it is not the Nature of habits or acts of will that makes them virtuous or faulty, but the Cause, must immediately run himself out of his own assertion; and in maintaining it, will insensibly contradict and deny it.

This is certain, that if effects are vicious and faulty, not from their Nature, or from any thing inherent in them, but because they are from a bad Cause, it must be on account of the *badness* of the Cause: a bad effect in the will must be bad, because the Cause is *bad*, or *of an evil Nature*, or *has badness* as a quality inherent in it: and a *good* effect

effect in the will muſt be *good*, by reaſon of the *goodneſs* of the Cauſe, or its being *of a good Kind and Nature*. And if this be what is meant, the very ſuppoſition of fault and praiſe lying not in the Nature of the thing, but the Cauſe, contradicts itſelf, and does at leaſt reſolve the Eſſence of virtue and vice into the Nature of things, and ſuppoſes it originally to conſiſt in that.—And if a caviller has a mind to run from the abſurdity, by ſaying, "No, the fault of the thing which is the Cauſe, lies not in this, that the Cauſe itſelf is *of an evil Nature*, but that the Cauſe is evil in that ſenſe, that it is from another bad Cauſe." Still the abſurdity will follow him; for, if ſo, then the Cauſe before charged is at once acquitted, and all the blame muſt be laid to the higher Cauſe, and muſt conſiſt in that's being *evil*, or *of an evil Nature*. So now, we are come again to lay the blame of the thing blame-worthy, to the Nature of the thing, and not to the Cauſe. And if any is ſo fooliſh as to go higher ſtill, and aſcend from ſtep to ſtep, till he is come to that, which is the firſt Cauſe concerned in the whole affair, and will ſay, all the blame lies in that; then, at laſt, he muſt be forced to own, that the faultineſs of the thing, which he ſuppoſes alone blame-worthy, lies wholly *in the Nature* of the thing, and not in the Original or Cauſe of it; for the ſuppoſition is, that it has no Original, it is determined by no act of our's, is cauſed by nothing faulty in us, being abſolutely *without any Cauſe*. And ſo the race is at an end, but the evader is taken in his flight.

It is agreable to the natural notions of mankind; that moral evil, with its deſert of diſlike and abhorrence, and all its other ill-deſervings, conſiſts in a certain *deformity* in the *Nature* of certain diſpoſitions of the heart and acts of the will;

will; and not in the deformity of *ſomething elſe*, diverſe from the very thing itſelf, which deſerves abhorrence, ſuppoſed to be the Cauſe of it. Which would be abſurd, becauſe that would be to ſuppoſe a thing, that is innocent and not evil, is truly evil and faulty, becauſe another thing is evil. It implies a contradiction; for it would be to ſuppoſe, the very thing, which is morally evil and blame-worthy, is innocent and not blame-worthy; but that ſomething elſe, which is its Cauſe, is only to blame. To ſay, that vice does not conſiſt in the thing which is vicious, but in its Cauſe, is the ſame as to ſay, that vice does not conſiſt in vice, but in that which produces it.

It is true, a Cauſe may be to blame, for being the cauſe of vice: it may be wickedneſs in the Cauſe, that it produces wickedneſs. But it would imply a contradiction, to ſuppoſe that theſe two are the ſame individual wickedneſs. The wicked act of the Cauſe in producing wickedneſs, is one wickedneſs; and the wickedneſs produced, if there be any produced, is another. And therefore, the wickedneſs of the latter does not lie in the former, but is diſtinct from it: and the wickedneſs of both lies in the *evil Nature* of the things, which are wicked.

The thing, which makes ſin hateful, is that by which it deſerves puniſhment; which is but the expreſſion of hatred. And that, which renders virtue lovely, is the ſame with that, on the account of which, it is fit to receive praiſe and reward; which are but the expreſſions of eſteem and love. But that which makes vice hateful, is its hateful Nature; and that which renders virtue lovely, is its amiable Nature. It is a certain beauty or deformity that are *inherent* in that good

good or evil will, which is the *ſoul* of virtue and vice (and not in the *occaſion* of it) which is their worthineſs of eſteem or diſeſteem, praiſe or diſpraiſe, according to the common ſenſe of mankind. If the Cauſe or occaſion of the riſe of an hateful diſpoſition or act of will, be alſo hateful; ſuppoſe another antecedent evil will; that is entirely another ſin, and deſerves puniſhment by itſelf, under a diſtinct conſideration. There is worthineſs of diſpraiſe in the Nature of an evil volition, and not wholly in ſome foregoing act, which is its Cauſe; otherwiſe the evil volition, which is the effect, is no moral evil, any more than ſickneſs, or ſome other natural calamity, which ariſes from a Cauſe morally evil.

Thus, for inſtance, ingratitude is hateful and worthy of diſpraiſe, according to common ſenſe; not becauſe ſomething as bad, or worſe than ingratitude, was the Cauſe that produced it; but becauſe it is hateful in itſelf, by its own inherent deformity. So the love of virtue is amiable, and worthy of praiſe, not merely becauſe ſomething elſe went before this love of virtue in our minds, which cauſed it to take place there; for inſtance, our own choice; we choſe to love virtue, and, by ſome method or other, wrought ourſelves into the love of it; but becauſe of the amiableneſs and condeſcendency of ſuch a diſpoſition and inclination of heart. If that *was* the caſe, that we *did* chuſe to love virtue, and ſo produced that love in ourſelves, this choice itſelf could be no otherwiſe amiable or praiſe worthy, than as love to virtue, or ſome other amiable inclination, was exerciſed and implied in it. If that choice was amiable at all, it muſt be ſo on account of ſome amiable quality in the Nature of the choice. If we choſe to love virtue,

T not

not in love to virtue, or any thing that was good, and exerciſed no ſort of good diſpoſition in the choice, the choice itſelf was not virtuous, nor worthy of any praiſe, according to common ſenſe, becauſe the choice was not of a *good Nature.*

It may not be improper here to take notice of ſomething ſaid by an author, that has lately made a mighty noiſe in *America.* "A neceſſary holineſs (ſays he*) is no holineſs.——*Adam* could not be originally created in righteouſneſs and true holineſs, becauſe he muſt *chuſe* to be righteous, *before* he could be righteous. And therefore he muſt exiſt, he muſt be created, yea, he muſt exerciſe thought and reflection, before he was righteous." There is much more to the ſame effect in that place, and alſo in p. 437, 438, 439, 440. If theſe things are ſo, it will certainly follow, that the firſt chuſing to be righteous is no righteous choice; there is no righteouſneſs or holineſs in it; becauſe no chuſing to be righteous goes before it. For he plainly ſpeaks of *chuſing to be righteous,* as what *muſt go before righteouſneſs:* and that which follows the choice, being the effect of the choice, cannot be righteouſneſs or holineſs: for an effect is a thing neceſſary, and cannot prevent the influence or efficacy of its Cauſe; and therefore is unavoidably dependent upon the Cauſe: and he ſays, *a neceſſary holineſs is no holineſs.* So that neither can a choice of righteouſneſs be righteouſneſs or holineſs, nor can any thing that is conſequent on that choice, and the effect of it, be righteouſneſs or holineſs; nor can any thing that is without choice, be righteouſneſs or holi-

* Scrip. Doc. of *Original Sin,* p. 180. 3d. Edit.

Dr. John Taylor

neſs.

ness. So that by his scheme, all righteousness and holiness is at once shut out of the world, and no door left open, by which it can ever possibly enter into the world.

I SUPPOSE, the way, that men came to entertain this absurd inconsistent notion, with respect to *internal inclinations and volitions* themselves, (or notions that imply it,) *viz.* that the Essence of their moral good or evil lies not in their Nature, but their Cause; was, that it is indeed a very plain dictate of common sence, that it is so with respect to all *outward actions*, and sensible motions of the body; that the moral good or evil of them does not lie at all in the motions themselves; which, taken by themselves, are nothing of a moral nature; and the Essence of all the moral good or evil that concerns them, lies in those internal dispositions and volitions, which are the Cause of them. Now, being always used to determine this, without hesitation or dispute, concerning *external Actions*; which are the things, that in the common use of language are signified by such phrases, as men's *actions*, or their *doings*; hence, when they came to speak of volitions, and *internal exercises* and their inclinations, under the same denominations of their *actions*, or *what they do*, they unwarily determined the case must also be the same with these, as with *external actions*; not considering the vast difference in the Nature of the case.

IF any shall still object and say, why is it not necessary that the Cause should be considered, in order to determine whether any thing be worthy of blame or praise? is it agreable to reason and common sense, that a man is to be praised or blamed

blamed for that, which he is not the Cauſe or author of, and has no hand in?

I ANSWER, ſuch phraſes as *being the Cauſe*, *being the author*, *having a hand*, and the like, are ambiguous. They are moſt vulgarly underſtood for being the deſigning voluntary Cauſe, or Cauſe by antecedent choice: and it is moſt certain, that men are not, in this ſenſe, the Cauſes or authors of the firſt act of their wills, in any caſe; as certain as any thing is, or ever can be; for nothing can be more certain, than that a thing is not before it is, nor a thing of the ſame kind before the firſt thing of that kind; and ſo no choice before the firſt choice.—As the phraſe, *being the author*, may be underſtood, not of being the producer by an antecedent act of will; but as a perſon may be ſaid to be the author of the act of will itſelf, by his being the immediate agent, or the being that *is acting*, or *in exerciſe* in that act; if the phraſe of *being the author*, is uſed to ſignify this, then doubtleſs common ſenſe requires men's being the authors of their own acts of will, in order to their being eſteemed worthy of praiſe or diſpraiſe, on account of them. And common ſenſe teaches, that they muſt be the authors of *external actions*, in the former ſenſe, namely, their being the Cauſes of them by an act of will or choice, in order to their being juſtly blamed or praiſed: but it teaches no ſuch thing with reſpect to the acts of the will themſelves:——But this may appear more manifeſt by the things, which will be obſerved in the following ſection.

S E C-

SECTION II.

The Falseness and Inconsistence of that metaphysical Notion of Action, *and* Agency, *which seems to be generally entertained by the Defenders of the* Arminian *Doctrine concerning Liberty, moral Agency,* &c.

ONE thing, that is made very much a ground of argument and supposed demonstration by *Arminians*, in defence of the fore-mentioned principles, concerning moral agency, virtue, vice, &c. is their metaphysical notion of *Agency* and *Action*. They say, unless the soul has a self-determining power, it has no power of *Action*; if its volitions be not caused by itself, but are excited, and determined by some extrinsic cause, they cannot be the soul's own *acts*; and that the soul cannot be *active*, but must be wholly *passive*, in those effects which it is the subject of necessarily, and not from its own free determination.

Mr. *Chubb* lays the foundation of his scheme of liberty, and of his arguments to support it, very much in this position, that *man is an agent, and capable of action*. Which doubtless is true: but *self-determination* belongs to his notion of *Action*, and is the very essence of it. Whence he infers that it is impossible for a man to act and be acted upon, in the same thing, at the same time; and that nothing, that is an action, can be the effect of the action of another: and he insists, that a *necessary Agent*, or an Agent that is necessarily determined to act, is a *plain contradiction*.

But those are a precarious sort of demonstration, which men build on the meaning that they arbitarily affix to a word; especially when that meaning is abstruse, inconsistent, and intirely diverse from the original sense of the word in common speech.

That the meaning of the word *Action*, as Mr. *Chubb* and many others use it, is utterly unintelligible and inconsistent, is manifest, because it belongs to their notion of an Action, that it is something wherein is no passion or passiveness; that is (according to their sense of passiveness) it is under the power, influence or action of no cause. And this implies, that Action has no cause, and is no effect; for to be an effect implies *passiveness*, or the being subject to the power and Action of its cause. And yet they hold, that the mind's *Action* is the effect of its own determination, yea, the mind's free and voluntary determination; which is the same with free choice. So that Action is the effect of something preceding, even a preceding act of choice: and consequently, in this effect the mind is passive, subject to the power and Action of the preceding cause, which is the foregoing choice, and therefore cannot be active. So that here we have this contradiction, that action is always the effect of foregoing choice; and therefore cannot be Action; because it is *passive* to the power of that preceding causal choice; and the mind cannot be active and passive in the same thing, at the same time. Again, they say, necessity is utterly inconsistent with Action, and a necessary Action is a contradiction: and so their notion of Action implies contingence, and excludes all necessity. And therefore, their notion of Action implies, that it has no necessary dependence or connection with any

any thing foregoing; for such a dependence or connectton excludes contingence, and implies necessity. And yet their notion of Action implies necessity, and supposes that it is necessary, and cannot be contingent. For they suppose, that whatever is properly called Action, must be determined by the will and free choice; and this is as much as to say, that it must be necessary, being dependent upon, and determined by something foregoing; namely, a foregoing act of choice. Again, it belongs to their notion of Action, of that which is a proper and mere act, that it is the beginning of motion, or of exertion of power; but yet it is implied in their notion of Action, that it is not the beginning of motion or exertion of power, but is consequent and dependent on a preceding exertion of power, *viz.* the power of will and choice: for they say there is no proper Action but what is freely *chosen*; or, which is the same thing, determined by a foregoing act of free choice. But if any of them shall see cause to deny this, and say they hold no such thing as that every Action is chosen or determined by a foregoing choice; but that the very first exertion of will only, undetermined by any preceding act, as properly called Action; then I say, such a man's notion of Action implies necessity; for what the mind is the subject of, without the determination of its own previous choice, it is the subject of necessarily, as to any hand, that free choice has in the affair, and, without any ability, the mind has to prevent it, by any will or election of its own; because by the supposition it precludes all previous acts of the will or choice in the case, which might prevenr it. So that it is again, in this other way, implied in their notion of act, that it is both necessary and not necessary. Again, it belongs to their notion of an *act*, that it is no effect of a pre-determining bias or preponderation, but ſprings immediately out of indifference; and this implies, that it cannot be from foregoing choice, which is foregoing preponderation: if it be not habitual, but occaſional, yet if it cauſes the act, it is truly previous, efficacious and determining. And yet, at the ſame time, it is eſſential to their notion of the act, that it is what the Agent is the Author of freely and voluntarily, and that is, by previous choice and deſign.

So that, according to their notion of the act, conſidered with regard to its conſequences, theſe following things are all eſſential to it; *viz.* That it ſhould be neceſſary, and not neceſſary; that it ſhould be from a cauſe, and no cauſe; that it ſhould be the fruit of choice and deſign, and not the fruit of choice and deſign; that it ſhould be the beginning of motion or exertion, and yet conſequent on previous exertion; that it ſhould be before it *is*; that it ſhould ſpring immdiately out of indifference and equilibrium, and yet be the effect of preponderation; that it ſhould be ſelf-originated, and alſo have its original from ſomething elſe; that it is what the mind cauſes itſelf, of its own will, and can produce or prevent, according to its choice or pleaſure, and yet what the mind has no power to prevent, precluding all previous choice in the affair.

So that an act, according to their metaphyſical notion of it, is ſomething of which there is no idea; it is nothing but a confuſion of the mind, excited by words without any diſtinct meaning, and is an abſolute non-entity; and that in two reſpects: (1.) There is nothing in the world that ever was, is, or can be, to anſwer the things which

which must belong to its description, according to what they suppose to be essential to it. And (2.) There neither is, nor ever was, nor can be, any notion or idea to answer the word, as they use and explain it. For if we should suppose any such notion, it would many ways destroy itself. But it is impossible any idea or notion should subsist in the mind, whose very nature and essence, which constitutes it, destroys it.—If some learned philosopher, who had been abroad, in giving an account of the curious observations he had made in his travels, should say, "He had been in *Terra del Fuego*, and there had seen an animal, which he calls by a certain name, that begat and brought forth itself, and yet had a sire and dam distinct from itself; that it had an appetite, and was hungry before it had a being; that his master, who led him, and governed him at his pleasure, was always governed by him, and driven by him where he pleased; that when he moved, he always took a step before the first step; that he went with his head first, and yet always went tail foremost; and this, though he had neither head nor tail:" it would be no impudence at all, to tell such a traveller, though a learned man, that he himself had no notion or idea of such an animal, as he gave an account of, and never had, nor ever would have.

As the forementioned notion of Action is very inconsistent, so it is wholly diverse from the original meaning of the word. The more usual signification of it, in vulgar speech, seems to be some *motion* or *exertion of power*, that is voluntary, or that is *the effect of the will*; and is used in the same sense as *doing*: and most commonly it is used to signify *outward Actions*. So *thinking* is often

often diſtinguiſhed from *acting*; and *deſiring* and *willing*, from *doing*.

Besides this more uſual and proper ſignification of the word *Action*, there are other ways in which the word is uſed, that are leſs proper, which yet have place in common ſpeech Oftentimes it is uſed to ſignify ſome motion or alteration in inanimate things, with relation to ſome object and effect. So the ſpring of a watch is ſaid to *act* upon the chain and wheels; the ſun-beams, to act upon plants and trees; and the fire, to act upon wood. Sometimes, the word is uſed to ſignify motions, alterations, and exertions of power, which are ſeen in corporal things, *conſidered abſolutely*; eſpecially when theſe motions ſeem to ariſe from ſome internal cauſe which is *hidden*; ſo that they have a greater reſemblance of thoſe motions of our bodies, which are the effects of natural volition, or inviſible exertions of will. So the fermentation of liquor, the operations of the loadſtone, and of electrical bodies, are called the *Action* of theſe things. And ſometimes, the word *Action* is uſed to ſignify the exerciſe of thought, or of will and inclination: ſo meditating, loving, hating, inclining, diſinclining, chuſing and refuſing, may be ſometimes called acting; though more rarely (unleſs it be by philoſophers and metaphyſicians) than in any of the other ſenſes.

But the word is never uſed in vulgar ſpeech in that ſenſe, which *Arminian* divines uſe it in, namely, for the ſelf-determinate exerciſe of the will, or an exertion of the ſoul that ariſes without any neceſſary connection, with any thing foregoing. If a man does ſomething voluntarily, or as the effect of his choice, then in the moſt proper

per ſenſe, and as the word is moſt originally and commonly uſed, he is ſaid to *act:* but whether that choice or volition be ſelf determined, or no, whether it be connected with foregoing habitual bias, whether it be the certain effect of the ſtrongeſt motive, or ſome intrinſic cauſe, never comes into conſideration in the meaning of the word.

And if the word *action* is arbitarily uſed by ſome men otherwiſe, to ſuit ſome ſcheme of metaphyſic or morality, no argument can reaſonably be founded on ſuch a uſe of this term, to prove any thing but their own pleaſure. For divines and philoſophers ſtrenuouſly to urge ſuch arguments, as though they were ſufficient to ſupport and demonſtrate a whole ſcheme of moral philoſophy and divinity, is certainly to erect a mighty edifice on the ſand, or rather on a ſhadow. And though it may now perhaps, through cuſtom, have become natural for them to uſe the word in this ſenſe (if that may be called a ſenſe or meaning, which is inconſiſtent with itſelf) yet this does not prove, that it is agreable to the natural notions men have of things, or that there can be any thing in the creation that ſhould anſwer ſuch a meaning. And though they appeal to experience, yet the truth is, that men are ſo far from experiencing any ſuch thing, that it is impoſſible for them to have any conception of it.

If it ſhould be objected, that *Action* and *Paſſion* are doubtleſs words of a contrary ſignification; but to ſuppoſe that the Agent, in its Action, is under the power and influence of ſomething intrinſic, is to confound Action and Paſſion, and make them the ſame thing.

I an-

I ANSWER, that Action and Passion are doubtless, as they are sometimes used, words of opposite signification; but not as signifying opposite *existences*, but only opposite *relations*. The words *cause* and *effect* are terms of opposite signification; but, nevertheless, if I assert, that the same thing may, at the same time, in different respects and relations, be both *cause* and *effect*, this will not prove that I confound the terms. The soul may be both *active* and *passive* in the same thing in different respects; *active* with relation to one thing, and *passive* with relation to another. The word *Passion*, when set in opposition to *Action*, or rather *activeness*, is merely a relative: it signifies no effect or cause, nor any proper existence; but is the same with *Passiveness*, or a being passive, or a being acted upon by some thing. Which is a mere relation of a thing to some power or force exerted by some cause, producing some effect in it, or upon it. And *Action*, when set properly in opposition to *Passion*, or *Passiveness*, is no real existence; it is not the same with *AN Action*, but is a mere relation: it is the *Activeness* of something on another thing, being the opposite relation to the other, *viz.* a relation of power, or force, exerted by some cause, towards another thing, which is the subject of the effect of that power. Indeed, the word *action* is frequently used to signify something not merely *relative*, but more *absolute*, and a real existence; as when we say *an Action*; when the word is not used transitively, but absolutely, for some motion or exercise of body or mind, without any relation to any object or effect: and as used thus, it is not properly the opposite of *Passion*; which ordinarily signifies nothing absolute, but merely the *relation of being acted upon*. And therefore if the word *Action* be used in the like relative sense, then

then Action and Passion are only two contrary relations. And it is no absurdity to suppose, that contrary relations may belong to the same thing, at the same time, with respect to different things. So to suppose, that there are acts of the soul by which a man voluntarily moves, and acts upon objects, and produces effects, which yet themselves are effects of something else, and wherein the soul itself is the object of something acting upon, and influencing that, do not at all confound Action and Passion. The words may nevertheless be properly of opposite signification: there may be as true and real a difference between *acting* and being *caused to act*, though we should suppose the soul to be both in the same volition, as there is between *living* and *being quickened*, or *made to live*. It is no more a contradiction, to suppose that Action may be the effect of some other cause, besides the Agent, or Being that acts, than to suppose, that life may be the effect of some other cause, besides the Liver, or the Being that lives, in whom life is caused to be.

The thing which has led men into this inconsistent notion of Action, when applied to volition, as though it were essential to this internal Action, that the Agent should be self-determined in it, and that the will should be the cause of it, was probably this; that according to the sense of mankind, and the common use of language, it is so, with respect to men's external Actions; which are what originally, and according to the vulgar use and most proper sense of the word, are called *Actions*. Men in these are self-directed, self determined, and their wills are the cause of the motions of their bodies, and the external things that are done; so that unless men do them voluntarily, and of choice, and the Action be deter-

determined by their antecedent volition, it is no Action or Doing of theirs. Hence some metaphysicians have been led unwarily, but exceeding absurdly, to suppose the same concerning volition itself, that *that* also must be determined by the will; which is to be determined by antecedent volition, as the motion of the body is; not considering the contradiction it implies.

But it is very evident, that in the metaphysical distinction between Action and Passion (though long since become common and the general vogue) due care has not been taken to conform language to the nature of things, or to any distinct clear ideas. As it is in innumerable other philosophical, metaphysical terms, used in these disputes; which has occasioned inexpressible difficulty, contention, error and confusion.

And thus probably it came to be thought, that necessity was inconsistent with Action, as these terms are applied to volition. First, these terms *Action* and *Necessity* are changed from their original meaning, as signifying external voluntary Action and Constraint, (in which meaning they are evidently inconsistent) to signify quite other things, *viz.* volition itself, and certainty of existence. And when the change of signification is made, care is not taken to make proper allowances and abatements for the difference of sense; but still the same things are unwarily attributed to *Action* and *Necessity*, in the new meaning of the words, which plainly belonged to them in their first sense; and on this ground, maxims are established without any real foundation, as though they were the most certain truths, and the most evident dictates of reason.

But

But however ftrenuoufly it is maintained, that what is neceffary cannot be properly called Action, and that a neceffary Action is a contradiction, yet it is probably there are few *Arminian* divines, who, if thorougly tried, would ftand to thefe principles. They will allow, that God is, in the higheft fenfe, an active Being, and the higheft Fountain of Life and Action; and they would not probably deny, that thofe, that are called God's acts of righteoufnefs, holinefs and faithfulnefs, are truly and properly God's *acts*, and God is really a holy *Agent* in them; and yet, I truft, they will not deny, that God neceffarily acts juftly and faithfully, and that it is impoffible for Him to act unrighteoufly and unholily.

SECTION III.

The Reafons why fome think it contrary to common Senfe, *to fuppofe thofe Things which are* neceffary, *to be worthy of either* Praife *or* Blame.

IT is abundantly affirmed and urged by *Arminian* writers, that it is contrary to *common Senfe*, and the natural notions and apprehenfions of mankind, to fuppofe otherwife than that neceffity (making no diftinction between natural and moral neceffity) is inconfiftent with Virtue and Vice, Praife and Blame, Reward and Punifhment. And their arguments from hence have been greatly triumphed in; and have been not a little perplexing to many, who have been friendly to the truth, as clearly revealed in the holy Scriptures: it has feemed to them indeed difficult, to reconcile *Calviniftic* doctrines with the notions, men commonly have of juftice and equity. And the

the true reasons of it seem to be these that follow.

I. It is indeed a very plain dictate of common Sense, that natural necessity is wholly inconsistent with just Praise or Blame. If men do things which in themselves are very good, fit to be brought to pass, and very happy effects, properly against their wills, and cannot help it; or do them from a necessity that is without their wills, or with which their wills have no concern or connection; then it is a plain dictate of common sense, that it is none of their virtue, nor any moral good in them; and that they are not worthy to be rewarded or praised; or at all esteemed, honoured or loved on that account. And, on the other hand, that if, from like necessity, they do those things which in themselves are very unhappy and pernicious, and do them, because they cannot help it; the necessity is such, that it is all one whether they will them, or no; and the reason why they are done, is from necessity only, and not from their wills; it is a very plain dictate of common Sense, that they are not at all to blame; there is no vice, fault, or moral evil at all in the effect done; nor are they, who are thus necessitated, in any wise worthy to be punished, hated, or in the least disrespected, on that account.

In like manner, if things, in themselves good and desirable, are absolutely impossible, with a natural impossibily, the universal reason of mankind teaches, that this *wholly and perfectly* excuses persons in their not doing them.

And it is also a plain dictate of common Sense, that if the doing things, in themselves good, or avoid-

avoiding things in themſelves evil, is not *abſolutely impoſſible*, with ſuch a natural impoſſibility, but very *difficult*, with a natural difficulty; that is, a difficulty prior *to*, and not at all conſiſting *in* will and inclination itſelf, and which would remain the ſame, let the inclination be what it will; then a perſon's neglect or omiſſion is excuſed *in ſome meaſure*, though not wholly; his ſin is leſs aggravated, than if the thing to be done were eaſy. And if inſtead of difficulty and hinderance, there be a contrary natural propenſity in the ſtate of things, to the thing to be done, or effect to be brought to paſs, abſtracted from any conſideration of the inclination of the heart; though the propenſity be not ſo great as to mount to a natural neceſſity; yet being ſome approach to it, ſo that the doing the good thing be very much from this natural tendency in the ſtate of things, and but little from a good inclination; then it is a dictate of common Senſe, that there is ſo much the leſs virtue in what is done; and ſo it is leſs praiſe-worthy and rewardable. The reaſon is eaſy, *viz.* becauſe ſuch a natural propenſity or tendency is an approach to natural neceſſity; and the greater the propenſity, ſtill ſo much the nearer is the approach to neceſſity. And, therefore, as natural neceſſity takes away or ſhuts out *all* virtue, ſo this propenſity approaches to an abolition of virtue; that is, it *diminiſhes* it. And, on the other hand, natural difficulty, in the ſtate of things, is an approach to natural impoſſibility. And as the latter, when it is compleat and abſoſolute, *wholly* takes away Blame; ſo ſuch difficulty takes away *ſome* Blame, or diminiſhes Blame; and makes the things done to be leſs worthy of puniſhment.

II. Men, in their firft ufe of fuch phrafes as thefe, *muft*, *cannot*, *cannot help it*, *cannot avoid it*, *neceffary*, *unable*, *impoffible*, *unavoidable*, *irrefiftible*, &c. ufe them to fignify a neceffity of conftraint or reftraint, a natural neceffity or impoffibility; or fome neceffity that the will has nothing to do in; which may be, whether men will or no; and which may be fuppofed to be juft the fame, let men's inclinations and defires be what they will. Such kind of terms in their original ufe, I fuppofe, among all nations, are relative; carrying in their fignification (as was before obferved) a reference or refpect to fome contrary will, defire or endeavour, which, it is fuppofed, is, or may be, in the cafe. All men find, and begin to find in early childhood, that there are innumerable things that cannot be done, which they defire to do; and innumerable things which they are averfe to, that muft be, they cannot avoid them, they will be, whether they chufe them or no. It is to exprefs this neceffity, which men fo foon and fo often find, and which fo greatly and early affects them in innumerable cafes, that fuch terms and phrafes are firft formed; and it is to fignify fuch a neceffity, that they are firft ufed, and that they are moft conftantly ufed, in the common affairs of life; and not to fignify any fuch metaphyfical, fpeculative and abftract notion, as that connection in the nature or courfe of things, which is between the fubject and predicate of a propofition, and which is the foundation of the certain truth of that propofition; to fignify which, they who employ themfelves in philofophical inquiries into the firft origin and metaphyfical relations and dependences of things, have borrowed thefe terms, for want of others. But we grow up from our cradles in a ufe of fuch terms and phrafes entirely different from this, and

and carrying a ſenſe exceeding diverſe from that, in which they are commonly uſed in the controverſy between *Arminians* and *Calviniſts*. And it being, as was ſaid before, a dictate of the univerſal ſenſe of mankind, evident to us as ſoon as we begin to think, that the neceſſity ſignified by theſe terms, in the ſenſe in which we firſt learn them, does excuſe perſons, and free them from all Fault or Blame; hence our ideas of excuſableneſs or faultleſſneſs is tied to theſe terms and phraſes by a ſtrong habit, which is begun in childhood, as ſoon as we begin to ſpeak, and grows up with us, and is ſtrengthened by conſtant uſe and cuſtom, the connection growing ſtronger and ſtronger.

The habitual connection, which is in men's minds between Blameleſſneſs and thoſe forementioned terms, *muſt*, *cannot*, *unable*, *neceſſary*, *impoſſible*, *unavoidable*, &c. becomes very ſtrong; becauſe, as ſoon as ever men begin to uſe reaſon and ſpeech they have occaſion to excuſe themſelves, from the natural neceſſity ſignified by theſe terms, in numerous inſtances.—*I cannot do it—I could not help it.*—And all mankind have conſtant and daily occaſion to uſe ſuch phraſes in this ſenſe, to excuſe themſelves and others, in almoſt all the concerns of life, with reſpect to diſappointments, and things that happen, which concern and affect ourſelves and others, that are hurtful, or diſagreeable to us or them, or things deſirable, that we or others fail of.

That a being accuſtomed to an union of different ideas, from early childhood, makes the habitual connection exceeding ſtrong, as though ſuch connection were owing to *nature*, is manifeſt in innumerable inſtances. It is altogether by ſuch an habitual connection of ideas, that men judge of the bigness or distance of the objects of sight, from their appearance. Thus it is owing to such a connection early established, and growing up with a person, that he judges a mountain, which he sees at ten miles distance, to be bigger than his nose, or further off than the end of it. Having been used so long to join a considerable distance and magnitude with such an appearance, men imagine it is by a dictate of natural sense: whereas, it would be quite otherwise with one that had his eyes newly opened, who had been born blind: he would have the same visible appearance, but natural sense would dictate no such thing, concerning the magnitude or distance of what appeared.

III. When men, after they had been so habituated to connect ideas of Innocency or Blamelessness with such terms, that the union seems to be the effect of mere nature, come to hear the same terms used, and learn to use them themselves in the forementioned new and metaphysical sense, to signify quite another sort of necessity, which has no such kind of relation to a contrary supposable will and endeavour; the notion of plain and manifest Blamelessness, by this means, is, by a strong prejudice, insensibly and unwarily transferred to a case to which it by no means belongs: the change of the use of the terms, to a signification which is very diverse, not being taken notice of, or adverted to. And there are several reasons, why it is not.

1. The terms, as used by philosophers, are not very distinct and clear in their meaning: few use them in a fixed determined sense. On the contrary, their meaning is very vague and confused. Which is what commonly appears to the

words

words uſed to ſignify things intellectual and moral, and to expreſs what Mr. *Locke* calls *mixt modes*. If men had a clear and diſtinct underſtanding of what is intended by theſe metaphyſical terms, they would be able more eaſily to compare them with their original and common Senſe; and ſo would not be ſo eaſily led into deluſion by no ſort of terms in the world, as by words of this ſort.

2. The change of the ſignification of the terms is the more inſenſible, becauſe the things ſignified, though indeed very different, yet do in ſome generals agree. In *neceſſity*, that which is *vulgarly* ſo called, there is a ſtrong connection between the thing ſaid to be neceſſary, and ſomething antecedent to it, in the order of nature; ſo there is alſo in *philoſophical neceſſity*. And though in both kinds of neceſſity, the connection cannot be called by that name, with relation to an oppoſite will or endeavour, to which it is *ſuperior*; which is the caſe in vulgar neceſſity; yet in both, the connection is *prior* to will and endeavour, and ſo, in ſome reſpect, *ſuperior*. In both kinds of neceſſity, there is a foundation for ſome certainty of the propoſition, that affirms the event.—The terms uſed being the ſame, and the things ſignified agreeing in theſe and ſome other general circumſtances, and the expreſſions as uſed by philoſophers being not well defined, and ſo of obſcure and looſe ſignification; hence perſons are not aware of the great difference; had the notions of innocence or faultineſs, which were ſo ſtrongly aſſociated with them, and were ſtrictly united in their minds, ever ſince they can remember, remain united with them ſtill, as if the union were altogether natural and neceſſary; and they

that go about to make a separation, seem to them to do great violence even to nature itself.

IV. Another reason why it appears difficult to reconcile it with reason, that men should be blamed for that which is necessary with a moral necessity (which, as was observed before, is a species of philosophical necessity) is, that for want of due consideration, men inwardly entertain that apprehension, that this necessity may be against men's wills and sincere endeavours. They go away with that notion, that men may truly will, and wish and strive that it may be otherwise; but that invincible necessity stands in the way. And many think thus concerning themselves: some, that are wicked men, think they wish that they were good, that they loved God and holiness: but yet do not find that their wishes produce the effect.—The reasons, why men think, are as follow: (1.) They find what may be called an *indirect willingness* to have a better will, in the manner before observed. For it is impossible, and a contradiction to suppose the will to be directly and properly against itself. And they do not consider, that this indirect willingness is entirely a different thing from properly willing the thing that is the duty and virtue required; and that there is no virtue in that sort of willingness which they have. They do not consider, that the volitions, which a wicked man may have that he loved God, are no acts of the will at all against the moral evil of not loving God; but only some disagreable consequences. But the making the requisite distinction requires more care of reflection and thought, than most men are used to. And men, through a prejudice in their own favour, are disposed to think well of their own desires and dispositions, and to account them good and virtuous, though their respect to virtue

tue be only *indirect* and *remote*, and it is nothing at all that is virtuous that truly excites or terminates their inclination. (2.) Another thing, that inſenſibly leads and beguiles men into a ſuppoſition that this moral neceſſity or impoſſibility is, or may be, againſt men's wills and true endeavours, is the derivation and formation of the terms themſelves, that are often uſed to expreſs it, which is ſuch as ſeems directly to point to, and holds this forth. Such words, for inſtance, as *unable*, *unavoidable*, *impoſſible*, *irreſtible*; which carry a plain reference to a ſuppoſable power exerted, endeavours uſed, reſiſtence made, in oppoſition to the neceſſity: and the perſons that hear them, not conſidering nor ſuſpecting, but that they are uſed in their proper ſenſe: that ſenſe being therefore underſtood, there does naturally, and as it were neceſſarily ariſe in their minds a ſuppoſition, that it may be ſo indeed, that true deſires and endeavours may take place, but that invincible neceſſity ſtands in the way, and renders them vain and to no effect.

V. Another thing, which makes perſons more ready to ſuppoſe it to be contrary to reaſon, that men ſhould be expoſed to the puniſhments threatened to ſin, for doing thoſe things which are morally neceſſary, or not doing thoſe things morally impoſſible, is, that imagination ſtrengthens the argument, and adds greatly to the power and influence of the ſeeming reaſons againſt it, from the greatneſs of that puniſhment. To allow that they may be juſtly expoſed to a ſmall puniſhment, would not be ſo difficult. Whereas, if there were any good reaſon in the caſe, if it were truly a dictate of reaſon, that ſuch neceſſity was inconſiſtent with faultineſs, or juſt puniſhment, the demonſtration would be equally certain with reſpect to a ſmall puniſhment, or any puniſhment at all, as a very great one: but it is not equally eaſy to the imagination. They that argue againſt the juſtice of *damning* men for thoſe things that are thus neceſſary, ſeem to make their argument the ſtronger, by ſetting forth the greatneſs of the puniſhment in ſtrong expreſſions:—*That a man ſhould be caſt into eternal burnings, that he ſhould be made to fry in hell to all eternity for thoſe things which he had no power to avoid, and was under a fatal, unfruſtrable, invincible neceſſity of doing.*——

SECTION IV.

It is agreable to common Senſe, *and* the natural Notions of Mankind, *to ſuppoſe moral Neceſſity to be conſiſtent with Praiſe and Blame, Reward and Puniſhment.*

WHETHER the reaſons, that have been given, why it appears difficult to ſome perſons, to reconcile with common Senſe the praiſing or blaming, rewarding or puniſhing thoſe things which are morally neceſſary, are thought ſatisfactory, or not; yet it moſt evidently appears, by the following things, that if this matter be rightly underſtood, ſetting aſide all deluſion ariſing from the impropriety and ambiguity of terms, this is not at all inconſiſtent with the natural apprehenſions of mankind, and that ſenſe of things which is found every where in the common people; who are furtheſt from having their thoughts perverted from their natural channel, by metaphyſical and philoſophical ſubtilties; but, on the contrary, altogether agreable *to*, and the very

very voice and dictate *of* this natural and vulgar Senſe.

I. This will appear, if we conſider what the vulgar Notion of *blame-worthineſs* is. The idea, which the common people, through all ages and nations, have of faultineſs, I ſuppoſe to be plainly this; *a perſon's being or doing wrong, with his own will and pleaſure*; containing theſe two things; 1. *His doing wrong, when he does as he pleaſes.* 2. *His pleaſures being wrong.* Or, in other words, perhaps more intelligibly expreſſing their Notion; *a perſon having his heart wrong, and doing wrong from his heart.* And this is the ſum total of the matter.

The common people do not aſcend up in their reflections and abſtractions to the metaphyſical ſources, relations and dependencies of things, in order to form their Notion of faultineſs or blame-worthineſs. They do not wait till they have decided by their refinings, what firſt determines the will; whether it be determined by ſomething extrinſic, or intrinſic; whether volition determines volition, or whether the underſtanding determines the will; whether there be any ſuch thing as metaphyſicians mean by contingence (if they have any meaning;) whether there be a ſort of a ſtrange unaccountable ſovereignty in the will, in the exerciſe of which, by its own ſovereign acts, it brings to paſs all its own ſovereign acts. They do not take any part of their Notion of fault or blame from the reſolution of any ſuch queſtions. If this were the caſe, there are multitudes, yea the far greater part of mankind, nine hundred and ninety-nine out of a thouſand, would live and die, without having any ſuch Notion, as that of fault, ever entering into their heads,

heads, or without so much as one having any conception that any body was to be either blamed or commended for any thing. To be sure, it would be a long time before men came to have such Notions. Whereas it is manifest, they are some of the first Notions that appear in children; who discover, as soon as they can think, or speak, or act at all as rational creatures, a Sense of desert. And, certainly, in forming their Notion of it, they make no use of metaphysics. All the ground they go upon, consists in these two things; *experience* and a *natural sensation* of a certain fitness or agreeableness, which there is in uniting such moral evil as is above described, *viz. a being or doing wrong with the will*, and resentment in others, and pain inflicted on the person in whom this moral evil is. Which *natural Sense* is what we call by the name of *conscience.*

It is true, the common people and children, in their Notion of any faulty act or deed, of any person, do suppose that it is the person's *own act and deed.* But this is all that belongs, to what they understand by a thing's being a person's *own deed or action*; even that it is something done by him of choice. That some exercise or motion should begin of itself, does not belong to their Notion of *an action*, or *doing*. If so, it would belong to their notion of it, that it is something, which is the cause of its own beginning: and that is as much as to say, that it is before it begins to be. Nor is their notion of *an action* some motion or exercise, that begins accidentally, without any cause or reason; for that is contrary to one of the prime dictates of common Sense, namely, that every thing that begins to be, has some cause or reason why it is.

The common people, in their Notion of a faulty or praiſe worthy deed or work done by any one, do ſuppoſe, that the man does it in the exerciſe of *liberty*. But then their Notion of liberty is only a perſon's having opportunity of doing as he pleaſes. They have no Notion of liberty conſiſting in the will's firſt acting, and ſo cauſing its own acts; and determining, and ſo cauſing its own determinations; or chuſing, and ſo cauſing its own choice. Such a Notion of liberty is what none have, but thoſe that have darkened their own minds with confuſed metaphyſical ſpeculation, and abſtruſe and ambiguous terms. If a man is not reſtrained from acting as his will determines, or conſtrained to act otherwiſe; then he has liberty, according to common Notions of liberty, without taking into the idea that grand contradiction of all, the determinations of a man's free will being the effects of the determinations of his free will.—— Nor have men commonly any Notion of freedom conſiſting in indifference. For if ſo, then it would be agreable to their Notion, that the greater indifference men act with, the more freedom they act with; whereas, the reverſe is true. He that in acting, proceeds with the fulleſt inclination, does what he does with the greateſt freedom, according to common Senſe. And ſo far is it from being agreable to common Senſe, that ſuch liberty as conſiſts in indifference is requiſite to praiſe or blame, that, on the contrary, the dictate of every man's natural ſenſe through the world is, that the further he is from being indifferent in his acting good or evil, and the more he does either with full and ſtrong inclination, the more is he eſteemed or abhorred, commended or condemned.

II. If

II. If it were inconsistent with the common Sense of mankind, that men should be either to be blamed or commended in any volitions, they have, or fail of, in case of moral necessity or impossibility; then it would surely also be agreable to the same Sense and reason of Mankind, that the nearer the case approaches to such a moral necessity or impossibility, either through a strong antecedent moral propensity, on the one hand,* or a great antecedent opposition and difficulty, on the other, the nearer does it approach to a being neither blameable nor commendable; so that acts exerted with such preceding propensity, would be worthy of proportionably less praise; and when omitted, the act being attended with such difficulty, the omission would be worthy of the less blame. It is so, as was observed before, with natural necessity and impossibility, propensity and difficulty: as it is a plain dictate of the sense of all mankind, that natural necessity and impossibility take away *all* blame and praise; and therefore, that the nearer the approach is to these, through previous propensity or difficulty, so praise and blame are proportionably *diminished*. And if it were as much a dictate of common Sense, that moral necessity of doing, or impossibility of avoiding, takes away *all* praise and blame, as that natural necessity or impossibility does this; then, by a perfect parity of reason, it would be as much the dictate of common Sense, that an *approach* to moral necessity of doing, or impossibility of avoiding, *diminishes* praise and blame, as that an approach to natural necessity and impossibility does so. It is equally the voice of common Sense, that persons are *excusable*

* It is here argued, on supposition that not all propensity implies moral necessity, but only some very high degree; which none will deny.

in

in part, in neglecting things difficult againſt their wills, as that they are *excuſable wholly* in neglecting things impoſſible againſt their wills. And if it made no difference, whether the impoſſibility were natural and againſt the will, or moral, lying in the will, with regard to excuſableneſs; ſo neither would it make any difference, whether the difficulty, or approach to neceſſity be natural againſt the will, or moral, lying in the propenſity of the will.

But it is apparent, that the reverſe of theſe things is true. If there be an approach to a moral neceſſity in a man's exertion of good acts of will, they being the exerciſe of a ſtrong propenſity to good, and a very powerful love to virtue; it is ſo far from being the dictate of common Senſe, that he is leſs virtuous, and the leſs to be eſteemed, loved and praiſed; that it is agreable to the natural Notions of all mankind, that he is ſo much the better man, worthy of greater reſpect, and higher commendation. And the ſtronger the inclination is, and the nearer it approaches to neceſſity in that reſpect; or to impoſſibility of neglecting the virtuous act, or of doing a vicious one; ſtill the more virtuous, and worthy of higher commendation. And, on the other hand, if a man exerts evil acts of mind; as, for inſtance, acts of pride or malice from a rooted and ſtrong habit or principle of haughtineſs and maliciouſneſs, and a violent propenſity of heart to ſuch acts; according to the natural Senſe of men, he is ſo far from being the leſs hateful and blameable on that account, that he is ſo much the more worthy to be deteſted and condemned, by all that obſerve him.

Moreover, it is manifest that it is no part of the Notion, which mankind commonly have of a blameable or praise worthy act of the will, that it is an act which is not determined by any antecedent bias or motive, but by the sovereign power of the will itself; because, if so, the greater hand such causes have in determining any acts of the will, so much the less virtuous or vicious would they be accounted; and the less hand, the more virtuous or vicious. Whereas, the reverse is true: men do not think a good act to be the less praise-worthy, for the agent's being much determined in it by a good inclination or a good motive, but the more. And if good inclination or motive, has but little influence in determining the agent, they do not think his act so much the more virtuous, but the less. And so concerning evil acts, which are determined by evil motives or inclinations.

Yea, if it be supposed, that good or evil dispositions are implanted in the hearts of men, by nature itself (which, it is certain, is vulgarly supposed in innumerable cases) yet it is not commonly supposed, that men are worthy of no praise or dispraise for such dispositions; although what is natural, is undoubtedly necessary, nature being prior to all acts of the will whatsoever. Thus, for instance, if a man appears to be of a very haughty or malicious disposition, and is supposed to be so by his natural temper, it is no vulgar Notion, no dictate of the common Sense and apprehension of men, that such dispositions are no vices or moral evils, or that such persons are not worthy of disesteem, or odium and dishonour; or that the proud or malicious acts which flow from such natural dispositions, are worthy of no resentment. Yea, such vile natural dispositions, and

and the ſtrength of them, will commonly be mentioned rather as an aggravation of the wicked acts that come from ſuch a fountain, than an extenuation of them. It being natural for men to act thus, is often obſerved by men in the height of their indignation: they will ſay, "It is his very nature: he is of a vile natural temper; it is as natural to him to act ſo, as it is to breathe; he cannot help ſerving the devil, *&c.*" But it is not thus with regard to hurtful miſchievous things, that any are the ſubjects or occaſions of, by *natural neceſſity*, againſt their inclinations. In ſuch a caſe, the neceſſity, by the common voice of mankind, will be ſpoken of as a full excuſe.——Thus it is very plain, that common Senſe makes a vaſt difference between theſe two kinds of neceſſity, as to the judgment it makes of their influence on the moral quality and deſert of men's actions.

And theſe dictates of men's minds are ſo natural and neceſſary, that it may be very much doubted whether the *Arminians* themſelves have ever got rid of them; yea, their greateſt doctors, that have gone furtheſt in defence of their metaphyſical Notions of liberty, and have brought their arguments to their greateſt ſtrength, and, as they ſuppoſe, to a demonſtration, againſt the conſiſtence of virtue and vice with any neceſſity: it is to be queſtioned, whether there is ſo much as one of them, but that, if he ſuffered very much from the injurious acts of a man, under the power of an invincible haughtineſs and malignancy of temper, would not, from the forementioned natural ſenſe of mind, reſent it far otherwiſe, than if as great ſufferings came upon him from the wind that blows, and fire that burns by natural neceſſity; and otherwiſe than he would,

would, if he suffered as much from the conduct of a man perfectly delirious; yea, though he first brought his distraction upon him some way by his own fault.

Some seem to disdain the distinction that we make between *natural* and *moral necessity* as though it were altogether impertinent in this controversy: "that which is necessary (say they) is necessary; it is that which must be, and cannot be prevented. And that which is impossible, is impossible, and cannot be done: and, therefore, none can be to blame for not doing it." And such comparisons are made use of, as the commanding of a man to walk, who has lost his legs, and condemning and punishing him for not obeying; inviting and calling upon a man, who is shut up in a strong prison, to come forth, *&c.* But, in these things, *Arminians* are very unreasonable. Let common Sense determine whether there be not a great difference between those two case; the one, that of a man who has offended his Prince, and is cast into prison; and after he has lain there awhile, the King comes to him, calls him to come forth to him; aud tells him, that if he will do so, and will fall down before him, and humbly beg his pardon, he shall be forgiven, and set at liberty, and also be greatly enriched, and advanced to honour: the prisoner heartily repents of the folly and wickedness of his offence against his Prince, is thoroughly disposed to abase himself, and accept of the King's offer; but is confined by strong walls, with gates of brass, and bars of iron. The other case is, that of a man who is of a very unreasonable spirit, of a haughty, ungrateful, wilful disposition; and, moreover, has been brought up in traiterous principles; and has his heart possessed with an extreme

treme and inveterate enmity to his lawful ſovereign; and for his rebellion is caſt into priſon, and lies long there, loaded with heavy chains, and in miſerable circumſtances. At length the compaſſionate Prince comes to the priſon, orders his chains to be knocked off, and his priſon-doors to be ſet wide open; calls to him, and tells him, if he will come forth to him, and fall down before him, acknowledge that he has treated him unworthily, and aſk his forgiveneſs; he ſhall be forgiven, ſet at liberty, and ſet in a place of great dignity and profit in his court, But he is ſtout and ſtomachful, and full of haughty malignity, that he cannot be willing to accept the offer: his rooted ſtrong pride and malice have perfect power over him, and as it were bind him, by binding his heart: the oppoſition of his heart has the maſtery over him, having an influence on his mind far ſuperior to the King's grace and condeſcenſion, and to all his kind offers and promiſes. Now, is it agreable to common Senſe, to aſſert and ſtand to it, that there is no difference between theſe two caſes, as to any worthineſs of blame in the priſoners; becauſe, forſooth, there is a neceſſity in both, and the required act in each caſe is impoſſible? It is true, a man's evil diſpoſitions may be as ſtrong and immoveable as the bars of a caſtle. But who cannot ſee, that when a man, in the latter caſe, is ſaid to be *unable* to obey the command, the expreſſion is uſed improperly, and not in the ſenſe it has originally and in common ſpeech? and that it may properly be ſaid to be in the rebel's power to come out of priſon, ſeeing he can eaſily do it if he pleaſes; though by reaſon of his vile temper of heart, which is fixed and rooted, it is impoſſible that it ſhould pleaſe him?

Upon the whole, I presume there is no person of good understanding, who impartially considers the things which have been observed, but will allow, that it is not evident, from the dictates of the common Sense, or natural Notions of mankind, that moral necessity is inconsistent with Praise and Blame. And, therefore, if the *Arminians* would prove any such inconsistency, it must be by some philosophical and metaphysical arguments, and not common Sense.

There is a grand illusion in the pretended demonstration of *Arminians* from common Sense. The main strength of all these demonstrations lies in that prejudice, that arises through the insensible change of the use and meaning of such terms as *liberty*, *able*, *unable*, *necessary*, *impossible*, *unavoidable*, *invincible*, *action*, &c. from their original and vulgar Sense, to a metaphysical Sense, entirely diverse; and the strong connection of the ideas of Blamelessness, &c. with some of these terms, by an habit contracted and established, while these terms were used in their first meaning. This prejudice and delusion, is the foundation of all those positions, they lay down as maxims, by which most of the Scriptures, which they alledge in this controversy, are interpreted, and on which all their pompous demonstrations from Scripture and reason depend. From this secret delusion and prejudice they have almost all their advantages: it is the strength of their bulwarks, and the edge of their weapons. And this is the main ground of all the right they have to treat their neighbours in so assuming a manner, and to insult others, perhaps as wise and good as themselves, as *weak bigots, men that dwell in the dark caves of superstition, perversely set, obstinately shutting their eyes against the noon-day light, enemies*

mies to common Senſe, maintaining the firſt-born of abſurdities, &c. &c. But perhaps an impartial conſideration of the things, which have been obſerved in the preceding parts of this enquiry, may enable the lovers of truth better to judge whoſe doctrine is indeed *abſurd, abſtruſe, ſelf-contradictory,* and inconſiſtent with common Senſe, and many ways repugnant to the univerſal dictates of the reaſon of mankind.

Corol. From things which have been obſerved, it will follow, that it is agreable to common Senſe to ſuppoſe, that the glorified ſaints have not their freedom at all diminiſhed, in any reſpect; and that God himſelf has the higheſt poſſible freedom, according to the true and proper meaning of the term; and that he is in the higheſt poſſible reſpect, an agent, and active in the exerciſe of his infinite holineſs; though he acts therein, in the higheſt degree, neceſſarily: and his actions of this kind are in the higheſt, moſt abſolutely perfect manner virtuous and praiſe-worthy; and are ſo, for that very reaſon, becauſe they are moſt perfectly neceſſary.

SECTION V.

Concerning those Objections, *that this Scheme of Necessity renders all* Means and Endeavours *for the avoiding of Sin, or the obtaining Virtue and Holiness*, vain, and to no Purpose; *and that it makes Men no more than mere* Machines *in Affairs of Morality and Religion.*

ARMINIANS say, if it be so, that sin and virtue come to pass by a necessity consisting in a sure connection of causes and effects, antecedents, and consequents, it can never be worth the while to use any Means or Endeavours to obtain the one, and avoid the other; seeing no endeavours can alter the futurity of the event, which is become necessary by a connection already established.

But I desire, that this matter may be fully considered; and that it may be examined with a thorough strictness, whether it will follow that Endeavours and Means, in order to avoid or obtain any future thing, must be more in vain, on the supposition of such a connection of antecedents and consequents, than if the contrary be supposed.

For Endeavours to be in vain, is for them not to be successful; that is to say, for them not eventually to be the means of the thing aimed at, which cannot be, but in one of these two ways; either *first*, that although the Means are used, yet the event aimed at does not follow: or, *secondly*,

condly, If the event does follow, it is not becauſe of the Means, or from any connection or dependence of the event of the Means, the event would have come to paſs, as well without the Means, as with them. If either of theſe two things are the caſe, then the Means are not properly ſucceſsful, and are truly in vain. The ſucceſsfulneſs or unſucceſsfulneſs, of Means, in order to an effect, or their being in vain or not in vain, conſiſts in thoſe Means being connected, or not connected, with the effect, in ſuch a manner as this, *viz.* That the effect is *with* the Means, and not *without* them; or, that the being of the effect is, on the one hand, connected with Means, and the want of the effect, on the other hand, is connected with the want of the Means. If there be ſuch a connection as this between Means and end, the Means are not in vain: the more there is of ſuch a connection, the further they are from being in vain; and the leſs of ſuch a connection, the more they are in vain.

Now, therefore, the queſtion to be anſwered, (in order to determine, whether it follows from this doctrine of the neceſſary connection between foregoing things, and conſequent ones, that Means uſed in order to any effect, are more in vain than they would be otherwiſe) is, whether it follows from it, that there is leſs of the forementioned connection between Means and effect; that is, whether, on the ſuppoſition of there being a real and true connection between antecedent things and conſequent ones, there muſt be leſs of a connection between Means and effect, than on the ſuppoſition of there being no fixed connection, between antecedent things and conſequent ones: and the very ſtating of this queſtion is ſufficient to anſwer it. It muſt appear to every one that will open his eyes, that this queſtion cannot be affirmed, without the groſſeſt abſurdity and inconſiſtence. Means are foregoing things, and effects are following things: And if there were no connection between foregoing things and following ones, there could be no connection between Means and end; and ſo all Means would be wholly vain and fruitleſs. For it is by virtue of ſome connection only, that they become ſucceſsful: It is ſome connection obſerved, or revealed, or otherwiſe known, between antecedent things and following ones that is what directs in the choice of Means. And if there were no ſuch thing as an eſtabliſhed connection, there could be no choice, as to Means; one thing would have no more tendency to an effect, than another; there would be no ſuch thing as tendency in the caſe. All thoſe things, which are ſucceſsful Means of other things, do therein prove connected antecedents of them: and therefore to aſſert, that a fixed connection between antecedents and conſequents makes Means vain and uſeleſs, or ſtands in the way to hinder the connection between Means and end, is juſt ſo ridiculous, as to ſay, that a connection between antecedents and conſequents ſtands in the way to hinder a connection between antecedents and conſequents..

Nor can any ſuppoſed connection of the ſucceſſion or train of antecedents and conſequents, from the very beginning of all things, the connection being made already ſure and neceſſary, either by eſtabliſhed laws of nature, or by theſe together, with a degree of ſovereign immediate interpoſitions of divine power, on ſuch and ſuch occaſions, or any other way (if any other there be;) I ſay, no ſuch neceſſary connection of a ſe-

ries

ries of antecedents and consequents can in the least tend to hinder, but that the Means we use may belong to the series; and so may be some of those antecedents which are connected with the consequents we aim at, in the established course of things. Endeavours which we use, are things that exist; and, therefore, they belong to the general chain of events; all the parts of which chain are supposed to be connected: and so Endeavours are supposed to be connected with some effects, or some consequent things or other. And certainly this does not hinder but that the events they are connected with, may be those which we aim at, and which we chuse, because we judge them most likely to have a connection with those events, from the established order and course of things which we observe, or from something in divine Revelation.

Let us suppose a real and sure connection between a man's having his eyes open in the clear day-light, with good organs of sight, and seeing; so that seeing is connected with his opening his eyes, and not seeing with his not opening his eyes; and also the like connection between such a man's attempting to open his eyes, and his actually doing it: the supposed established connection between these antecedents and consequents, let the connection be never so sure and necessary, certainly does not prove that it is in vain, for a man in such circumstances, to attempt to open his eyes, in order to seeing: his aiming at that event, and the use of the Means, being the effect of his will, does not break the connection, or hinder the success.

So that the objection we are upon does not lie against the doctrine of the necessity of events by a certainty of connection and consequence:

On the contrary, it is truly forcible againſt the *Arminian* doctrine of contingence and ſelf-determination; which is inconſiſtent with ſuch a connection. If there be no connection between thoſe events, wherein virtue and vice conſiſt, and any thing antecedent; then there is no connection between theſe events and any Means or Endeavours uſed in order to them: and if ſo, then thoſe means muſt be in vain. The leſs there is of connection between foregoing things and following ones, ſo much the leſs there is between Means and end, Endeavours and ſucceſs; and in the ſame proportion are Means and Endeavours ineffectual and in vain.

It will follow from *Arminian* principles, that there is no degree of connection between virtue or vice, and any foregoing event or thing: or, in other words, that the determination of the exiſtence of virtue or vice do not in the leaſt depend on the influence of any thing that comes to paſs antecedently, from which the determination of its exiſtence is, as its cauſe, Means, or ground; becauſe, ſo far as it is ſo, it is not from ſelf-determination: and, therefore, ſo far there is nothing of the nature of virtue or vice. And ſo it follows, that virtue and vice are not at all, in any degree dependent upon, or connected with, any foregoing event or exiſtence, as its cauſe, ground, or Means. And if ſo, then all foregoing Means muſt be totally in vain.

Hence it follows, that there cannot, in any conſiſtence with the *Arminian* ſcheme, be any reaſonable ground of ſo much as a conjecture concerning the conſequence of any Means and Endeavours, in order to eſcaping vice or obtaining virtue, or any choice or preference of Means,

as

as having a greater probability of success by some than others; either from any natural connection or dependence of the end on the Means, or through any divine constitution, or revealed way of God's bestowing or bringing to pass these things, in consequence of any Means, Endeavours, Prayers, or Deeds. Conjectures, in this latter case, depend on a supposition, that God himself is the Giver, or determining Cause of the events sought: but if they depend on self-determination, then God is not the determining or disposing Author of them: and if these things are not of his disposal, then no conjecture can be made, from any revelation he has given, concerning any way or method of his disposal of them.

YEA, on these principles, it will not only follow, that men cannot have any reasonable ground of judgment or conjecture, that their Means and Endeavours to obtain virtue or avoid vice, will be successful, but they may be sure, they will not; they may be certain, that they will be in vain; and that if ever the thing, which they seek, comes to pass, it will not be at all owing to the Means they use. For Means and Endeavours can have no effect at all, in order to obtain the end, but in one of these two ways: either, (1.) Through a natural tendency and influence, to prepare and dispose the mind more to virtuous acts, either by causing the disposition of the heart to be more in favour of such acts, or by bringing the mind more into the view of powerful motives and inducements: or, (2.) By putting persons more in the way of God's bestowment of the benefit. But neither of these can be the case. *Not the latter*; for, as has been just now observed, it does not consist with the *Arminian* notion of self-determination,

mination, which they fuppofe effential to virtue, that God fhould be the Beftower, or (which is the fame thing) the determining, difpofing Author of Virtue. *Not the former*; for natural influence and tendency fuppofes caufality and connection; and fuppofes neceffity of event, which is inconfiftent with *Arminian* liberty. A tendency of Means, by biaffing the heart in favour of virtue, or by bringing the will under the influence and power of motives in its determinations, are both inconfiftent with *Arminian* liberty of will, confifting in indifference, and fovereign felf-determination, as has been already demonftrated.

But for the more full removal of this prejudice againft the doctrine of neceffity, which has been maintained, as though it tended to encourage a total neglect of all Endeavours as vain; the following things may be confidered.

The queftion is not, Whether men may not thus improve this doctrine: we know that many true and wholefome doctrines are abufed: but, whether the doctrine gives any juft occafion for fuch an improvement; or whether, on the fuppofition of the truth of the doctrine, fuch a ufe of it would not be unreafonable? If any fhall affirm, that it would not, but that the very nature of the doctrine is fuch as gives juft occafion for it, it muft be on this fuppofition; namely, that fuch an invariable neceffity of all things already fettled, muft render the interpofition of all Means, Endeavours, Conclufions or Actions of ours, in order to the obtaining any future end whatfoever, perfectly infignificant; becaufe they cannot in the leaft alter or vary the courfe and feries of things, in any event or circumftance; all

all being already fixed unalterably by necessity: and that therefore it is folly, for men to use any Means *for any end*; but their wisdom, to save themselves the trouble of Endeavours, and take their ease. No person can draw such an inference from this doctrine, and come to such a conclusion, without contradicting himself, and going counter to the very principles he pretends to act upon: for he comes to a conclusion, and takes a course, *in order to an end*, even *his ease*, or the saving himself from trouble; he seeks something future, and uses Means in order to a future thing, even in his drawing up that conclusion, that he will seek nothing, and use no Means in order to any thing in future; he seeks his future ease, and the benefit and comfort of indolence. If prior necessity, that determines all things, makes vain all actions or conclusions of ours, in order to any thing future; then it makes vain all conclusions and conduct of ours, in order to our future ease. The measure of our ease, with the time, manner and every circumstance of it, is already fixed, by all-determining necessity, as much as any thing else. If he says within himself, "What future happiness or misery I shall have, is already, in effect, determined by the necessary course and connection of things; therefore, I will save myself the trouble of labour and diligence, which cannot add to my determined degree of happiness, or diminish my misery; but will take my ease, and will enjoy the comfort of sloth and negligence." Such a man contradicts himself: he says, the measure of his future happiness and misery is already fixed, and he will not try to diminish the one, or add to the other: but yet, in his very conclusion, he contradicts this; for, he takes up this conclusion, *to add to his future happiness*, by the ease and comfort

fort of his negligence; and to diminish his future trouble and misery, by saving himself the trouble of using Means and taking Pains.

Therefore persons cannot reasonably make this improvement of the doctrine of necessity, that they will go into a voluntary negligence of Means for their own happiness. For the principles they must go upon, in order to this, are inconsistent with their making any improvement at all of the doctrine: for to make some improvement of it, is to be influenced by it, to come to some voluntary conclusion, in regard to their own conduct, with some view or aim: but this, as has been shown, is inconsistent with the principles they pretend to act upon. In short, the principles are such as cannot be acted upon at all, or, in any respect, consistently. And, therefore, in every pretence of acting upon them, or making any improvement at all of them, there is a self-contradiction.

As to that Objection against the doctrine, which I have endeavoured to prove, that it makes men no more than mere Machines; I would say, that notwithstanding this doctrine, Man is entirely, perfectly and unspeakably different from a mere Machine, in that he has reason and understanding, and has a faculty of will, and so is capable of volition and choice; and in that, his will is guided by the dictates or views of his understanding; and in that his external actions and behaviour, and, in many respects, also his thoughts, and the exercises of his mind, are subject to his will; so that he has liberty to act according to his choice, and do what he pleases; and by Means of these things, is capable of moral habits and moral acts, such inclinations and actions as, according

cording to the common sense of mankind, are worthy of praise, esteem, love and reward; or, on the contrary, of disesteem, detestation, indignation and punishment.

In these things is all the difference from mere Machines, as to liberty and agency, that would be any perfection, dignity or privilege, in any respect: all the difference that can be desired, and all that can be conceived of; and indeed all that the pretensions of the *Arminians* themselves come to, as they are forced often to explain themselves. (Though their explications overthrow and abolish the things asserted, and pretended to be explained) For they are forced to explain a self-determining power of will, by a power in the soul, to determine as it chuses or wills; which comes to no more than this, that a man has a power of chusing, and, in many instances, can do as he chuses. Which is quite a different thing from that contradiction, his having power of chusing his first act of choice in the case.

Or, if their scheme makes any other difference than this, between Men and Machines, it is for the worse: it is so far from supposing Men to have a dignity and privilege above Machines, that it makes the manner of their being determined still more unhappy. Whereas, Machines are guided by an understanding cause, by the skilful hand of the workman or owner; the will of Man is left to the guidance of nothing, but absolute blind contingence.

SECT.

SECTION VI.

Concerning that Objection *against the Doctrine which has been maintained, that it agrees with the* Stoical *Doctrine of* Fate, *and the Opinions of Mr.* Hobbes.

WHEN *Calvinists* oppose the *Arminian* notion of the freedom of will, and contingence of volition, and insist that there are no acts of the will, nor any other events whatsoever, but what are attended with some kind of necessity; their opposers cry out of them, as agreeing with the antient *Stoics* in their doctrine of *Fate*, and with Mr. *Hobbes* in his opinion of *Necessity*.

It would not be worth while to take notice of so impertinent an Objection, had it not been urged by some of the chief *Arminian* writers.—There were many important truths maintained by the antient *Greek* and *Roman* philosophers, and especially the *Stoics*, that are never the worse for being held by them. The *Stoic* philosophers, by the general agreement of Christian divines, and even *Arminian* divines, were the greatest, wisest, and most virtuous of all the heathen philosophers; and, in their doctrine and practice, came the nearest to Christianity of any of their sects. How frequently are the sayings of these philosophers, in many of the writings and sermons, even of *Arminian* divines, produced, not as arguments of the falseness of the doctrines which they delivered, but as a confirmation of some of the greatest trtuths of the Christian Religion, relating to the Unity and Perfections

fections of the Godhead, a future ſtate, the duty and happineſs of mankind, &c. as obſerving how the light of nature and reaſon, in the wiſeſt and beſt of the Heathen, harmonized with, and confirms the Goſpel of Jeſus Chriſt.

And it is very remarkable, concerning Dr. *Whitby*, that although he alledges the agreement of the *Stoics* with us, wherein he ſuppoſes they maintained the like doctrine with us, as an argument againſt the truth of our doctrine; yet, this very Dr. *Whitby* alledges the agreement of the *Stoics* with the *Arminians*, wherein he ſuppoſes they taught the ſame doctrine with them, as an argument for the truth of their doctrine*. So that when the *Stoics* agree with them, this (it ſeems) is a confirmation of their doctrine, and a confutation of ours, as ſhewing that our opinions are contrary to the natural ſenſe and common reaſon of mankind: nevertheleſs, when the *Stoics* agree with *us*, it argues no ſuch thing in our favour; but, on the contrary, is a great argument againſt us, and ſhews our doctrine to be heatheniſh.

It is obſerved by ſome *Calviniſtic* writers, that the *Arminians* ſymbolize with the *Stoics*, in ſome of thoſe doctrines wherein they are oppoſed by the *Calviniſts*; particularly in their denying an original, innate, total corruption and depravity of heart; and in what they held of man's ability to make himſelf truly virtuous and conformed to God;—and in ſome other doctrines.

It may be further obſerved, it is certainly no better Objection againſt our doctriue, that it agrees, in ſome reſpects with the doctrine of the antient

* *Whitby* on the five Points, Edit. 3. p. 325, 326, 327.

antient *Stoic* philosophers, than it is against theirs, wherein they differ from us, that it agrees, in some respects, with the opinion of the very worst of the heathen philosophers, the followers of *Epicurus*, that father of atheism and licentiousness, and with the doctrine of the *Sadducees* and *Jesuits*.

I AM not much concerned to know precisely, what the antient *Stoic* philosophers held concerning *Fate*, in order to determine what is truth; as though it were a sure way to be in the right, to take good heed to differ from them. It seems, that they differed among themselves; and probably the doctrine of *Fate*, as maintained by most of them, was, in some respects, erroneous. But what ever their doctrine was, if any of them held such a Fate, as is repugnant to any liberty, consisting in our doing as we please, I utterly deny such a Fate. If they held any such fate, as is not consistent with the common and universal notions that mankind have of liberty, activity, moral agency, virtue and vice; I disclaim any such thing, and think I have demonstrated, that the scheme I maintain is no such scheme. If the *Stoics*, by *Fate*, meant any thing of such a nature, as can be supposed to stand in the way of the advantage and benefit of the use of means and endeavours, or make it less worth the while for men to desire, and seek after any thing wherein their virtue and happinness consists; I hold no doctrine that is clogged with any such inconvenience, any more than any other scheme whatsoever; and by no means so much as the *Arminian* scheme of contingence; as has been shewn. If they held any such doctrine of universal fatality, as is inconsistent with any kind of liberty, that is or can be any perfection, dignity, privilege or benefit, or any thing desirable, in any respect, for any

any intelligent creature, or indeed with any liberty that is possible or conceivable; I embrace no such doctrine. If they held any such doctrine of Fate, as is inconsistent with the world's being in all things subject to the disposal of an intelligent wise agent, that presides, not as the *soul* of the world, but as the Sovereign *Lord* of the Universe, governing all things by proper will, choice and design, in the exercise of the most perfect liberty conceivable, without subjection to any constraint, or being properly under the power or influence of any thing before, above or without himself; I wholly renounce any such doctrine.

As to Mr. *Hobbes*'s maintaining the same doctrine concerning necessity;—I confess, it happens I never read Mr. *Hobbes.* Let his opinion be what it will, we need not reject all truth which is demonstrated by clear evidence, merely because it was once held by some bad man. This great truth, *that Jesus is the Son of God,* was not spoiled because it was once and again proclaimed with a loud voice by the devil. If truth is so defiled, because it is spoken by the mouth, or written by the pen of some ill-minded mischievous man, that it must never be received, we shall never know, when we hold any of the most precious and evident truths by a sure tenure. And if Mr. *Hobbes* has made a bad use of this truth, that is to be lamented; but the truth is not to be thought worthy of rejection on that account. It is common for the corruptions of the hearts of evil men to abuse the best things to vile purposes.

I MIGHT also take notice of its having been observed, that the *Arminians* agree with Mr. *Hobbes* in

* in many more things than the *Calviniſts*. As, in what he is ſaid to hold concerning original ſin, in denying the neceſſity of ſupernatural illumination, in denying infuſed grace, in denying the doctrine of juſtification by faith alone; and other things.

SECTION VII.

Concerning the Neceſſity *of the* Divine Will.

SOME may poſſibly, object againſt what has been ſuppoſed of the abſurdity and inconſiſtence of a ſelf-determining power in the will, and the impoſſibility of its being otherwiſe, than that the will ſhould be determined in every caſe by ſome motive, and by a motive which (as it ſtands in the view of the underſtanding) is of ſuperior ſtrength to any appearing on the other ſide; that if theſe things are true, it will follow, that not only the will of created minds, but the will of *God Himſelf* is neceſſary in all its determinations. Concerning which, ſays the Author of the *Eſſay on the Freedom of Will in God and in the Creature* (pag. 85, 86.) "What ſtrange doctrine is "this, contrary to all our ideas of the dominion "of God? does it not deſtroy the glory of his "liberty of choice, and take away from the "Creator and Governor and Benefactor of the "world, that moſt free and Sovereign Agent, all "the glory of this ſort of freedom? does it "not ſeem to make him a kind of mechanical "medium of fate, and introduce Mr. *Hobbes*'s "doctrine of fatality and Neceſſity, into all "things that God hath to do with? Does it not "ſeem to repreſent the bleſſed God, as a Being "of vaſt underſtanding, as well as power and "efficiency,

* Dr. *Gill*, in his Anſwer to Dr. *Whitby*. Vol. III. p. 183, &c.

" efficiency, but ſtill to leave him without a " will to chuſe among all the objects within his " view? In ſhort, it ſeems to make the bleſſed " God a ſort of Almighty Miniſter of Fate, un- " der its univerſal and ſupreme influence; as it " was the profeſſed ſentiment of ſome of the an- " tients, that Fate was above the gods."

This is declaiming, rather than arguing, and an application to men's imaginations and prejudices, rather than to mere reaſon.—But I would calmly endeavour to conſider, whether there be any reaſon in this frightful repreſentation.—But, before I enter upon a particular conſideration of the matter, I would obſerve this: that it is reaſonable to ſuppoſe, it ſhould be much more difficult to expreſs or conceive things according to exact metaphyſical truth, relating to the nature and manner of the exiſtence of things in the Divine Underſtanding and Will, and the operation of theſe faculties (if I may ſo call them) of the Divine Mind, than in the human mind; which is infinitely more within our view, and nearer to a proportion to the meaſure of our comprehenſion, and more commenſurate to the uſe and import of human ſpeech. Language is indeed very deficient, in regard of terms to expreſs preciſe truth, concerning our own minds, and ther faculties and operations. Words were firſt formed to expreſs external things; and thoſe that are applied to expreſs things internal and ſpiritual, are almoſt all borrowed, and uſed in a ſort of figurative ſenſe. Whence they are, moſt of them, attended with a great deal of ambiguity and unfixedneſs in their ſignification, occaſioning innumerable doubts, difficulties and confuſions, in enquiries and controverſies, about things of this nature. But language is much leſs adapted to expreſs things in the mind of the incomprehenſible Deity, preciſely as they are.

We find a great deal of difficulty in conceiving exactly of the nature of our own ſouls. And notwithſtanding all the progreſs, which has been made, in paſt and preſent ages, in this kind of knowledge, whereby our metaphyſics, as it relates to theſe things, is brought to greater perfection than once it was; yet, here is ſtill work enough left for future enquiries and reſearches, and room for progreſs ſtill to be made, for many ages and generations. But we had need to be infinitely able metaphyſicians, to conceive with clearneſs, according to ſtrict, proper and perfect truth, concerning the nature of the Divine Eſſence, and the modes of the action and operation of the powers of the Divine Mind.

And it may be noted particularly, that though we are obliged to conceive of ſome things in God as conſequent and dependent on others, and of ſome things pertaining to the Divine Nature and Will as the foundation of others, and ſo before others in the order of nature: as, we muſt conceive of the knowledge and holineſs of God as prior, in the order of nature, to his happineſs; the perfection of his underſtanding, as the foundation of his wiſe purpoſes and decrees; the holineſs of his nature, as the cauſe and reaſon of his holy determinations. And yet, when we ſpeak of cauſe and effect, antecedent and conſequent, fundamental and dependent, determining and determined, in the firſt Being, who is ſelf-exiſtent, independent, of perfect and abſolute ſimplicity and immutability, and the firſt cauſe of all things; doubtleſs there muſt be leſs propriety in ſuch repreſentations, than when we ſpeak of derived dependent

pendent beings, who are compounded, and liable to perpetual mutation and succession.

Having premised this, I proceed to observe concerning the forementioned Author's exclamation, about the *necessary Determination of God's Will*, in all things, by what he sees to be *fittest* and *best*.

That all the seeming force of such objections and exclamations must arise from an imagination, that there is some sort of privilege or dignity in being without such a moral Necessity, as will make it impossible to do any other, than always chuse what is wisest and best; as though there were some disadvantage, meanness and subjection, in such a Necessity; a thing by which the will was confined, kept under, and held in servitude by something, which, as it were, maintained a strong and invincible power and dominion over it, by bonds that held him fast, and that he could, by no means, deliver himself from Whereas, this must be all mere imagination and delusion. It is no disadvantage or dishonour to a being, necessarily to act in the most excellent and happy manner, from the necessary perfection of his own nature. This argues no imperfection, inferiority or dependance, nor any want of dignity, privilege or ascendency*. It is not inconsistent with the absolute

* "It might have been objected, with more plausibleness, that the Supreme Cause cannot be free, because he must needs do always what is best in the whole. But this would not at all serve *Spinoza*'s purpose; for this is a Necessity, not of nature and of fate, but of fitness and wisdom; a Necessity consistent with the greatest freedom, and most perfect choice. For the only foundation of this Necessity is such an unalterable rectitude of will, and perfection of wisdom, as makes it impossible for a wise being to act foolishly." *Clark*'s Demonstration of the Being and Attributes of God. Edit. 6. p. 64.

"Though

absolute and most perfect sovereignty of God, The sovereignty of God is his ability and authority to do whatever pleases him; whereby *He doth according to his will in the armies of heaven, and amongst the inhabitants of the earth, and none can stay his hand, or say unto him, what dost thou?*—The following things belong to the *sovereignty* of God; *viz.* (1.) Supreme, Universal, and Infinite *Power*; whereby he is able to do what he pleases, without controul, without any confinement of that power, without any subjection, in the least measure, to any other power; and so without any hinderance or restraint, that it should be either impossible, or at all difficult, for him to accomplish his Will; and without any dependence of his power on any other power, from whence it should be derived, or which it should stand in any need of: so far from this, that all other power is derived from him, and is absolutely dependent on him. (2.) That He has supreme *authority*; absolute

" Though God is a most perfect free Agent, yet he cannot " but do always what is best and wisest in the whole. The " reason is evident; because perfect wisdom and goodness " are as steady and certain principles of action, as Necessity " itself; and an infinitely wise and good being, indued with " the most perfect liberty, can no more chuse to act in con" tradiction to wisdom and goodness, than a necessary agent " can act contrary to the Necessity by which it is acted; it " being as great an absurdity and impossiblity in choice, for " Infinite Wisdom to chuse to act unwisely, or Infinite Good" ness to chuse what is not good, as it would be in nature, " for absolute necessity to fail of producing its necessary " effect. There was, indeed, no Necessity in nature, that God " should at first create such beings as he has created, or indeed " any being at all; because he is, in Himself, infinitely happy " and all-sufficient. There was, also, no Necessity in nature, " that he should preserve and continue things in being, after " they were created; because he would be self-sufficient with" out their continuance, as he was before their creation. " But it was fit and wise and good, that Infinite Wisdom should " manifest absolute and most perfect right to do what he wills, without subjection to any superior authority, or any derivation of authority from any other, or limitation by any distinct independent authority, either superior, equal, or inferior; he being the head of all dominion, and fountain of all authority; and also without restraint by any obligation, implying either subjection, derivation, or dependence, or proper limitation. (3.) That his *Will* is supreme, underived, and independent on any thing without himself; being in every thing determined by his own counsel, having no other rule but his own wisdom; his will not being subject to, or restrained by the will of any other, and other wills being perfectly subject to his. (4.) That his *Wisdom*, which determines his will, is supreme, perfect, underived, self-sufficient and independent; so that it may be said, as in Isai. xl. 14 *With whom took He counsel? And who instructed Him and taught him in the*

" manifest, and Infinite Goodness communicate itself; and " therefore it was necessary, in the sense of Necessity I am " now speaking of, that things should be made *at such a time*, " and continued *so long*, and indeed with various perfections " in such degrees, as Infinite Wisdom and Goodness saw it " wisest and best that they should." *Ibid*, p. 112, 113.

" It is not a fault, but a perfection of our nature, to de- " sire, will and act, according to the last result of a fair ex- " amination.—This is so far from being a restraint or di- " munition of freedom, that it is the very improvement and " benefit of it: it is not an abridgement, it is the end and " use of our liberty; and the further we are removed from " such a determination, the nearer we are to misery and sla- " very. A perfect indifference in the mind, not determin- " able by its last judgment, of the good or evil that is thought " to attend its choice, would be so far from being an advan- " tage and excellency of any intellectual nature, that it " would be as great an imperfection, as the want of indiffe- " rency to act, or not to act, till determined by the will, " would be an imperfection on the other side—It is as " much *the path of judgment, and taught Him knowledge, and shewed him the way of understanding?*—There is no other Divine Sovereignty but this: and this is properly *absolute sovereignty:* no other is desirable; nor would any other be honourable, or happy: and indeed, there is no other conceivable or possible. It is the glory and greatness of the Divine Sovereign, that God's Will is determined by his own infinite all-sufficient wisdom in every thing; and in nothing at all is either directed by any inferior wisdom, or by no wisdom; whereby it would become senseless arbitrariness, determining and acting without reason, design or end.

If God's Will is steadily and surely determined in every thing by *supreme* wisdom, then it is in every thing necessarily determined to that which is *most* wise. And, certainly, it would be a disadvantage and indignity, to be otherwise. For if the

" much a perfection, that desire or the power of preferring " should be determined by good, as that the power of acting " should be determined by the will: and the certainer such " determination is, the greater the perfection. Nay, were " we determined by any thing but the last result of our own " minds, judging of the good or evil of any action, we were " not free. This very end of our freedom being, that we " might attain the good we chuse; and, therefore, every man " is brought under a Necessity by his constitution, as an intelligent being, to be determined in willing by his own " thought and judgment, what is best for him to do; else " he would be under the determination of some other than " himself, which is want of liberty. And to deny that a " man's will, in every determination, follows his own judgment, is to say, that a man wills and acts for an end that " he would not have, at the same time that he wills and acts " for it. For if he prefers it in his present thoughts, before any other, it is plain he then thinks better of it, and " would have it before any other; unless he can have, and " not have it; will, and not will it, at the same time; a " con-the Divine Will was not neceſſarily determined to that, which in every caſe is wiſeſt and beſt, it muſt be ſubject to ſome degree of undeſigning contingence; and ſo in the ſame degree liable to evil. To ſuppoſe the Divine Will liable to be carried hither and thither at random, by the uncertain wind of blind contingence, which is guided by no wiſdom, no motive, no intelligent dictate whatſoever, (if any ſuch thing were poſſible) would certainly argue a great degree of imperfection and meanneſs, infinitely unworthy of the Deity.—If it be a diſadvantage, for the Divine Will to be attended with this moral Neceſſity, then the more free from it, and the more

" contradiction too manifeſt to be admitted—If we look up-" on thoſe ſuperior beings above us, who enjoy perfect hap-" pineſs, we ſhall have reaſon to judge, that they are more " ſteadily determined in their choice of good than we; and " yet we have no reaſon to think they are leſs happy, or leſs " free, than we are. And if it were fit for ſuch poor finite " creatures as we are, to pronounce what Infinite Wiſdom " and Goodneſs could do, I think we might ſay, that God " himſelf cannot chuſe what is not good. *The freedom of the* " *Almighty hinders not his being determined by what is beſt.*— " But to give a right view of this miſtaken part of liberty, " let me aſk, Would any one be a changeling, becauſe he is " leſs determined by wiſe determination, than a wiſe man? " Is it worth the name of freedom, to be at liberty to play " the fool, and draw ſhame and miſery upon a man's ſelf? " If to break looſe from the conduct of reaſon, and to want " that reſtraint of examination and judgment, that keeps us " from doing or chuſing the worſe, be liberty, true liberty, " mad men and fools are the only free men. Yet, I think, " no body would chuſe to be mad, for the ſake of ſuch li-" berty, but he that is mad already. *Lock*, Hum. Und. " Vol. I. Edit. 7. p. 215, 216.

" This Being, having all things always neceſſarily in view, " muſt always, and eternally will, according to his infinite " comprehenſion of things; that is, muſt will all things " that are wiſeſt and beſt to be done. There is not getting " free of this conſequence. If it can will at all, it muſt will " this way. To be capable of knowing, and not capable of " willing, more left at random, the greater dignity and advantage. And, consequently, to be perfectly free from the direction of understanding, and universally and entirely left to senseless unmeaning contingence, to act absolutely at random, would be the supreme glory.

It no more argues any dependence of God's Will, that his supremely wise volition is necessary, than it argues a dependence of his being, that his existence is necessary. If it be something too low, for the Supreme Being to have his Will determined by moral Necessity, so as necessarily, in every case, to will in the highest degree holily and happily; then why is it not also something too low, for him to have his existence, and the infinite

" willing, is not to be understood. And to be capable of " willing otherwise than what is wisest and best, contradicts " that knowledge which is infinite. Infinite Knowledge must " direct the will without error. *Here then, is the origin of* " *moral Necessity; and that is really, of freedom*—Perhaps it " may be said, when the Divine Will is determined, from the " consideration of the eternal aptitudes of things, it is as " necessarily determined, as if it were physically impelled, if " that were possible. But it is unskilfulness, to suppose this " an objection. The great principle is once established, *viz.* " That the Divine Will is determined by the eternal reason " and aptitudes of things, instead of being physically im- " pelled; and after that, the more strong and necessary this " determination is, the more perfect the Deity must be al- " lowed to be: it is this that makes him an amiable and " adorable Being, whose Will and Power are constantly, im- " mutably determined, by the consideration of what is wisest " and best; instead of a surd Being, with power, but without " discerning and reason. *It is the beauty of this Necessity,* " *that it is strong as fate itself, with all the advantage of reason* " *and goodness.*—It is strange, to see men contend, that the " Deity is not free, because he is necessarily rational, im- " mutably good and wise; when a man is allowed still the " perfecter being, the more fixedly and constantly his will is " determined by reason and truth." *Enquiry into the Nature of the Hum. Soul.* Edit. 3. Vol. II. p. 403, 404.

finite perfection of his nature, and his infinite happineſs determined by Neceſſity? It is no more to God's diſhonour, to be neceſſarily wiſe, than to be neceſſarily holy. And, if neither of them be to his diſhonour, then it is not to his diſhonour neceſſarily to act holily and wiſely. And if it be not diſhonourable to be neceſſarily holy and wiſe, in the higheſt poſſible degree, no more is it mean and diſhonourable, neceſſarily to act holily and wiſely in the higheſt poſſible degree; or, which is the ſame thing, to do that, in every caſe, which, above all other things, is wiſeſt and beſt.

THE reaſon why it is not diſhonourable, to be neceſſarily *moſt* holy, is, becauſe holineſs in itſelf is an excellent and honourable thing. For the ſame reaſon, it is no diſhonour to be neceſſarily *moſt* wiſe, and, in every caſe, to act moſt wiſely, or do the thing which is the wiſeſt of all; for wiſdom is alſo in itſelf excellent and honourable.

THE forementioned Author of the *Eſſay on the Freedom of Will*, &c. as has been obſerved, repreſents that doctrine of the Divine Will's being in every thing neceſſarily determined by ſuperior fitneſs, as making the bleſſed God a kind of Almighty Miniſter and mechanical medium of fate: and he inſiſts, p. 93, 94. that this moral Neceſſity and impoſſibility is, in effect, the ſame thing with phyſical and natural Neceſſity and impoſſibility: and in p. 54, 55. he ſays, "The ſcheme which determines the will always and certainly by the underſtanding, and the underſtanding by the appearance of things, ſeems to take away the true nature of vice and virtue. For the ſublimeſt of virtues, and the

the vilest of vices, seem rather to be matters of fate and Necessity, flowing naturally and necessarily from the existence, the circumstances, and present situation of persons and things: for this existence and situation necessarily makes such an appearance to the mind; from this appearance flows a necessary perception and judgment, concerning these things; this judgment necessarily determines the will: and thus, by this chain of necessary causes, virtue and vice would lose their nature, and become natural ideas and necessary things, instead of moral and free actions."

AND yet this same Author allows. p. 30, 31. That a perfectly wise being will constantly and certainly chuse what is most fit; and says, p. 102, 103. "I grant, and always have granted, that wheresoever there is such antecedent superior fitness of things, God acts according to it, so as never to contradict it; and, particularly, in all his judicial proceedings as a Governor and Distributer of rewards and punishments." Yea, he says expresly, p. 42. "That it is not possible for God to act otherwise, than according to this fitness and goodness in things."

So that, according to this Author, putting these several passages of this Essay together, there is *no virtue, nor any thing of a moral nature*, in the most sublime and glorious acts and exercises of God's holiness, justice, and faithfulness; and he never does any thing which is in itself supremely worthy, and, above all other things, fit and excellent, but only as a kind of mechanical medium of fate; and in *what he does as the Judge, and moral Governor of the world*, he exercises no moral

moral excellency; exerciſing no freedom in theſe things, becauſe he acts by moral Neceſſity, which is, in effect, the ſame with phyſical or natural Neceſſity; and therefore, he only acts by an *Hobbiſtical* fatality; *as a Being indeed of vaſt underſtanding, as well as power and efficiency* (as he ſaid before) *but without a will to chuſe, being a kind of Almighty Miniſter of fate, acting under a ſupreme influence.* For he allows, that in all theſe things, God's Will is determined conſtantly and certainly by a ſuperior fitneſs, and that it is not poſſible for him to act otherwiſe. And if theſe things are ſo, what glory or praiſe belongs to God for doing holily and juſtly, or taking the moſt fit, holy, wiſe and excellent courſe, in any one inſtance? Whereas, according to the Scriptures, and alſo the common ſenſe of mankind, it does not, in the leaſt, derogate from the honour of any being, that through the moral perfection of his nature, he neceſſarily acts with ſupreme wiſdom and holineſs: but, on the contrary, his praiſe is the greater: herein conſiſts the height of his glory.

The ſame Author, p. 56. ſuppoſes, that herein appears the excellent *character of a wiſe and good man, that though he can chuſe contrary to the fitneſs of things, yet he does not; but ſuffers himſelf to be directed by fitneſs*; and that, in this conduct, *he imitates the bleſſed God.* And yet, he ſuppoſes it is contrariwiſe with the bleſſed God; not that he ſuffers himſelf to be directed by fitneſs, when *he can chuſe, contrary to the fitneſs of things*, but that *he cannot chuſe contrary to the fitneſs of things*; as he ſays, p. 42.—*That it is not poſſible for God to act otherwiſe than according to this fitneſs, where there is any fitneſs or goodneſs in things*: Yea, he ſuppoſes, p. 31. That if a man *were perfectly wiſe and*

and good, he could not do otherwise than be constantly and certainly determined by the fitness of things.

One thing more I would observe, before I conclude this section; and that is, that if it derogates nothing from the glory of God, to be necessarily determined by superior fitness in some things, then neither does it to be thus determined in all things; from any thing in the nature of such necessity, as at all detracting from God's freedom, independence, absolute supremacy, or any dignity or glory of his nature, state or manner of acting; or as implying any infirmity, restraint, or subjection. And if the thing be such as well consists with God's glory, and has nothing tending at all to detract from it; then we need not be afraid of ascribing it to God in too many things, lest thereby we should detract from God's glory too much.

SECTION VIII.

Some further Objections against the moral Necessity of God's Volitions *considered.*

THE Author last cited, as has been observed, owns that God, being perfectly wise, will constantly and certainly chuse what appears most fit, where there is a superior fitness and goodness in things; and that it is not possible for him to do otherwise. So that it is in effect confessed, that in those things where there is any real preferableness, it is no dishonour, nothing in any respect unworthy of God, for him to act from Necessity; notwithstanding all that can be objected from the agreement of such a Necessity, with

with the fate of the *Stoicks*, and the Necessity maintained by Mr. *Hobbes*. From which it will follow, that if it were so, that in all the different things, among which God chuses, there were evermore a superior fitness or preferableness on one side, then it would be no dishonour, or any thing, in any respect unworthy, or unbecoming of God, for his will to be necessarily determined in every thing. And if this be allowed, it is a giving up entirely the argument, from the unsuitableness of such a Necessity to the liberty, supremacy, independence and glory of the Divine Being; and a resting the whole weight of the affair on the decision of another point wholly diverse; *viz. Whether it be so indeed*, that in all the various possible things, which are in God's view, and may be considered as capable objects of his choice, there is not evermore a preferableness in one thing above another. This is denied by this Author; who supposes, that in many instances, between two or more possible things, which come within the view of the Divine Mind, there is a perfect indifference and equality, as to fitness or tendency, to attain any good end which God can have in view, or to answer any of his designs. Now, therefore, I would consider whether this be evident.

THE arguments brought to prove this, are of two kinds. (1.) It is urged, that, in many instances, we must suppose there is absolutely no difference between various possible objects of choice, which God has in view: and (2.) that the difference between many things is so inconsiderable, or of such a nature, that it would be unreasonable to suppose it to be of any consequence; or to suppose that any of God's wise designs

ſigns, would not be anſwered in one way as well as the other. Therefore,

I. The firſt thing to be conſidered is, whether there are any inſtances wherein there is a perfect likeneſs, and abſolutely no difference, between different objects of choice, that are propoſed to the divine underſtanding?

And here, in the *firſt* place, it may be worthy to be conſidered, whether the contradiction there is in the *terms* of the queſtion propoſed, does not give reaſon to ſuſpect, that there is an inconſiſtency in the *thing* ſuppoſed. It is inquired, whether *different* objects of choice may not be abſolutely *without difference?* If they are abſolutely *without difference*, then how are they *different* objects of choice? If there be abſolutely *no difference*, in any reſpect, then there is *no variety* or *diſtinction:* for diſtinction is only by ſome difference. And if there be no *variety* among propoſed *objects of choice*, then there is no opportunity for *variety of choice*, or difference of determination. For that determination of a thing, which is not different in any reſpect, is not a different determination, but the ſame. That this is no quibble, may appear more fully anon.

The arguments, to prove that the Moſt High, in ſome inſtances, chuſes to do one thing rather than another, where the things themſelves are perfectly without difference, are two.

1. That the various parts of infinite time and ſpace, abſolutely conſidered, are perfectly alike, and do not differ at all one from another: and that therefore, when God determined to create the

the world in such a part of infinite duration and space, rather than others, he determined and preferred, among various objects, between which there was no preferableness, and absolutely no difference.

Answ. This objection supposes an infinite length of time before the world was created, distinguished by successive parts, properly and truly so; or a succession of limited and unmeasurable periods of time, following one another, in an infinitely long series: which must needs be a groundless imagination. The eternal duration which was before the world, being only the eternity of God's existence; which is nothing else but his immediate, perfect and invariable possession of the whole of his unlimited life, together and at once; *Vitæ interminabilis, tota simul & perfecta possessio.* Which is so generally allowed, that I need not stand to demonstrate it *.

* "If all created beings were taken away, all possibility "of any mutation or succession, of one thing to another, "would appear to be also removed. Abstract succession in "eternity is scarce to be understood. What is it that suc-"ceeds? one minute to another, perhaps *velut unda super-"venit undam.* But when we imagine this, we fancy that "the minutes are things separately existing. This is the "common notion; and yet it is a manifest prejudice. Time "is nothing but the existence of created successive beings, "and eternity the necessary existence of the Deity. Therefore, "if this necessary being hath no change or succession in his "nature, his existence must of course be unsuccessive. We "seem to commit a double oversight in this case; *first*, we "find succession in the necessary nature and existence of the "Deity himself: which is wrong, if the reasoning above be "conclusive. And *then*, we ascribe this succession to eternity, "considered abstractedly from the Eternal Being; and sup-"pose it, one knows not what, a thing subsisting by itself, "and flowing, one minute after another. This is the work "of pure imagination, and contrary to the reality of things.

"Hence

So this objection ſuppoſes an extent of ſpace beyond the limits of the creation, of an infinite length, breadth and depth, truely and properly diſtinguiſhed into different meaſurable parts, limited at certain ſtages, one beyond another, in an infinite ſeries. Which notion of abſolute and infinite ſpace is doubtleſs as unreaſonable, as that now mentioned, of abſolute and infinite duration. It is as improper, to imagine that the immenſity and omnipreſence of God is diſtinguiſhed by a ſeries of miles and leagues, one beyond another; as that the infinite duration of God is diſtinguiſhed by months and years, one after another. A diverſity and order of diſtinct parts, limited by certain periods, is as conceivable, and does as naturally obtrude itſelf on our imagination, in one caſe as the other; and there is equal reaſon in each caſe, to ſuppoſe that our imagination deceives us. It is equally improper, to talk of months and years of the Divine Exiſtence, and mile-ſquares of Deity: and we equally deceive our ſelves

" Hence the common metaphorical expreſſions; *Time runs* " *a-pace, let us lay hold on the preſent minute,* and the like. The " philoſophers themſelves miſlead us by their illuſtration. " They compare eternity to the motion of a point running " on for ever, and making a traceleſs infinite line. Here the " point is ſuppoſed a thing actually ſubſiſting, repreſenting " the preſent minute; and then they aſcribe motion or ſuc- " ceſſion to it: that is, they aſcribe motion to a mere non- " entity, to illuſtrate to us a ſucceſſive eternity, made up of " finite ſucceſſive parts.——If once we allow an all-perfect " mind, which hath an eternal, immutable and infinite com- " prehenſion of all things, always (and allow it we muſt) " the diſtinction of paſt and future vaniſhes with reſpect to " ſuch a mind.—In a word, if we proceed ſtep by ſtep, as " above, the eternity or exiſtence of the Deity will appear " to be *Vitæ interminabilis, tota, ſimul & perfecta poſſeſſio*; " how much ſoever this may have been a paradox hitherto." *Enquiry into the Nature of the Human Soul.* Vol. ii. 409, 410. 411. Edit. 3.

selves, when we talk of the world's being differently fixed, with respect to either of these sorts of measures. I think, we know not what we mean, if we say, the world might have been differently placed from what it is, in the broad expanse of infinity; or, that it might have been differently fixed in the long line of eternity: and all arguments and objections, which are built on the imaginations we are apt to have of infinite extension or duration, are buildings founded on shadows, or castles in the air.

2. The second argument, to prove that the Most High wills one thing rather than another, without any superior fitness or preferableness in the thing preferred, is God's actually placing in different parts of the world, particles, or atoms of matter, that are perfectly equal and alike. The forementioned Author says, p. 78, *&c.* "If one would descend to the minute specific particles, of which different bodies are composed, we should see abundant reason to believe, that there are thousands of such little particles, or atoms of matter, which are perfectly equal and alike, and could give no distinct determination to the Will of God, where to place them." He there instances in particles of water, of which there are such immense numbers, which compose the rivers and oceans of this world; and the infinite myriads of the luminous and fiery particles, which compose the body of the Sun; so many, that it would be very unreasonable to suppose no two of them should be exactly equal and alike.

Answ. (1.) To this I answer: that as we must suppose matter to be infinitely divisible, it is very unlikely, that any two, of all these particles, are exactly equal and alike; so unlikely, that it is a thousand to one, yea, an infinite number to one, but it is otherwise: and that although we should allow a great similiarity between the different particles of water and fire, as to their general nature and figure; and however small we suppose those particles to be, it is infinitely unlikely, that any two of them should be exactly equal in dimensions and quantity of matter.—If we should suppose a great many globes of the same nature with the globe of the earth, it would be very strange, if there were any two of them that had exactly the same number of particles of dust and water in them. But infinitely less strange, than that two particles of light should have just the same quantity of matter. For a particle of light, according to the doctrine of the infinite divisibility of matter, is composed of infinitely more assignable parts, than there are particles of dust and water in the globe of the earth. And as it is infinitely unlikely, that any two of these particles should be *equal*; so it is, that they should be *alike* in other respects: to instance in the configuration of their surfaces. If there were very many globes, of the nature of the earth, it would be very unlikely that any two should have exactly the same number of particles of dust, water and stone, in their surfaces, and all posited exactly alike, one with respect to another, without any difference, in any part discernable either by the naked eye or microscope; but infinitely less strange, than that two particles of light should be perfectly of the same figure. For there are infinitely more assignable real parts on the surface of a particle of light, than there are particles of dust, water and stone, on the surface of the terrestrial Globe.

Answ.

Anſw. (2.) But then, ſuppoſing that there are two particles, or atoms of matter, perfectly equal and alike, which God has placed in different parts of the creation; as I will not deny it to be poſſible for God to make two bodies perfectly alike, and put them in different places; yet it will not follow, that two different or diſtinct acts or effects of the Divine Power have exactly the ſame fitneſs for the ſame ends. For theſe two different bodies are not different or diſtinct, in any other reſpects than thoſe wherein they *differ*: they are two in no other reſpects than thoſe wherein there is a difference. If they are perfectly equal and alike *in themſelves*, then they can be diſtinguiſhed, or be diſtinct, only in thoſe things which are called *circumſtances*; as place, time, reſt, motion, or ſome other preſent or paſt circumſtances or relations. For it is difference only that conſtitutes diſtinction If God makes two bodies, *in themſelves* every way equal and alike, and agreeing perfectly in all other circumſtances and relations, but only *their place*; then in this only is there any diſtin tion or duplicity. The figure is the ſame, the meaſure is the ſame, the ſolidity and reſiſtance are the ſame, and every thing the ſame, but only the place. Therefore what the Will of God determines, is this, namely, that there ſhould be the ſame figure, the ſame extenſion, the ſame reſiſtance, &c. in two different places. And for this determination he has ſome reaſon. There is ſome end, for which ſuch a determination and act has a peculiar fitneſs, above all other acts. Here is no one thing determined without an end, and no one thing without a fitneſs for that end, ſuperior to any thing elſe. If it be the pleaſure of God to cauſe the ſame reſiſtance, and the ſame figure, to be in two different places and ſituations, we can no more juſtly argue from it, that here muſt be ſome determination or act of God's will, that is wholly without motive or end, then we can argue, that whenever, in any caſe it is a man's will to ſpeak the ſame words, or make the ſame ſounds at two different times; there muſt be ſome determination or act of his will, without any motive or end. The difference of place, in the former caſe, proves no more than the difference of time does in the other. If any one ſhould ſay, with regard to the former caſe, that there muſt be ſomething determined without an end; *viz* that of thoſe two ſimilar bodies, this in particular ſhould be made in this place, and the other in the other, and ſhould enquire, why the Creator did not make them in a tranſpoſition, when both are alike, and each would equally have ſuited either place? The enquiry ſuppoſes ſomething that is not true; namely, that the two bodies differ and are diſtinct in other reſpects beſides their place. So that with this diſtinction *inherent* in them, they might, in their firſt creation, have been tranſpoſed, and each might have begun its exiſtence in the place of the other.

Let us, for clearneſs ſake, ſuppoſe, that God had, at the beginning, made two globes, each of an inch diameter, both perfect ſpheres, and perfectly ſolid, without pores, and perfectly alike in every reſpect, and placed them near one to another, one towards the right hand, and the other towards the left, without any difference as to time, motion or reſt, paſt or preſent, or any circumſtance, but only their place; and the queſtion ſhould be aſked, why God in their creation placed them ſo? Why that which is made on the right hand, was not made on the left, and *vice verſa?* Let it be well conſidered, whether there be be any sense in such a question; and whether the enquiry does not suppose something false and absurd. Let it be considered, what the Creator must have done otherwise than he did, what different act of will or power he must have exerted, in order to the thing proposed. All that could have been done, would have been to have made two spheres, perfectly alike, in the same places where he has made them, without any difference of the things made, either in themselves or in any circumstance; so that the whole effect would have been without any difference, and, therefore, just the same. By the supposition, the two spheres are different in no other respect but their place; and therefore in other respects they are the same. Each has the same roundness; it is not a distinct rotundity, in any other respect but its situation. There are, also, the same dimensions, differing in nothing but their place. And so of their resistance, and every thing else that belongs to them.

HERE, if any chuse to say, "that there is a difference in another respect, *viz.* that they are not NUMERICALLY the same: that it is thus with all the qualities that belong to them: that it is confessed, they are, in some respects, the same; that is, they are both exactly alike; but yet *numerically* they differ. Thus the roundness of one is not the same *numerical, individual* roundness with that of the other." Let this be supposed; then the question about the determination of the Divine Will in the affair, is, why did God will, that this *individual* roundness should be at the right hand, and the other *individual* roundness at the left? why did not he make them in a contrary position? Let any rational person consider, whether such questions be not words without a meaning; as much as if God should see fit for some ends, to cause the same sounds to be repeated, or made at two different times; the sounds being perfectly the same in every other respect, but only one was a minute after the other; and it should be asked, upon it, why God caused these sounds, numerically different, to succeed one the other in such a manner? Why he did not make that individual sound, which was in the first minute, to be in the second? And the individual sound of the last minute to be in the first; which enquiries would be even ridiculous; as, I think, every person must see, at once, in the case proposed of two sounds, being only the same repeated, absolutely without any difference, but that one circumstance of time. If the Most High sees it will answer some good end, that the same sound should be made by lightening at two distinct times, and therefore wills that it should be so, must it needs therefore be, that herein there is some act of God's will without any motive or end? God saw fit often, at distinct times, and on different occasions, to say the very same words to *Moses*; namely, those, *I am Jehovah*. And would it not be unreasonable to infer, as a certain consequence, from this, that here must be some act or acts of the Divine Will, in determining and disposing these words exactly alike, at different times, wholly without aim or inducement? But it would be no more unreasonable than to say, that there must be an act of God's without any inducement, if he sees it best, and, for some reasons, determines that there shall be the same resistance, the same dimensions, and the same figure, in several distinct places.

If, in the instance of the two spheres, perfectly alike, it be supposed possible that God might have made them in a contrary position; that which is made

made at the right hand, being made at the left; then I ask, Whether it is not evidently equally possible, if God had made but one of them, and that in the place of the right-hand globe, that he might have made that numerically different from what it is, and numerically different from what he did make it; though perfectly alike, and in the same place; and at the same time, and in every respect, in the same circumstances and relations? Namely, Whether he might not have made it numerically the same with that which he has now made at the left hand; and so have left that which is now created at the right hand, in a state of non-existence? And, if so, whether it would not have been possible to have made one in that place, perfectly like these, and yet numerically differing from both? And let it be considered, whether, from this notion of a numerical difference in bodies, perfectly equal and alike, which numerical difference is something inherent in the bodies themselves, and diverse from the difference of place or time, or any circumstance whatsoever; it will not follow, that there is an infinite number of numerically different possible bodies, perfectly alike, among which God chuses, by a self-determining power, when he goes about to create bodies.

THEREFORE let us put the case thus: Supposing that God, in the beginning, had created but one perfectly solid sphere, in a certain place; and it should be enquired, Why God created that individual sphere, in that place, at that time? And why he did not create another sphere perfectly like it, but numerically different, in the same place, at the same time? or why he chose to bring into being there, that very body, rather than any of the infinite number of other bodies, perfectly

perfectly like it; either of which he could have made there as well, and would have answered his end as well? Why he caused to exist, at that place and time, that individual roundness, rather than any other of the infinite number of individual rotundities, just like it? Why that individual resistance, rather than any other of the infinite number of possible resistances, just like it? And it might as reasonably be asked, Why, when God first caused it to thunder, he caused that individual sound then to be made, and not another just like it? Why did he make choice of this very sound, and reject all the infinite number of other possible sounds just like it, but numerically differing from it, and all differing one from another? I think, every body must be sensible of the absurdity and nonsense of what is supposed in such enquiries. And, if we calmly attend to the matter, we shall be convinced, that all such kind of objections as I am answering, are founded on nothing but the imperfection of our manner of conceiving things, and the obscureness of language, and great want of clearness and precision in the signification of terms.

IF any shall find fault with this reasoning, that it is going a great length into metaphysical niceties and subtilties: I answer, the objection which they are in reply to, is a metaphysical subtility, and must be treated according to the nature of it*.

II. ANOTHER thing alledged is, that innumerable things which are determined by the Divine Will,

* "For men to have recourse to subtilties, in raising difficulties, and then complain, that they should be taken off by minutely examining these subtilties, is a strange kind of procedure." *Nature of the Human Soul*, vol. 2, p. 331.

Will, and chofen and done by God rather than others, differ from thofe that are not chofen in fo inconfiderable a manner, that it would be unreafonable to fuppofe the difference to be of any confequence, or that there is any fuperior fitnefs or goodnefs, that God can have refpect to in the determination.

To which I anfwer; it is impoffible for us to determine, with any certainty or evidence, that becaufe the difference is very fmall, and appears to us of no confideration, therefore there is abfolutely no fuperior goodnefs, and no valuable end, which can be propofed by the Creator and Governor of the world, in ordering fuch a difference. The forementioned author mentions many inftances. One is, there being one atom in the whole univerfe more, or lefs. But, I think, it would be unreafonable to fuppofe, that God made one atom in vain, or without any end or motive. He made not one atom, but what was a work of his Almighty Power, as much as the whole globe of the earth, and requires as much of a conftant exertion of Almighty Power to uphold it; and was made and is upheld underftandingly, and on defign, as much as if no other had been made but that. And it would be as unreafonable to fuppofe, that he made it without any thing really aimed at in fo doing, as much as to fuppofe, that he made the planet *Jupiter* without aim or defign.

It is poffible, that the moft minute effects of the Creator's power, the fmalleft affignable difference between the things which God has made, may be attended, in the whole feries of events, and the whole compafs and extent of their influence, with very great and important confequences.

quences. If the laws of motion and gravitation, laid down by Sir *Iſaac Newton*, hold univerſally, there is not one atom, nor the leſt aſſignable part of an atom, but what has influence, every moment, throughout the whole material univerſe, to cauſe every part to be otherwiſe than it would be, if it were not for that particular corporeal exiſtence. And however the effect is inſenſible for the preſent, yet it may, in length of time, become great and important.

To illuſtrate this, let us ſuppoſe two bodies moving the ſame way, in ſtraight lines, perfectly parallel one to another; but to be diverted from this parallel courſe, and drawn one from another, as much as might be by the attraction of an atom, at the diſtance of one of the furtheſt of the fixed ſtars from the earth; theſe bodies being turned out of the lines of their parallel motion, will, by degrees, get further and further diſtant, one from the other; and though the diſtance may be imperceptible for a long time, yet at length it may become very great. So the revolution of a planet round the ſun being retarded or accelerated, and the orbit of its revolution made greater or leſs, and more or leſs elliptical: and ſo its periodical time longer or ſhorter, no more than may be by the influence of the leaſt atom, might, in length of time, perform a whole revolution ſooner or later than otherwiſe it would have done; which might make a vaſt alteration with regard to millions of important events. So the influence of the leaſt particle may, for ought we know, have ſuch effect on ſomething in the conſtitution of ſome human body, as to cauſe another thought to ariſe in the mind at a certain time, than otherwiſe would have been; which, in length of time, (yea, and that not very great) might occaſion

caſion a vaſt alteration through the whole world of mankind. And ſo innumerable other ways might be mentioned, wherein the leaſt aſſignable alteration may poſſibly be attended with great conſequences.

Another *argument*, which the fore-mentioned author brings againſt a neceſſary determination of the Divine Will, by a ſuperior fitneſs, is, that ſuch doctrine derogates from the *freeneſs* of God's *grace* and *goodneſs*, in chuſing the objects of his favour and bounty, and from the *obligation* upon men to *thankfulneſs* for ſpecial benefits. P. 89, *&c.*

In anſwer to this objection, I would obſerve,

1. That it derogates no more from the goodneſs of God, to ſuppoſe the exerciſe of the benevolence of his nature to be determined by wiſdom, than to ſuppoſe it determined by chance, and that his favours are beſtowed altogether at random, his will being determined by nothing but perfect accident, without any end or deſign whatſoever: which muſt be the caſe, as has been demonſtrated, if Volition be not determined by a prevailing motive. That which is owing to perfect contingence, wherein neither previous inducement, nor antecedent choice has any hand, is not owing more to goodneſs or benevolence, than that which is owing to the influence of a wiſe end.

2. It is acknowledged, that if the motive that determines the Will of God, in the choice of the objects of his favours, be any moral quality in the object, recommending that object to his benevolence above others, his chuſing that object is not ſo great a manifeſtation of the freeneſs and ſovereignty of his Grace, as if it were otherwiſe.

But

But there is no Necessity of supposing this, in order to our supposing that he has some wise end in view, in determining to bestow his favours on one person rather than another. We are to distinguish between the *merit of the object of God's Favour*, or a moral qualification of *the object* attracting that favour and recommending to it, and the *natural fitness* of such a determination *of the act of God's goodness*, to answer some wise design of his own, some end in the view of God's Omniscience. —It is God's own act, that is the proper and immediate object of his Volition.

3. I SUPPOSE that none will deny, but that, in some instances, God acts from wise design in determining the particular subjects of his favours: none will say, I presume, that when God distinguishes, by his bounty, particular societies or persons, He never, in any instance, exercises any wisdom in so doing, aiming at some happy consequence. And, if it be not denied to be so in some instances, then I would enquire, whether, in these instances, God's goodness is less manifested, than in those wherein God has no aim or end at all? And whether the subjects have less cause of thankfulness? And if so, who shall be thankful for the bestowment of distinguishing mercy, with that enhancing circumstance of the distinction's being made without an end? How shall it be known when God is influenced by some wise aim, and when not? It is very manifest, with respect to the apostle *Paul*, that God had wise ends in chusing him to be a Christian and an Apostle, who had been a persecutor, &c. The apostle himself mentions one end. 1 *Tim.* i. 15, 16. *Christ Jesus came into the world to save sinners, of whom I am chief. Howbeit, for this cause I obtained mercy, that in me first, Jesus Christ might shew forth*

all

all long-suffering, for a pattern to them who should hereafter believe on Him to life everlasting. But yet the apostle never looked on it as a diminution of the freedom and riches of Divine Grace in his election, which he so often and so greatly magnifies. This brings me to observe,

4. Our supposing such a moral Necessity in the acts of God's will, as has been spoken of, is so far from necessarily derogating from the riches of God's grace to such as are the chosen objects of his favour, that, in many instances, this moral Necessity may arise from goodness, and from the great degree of it. God may chuse this object rather than another, as having a superior fitness to answer the ends, designs and inclinations of his goodness; being more sinful, and so more miserable and necessitous than others; the inclinations of Infinite Mercy and Benevolence may be more gratified, and the gracious design of God's sending his Son into the world, may be more abundantly answered, in the exercises of mercy towards such an object, rather than another.

One thing more I would observe, before I finish what I have to say on the head of the Necessity of the acts of God's will; and that is, that something much more like a servile subjection of the Divine Being to fatal Necessity, will follow from *Arminian* principles, than from the doctrines which they oppose. For they (at least most of them) suppose, with respect to all events that happen in the moral world, depending on the Volitions of moral agents, which are the most important events of the universe, to which all others are subordinate; I say, they suppose, with respect to these, that God has a certain foreknowledge of them, antecedent to any purposes or decrees

decrees of his about them. And if so they have a fixed certain futurity, prior to any designs or volitions of his, and independent on them, and to which his volitions must be subject, as he would wisely accommodate his affairs to this fixed futurity of the state of things in the moral world. So that here, instead of a moral necessity of God's Will, arising from, or consisting in, the infinite perfection and blessedness of the Divine Being, we have a fixed unalterable state of things, properly distinct from the perfect nature of the Divine Mind, and the state of the Divine Will and Design, and entirely independent on these things, and which they have no hand in, because they are prior to them; and which God's Will is truly subject to, being obliged to conform or accommodate himself to it, in all his purposes and decrees, and in every thing he does in his disposals and government of the world; the moral world being the end of the natural; so that all is in vain, that is not accommodated to that state of the moral world, which consists in, or depends upon, the acts and state of the wills of moral agents, which had a fixed futurition from eternity. Such a subjection to necessity as this, would truly argue an inferiority and servitude, that would be unworthy of the Supreme Being; and is much more agreeable to the notion which many of the heathen had of Fate, as above the gods, than that moral necessity of fitness and wisdom which has been spoken of; and is truly repugnant to the absolute sovereignty of God, and inconsistent with the supremacy of his will; and really subjects the will of the Most High, to the will of his creatures, and brings him into dependence upon them.

SECTION IX.

Concerning that Objection against the Doctrine which has been maintained, that it makes GOD *the* Author of Sin.

IT is urged by *Arminians*, that the doctrine of the neceſſity of men's volitions, or their neceſſary connection with antecedent events and circumſtances, makes the firſt cauſe, and ſupreme orderer of all things, the Author of Sin; in that he has ſo conſtituted the ſtate and courſe of things, that ſinful volitions become neceſſary, in conſequence of his diſpoſal. Dr. *Whitby*, in his Diſcourſe on the Freedom of the Will *, cites one of the ancients, as on his ſide, declaring that this opinion of the neceſſity of the will "abſolves Sinners, as doing nothing of their own accord which was evil, and would caſt all the blame of all the wickedneſs committed in the world, upon God, and upon his Providence, if that were admitted by the aſſertors of this fate; whether he himſelf did neceſſitate them to do theſe things, or ordered matters ſo, that they ſhould be conſtrained to do them by ſome other cauſe." And the doctor ſays, in another place †, "In the nature of the thing, and in the opinion of philoſophers, *cauſa deficiens, in rebus neceſſariis, ad cauſam per ſe efficientem reducenda eſt.* In things neceſſary, the deficient cauſe muſt be reduced to the efficient. And in this caſe the reaſon is evident; becauſe the not doing what is required, or not avoiding what is forbidden, being a defect, muſt follow

 from

* On the five Points, p. 361. † *Ibid.* p. 486.

from the position of the necessary cause of that deficiency."

Concerning this, I would observe the following things.

I. If there be any difficulty in this matter, it is nothing peculiar to this scheme; it is no difficulty or disadvantage, wherein it is distinguished from the scheme of *Arminians*; and, therefore, not reasonably objected by them.

Dr. Whitby supposes, that if Sin necessarily follows from God's withholding assistance, or if that assistance be not given, which is absolutely necessary to the avoiding of Evil; then, in the nature of the thing, God must be as properly the Author of that Evil, as if he were the efficient cause of it. From whence, according to what he himself says of the devils and damned spirits, God must be the proper Author of their perfect unrestrained wickedness: he must be the efficient cause of the great pride of the devils, and of their perfect malignity against God, Christ, his saints, and all that is good, and of the insatiable cruelty of their disposition. For he allows, that God has so forsaken them, and does so withhold his assistance from them, that they are incapacitated from doing good, and determined only to evil *. Our doctrine, in its consequence, makes God the Author of men's Sin in this world, no more, and in no other sense, than his doctrine, in its consequence, makes God the Author of the hellish pride and malice of the devils. And doubtless the latter is as odious an effect as the former.

Again, if it will *follow at all*, that God is the Author of Sin, from what has been supposed of

* On the five points, p. 302, 305.

of a ſure and infallible connection between antecedents and conſequents, it will *follow becauſe of this*, *viz.* that for God to be Author or Orderer of thoſe things which, he knows before-hand, will infallibly be attended with ſuch a conſequence, is the ſame thing, in effect, as for him to be the Author of that conſequence. But, if this be ſo, this is a difficulty which equally attends the doctrine of *Arminians* themſelves; at leaſt, of thoſe of them who allow God's certain fore-knowledge of all events. For, on the ſuppoſition of ſuch a fore-knowledge, this is the caſe with reſpect to every Sin that is committed: God knew, that if he ordered and brought to paſs ſuch and ſuch events, ſuch Sins would infallibly follow. As for inſtance, God certainly foreknew, long before *Judas* was born, that if he ordered things ſo, that there ſhould be ſuch a man born, at ſuch a time, and at ſuch a place, and that his life ſhould be preſerved, and that he ſhould, in Divine Providence, be led into acquaintance with Jeſus; and that his heart ſhould be ſo influenced by God's Spirit or Providence, as to be inclined to be a follower of Chriſt; and that he ſhould be one of thoſe twelve, which ſhould be choſen conſtantly to attend him as his family; and that his health ſhould be preſerved, ſo that he ſhould go up to *Jeruſalem*, at the laſt Paſſover in Chriſt's life; and it ſhould be ſo ordered, that *Judas* ſhould ſee Chriſt's kind treatment of the woman which anointed him at *Bethany*, and have that reproof from Chriſt, which he had at that time, and ſee and hear other things, which excited his enmity againſt his Maſter, and other circumſtances ſhould be ordered, as they were ordered; it would be what would moſt certainly and infallibly follow, that *Judas* would betray his Lord, and would ſoon

 after

after hang himſelf, and die impenitent, and be ſent to hell, for his horrid wickedneſs.

THEREFORE, this ſuppoſed difficulty ought not to be brought as an objection againſt the ſcheme which has been maintained, as *diſagreeing* with the *Arminian* ſcheme, ſeeing it is no difficulty owing to ſuch a *diſagreement*; but a difficulty wherein the *Arminians* ſhare with us. That muſt be unreaſonably made an objection againſt our differing from them, which we ſhould not eſcape or avoid at all by agreeing with them.

AND therefore I would obſerve,

II. THEY who object, that this doctrine makes God the Author of Sin, ought diſtinctly to explain what they mean by that phraſe, *The Author of Sin*. I know the phraſe, as it is commonly uſed, ſignifies ſomething very ill. If by *the Author of Sin*, be meant *the Sinner*, *the Agent*, or *Actor of Sin*, or *the Doer of a wicked thing*; ſo it would be a reproach and blaſphemy, to ſuppoſe God to be the Author of Sin. In this ſenſe, I utterly deny God to be the Author of Sin; rejecting ſuch an imputation on the Moſt High, as what is infinitely to be abhorred; and deny any ſuch thing to be the conſequence of what I have laid down. But if, by *the Author of Sin*, is meant the permitter, or not a hinderer of Sin; and, at the ſame time, a diſpoſer of the ſtate of events, in ſuch a manner, for wiſe, holy, and moſt excellent ends and purpoſes, that Sin, if it be permitted or not hindered, will moſt certainly and infallibly follow: I ſay, if this be all that is meant, by being the Author of Sin, I do not deny that God is the Author of Sin, (though I diſlike and reject the phraſe, as that which by uſe and cuſtom is apt to carry another ſenſe) it is no reproach

for

for the Most High to be thus the Author of Sin. This is not to be the *Actor of Sin*, but, on the contrary, *of holiness*. What God doth herein, is holy; and a glorious exercise of the infinite excellency of his nature. And, I do not deny, that God's being thus the Author of Sin, follows from what I have laid down; and, I assert, that it equally follows from the doctrine which is maintained by most of the *Arminian* divines.

THAT it is most certainly so, that God is in such a manner the Disposer and Orderer of Sin, is evident, if any credit is to be given to the Scriptures; as well as because it is impossible, in the nature of things, to be otherwise. In such a manner God ordered the obstinacy of *Pharaoh*, in his refusing to obey God's Commands, to let the people go. Exod iv. 21. *I will harden his heart, and he shall not let the people go.* Chap. vii. 2—5. Aaron *thy brother shall speak unto* Pharaoh, *that he send the children of* Israel *out of his land. And I will harden* Pharaoh's *heart, and multiply my signs and my wonders in the land of* Egypt. *But* Pharaoh *shall not hearken unto you; that I may lay mine hand upon* Egypt, *by great judgments*, &c. Chap. ix. 12. *And the Lord hardened the heart of* Pharaoh, *and he hearkened not unto them, as the Lord had spoken unto* Moses. Chap. x. 1, 2. *And the Lord said unto* Moses, *Go in unto* Pharaoh; *for I have hardened his heart, and the heart of his servants, that I might shew these my signs before him, and that thou mayest tell it in the ears of thy son, and thy son's son, what things I have wrought in* Egypt, *and my signs which I have done amongst them, that ye may know that I am the Lord.* Chap. xiv. 4. *And I will harden* Pharaoh's *heart, that he shall follow after them: and I will be honoured upon* Pharaoh, *and upon all his Host.* Ver. 8. *And the Lord hardened the heart of*

Pharaoh *King of* Egypt, *and he pursued after the Children of* Israel. And it is certain, that in such a manner God, for wise and good ends, ordered that event, *Joseph* being sold into *Egypt*, by his brethren. Gen. xlv. 5. *Now, therefore, be not grieved, nor angry with yourselves, that ye sold me hither; for God did send me before you to preserve life.* Ver 7, 8. *God did send me before you to preserve a posterity in the earth, and to save your lives by a great deliverance: so that now it was not you, that sent me hither, but God.* Psal. cvii. 17. *He sent a man before them, even* Joseph, *who was sold for a servant.* It is certain, that thus God ordered the Sin and Folly of *Sihon* King of the *Amorites*, in refusing to let the people of *Israel* pass by him peaceably. Deut. ii. 30. *But* Sihon *King of* Heshbon *would not let us pass by him; for the Lord thy God hardened his spirit, and made his heart obstinate, that he might deliver him into thine hand.* It is certain, that God thus ordered the Sin and Folly of the Kings of *Canaan*, that they attempted not to make peace with *Israel*, but, with a stupid boldness and obstinacy, set themselves violently to oppose them and their God. Josh. xi. 20. *For it was of the Lord, to harden their hearts, that they should come against* Israel *in battle, that he might destroy them utterly, and that they might have no favour; but that he might destroy them, as the Lord commanded* Moses. It is evident, that thus God ordered the treacherous rebellion of *Zedekiah* against the King of *Babylon*. Jer. lii. 3. *For through the anger of the Lord it came to pass in* Jerusalem, *and* Judah, *until he had cast them out from his presence, that* Zedekiah *rebelled against the King of* Babylon. So 2 Kings xxiv. 20. And it is exceeding manifest, that God thus ordered the rapine and unrighteous ravages of *Nebuchadnezzar*, in spoiling and ruining the nations round about. Jer. xxv. 9. *Behold, I will ſend and take all the families of the north, ſaith the Lord, and* Nebuchadnezzar *my ſervant, and will bring them againſt this land, and againſt all the nations round about; and will utterly deſtroy them, and make them an aſtoniſhment, and an hiſſing, and perpetual deſolations.* Chap. xliii. 10, 11. *I will ſend and take* Nebuchadnezzar *the king of* Babylon, *my ſervant: and I will ſet his throne upon theſe ſtones that I have hid, and he ſhall ſpread his royal pavilion over them. And when he cometh, he ſhall ſmite the land of* Egypt, *and deliver ſuch as are for death to death, and ſuch as are for captivity to captivity, and ſuch as are for the ſword to the ſword.* Thus God repreſents himſelf as *ſending* for *Nebuchadnezzar*, and *taking* of him and his armies, and *bringing* him againſt the nations, which were to be deſtroyed by him, to that very end, that he might utterly deſtroy them, and make them deſolate; and as appointing the work that he ſhould do, ſo particularly, that the very perſons were deſigned, that he ſhould kill with the ſword; and thoſe that ſhould be killed with famine and peſtilence, and thoſe that ſhould be carried into captivity; and that in doing all theſe things, he ſhould act as his ſervant; by which, leſs cannot be intended, than that he ſhould ſerve his purpoſes and deſigns. And in *Jer.* xxvii. 4, 5, 6. God declares, how he would cauſe him thus to ſerve his deſigns, *viz.* by bringing this to paſs in his ſovereign diſpoſals, as the great Poſſeſſor and Governor of the Univerſe, that diſpoſes all things juſt as pleaſes him. *Thus ſaith the Lood of Hoſts, the God of* Iſrael; *I have made the earth, the man and the beaſt, that are upon the ground, by my great power, and my ſtretched out arm, and have given it unto whom it ſeemed meet unto me: and now I have given all theſe lands into the hands of* Nebuchadnezzar MY SERVANT, *and the beaſts of the field have I given also to serve him.* And *Nebuchadnezzar* is spoken of as doing these things, by having his *arms strengthened* by God, and having *God's sword put into his hands, for this end.* Ezek. xxx. 24, 25, 26. Yea, God speaks of his terribly ravaging and wasting the nations, and cruelly destroying all sorts, without distinction of sex or age, as the weapon in God's hand, and the instrument of his indignation, which God makes use of to fulfill his own purposes, and execute his own vengeance. Jer li. 20, &c. *Thou art my battle-axe, and weapons of war. For with thee will I break in pieces the nations, and with thee I will destroy kingdoms, and with thee I will break in pieces the horse and his rider, and with thee I will break in pieces the chariot and his rider; with thee also will I break in pieces man and woman; and with thee will I break in pieces old and young; and with thee will I break in pieces the young man and the maid,* &c. It is represented, that the designs of *Nebuchadnezzar*, and those that destroyed *Jerusalem*, never could have been accomplished, had not God determined them, as well as they; Lam. iii. 37. *Who is he that saith, and it cometh to pass, and the Lord commandeth it not?* And yet the King of *Babylon*'s thus destroying the nations, and especially the *Jews*, is spoken of as his great wickedness, for wihch God finally destroyed him. *Isa.* xiv. 4, 5, 6, 12. *Hab.* ii. 5—12. and *Jer.* chap. l. and li It is most manifest, that God, to serve his own designs, providentially ordered *Shimei*'s cursing *David.* 2 Sam. xvi. 10, 11. *The Lord hath said unto him curse* David.—*Let him curse, for the Lord hath bidden him.*

It is certain, that God thus, for excellent, holy, gracious and glorious ends, ordered the fact which they committed, who were concerned in

Christ's death; and that therein they did but fulfill God's designs. As, I trust, no Christian will deny it was the design of God, that Christ should *be crucified*, and that for this end, he came into the world. It is very manifest, by many Scriptures, that the whole affair of Christ's crucifixion, with its circumstances, and the treachery of *Judas*, that made way for it, was ordered in God's providence, in pursuance of his purpose; notwithstanding the violence that is used with those plain Scriptures, to obscure and pervert the sense of them. Acts ii. 23. *Him being delivered, by the determinate counsel and foreknowledge of God*, ye have taken, and with wicked hands, have crucified and slain.* Luke xxii. 21, 22. † *But behold the hand of him that betrayeth me, is with me on the table: and truly the Son of Man goeth, as it was determined.* Acts iv. 27, 28. *For of a truth, against the holy child Jesus, whom thou hast anointed, both* Herod *and* Pontius Pilate, *with the Gentiles, and the people of* Israel, *were gathered together, for to do whatsoever thy hand and thy counsel determined before to be done.* Acts iii. 17, 18. *And now, brethren, I wot that through ignorance ye did it, as did also*

* "*Grotius*, as well as *Beza*, observes, προγνωσις must "here signify decree; and *Elsner* has shewn that it has that "signification, in approved Greek writers. And it is certain εκδοτος signifies one given up into the hands of an "enemy." *Doddridge* in *Loc.*

† "As this passage is not liable to the ambiguities, which "some have apprehended in *Acts* ii. 23. and iv 28. (which "yet seem on the whole to be parallel to it, in their most "natural construction) I look upon it as an evident proof, "that these things are, in the language of Scripture, said "to be determined or decreed (or exactly bounded and "marked out by God, as the word ὁριζω most naturally signifies) which he sees in fact will happen, in consequence "of his volitions, without any necessitating agency; as well "as those events, of which he is properly the Author." *Dodd.* in *Loc.*

also your rulers: but these things, which God before had shewed by the mouth of all his prophets, that Christ should suffer, he hath so fulfilled. So that what these murderers of Christ did, is spoken of as what God brought to pass or ordered, and that by which he fulfilled his own word.

In Rev. xvii. 17. *The agreeing of the Kings of the earth to give their kingdom to the beast*, though it was a very wicked thing in them, is spoken of as *a fulfilling God's Will*, and what *God hath put into their hearts to do.* It is manifest that God sometimes permits Sin to be committed, and at the same time orders things so, that if he permits the fact, it will come to pass, because, on some accounts, he sees it needful and of importance, that it should come to pass. Matt. xviii. 7. *It must needs be, that offences come; but wo to that man by whom the offence cometh.* With 1 Cor. xi. 19. *For there must also be heresies among you, that they which are approved may be made manifest among you.*

THUS it is certain and demonstrable, from the holy Scriptures, as well as the nature of things, and the principles of *Arminians*, that God permits Sin; and at the same time, so orders things, in his Providence, that it certainly and infallibly will come to pass, in consequence of his permission.

I PROCEED to observe in the next place,

III. THAT there is a great difference between God's being concerned thus, by his *permission*, in an event and act, which, in the inherent subject and agent of it, is Sin, (though the event will certainly follow on his permission) and his being concerned in it by *producing* it and exerting the act of Sin; or between his being the *Orderer* of its certain existence, by *not hindering* it, under certain

certain circumstances, and his being the proper *Actor* or *Author* of it, by a *positive Agency* or *Efficiency*. And this, notwithstanding what Dr. *Whitby* offers about a saying of philosophers, that *causa deficiens in rebus necessariis, ad causam per se efficientem reducenda est*. As there is a vast difference between the sun's being the cause of the lightsomeness and warmth of the atmosphere, and brightness of gold and diamonds, by its presence and possitive influence; and its being the occasion of darkness and frost, in the night, by its motion, whereby it descends below the horizon. The motion of the sun is the occasion of the latter kind of events; but it is not the proper cause, efficient or producer of them; though they are necessarily consequent on that motion, under such circumstances: no more is any action of the Divine Being the Cause of the Evil of men's wills. If the sun were the proper *cause* of cold and darkness, it would be the *fountain* of these things, as it is the fountain of light and heat: and then something might be argued from the nature of cold and darkness, to a likeness of nature in the sun; and it might be justly inferred, that the sun itself is dark and cold, and that his beams are black and frosty. But from its being the cause no otherwise than by its departure, no such thing can be inferred, but the contrary; it may justly be argued, that the sun is a bright and hot body, if cold and darkness are found to be the consequence of its withdrawment; and the more constantly and necessarily these effects are connected with, and confined to its absence, the more strongly does it argue the sun to be the fountain of light and heat. So, inasmuch as Sin is not the Fruit of any positive Agency or Influence of the Most High, but, on the contrary, arises from the withholding of his action

action and energy, and, under certain circumstances, necessarily follows on the want of his influence; this is no argument that he is sinful, or his operation evil, or has any thing of the nature of Evil; but, on the contrary, that He, and his Agency, are altogether good and holy, and that He is the Fountain of all Holiness. It would be strange arguing, indeed, because men never commit sin, but only when God leaves them *to themselves*, and necessarily sin, when he does so, and therefore their Sin is not *from themselves*, but from God; and so, that God must be a sinful Being: as strange as it would be to argue, because it is always dark when the sun is gone, and never dark when the sun is present, that therefore all darkness is from the sun, and that his disk and beams must needs be black.

IV. It properly belongs to the Supreme and Absolute Governor of the Universe, to order all important events within his dominion, by his wisdom: but the events in the moral world are of the most important kind: such as the moral actions of intelligent creatures, and their consequences.

These events will be ordered by something. They will either be disposed by wisdom, or they will be disposed by chance; that is, they will be disposed by blind and undesigning causes, if that were possible, and could be called a disposal. Is it not better, that the good and evil which happens in God's world, should be ordered, regulated, bounded and determined by the good pleasure of an infinitely wise Being, who perfectly comprehends within his understanding and constant view, the universality of things, in all their extent and duration, and sees all the influence

ence of every event, with reſpect to every individual thing and circumſtance, throughout the grand ſyſtem, and the whole of the eternal ſeries of conſequences; than to leave theſe things to fall out by chance, and to be determined by thoſe cauſes which have no underſtanding or aim? Doubtleſs, in theſe important events, there is a better and a worſe, as to the time, ſubject, place, manner and circumſtances of their coming to paſs, with regard to their influence on the ſtate and courſe of things. And if there be, it is certainly beſt that they ſhould be determined to that time, place, *&c.* which is beſt. And therefore it is in its own nature fit, that wiſdom, and not chance, ſhould order theſe things. So that it belongs to the Being, who is the poſſeſſor of infinite wiſdom, and is the Creator and Owner of the whole ſyſtem of created exiſtences, and has the care of all; I ſay, it belongs to him, to take care of this matter; and he would not do what is proper for him, if he ſhould neglect it. And it is ſo far from being unholy in him, to undertake this affair, that it would rather have been unholy to neglect it; as it would have been a neglecting what fitly appertains to him; and ſo it would have been a very unfit and unſuitable neglect.

Therefore the ſovereignty of God doubleſs extends to this matter: eſpecially conſidering, that if it ſhould be ſuppoſed to be otherwiſe, and God ſhould leave men's volitions, and all moral events, to the determination and diſpoſition of blind unmeaning cauſes, or they ſhould be left to happen perfectly without a cauſe; this would be no more conſiſtent with liberty, in any notion of it, and particularly not in the *Arminian* notion of it, than if theſe events were ſubject to the

the diſpoſal of Divine Providence, and the will of man were determined by circumſtances which are ordered and diſpoſed by Divine Wiſdom; as appears by what has already been obſerved. But it is evident, that ſuch a providential diſpoſing and determining men's moral actions, though it infers a moral neceſſity of thoſe actions, yet it does not in the leaſt infringe the real liberty of mankind; the only liberty that common ſenſe teaches to be neceſſary to moral agency, which, as has been demonſtrated, is not inconſiſtent with ſuch neceſſity.

On the whole, it is manifeſt, that God may be, in the manner which has been deſcribed, the Order and Diſpoſer of that event, which, in the inherent ſubject and agent, is moral Evil; and yet His ſo doing may be no moral Evil. He may will the diſpoſal of ſuch an event, and its coming to paſs for good ends, and his will not be an immoral or ſinful will, but a perfect holy will. And he may actually, in his Providence, ſo diſpoſe and permit things, that the event may be certainly and infalliby connected with ſuch diſpoſal and permiſſion, and his act therein not be an immoral or unholy, but a perfect holy act. Sin may be an evil thing, and yet that there ſhould be ſuch a diſpoſal and permiſſion, as that it ſhould come to paſs, may be a good thing. This is no contradiction, or inconſiſtence. *Joſeph's* brethren's ſelling him into *Egypt*, conſider it only as it was acted by them, and with reſpect to their views and aims which were evil, was a very bad thing; but it was a good thing, as it was an event of God's ordering, and conſidered with reſpect to his views and aims which were good. Gen. l. 20. *As for you, ye thought Evil againſt me; but God meant it unto Good.* So the crucifixion of Chriſt,

Chriſt, if we conſider only thoſe things which belong to the event as it proceeded from his murderers, and are comprehended within the compaſs of the affair conſidered as their act, their principles, diſpoſitions, views and aims; ſo it was one of the moſt heinous things that ever was done; in many reſpects the moſt horrid of all acts; but conſider it, as it was willed and ordered of God, in the extent of his deſigns and views, it was the moſt admirable and glorious of all events; and God's willing the event was the moſt holy volition of God, that ever was made known to men; and God's act in ordering it, was a divine act, which, above all others, manifeſts the moral excellency of the Divine Being.

The conſideration of theſe things may help us to a ſufficient anſwer to the cavils of *Arminians*, concerning what has been ſuppoſed by many *Calviniſts*, of a diſtinction between a *ſecret* and *revealed* Will of God, and their diverſity one from the other; ſuppoſing that the *Calviniſts* herein aſcribe inconſiſtent Wills to the Moſt High: which is without any foundation. God's *ſecret* and *revealed* Will, or, in other words, his *diſpoſing* and *perceptive* Will may be diverſe, and exerciſed in diſſimilar acts, the one in diſapproving and oppoſing, the other in willing and determining, without any inconſiſtence. Becauſe, although theſe diſſimilar exerciſes of the Divine Will may, in ſome reſpects, relate to the ſame things, yet, in ſtrictneſs, they have different and contrary objects, the one evil and the other good. Thus, for inſtance, the crucifixion of Chriſt was a thing contrary to the revealed or perceptive Will of God; becauſe, as it was viewed and done by his malignant murderers, it was a thing infinitely contrary to the holy Nature of God, and ſo neceſſarily contrary to the

holy

holy inclination of his heart revealed in his law. Yet this does not at all hinder but that the crucifixion of Christ, considered with all those glorious consequences, which were within the view of the Divine Omniscience, might be indeed, and therefore might appear to God to be, a glorious event; and consequently be agreeable to his will, though this Will may be secret, *i. e.* not revealed in God's law. And thus considered, the Crucifixion of Christ was not evil, but good. If the secret exercises of God's Will were of a kind that is dissimilar, and contrary to his revealed Will, respecting the same, or like objects; if the objects of both were good, or both evil; then, indeed, to ascribe contrary kinds of volition or inclination to God, respecting these objects, would be to ascribe an inconsistent Will to God: but to ascribe to Him different and opposite exercises of heart; respecting different objects, and objects contrary one to another, is so far from supposing God's Will to be *inconsistent* with itself, that it cannot be supposed *consistent* with itself any other way. For any Being to have a Will of choice respecting good, and, at the same time, a Will of rejection and refusal respecting evil, is to be very consistent: but the contrary, *viz.* to have the same Will towards these contrary objects, and to chuse and love both good and evil, at the same time, is to be very inconsistent.

THERE is no inconsistence in supposing, that God may hate a thing as it is in itself, and considered simply as evil, and yet that it may be his Will it should come to pass, considering all consequences. I believe, there is no person of good understanding, who will venture to say, he is certain that it is impossible it should be best, taking in the whole compass and extent of existence,

and

and all consequences in the endless series of events, that there should be such a thing as moral evil in the world *. And, if so, it will certainly

follow,

* Here are worthy to be observed some passages of a late noted writer, of our nation, that no body who is acquainted with him, will suspect to be very favourable to *Calvinism.* " It is difficult (says he) to handle the *necessity of evil* in such " a manner, as not to stumble such as are not above being " alarmed at propositions which have an uncommon sound. " But if philosophers will but reflect calmly on the matter, " they will find, that consistently with the unlimited power " of the Supreme Cause, it may be said, that in the best or- " dered system, *evils* must have place."—*Turnbull's* PRINCIPLES *of moral Philosophy*, p. 327, 328. He is there speaking of *moral* evils, as may be seen.

Again the same Author, in his *second Vol.* entitled, *Christian Philosophy*, p. 35. has these words: " If the Author and " Governor of all things be infinitely *perfect*, then whatever " is, is *right*; of all possible systems he hath chosen the *best*: " and, consequently, there is *no absolute evil* in the universe.— " This being the case, all the seeming *imperfections* or *evils* " in it are such only in a *partial* view; and, with respect to " the *whole* system, they are *goods*.

" Ibid. p. 37. " *Whence then comes evil*, is the question that " hath, in all ages, been reckoned the *Gordian* knot in philo- " sophy. And, indeed, if we own the existence of evil in the " world in an *absolute* sense, we diametrically contradict what " hath been just now proved of God. For if there be any " *evil* in the system, that is not good with respect to the *whole*, " then is the *whole* not good, but evil: or, at best, very im- " perfect: and an *Author* must be as his *workmanship* is; as " is the effect, such is the cause. But the solution of this " difficulty is at hand; *That there is no evil in the universe.* " What! are there no pains, no imperfections? Is there no " misery, no vice in the world? or are not these *evils?* " Evils indeed they are; that is, those of one sort are hurt- " ful, and those of the other sort are equally hurtful, and " abominable: but they are *not* evil or mischievous with re- " spect to the *whole*."

Ibid. p. 42 " But He is, at the same time, said to *create* " evil, darkness, confusion; and yet to do no evil, but to be " the Author of good only. He is called the *Father of Lights*, " the Author of *every perfect and good gift, with whom there* " *is no variableness nor shadow of turning*, who *tempteth no* " *man*, follow, that an infinitely wiſe Being, who always chuſes what is beſt, muſt chuſe that there ſhould be ſuch a thing. And, if ſo, then ſuch a choice is not an evil, but a wiſe and holy choice. And if ſo, then that Providence which is agreeable to ſuch a choice, is a wiſe and holy Providence. Men do *will* ſin as ſin, and ſo are the authors and actors of it: they love it as ſin, and for evil ends and purpoſes. God does not will ſin as ſin, or for the ſake of any thing evil; though it be his pleaſure ſo to order things, that, He permitting, ſin will come to paſs; for the ſake of the great good that by his diſpoſal ſhall be the conſequence. His willing to order things ſo that evil ſhould come to paſs, for the ſake of the contrary good, is no argument that He does not hate evil, as evil: and if ſo, then it is no reaſon why he may not reaſonably forbid evil as evil, and puniſh it as ſuch.

The *Arminians* themſelves muſt be obliged, whether they will or no, to allow a diſtinction of God's Will, amounting to juſt the ſame thing that *Calviniſts* intend by their diſtinction of a *ſecret and revealed Will.* They muſt allow a diſtinction of thoſe things which God thinks beſt ſhould be, conſidering all circumſtances and conſequences, and ſo are agreeable to his diſpoſing Will, and thoſe things which he loves, and are agreeable to his nature

" *man,* but *giveth to all men liberally, and upbraideth not.* And " yet, by the prophet *Iſaias,* He is introduced ſaying of " Himſelf, *I form light, and create darkneſs; I make peace, and* " *create evil: I the Lord, do all theſe things.* What is the " meaning, the plain language of all this, but that the Lord " delighteth in goodneſs, and (as the Scripture ſpeaks) evil " is *his ſtrange work?* He intends and purſues the univerſal " *good* of his creation: and the *evil* which happens, is not " permitted for its own ſake, or through any pleaſure in evil, " but becauſe it is requiſite to the *greater good* purſued.

nature, in themselves considered. Who is there that will dare to say, that the hellish pride, malice and cruelty of devils, are agreeable to God, and what He likes and approves? And yet, I trust, there is no Christian divine but what will allow, that it is agreeable to God's Will so to order and dispose things concerning them, so to leave them to themselves, and give them up to their own wickedness, that this perfect wickedness should be a necessary consequence. Be sure Dr. *Whitby*'s words do plainly suppose and allow it *.

These following things may be laid down as maxims of plain truth, and indisputable evidence.

1. That God is a *perfectly happy* Being, in the most absolute highest sense possible.

2. That it will follow from hence, that God is free from every thing that is *contrary to happiness*; and so, that in strict propriety of speech, there is no such thing as any pain, grief, or trouble, in God.

3. When any intelligent being is really crossed and disappointed, and things are contrary to what he truly desires, he is the *less pleased*, or has *less pleasure*, his *pleasure and happiness is diminished*, and he suffers what is disagreeable to him, or is the subject of something that is of a nature contrary to joy and happiness, even pain and grief †.

* *Whitby* on the five points, Edit. 2. 300, 305, 309.

† Certainly it is not less absurd and unreasonable, to talk of God's Will and Desires being truly and properly crossed, without his suffering any uneasiness, or any thing grievous or disagreeable than it is to talk of something that may be called a *revealed Will*, which may, in some respect, be different from a *secret* purpose; which purpose may be fulfilled, when the other is opposed.

From this last axiom, it follows, that if no distinction is to be admitted between God's hatred of sin, and his Will with respect to the event and the existence of sin, as the all-wise Determiner of all events, under the view of all consequences through the whole compass and series of things; I say, then it certainly follows, that the coming to pass of every individual act of sin is truly, all things considered, contrary to his Will, and that his Will is really crossed in it; and this in proportion as He hates it. And as God's hatred of sin is infinite, by reason of the infinite contrariety of his Holy Nature to sin; so his Will is infinitely crossed, in every act of sin that happens. Which is as much as to say, He endures that which is infinitely disagreeable to Him, by means of every act of sin that He sees committed. And, therefore, as appears by the preceding positions, He endures truly and really, infinite grief or pain from every sin. And so He must be infinitely crossed, and suffer infinite pain, every day, in millions and millions of instances: He must continually be the subject of an immense number of *real*, and truly infinitely *great* crosses and vexations. Which would be to make him infinitely the most miserable of all Beings.

If any objector should say; all that these things amount to, is, that *God may do evil that good may come*; which is justly esteemed immoral and sinful in men; and therefore may be justly esteemed inconsistent with the moral perfections of God. I answer, that for God to dispose and permit evil, in the manner that has been spoken of, is not to do evil that good may come; for it is not to do evil at all.—In order to a thing's being morally evil, there must be one of these things belonging to it: either it must be a thing *unfit*

unfit and *unsuitable* in its own nature; or it must have a *bad tendency*; or it must proceed from an *evil disposition*, and be done for an evil end. But neither of these things can be attributed to God's ordering and permitting such events, as the immoral acts of creatures, for good ends. (1.) It is not *unfit in its own nature*, that He should do so. For it is in its own nature *fit*, that *infinite wisdom*, and not blind chance, should dispose moral good and evil in the world. And it is *fit*, that the Being who has *infinite wisdom*, and is the Maker, Owner, and Supreme Governor of the World, should take care of that matter. And, therefore, there is no *unfitness*, or unsuitableness in his doing it. It may be unfit, and so immoral, for any other beings to go about to order this affair; because they are not possessed of a wisdom, that in any manner fits them for it; and, in other respects, they are not fit to be trusted with this affair; nor does it belong to them, they not being the owners and lords of the universe.

We need not be afraid to affirm, that if a wise and good man knew with absolute certainty, it would be best, all things considered, that there should be such a thing as moral evil in the world, it would not be contrary to his wisdom and goodness, for him to chuse that it should be so. It is no evil desire, to desire good, and to desire that which, all things considered, is best. And it is no unwise choice, to chuse that that should be, which is best should be; and to chuse the existence of that thing concerning which this is known, *viz.* that it is best it should be, and so is known in the whole to be most worthy to be chosen. On the contrary, it would be a plain defect in wisdom and goodness, for him not to chuse it. And the reason why he might not *or-*

der it, if he were able, would not be becauſe he might not deſire it, but only the ordering of that matter does not belong to him. But it is no harm for Him who is, by right, and in the greateſt propriety, the Supreme Orderer of all things, to order every thing in ſuch a manner, as it would be a point of wiſdom in Him to chuſe that they ſhould be ordered. If it would be a plain defect of wiſdom and goodneſs in a Being, not to chuſe that that ſhould be, which He certainly knows it would, all things conſidered, be beſt ſhould be (as was but now obſerved) then it muſt be impoſſible for a Being who has no defect of wiſdom and goodneſs, to do otherwiſe than chuſe it ſhould be; and that, for this very reaſon, becauſe He is perfectly wiſe and good. And if it be agreable to perfect wiſdom and goodneſs for him to chuſe that it ſhould be, and the ordering of all things ſupremely and perfectly belongs to him, it muſt be agreeable to infinite wiſdom and goodneſs, to order that it ſhould be. If the choice is good, the ordering and diſpoſing things according to that choice muſt alſo be good. It can be no harm in one to whom it belongs *to do his Will in the armies of heaven, and amongſt the inhabitants of the earth*, to execute a good volition. If this Will be good, and the object of his Will be, all things conſidered, good and beſt, then the chuſing or willing it is not *willing evil* that good may come. And if ſo, then his ordering, according to that Will, is not *doing evil*, that good may come.

2. It is not of a *bad tendency*, for the Supreme Being thus to order and permit that moral evil to be, which is beſt ſhould come to paſs. For that it is of good tendency, is the very thing ſuppoſed in the point now in queſtion.—Chriſt's Crucifixion, though a moſt horrid fact in them that perpe-

perpetrated it, was of moſt glorious tendency as permitted and ordered of God.

3. Nor is there any need of ſuppoſing, it *proceeds from any evil diſpoſition or aim:* for by the ſuppoſition, what is aimed at is good, and good is the actual iſſue, in the final reſult of things.

SECTION X.

Concerning Sin's firſt Entrance *into the World.*

THE things, which have already been offered, may ſerve to obviate or clear many of the objections which might be raiſed concerning Sin's firſt coming into the world; as though it would follow from the doctrine maintained, that God muſt be the Author of the firſt Sin, through his ſo diſpoſing things, that it ſhould neceſſarily follow from his permiſſion, that the ſinful act ſhould be committed, &c. I need not, therefore, ſtand to repeat what has been ſaid already, about ſuch a neceſſity's not proving God to be the Author of Sin, in any ill ſenſe, or in any ſuch ſenſe as to infringe any liberty of man, concerned in his moral agency, or capacity of blame, guilt and puniſhment.

But, if it ſhould nevertheleſs be ſaid, ſuppoſing the caſe ſo, that God, when he had made man, might ſo order his circumſtances, that from theſe circumſtances, together with his withholding further aſſiſtance and Divine Influence, his Sin would infallibly follow, why might not God as well have firſt made man with a fixed prevailing principle of Sin in his heart?

I answer,

I ANSWER, 1. It was meet, if Sin did come into exiſtence, and appear in the world, it ſhould ariſe from the imperfection which properly belongs to a creature, as ſuch, and ſhould appear ſo to do, that it might appear not to be from God as the efficient or fountain. But this could not have been, if man had been made at firſt with Sin in his heart; nor unleſs the abiding principle and habit of Sin were firſt introduced by an evil act of the creature. If Sin had not aroſe from the imperfection of the creature, it would not have been ſo viſible, that it did not ariſe from God, as the poſitive cauſe, and real ſource of it.—But it would require room that cannot be here allowed, fully to conſider all the difficulties which have been ſtarted, concerning the firſt Entrance of Sin into the world.

AND therefore,

2. I WOULD obſerve, that objections againſt the doctrine that has been laid down, in oppoſition to the *Arminian* notion of liberty, from theſe difficulties, are altogether impertinent; becauſe no additional difficulty is incurred, by adhering to a ſcheme in this manner differing from theirs, and none would be removed or avoided, by agreeing with, and maintaining theirs. Nothing that the *Arminians* ſay, about the contingence, or ſelf-determining power of man's will, can ſerve to explain, with leſs difficulty, how the firſt ſinful volition of mankind could take place, and man be juſtly charged with the blame of it. To ſay, the will was ſelf-determined, or determined by free choice, in that ſinful volition; which is to ſay, that the firſt ſinful volition was determined by a foregoing ſinful volition; is no ſolution of the difficulty. It is an odd way of ſolving difficulties, to advance greater, in order to it. To ſay, two and two

two makes nine; or, that a child begat his father, ſolves no difficulty: no more does it, to ſay, the firſt ſinful act of choice was before the firſt ſinful act of choice, and choſe and determined it, and brought it to paſs. Nor is it any better ſolution, to ſay, the firſt ſinful volition choſe, determined and produced itſelf; which is to ſay, it was before it was. Nor will it go any further towards helping us over the difficulty, to ſay, the firſt ſinful volition aroſe accidentally, without any cauſe at all; any more than it will ſolve that difficult queſtion, *How the world could be made out of nothing?* to ſay, it came into being out of nothing, without any cauſe; as has been already obſerved. And if we ſhould allow that *that* could be, that the firſt evil volition ſhould ariſe by perfect accident, without any cauſe; it would relieve no difficulty, about God's laying the blame of it to man. For how was man to blame for perfect accident, which had no cauſe, and which, therefore, he (to be ſure) was not the cauſe of, any more than if it came by ſome external cauſe?—Such kind of ſolutions are no better, than if ſome perſon, going about to ſolve ſome of the ſtrange mathematical paradoxes, about infinitely great and ſmall quantities; as, that ſome infinitely great quantities are infinitely greater than ſome other infinitely great quantities; and alſo that ſome infinitely ſmall quantities, are infinitely leſs than others, which yet are infinitely little; in order to a ſolution, ſhould ſay, that mankind have been under a miſtake, in ſuppoſiog a grea er quantity to exceed a ſmaller; and that a hundred, multiplied by ten, makes but a ſingle unit.

SECT.

SECTION XI.

Of a supposed Inconsistence of those Principles with GOD's moral Character.

THE things which have been already observed, may be sufficient to answer most of the objections, and silence the great exclamations of *Arminians* against the *Calvinists*, from the supposed inconsistence of *Calvinistic* principles with the moral perfections of God, as exercised in his government of mankind. The consistence of such a doctrine of necessity as has been maintained, with the fitness and reasonableness of God's commands, promises and threatenings, rewards and punishments, has been particularly considered: the cavils of our opponents, as though our doctrine of necessity made God the author of sin, have been answered; and also their objection against these principles, as inconsistent with God's sincerity, in his counsels, invitations and persuasions, has been already obviated, in what has been observed, respecting the consistence of what *Calvinists* suppose, concerning the secret and revealed will of God: by that it appears, there is no repugnance in supposing it may be the secret will of God, that his ordination and permission of events should be such, that it shall be a certain consequence, that a thing never will come to pass; which yet it is man's duty to do, and so God's perceptive will, that he should do; and this is the same thing as to say, God may sincerely command and require him to do it. And if he may be sincere in commanding him, he may, for the same reason, be sincere in counselling, inviting and using persuasions with him to do it. Counsels and

and invitations are manifestations of God's perceptive will, or of what God loves, and what is in itself, and as man's act, agreeable to his heart; and not of his disposing will, and what he chuses as a part of his own infinite scheme of things. It has been particularly shewn, Part III. Sect. IV. that such a necessity as has been maintained, is not inconsistent with the propriety and fitness of divine commands; and for the same reason, not inconsistent with the sincerity and invitations and counsels, in the Corollary at the end of that Section. Yea, it hath been shewn, Part III. Sect. VII. Corol. 1. that this objection of *Arminians*, concerning the sincerity and use of divine exhortations, invitations and counsels, is demonstrably against themselves.

Notwithstanding, I would further observe, that the difficulty of reconciling the sincerity of counsels, invitations and persuasions with such an antecedent known fixedness of all events, as has been supposed, is not peculiar to this scheme, as distinguished from that of the generality of *Arminians*, which acknowledge the absolute foreknowledge of God: and therefore, it would be unreasonably brought as an objection against my differing from them. The main seeming difficulty in the case is this: that God, in counselling, inviting and persuading, makes a shew of aiming at, seeking and using endeavours for the thing exhorted and persuaded to; whereas, it is impossible for any intelligent being truly to seek, or use endeavours for a thing, which he at the same time knows, most perfectly, will not come to pass; and that it is absurd to suppose, he makes the obtaining of a thing his end, in his calls and counsels, which he, at the same time, infallibly knows will not be obtained by these means. Now,

Now, if God knows this, in the utmost certainty and perfection, the way by which he comes by this knowledge makes no difference. If he knows it is by the necessity which he sees in things, or by some other means, it alters not the case. But it is in effect allowed by *Arminians* themselves, that God's inviting and persuading men to do things, which he, at the same time, certainly knows will not be done, is no evidence of insincerity; because they allow, that God has a certain foreknowledge of all men's sinful actions and omissions. And as this is thus implicitly allowed by most *Arminians*, so all that pretend to own the Scriptures to be the word of God, must be constrained to allow it.—God commanded and counselled *Pharaoh* to let his people go, and used arguments and persuasions to induce him to it: he laid before him arguments taken from his infinite Greatness and almighty Power, (*Exod.* vii. 16.) and forewarned him of the fatal consequences of his refusal, from time to time; (*chap.* vii. 1, 2, 20, 21. *chap.* ix. 1,—5. 13—17. and x. 3, 6.) He commanded *Moses*, and the elders of *Israel*, to go and beseech *Pharaoh* to let the people go; and at the same time told them, he knew surely that he would not comply to it. Exod. iii 18, 19. *And thou shalt come, thou and the elders of* Israel, *unto the king of* Egypt, *and you shall say unto him; the Lord God of the* Hebrews *hath met with us; and now let us go, we beseech thee, three days journey into the wilderness, that we may sacrifice unto the Lord our God:* and, *I am sure, that the king of* Egypt *will not let you go.* So our Blessed Saviour, the evening wherein he was betrayed, knew that *Peter* would shamefully deny him, before the morning; for he declares it to him with asseverations, to shew the certainty of it; and tells the disciples, that all of them should be offended

fended because of him that night; *Matthew* xxvi. 31,—35. *John* xiii. 38. *Luke* xxii. 31,—34. *John* xvi. 32. And yet it was their duty to avoid these things; they were very sinful things, which God had forbidden, and which it was their duty to watch and pray against; and they were obliged to do so from the *counsels* and *persuasions* Christ used with them, at that very time, so to do; *Matthew* xxvi. 41. *Watch and pray, that ye enter not into temptation.* So that whatever difficulty there can be in this matter, it can be no objection against any principles which have been maintained in opposition to the principles of *Arminians*; nor does it any more concern me to remove the difficulty, than it does them, or indeed all, that call themselves Christians, and acknowledge the divine authority of the Scriptures.—Nevertheless, this matter may possibly (God allowing) be more particularly and largely considered, in some future discourse, on the doctrine of *predestination.*

But I would here observe, that however the defenders of that notion of liberty of will, which I have opposed, exclaim against the doctrine of *Calvinists*, as tending to bring men into doubts concerning the moral perfections of God; it is their scheme, and not the scheme of *Calvinists*, that indeed is justly chargeable with this. For it is one of the most fundamental points of their scheme of things, that a freedom of will, consisting in self-determination, without all necessity, is essential to *moral agency* This is the same thing as to say, that such a determination of the will, without all necessity, must be in all intelligent beings, in those things, wherein they are *moral agents*, or in their *moral acts:* and from this it will follow, that God's will is not neces-

sarily

sarily determined, in any thing he does, as *moral agent*, or in any of his *acts* that are of a *moral nature*: So that in all things, wherein he acts *holily*, *justly* and *truly*, he does not act necessarily; or his will is not necessarily determined to act holily and justly; because, if it were necessarily determined, he would not be a *moral agent* in thus acting his will would be attended with necessity; which, they say, is inconsistent with *moral agency*: "He can act no otherwise; He is at no liberty in the affair; He is determined by unavoidable invincible necessity: therefore such agency is no moral agency; yea, no agency at all, properly speaking: a necessary agent is no agent: He being passive, and subject to necessity, what he does is no act of his, but an effect of a necessity prior to any act of his." This is agreeable to their manner of arguing. Now then, what is become of all our proof of the moral perfections of God? How can we prove, that God certainly will, in any one instance, do that which is just and holy; seeing his will is determined in the matter by no necessity? We have no other way of proving that any thing *certainly* will be, but only by the necessity of the event. Where we can see no necessity, but that the thing may be, or may not be, there we are unavoidably left at a loss. We have no other way properly and truly to demonstrate the moral perfections of God, but the way that Mr. *Chubb* proves them, in p. 252, 261, 262, 263. of his Tracts, *viz.* that God must necessarily perfectly know, what is most worthy and valuable in itself, which, in the nature of things, is best and fittest to be done. And, as this is most eligible in itself, He, being omniscient, must see it to be so; and being both omniscient and self-sufficient, cannot have any temptation to reject it; and so must necessarily

neceſſarily will that which is beſt. And thus, by this neceſſity of the determination of God's will to what is good and beſt, we demonſtrably eſtabliſh God's moral character.

Corol. From things which have been obſerved, it appears, that moſt of the arguments from Scripture, which *Arminians* make uſe of to ſupport their ſcheme, are no other than *begging the queſtion*. For in theſe their arguments, they determine in the firſt place, that without ſuch a freedom of will as they hold, men cannot be proper moral agents, nor the ſubjects of command, counſel, perſuaſion, invitation, promiſes, threatenings, expoſtulations, rewards and puniſhments; and that without ſuch freedom it is to no purpoſe for men to take any care, or uſe any diligence, endeavours or means, in order to their avoiding ſin, or becoming holy, eſcaping puniſhment or obtaining happineſs: and having ſuppoſed theſe things, which are grand things in queſtion in the debate, then they heap up Scriptures, containing commands, counſels, calls, warnings, perſuaſions, expoſtulations, promiſes and threatenings; (as doubtleſs they may find enough ſuch; the Bible is confeſſedly full of them, from the beginning to the end) and then they glory, how full the Scripture is on their ſide, how many more texts there are that evidently favour their ſcheme, than ſuch as ſeem to favour the contrary. But let them firſt make manifeſt the things in queſtion, which they ſuppoſe and take for granted, and ſhew them to be conſiſtent with themſelves; and produce clear evidence of their truth; and they have gained their point, as all will confeſs, without bringing one Scripture. For none denies, that there are commands, counſels, promiſes, threatenings, *&c.* in the Bible. But unleſs they do theſe things, their

their multiplying such texts of Scripture is insignificant and vain.

It may further be observed, that such scriptures, as they bring, are really against them, and not for them. As it has been demonstrated, that it is their scheme, and not ours, that is inconsistent with the use of motives and persuasives, or any moral means whatsoever, to induce men to the practice of virtue, or abstaining from wickedness: their principles, and not ours, are repugnant to moral agency, and inconsistent with moral government, with law or precept, with the nature of virtue or vice, reward or punishment, and with every thing whatsoever of a moral nature, either on the part of the moral governor, or in the state, actions or conduct of the subject.

SECTION XII.

Of a supposed Tendency of these Printiples to Atheism *and* Licentiousness.

If any object against what has been maintained, that it tends to *Atheism*; I know not on what grounds such an objection can be raised, unless it be, that some Atheists have held a doctrine of necessity which they suppose to be like this. But if it be so, I am persuaded the *Arminians* would not look upon it just, that their notion of freedom and contingence should be charged with a tendency to all the errors that ever any embraced, who have held such opinions. The *Stoic* philosophers, whom the *Calvinists* are charged with agreeing with, were no Atheists, but the greatest Theists, and nearest a-kin to Christians in their opinions

opinions concerning the unity and the perfections of the Godhead, of all the heathen philosophers. And *Epicurus*, that chief father of Atheism, maintained no such doctrine of necessity, but was the greatest maintainer of contingence.

The doctrine of necessity, which supposes a necessary connection of all events, on some antecedent ground and reason of their existence, is the only medium we have to prove the being of a God. And the contrary doctrine of contingence, even as maintained by *Arminians* (which certainly implies or infers, that events may come into existence, or begin to be, without dependence on any thing foregoing, as their cause, ground or reason) takes away all proof of the being of God; which proof is summarily expressed by the apostle, in *Rom.* i. 20. And this is a tendency to *Atheism* with a witness. So that, indeed, it is the doctrine of *Arminians*, and not of the *Calvinists*, that is justly charged with a tendency to *Atheism*; it being built on a foundation that is the utter subversion of every demonstrative argument for the proof of a Deity; as has been shown, Part II. Sect. III.

And whereas it has often been said, that the *Calvinistic* doctrine of necessity saps the foundations of all religion and virtue, and tends to the greatest Licentiousness of practice: this objection is built on the pretence, that our doctrine renders vain all means and endeavours, in order to be virtuous and religious. Which pretence has been already particularly considered in the 5th *Section* of this *Part*; where it has been demonstrated, that this doctrine has no such tendency; but that such a tendency is truly to be charged on the contrary doctrine: inasmuch as the notion of contingence, which their doctrine implies, in its certain consequences, overthrows all connection in every degree, between endeavour and event, means and end.

And besides, if many other things, which have been observed to belong to the *Arminian* doctrine, or to be plain consequences of it, be considered, there will appear just reason to suppose that, it is *that* which must rather tend to Licentiousness. Their doctrine excuses all evil inclinations, which men find to be natural; because in such inclinations, they are not self-determined, as such inclinations are not owing to any choice or determination of their own wills. Which leads men wholly to justify themselves in all their wicked actions, so far as natural inclination has had a hand in determining their wills, to the commission of them. Yea, these notions, which suppose moral necessity and inability to be inconsistent with blame or moral obligation, will directly lead men to justify the vilest acts and practices, from the strength of their wicked inclinations of all sorts; strong inclinations inducing a moral necessity; yea, to excuse every degree of evil inclination, so far as this has evidently prevailed, and been the thing which has determined their wills: because, so far as antecedent inclination determined the will, so far the will was without liberty of indifference and self-determination. Which, at last, will come to this, that men will justify themselves in all the wickedness they commit. It has been observed already, that this scheme of things does exceedingly diminish the guilt of sin, and the difference between the greatest and smallest offences; *and if it be pursued in its real consequences, it leaves room for

* Part III. Sect. VI.

for no such thing, as either virtue or vice, blame or praise in the world. *And then again, how naturally does this notion of the sovereign self-determining power of the will, in all things, virtuous or vicious, and whatsoever deserves either reward or punishment, tend to encourage men to put off the work of religion and virtue, and turning from sin to God; it being that which they have a sovereign power to determine themselves to, just when they please; or if not, they are wholly excusable in going on in sin, because of their inability to do any other.

If it should be said, that the tendency of this doctrine of necessity, to Licentiousness, appears by the improvement many at this day actually make of it, to justify themselves in their dissolute courses; I will not deny that some men do unreasonably abuse this doctrine, as they do many other things, which are true and excellent in their own nature: but I deny that this proves, the doctrine itself has any tendency to Licentiousness. I think, the tendency of doctrines, by what now appears in the world, and in our nation in particular, may much more justly be argued, from the general effect which has been seen, to attend the prevailing of the principles of *Arminians*, and the contrary principles; as both have had their turn of general prevalence in our nation. If it be indeed, as is pretended, that *Calvinistic* doctrines undermine the very foundation of all religion and morality, and enervate and disannul all rational motives to holy and virtuous practice; and that the contrary doctrines give the inducements to virtue and goodness their proper force, and exhibit religion in a rational

* Part III. Sect. VI. Ibid. Sect. VII. Part IV. Sect. I. Part III. Sect. III. *Corol.* 1. after the first head.

tional light, tending to recommend it to the reason of mankind, and enforce it in a manner that is agreable to their natural notions of things: I say, if it be thus, it is remarkable, that virtue and religious practice should prevail most, when the former doctrines, so inconsistent with it, prevailed almost universally: and that ever since the latter doctrines, so happily agreeing with it, and of so proper and excellent a tendency to promote it, have been gradually prevailing, vice, prophaneness, luxury and wickedness of all sorts, and contempt of all religion, and of every kind of seriousness and strictness of conversation, should proportionably prevail; and that these things should thus accompany one another, and rise and prevail one with another, now for a whole age together. It is remarkable, that this happy remedy (discovered by the free enquiries, and superior sense and wisdom of this age) against the pernicious effects of *Calvinism*, so inconsistent with religion, and tending so much to banish all virtue from the earth, should, on so long a trial, be attended with no good effect; but that the consequence should be the reverse of amendment; that in proportion as the remedy takes place, and is thoroughly applied, so the disease should prevail; and the very same dismal effect take place, to the highest degree, which *Calvinistic* doctrines are supposed to have so great a tendency to; even the banishing of religion and virtue, and the prevailing of unbounded Licentiousness of manners. If these things are truly so, they are very remarkable, and matter of very curious speculation.

SEC-

SECTION XIII.

Concerning that Objection against the Reaſoning, *by which the* Calviniſtic *doctrine is ſupported, that it is* metaphyſical *and* abſtruſe.

IT has often been objected againſt the defenders of *Calviniſtic* principles, that in their reaſonings, they run into nice ſcholaſtic diſtinctions, and abſtruſe metaphyſical ſubtilties, and ſet theſe in oppoſition to common ſenſe. And it is poſſible, that, after the former manner, it may be alledged againſt the Reaſoning by which I have endeavoured to confute the *Arminian* ſcheme of liberty and moral agency, that it is very abſtracted and metaphyſical.——Concerning this, I would obſerve the following things:

I. If that be made an objection againſt the foregoing Reaſoning, that it is *metaphyſical*, or may properly be reduced to the ſcience of *metaphyſics*, it is a very impertinent objection; whether it be ſo or no, is not worthy of any diſpute or controverſy. If the Reaſoning be good, it is as frivolous to enquire what ſcience it is properly reduced to, as what language it is delivered in: and for a man to go about to confute the arguments of his opponent, by telling him, his arguments are *metaphyſical*, would be as weak as to tell him, his arguments could not be ſubſtantial, becauſe they were written in *French* or *Latin*. The queſtion is not, whether what is ſaid be metaphyſics, phyſics, logic, or mathematics, *Latin*, *French*, *Engliſh*, or *Mohawk?* But whether the reaſoning be good, and the arguments truly concluſive? The foregoing arguments are no more metaphyſical, than thoſe which we uſe againſt the Papiſts, to diſprove their doctrine of tranſubſtantiation; alledging, it is inconſiſtent with the notion of corporeal identity, that it ſhould be in ten thouſand places at the ſame time. It is by metaphyſical arguments only we are able to prove, that the rational ſoul is not corporeal; that lead or ſand cannot think; that thoughts are not ſquare or round, or do not weigh a pound. The arguments by which we prove the being of God, if handled cloſely and diſtinctly, ſo as to ſhew their clear and demonſtrative evidence, muſt be metaphyſically treated. It is by metaphyſics only, that we can demonſtrate, that God is not limited to a place, or is not mutable: that he is not ignorant, or forgetful; that it is impoſſible for him to lie, or be unjuſt; and that there is one God only, and not hundreds or thouſands. And, indeed, we have no ſtrict demonſtration of any thing, excepting mathematical truths, but by metaphyſics. We can have no proof, that is properly demonſtrative, of any one propoſition, relating to the being and nature of God, his creation of the world, the dependence of all things on him, the nature of bodies or ſpirits, the nature of our own ſouls, or any of the great truths of morality and natural religion, but what is metaphyſical. I am willing, my arguments ſhould be brought to the teſt of the ſtricteſt and juſteſt Reaſon, and that a clear, diſtinct and determinate meaning of the terms I uſe, ſhould be inſiſted on; but let not the whole be rejected, as if all were confuted, by fixing on it the epithet, *metaphyſical*.

II. If the reaſoning, which has been made uſe of, be in ſome ſenſe metaphyſical, it will not follow

low, that therefore it muſt needs be abſtruſe, unintelligible, and a-kin to the jargon of the ſch ols. I humbly conceive, the foregoing reaſoning, at leaſt to thoſe things which are moſt material belonging to it, depends on no abſtruſe definitions or diſtinctions, or terms without a meaning, or of very ambiguous and undetermined ſignification, or any points of ſuch abſtraction and ſubtilty, as tends to involve the attentive underſtanding in clouds and darkneſs. There is no high degree of refinement and abſtruſe ſpeculation, in determining, that a thing is not before it is, and ſo cannot be the cauſe of itſelf; or that the firſt act of free choice, has not another act of free choice going before that, to excite or direct it; or in determining, that no choice is made, while the mind remains in a ſtate of abſolute indifference; that preference and equilibrium never co-exiſt; and that therefore no choice is made in a ſtate of liberty, conſiſting in indifference: and that ſo far as the will is determined by motives, exhibited and operating previous to the act of the will, ſo far it is not determined by the act of the will itſelf; that nothing can begin to be, which before was not, without a cauſe, or ſome antecedent ground or reaſon, why it then begins to be; that effects depend on their cauſes, and are connected with them; that virtue is not the worſe, nor ſin the better, for the ſtrength of inclination, with which it is practiſed, and the difficulty which thence ariſes of doing otherwiſe; that when it is already infallibly known, that the thing will be, it is not a thing contingent whether it will ever be or no; or that it can be truly ſaid, notwithſtanding, that it is not neceſſary it ſhould be, but it either may be, or may not be. And the like might be obſerved of many other things which belong to the foregoing Reasoning.

If any shall still stand to it, that the foregoing Reasoning is nothing but metaphysical sophistry; and that it must be so, that the seeming force of the arguments all depends on some fallacy and wile that is hid in the obscurity, which always attends a great degree of metaphysical abstraction and refinement; and shall be ready to say, "Here is indeed something that tends to confound the mind, but not to satisfy it: for who can ever be truly satisfied in it, that men are fitly blamed or commended, punished or rewarded for those volitions which are not from themselves, and of whose existence they are not the causes. Men may refine, as much as they please, and advance their abstract notions, and make out a thousand seeming contradictions, to puzzle our understanding; yet there can be no satisfaction in such doctrine as this: the natural sense of the mind of man will always resist it."* I humbly conceive, that such

* A certain noted Author of the present age says, the arguments for *necessity* are nothing but *quibbling, or logomachy, using words without a meaning, or begging the question.*—I do not know what kind of necessity any authors, he may have reference to, are advocates for; or whether they have managed their arguments well, or ill. As to the arguments I have made use of, if they are *quibbles* they may be shewn so: such knots are capable of being untied, and the trick and cheat may be detected and plainly laid open. If this be fairly done, with respect to the grounds and reasons I have relied upon, I shall have just occasion, for the future, to be silent, if not to be ashamed of my argumentations. I am willing my proofs should be thoroughly examined; and if there be nothing but *begging the question*, or mere *logomachy*, or dispute of words, let it be made manifest, and shewn how the seeming strength of

such an objector, if he has capacity and humility and calmness of spirit, sufficient impartially and thoroughly to examine himself, will find that he knows not really what he would be at; and indeed, his difficulty is nothing but a mere prejudice, from an inadvertent customary use of words, in a meaning that is not clearly understood,

of the argument depends on my *using words without a meaning*, or arises from the ambiguity of terms, or my making use of words in an indeterminate and unsteady manner; and that the weight of my reasons rest mainly on such a foundation: and then, I shall either be ready to retract what I have urged, and thank the man that has done the kind part, or shall be justly exposed for my obstinacy.

The same Author is abundant in appealing, in this affair, from what he calls *logomachy and sophistry*, to *experience*.—— A person can experience only what passes in his own mind. But yet, as we may well suppose, that all men have the same human faculties; so a man may well argue from his own experience to that of others, in things that shew the nature of those faculties, and the manner of their operation. But then one has as good right to alledge his experience, as another. As to my own experience, I find, that in innumerable things I can do as I will; that the motions of my body, in many respects, instantaneously follow the acts of my will concerning those motions; and that my will has some command of my thoughts; and that the acts of my will are my own, *i. e.* that they are acts of my will, the volitions of my own mind; or, in other words, that what I will, I will. Which, I presume, is the sum of what others experience in this affair. But as to finding by experience, that my will is originally determined by itself; or that, my will first chusing what volition there shall be, the chosen volition accordingly follows; and that this is the first rise of the determination of my will in any affair; or that any volition rises in my mind contingently; I declare, I know nothing in myself, by experience, of this nature; and nothing that ever I experienced, carries the least appearance or shadow of any such thing, or gives me any more reason to suppose or suspect any such thing, than to suppose that my volitions existed twenty years before they existed. It is true, I find myself possessed of my volitions before I can see the effectual power of any cause to produce them (for the power and efficacy of the cause is not seen but ſtood, nor carefully reflected upon.——Let the objector reflect again, if he has candor and patience enough, and does not ſcorn to be at the trouble of cloſe attention in the affair.—He would have a man's volition be *from himſelf.* Let it be *from himſelf,* moſt primarily and originally of any way conceivable; that is, from his own choice: how will that help the matter, as to his being juſtly blamed or praiſed, unleſs that choice itſelf be blame or praiſe-worthy? And how is the choice itſelf (an ill choice, for inſtance) blame-worthy, according to theſe principles, unleſs that be from himſelf too, in the ſame manner; that is, from his own choice? But the original and firſt-determining choice in the affair is not from his choice: his choice is not the cauſe of it.——And if it be from himſelf ſome other way, and not from his choice, ſurely that will not help the matter. If it be not from himſelf of choice, then it is not from himſelf voluntarily; and if ſo, he is ſurely no more to blame, than if it were not from himſelf at all. It is a vanity to pretend it is a ſufficient anſwer to this, to ſay, that it is nothing but metaphyſical refinement and ſubtilty, and ſo attended with obſcurity and uncertainty.

If it be the natural ſenſe of our minds, that what is blame-worthy in a man muſt be from himſelf, then it doubtleſs is alſo, that it muſt be from ſomething *bad* in himſelf, a *bad choice,* or *bad*

but by the effect) and this, for aught I know, may make ſome imagine, that volition has no cauſe, or that it produces itſelf. But I have no more reaſon from hence to determine any ſuch thing, than I have to determine that I gave myſelf my own being, or that I came into being accidentally without a cauſe, becauſe I firſt found myſelf poſſeſſed of being, before I had knowledge of a cauſe of my being.

bad disposition. But then our natural sense is, that this bad choice or disposition is evil *in itself*, and the man blame-worthy for it, *on its own account*, without taking into our notion of its blame-worthiness, another bad choice, or disposition going before this, from whence this arises: for that is a ridiculous absurdity, running us into an immediate contradiction, which our natural sense of blame-worthiness has nothing to do with, and never comes into the mind, nor is supposed in the judgment we naturally make of the affair. As was demonstrated before, natural sense does not place the moral evil of volitions and dispositions in the cause of them, but the nature of them. An evil thing's being FROM a man, or from something antecedent in him, is not essential to the original notion we have of blame-worthiness: but it is its being the choice of the heart; as appears by this, that if a thing be *from* us, and not from our choice, it has not the nature of blame-worthiness or ill-desert, according to our natural sense. When a thing is *from* a man, in that sense, that it is from his will or choice, he is to blame for it, because his will is IN IT: so far as the will is *in it*, blame is *in it*, and no further. Neither do we go any further in our notion of blame, to enquire whether the bad will be FROM a bad will: there is no consideration of the original of that bad will; because, according to our natural apprehension, blame *originally consists in it.* Therefore a thing's being *from* a man, is a secondary consideration, in the notion of blame or ill-desert. Because those things, in our *external* actions, are most properly said to be *from* us, which are *from* our choice; and no other *external* actions, but those that are from us in this sense, have the nature of blame;

and

and they indeed, not so properly because they are *from us*, as because we are *in them*, i. e. our wills are in them; not so much because they are from some *property* of ours, as because they are our *properties*.

However, all these external actions being truly *from us*, as their cause; and we being so used, in ordinary speech, and in the common affairs of life, to speak of men's actions and conduct that we see, and that affect human society, as deserving ill or well, as worthy of blame or praise; hence it is come to pass, that philosophers have incautiously taken all their measures of good and evil, praise and blame, from the dictates of common sense, about these *overt acts* of men; to the running of every thing into the most lamentable and dreadful confusion. And, therefore, I observe,

III. It is so far from being true (whatever may be pretended) that the proof of the doctrine which has been maintained, depends on certain abstruse, unintelligible, metaphysical terms and notions; and that the *Arminian* scheme, without needing such clouds and darkness for its defence, is supported by the plain dictates of common sense; that the very reverse is most certainly true, and that to a great degree. It is fact, that they, and not we, have confounded things with metaphysical, unintelligible notions and phrases, and have drawn them from the light of plain truth, into the gross darkness of abstruse metaphysical propositions, and words without a meaning. Their pretended demonstrations depend very much on such unintelligible, metaphysical phrases, as *self-determination*, and *sovereignty of the will*; and the metaphysical sense

they

they put on ſuch terms, as *neceſſity*, *contingency*, *action*, *agency*, &c. quite diverſe from their meaning as uſed in common ſpeech; and which, as they uſe them, are without any conſiſtent meaning, or any manner of diſtinct conſiſtent ideas; as far from it as any of the abſtruſe terms and perplexed phraſes of the peripatetic philoſophers, or the moſt unintelligible jargon of the ſchools, or the cant of the wildeſt fanatics. Yea, we may be bold to ſay, theſe metaphyſical terms, on which they build ſo much, are what they uſe without knowing what they mean themſelves; they are pure metaphyſical ſounds, without any ideas whatſoever in their minds to anſwer them; inaſmuch as it has been demonſtrated, that there cannot be any notion in the mind conſiſtent with theſe expreſſions, as they pretend to explain them; becauſe their explanations deſtroy themſelves. No ſuch notions as imply ſelf-contradiction, and ſelf-abolition, and this a great many ways, can ſubſiſt in the mind; as there can be no idea of a whole which is leſs than any of its parts, or of ſolid extenſion without dimenſions, or of an effect which is before its cauſe.——*Arminians* improve theſe terms, as terms of art, and in their metaphyſical meaning, to advance and eſtabliſh thoſe things which are contrary to common ſenſe, in a high degree. Thus, inſtead of the plain vulgar notion of liberty, which all mankind, in every part of the face of the earth, and in all ages, have; conſiſting in opportunity to do as one pleaſes; they have introduced a new ſtrange liberty, conſiſting in indifference, contingence, and ſelf-determination; by which they involve themſelves and others in great obſcurity, and manifold groſs inconſiſtence. So, inſtead of placing virtue and vice, as common ſenſe places them very much, in fixed bias

and

and inclination, and greater virtue and vice in ſtronger and more eſtabliſhed inclination; theſe, through their refinings and abſtruſe notions, ſuppoſe a liberty conſiſting in indifference, to be eſſential to all virtue and vice. So they have reaſoned themſelves, not by metaphyſical diſtinctions, but by metaphyſical confuſion, into many principles about moral agency, blame, praiſe, reward and puniſhment, which are, as has been ſhewn, exceeding contrary to the common ſenſe of mankind; and perhaps to their own ſenſe, which governs them in common life.

THE

THE

CONCLUSION.

WHETHER the things which have been alledged, are liable to any tolerable anſwer in the ways of calm, intelligible and ſtrict reaſoning, I muſt leave others to judge: but I am ſenſible they are liable to one ſort of anſwer. It is not unlikely, that ſome, who value themſelves on the ſuppoſed rational and generous principles of the modern faſhionable divinity, will have their indignation and diſdain raiſed at the ſight of this diſcourſe, and on perceiving what things are pretended to be proved in it. And if they think it worthy of being read, or of ſo much notice as to ſay much about it, they may probably renew the uſual exclamations, with additional vehemence and contempt, about the *fate of the heathen*, Hobbes's *Neceſſity*, and *making men mere machines*; accumulating the terrible epithets of *fatal*, *unfruſtrable*, *inevitable*, *irreſiſtible*, &c. and it may be, with the addition of *horrid* and *blaſphemous*; and perhaps much ſkill may be uſed to ſet forth things, which have been ſaid, in colours which ſhall be ſhocking to the imaginations, and moving to the paſſions of thoſe, who have either too little capacity, or too much confidence of the opinions

opinions they have imbibed, and contempt of the contrary, to try the matter by any ſerious and circumſpect examination*. Or difficulties may be ſtarted and inſiſted on, which do not belong to the controverſy; becauſe, let them be more or leſs real, and hard to be reſolved, they are not what are owing to any thing diſtinguiſhing of this ſcheme from that of the *Arminians*, and would not be removed nor diminiſhed by renouncing the former, and adhering to the latter. Or ſome particular things may be picked out, which they may think will ſound harſheſt in the ears of the generality; and theſe may be gloſſed and deſcanted on, with tart and contemptuous words; and from thence, the whole treated with triumph and inſult.

It is eaſy to ſee, how the deciſion of moſt of the points in controverſy, between *Calviniſts* and *Arminians*, depends on the determination of this grand article concerning *the Freedom of the Will requiſite to moral agency*; and that by clearing and eſtabliſhing

* A writer of the preſent age, whom I have ſeveral times had occaſion to mention ſpeaks once and again of thoſe who hold the doctrine of *Neceſſity*, as ſcarcely worthy of the name of *philoſophers*.——I do not know, whether he has reſpect to any particular notion of neceſſity, that ſome may have maintained; and, if ſo, what doctrine of neceſſity is it that he means.——Whether I am worthy of the name of a philoſopher, or not, would be a queſtion little to the preſent purpoſe. If any, and ever ſo many, ſhould deny it, I ſhould not think it worth the while to enter into a diſpute on that queſtion: though at the ſame time I might expect, ſome better anſwer ſhould be given to the arguments brought for the truth of the doctrine I maintain; and I might further reaſonably deſire, that it might be conſidered, whether it does not become thoſe, who are *truly worthy* of the name of philoſophers, to be ſenſible, that there is a difference between *argument* and *contempt*; yea, and a difference between the contemptibleneſs of the *perſon* that argues, and the inconcluſiveneſs of the *arguments* he offers.

bliſhing the *Calviniſtic* doctrine in this point, the chief arguments are obviated, by which *Arminian* doctrines in general are ſupported, and the contrary doctrines demonſtratively confirmed. Hereby it becomes manifeſt, that God's moral government over mankind, his treating them as moral agents, making them the objects of his commands, counſels, calls, warnings, expoſtulations, promiſes, threatenings, rewards and puniſhments, is not inconſiſtent with a *determining diſpoſal* of all events, of every kind, throughout the univerſe, *in his Providence*; either by poſitive efficiency, or permiſſion. Indeed, ſuch an *univerſal determining Providence*, infers ſome kind of neceſſity of all events, ſuch a neceſſity as implies an infallible previous fixedneſs of the futurity of the event: but no other neceſſity of moral events, or volitions of intelligent agents, is needful in order to this, than *moral neceſſity*; which does as much aſcertain the futurity of the event, as any other neceſſity. But, as has been demonſtrated, ſuch a neceſſity is not at all repugnant to moral agency, and a reaſonable uſe of commands, calls, rewards, puniſhments, &c. Yea, not only are objections of this kind againſt the doctrine of an univerſal *determining Providence*, removed by what has been ſaid; but the truth of ſuch a doctrine is demonſtrated. As it has been demonſtrated, that the futurity of all future events is eſtabliſhed by previous neceſſity, either natural or moral; ſo it is manifeſt, that the ſovereign Creator and Diſpoſer of the world has ordered this neceſſity, by ordering his own conduct, either in deſignedly acting, or forbearing to act. For, as the being of the world is from God, ſo the circumſtances in which it had its being at firſt, both negative and poſitive, muſt be ordered by him, in one of theſe ways; and all the neceſſary conſequences of theſe circumſtances, muſt be ordered by him. And God's active and poſitive interpoſitions, after the world was created, and the conſequences of theſe interpoſitions; alſo every inſtance of his forbearing to interpoſe, and the ſure conſequences of this forbearance, muſt all be determined according to his pleaſure. And therefore every event, which is the conſequence of any thing whatſoever, or that is connected with any foregoing thing or circumſtance, either poſitive or negative, as the ground or reaſon of its exiſtence, muſt be ordered of God; either by a deſigning efficiency and interpoſition, or a deſigned forbearing to operate or interpoſe. But, as has been proved, all events whatſoever are neceſſarily connected with ſomething foregoing, either poſſitive or negative, which is the ground of its exiſtence. It follows, therefore, that the whole ſeries of events is thus connected with ſomething in the ſtate of things, either poſitive or negative, which is *original* in the ſeries; *i. e.* ſomething which is connected with nothing preceding that, but God's own immediate conduct, either his acting or forbearing to act From whence it follows, that as God deſignedly orders his own conduct, and its connected conſequences, it muſt neceſſarily be, that he deſignedly orders all things.

The things, which have been ſaid, obviate ſome of the chief objections of *Arminians* againſt the *Calviniſtic* doctrine of the *total depravity and corruption of man's nature*, whereby his heart is wholly under the power of ſin, and he is utterly unable, without the interpoſition of ſovereign grace, ſavingly to love God, believe in Chriſt, or do any thing that is truly good and acceptable in God's ſight. For the main objection againſt this doctrine is, that it is inconſiſtent with the freedom

freedom of man's will, confifting in indifference and felf-determining power; becaufe it fuppofes man to be under a neceffity of finning, and that God requires things of him, in order to his avoiding eternal damnation, which he is unable to do; and that this doctrine is wholly inconfiftent with the fincerity of counfels, invitations, &c. Now, this doctrine fuppofes *no other neceffity* of finning, than a moral neceffity; which, as has been fhewn, does not at all excufe fin; and fuppofes *no other inability* to obey any command, or perform any duty, even the moft fpiritual and exalted, but a moral inability, which, as has been proved, does not excufe perfons in the non-performance of any good thing, or make them not to be the proper objects of commands, counfels and invitations. And, moreover, it has been fhewn, that there is not, and never can be, either in exiftence, or fo much as in idea, any fuch freedom of will, confifting in indifference and felf-determination, for the fake of which, this doctrine of original fin is caft out; and that no fuch freedom is neceffary, in order to the nature of fin, and a juft defert of punifhment.

The things, which have been obferved, do alfo take off the main objections of *Arminians* againft the doctrine of *efficacious grace*; and, at the fame time, prove the grace of God in a finner's converfion (if there be any grace or divine influence in the affair) to be *efficacious*, yea, and *irrefiftible* too, if by irrefiftible is meant, that which is attended with a moral neceffity, which it is impoffible fhould ever be violated by any refiftance. The main objection of *Arminians* againft this doctrine is, that it is inconfiftent with their felf-determining freedom of will; and that it is repugnant to the nature of virtue, that it fhould be wrought in the heart by the determining efficacy and power of another, instead of its being owing to a self-moving power; that, in that case, the good which is wrought, would not be *our* virtue, but rather *God*'s virtue; because it is not the person in whom it is wrought, that is the determining author of it, but God that wrought it in him. But the things, which are the foundation of these objections, have been considered; and it has been demonstrated, that the liberty of moral agents does not consist in self-determining power; and that there is no need of any such liberty, in order to the nature of virtue; nor does it at all hinder, but that the state or act of the will may be the virtue of the subject, though it be not from self-determination, but the determination of an intrinsic cause: even so as to cause the event to be morally necessary to the subject of it. And as it has been proved, that nothing in the state or acts of the will of man is contingent; but that, on the contrary, every event of this kind is necessary, by a moral necessity; and has also been now demonstrated, that the doctrine of an universal determining Providence, follows from that doctrine of necessity, which was proved before: and so that God does decisively, in his Providence, order all the volitions of moral agents, either by positive influence or permission: and it being allowed, on all hands, that what God does in the affair of man's virtuous volitions, whether it be more or less, is by some positive influence, and not by meer permission, as in the affair of a sinful volition: if we put these things together, it will follow, that God's assistance or influence, must be determining and decisive, or must be attended with a moral necessity of the event; and so, that God gives virtue, holiness and conversion to sinners, by an influence which deter-

determines the effect, in such a manner, that the effect will infallibly follow by a moral necessity; which is what *Calvinists* mean by efficacious and irresistible grace.

The things, which have been said, do likewise answer the chief objections against the doctrine of God's *universal* and *absolute decree*, and afford infallible proof of this doctrine; and of the doctrine of *absolute*, *eternal*, *personal election* in particular. The main objections against these doctrines are, that they infer a necessity of the volitions of moral agents, and of the future moral state and acts of men; and so are not consistent with those eternal rewards and punishments, which are connected with conversion and impenitence; nor can be made to agree with the reasonableness and sincerity of the precepts, calls, counsels, warnings and expostulations of the Word of God; or with the various methods and means of grace, which God uses with sinners, to bring them to repentance; and the whole of that moral government, which God exercises towards mankind: and that they infer an inconsistence between the *secret* and *revealed Will of God*; and make God the author of sin. But all these things have been obviated in the preceding discourse. And the certain truth of these doctrines, concerning God's eternal purposes, will follow from what was just now observed concerning God's universal Providence; how it infallibly follows from what has been proved, that God orders all events, and the volitions of moral agents amongst others, by such a decisive disposal, that the events are infallibly connected with his disposal. For if God disposes all events, so that the infallible existence of the events is decided by his Providence, then he, doubtless, thus orders and decides things *knowingly*,

ingly, and *on design*. God does not do what he does, nor order what he orders, accidentally and unawares; either *without*, or *beside* his intention. And if there be a foregoing *design* of doing and ordering as he does, this is the same with a *purpose* or *decree*. And as it has been shewn, that nothing is new to God, in any respect, but all things are perfectly and equally in his view from eternity; hence it will follow, that his designs or purposes are not things formed anew, founded on any new views or appearances, but are all eternal purposes. And as it has been now shewn, how the doctrine of determining efficacious grace certainly follows from things proved in the foregoing discourse; hence will necessarily follow the doctrine of *particular*, *eternal*, *absolute election*. For if men are made true saints, no otherwise than as God makes them so, and distinguishes them from others, by an efficacious power and influence of his, that decides and fixes the event; and God thus makes some saints, and not others, on design or purpose, and (as has been now observed) no designs of God are new; it follows, that God thus distinguished from others, all that ever become true saints, by his eternal design or decree. I might also shew, how God's certain forenowledge must suppose an absolute decree, and how such a decree can be proved to a demonstration from it: but that this discourse may not be lengthened out too much, that must be omitted for the present.

From these things it will inevitably follow, that however Christ in some sense may be said to *die for all*, and to redeem all visible Christians, yea, the whole world by his death; yet there must be something *particular* in the design of his death, with respect to such as he intended should actu-

ally

ally be saved thereby. As appears by what has been now shewn, God has the actual salvation or redemption of a certain number in his proper absolute design, and of a certain number only; and therefore such a design only can be prosecuted in any thing God does, in order to the salvation of men. God pursues a proper design of the salvation of the elect in giving Christ to die, and prosecutes such a design with respect to no other, most strictly speaking; for it is impossible, that God should prosecute any other design than only such as he has: he certainly does not, in the highest propriety and strictness of speech, pursue a design that he has not.—And, indeed, such a particularity and limitation of redemption will as infalliby follow, from the doctrine of God's foreknowledge, as from that of the decree. For it is as impossible, in strictness of speech, that God should prosecute a design, or aim at a thing, which He at the same time most perfectly knows will not be accomplished, as that he should use endeavours for that which is beside his decree.

By the things which have been proved, are obviated some of the main objections against the doctrine of the infallible and necessary *perseverance* of saints, and some of the main foundations of this doctrine are established. The main prejudices of *Arminians* against this doctrine seem to be these; they suppose such a necessary, infallible perseverance to be repugnant to the freedom of the will; that it must be owing to man's own self determining power, that he *first becomes* virtuous and holy; and so, in like manner, it must be left a thing contingent, to be determined by the same freedom of will, whether he will *persevere* in virtue and holiness; and that otherwise his continuing stedfast in faith and obedience would not be his virtue, or at all praiſe-worthy and rewardable; nor could his perſeverance be properly the matter of divine commands, counſels and promiſes, nor his apoſtacy be properly threatened, and men warned againſt it. Whereas, we find all theſe things in ſcripture: there we find ſtedfaſtneſs and perſeverance in true Chriſtianity, repreſented as the virtue of the ſaints, ſpoken of as praiſe-worthy in them, and glorious rewards promiſed to it; and alſo find, that God makes it the ſubject of his commands, counſels and promiſes; and the contrary, of threatenings and warnings. But the foundation of theſe objections has been removed, in its being ſhewn that moral neceſſity and infallible certainty of events is not inconſiſtent with theſe things; and that, as to freedom of will lying in the power of the will to determine itſelf, there neither is any ſuch thing, nor need any of it, in order to virtue, reward, commands, counſels, &c.

And as the doctrines of efficacious grace and abſolute election do certainly follow from things, which have been proved in the preceding diſcourſe; ſo ſome of the main foundations of the doctrine of perſeverance, are thereby eſtabliſhed. If the beginning of true faith and holineſs, and a man's becoming a true ſaint at firſt, does not depend on the ſelf-determining power of the will, but on the determining efficacious grace of God; it may well be argued, that it is alſo with reſpect to men's being continued ſaints, or perſevering in faith and holineſs. The converſion of a ſinner being not owing to a man's ſelf-determination, but to God's determination, and eternal election, which is abſolute, and depending on the ſovereign will of God; and not on the free will of man; as is evident from what has been ſaid: and it being very evident from the Scriptures,

tures, that the eternal election which there is of ſaints to faith and holineſs, is alſo an election of them to eternal ſalvation: hence their appointment to ſalvation muſt alſo be abſolute, and not depending on their contingent, ſelf-determining will. From all which it follows, that it is abſolutely fixed in God's decree, that all true ſaints ſhall perſevere to actual eternal ſalvation.

But I muſt leave all theſe things to the conſideration of the fair and impartial reader; and when he has maturely weighed them, I would propoſe it to his conſideration, whether many of the firſt reformers, and others that ſucceeded them, whom God in their day made the chief pillars of his church, and greateſt inſtruments of their deliverance from error and darkneſs, and of the ſupport of the cauſe of piety among them, have not been injured, in the contempt with which they have been treated by many late writers, for their teaching and maintaining ſuch doctrines as are commonly called *Calviniſtic*. Indeed, ſome of theſe new writers, at the ſame time that they have repreſented the doctrines of theſe antient and eminent divines, as in the higheſt degree ridiculous, and contrary to common ſenſe, in an oſtentation of a very generous charity, have allowed that they were honeſt well-meaning men: yea, it may be ſome of them, as though it were in great condeſcenſion and compaſſion to them, have allowed, that they did pretty well for the day which they lived in, and conſidering the great diſadvantages they laboured under: when, at the ſame time, their manner of ſpeaking has naturally and plainly ſuggeſted to the minds of their readers, that they were perſons, who through the lowneſs of their genius, and greatneſs of the bigotry, with which their minds were ſhackled,

and

and thoughts confined, living in the gloomy caves of superstition, fondly embraced, and demurely and zealously taught the most absurd, silly and monstrous opinions, worthy of the greatest contempt of gentlemen possessed of that noble and generous freedom of thought, which happily prevails in this age of light and enquiry. When, indeed, such is the case, that we might, if so disposed, speak as big words as they, and on far better grounds. And really all the *Arminians* on earth might be challenged without arrogance or vanity, to make these principles of theirs, wherein they mainly differ from their fathers, whom they so much despise, consistent with common sense; yea, and perhaps to produce any doctrine ever embraced by the blindest bigot of the Church of *Rome*, or the most ignorant *Mussulman*, or extravagant enthusiast, that might be reduced to more demonstrable inconsistencies, and repugnancies to common sense, and to themselves; though their inconsistencies indeed may not lie so deep, or be so artfully vailed by a deceitful ambiguity of words, and an indeterminate signification of phrases.—I will not deny, that these gentlemen, many of them, are men of great abilities, and have been helped to higher attainments in philosophy, than those antient divines, and have done great service to the Church of God in some respects: but I humbly conceive, that their differing from their fathers, with such magisterial assurance, in these points in divinity, must be owing to some other cause than superior wisdom.

It may also be worthy of consideration, whether the great alteration, which has been made in the state of things in our nation, and some other parts of the Protestant world, in this and the past age, by the exploding so general *Calvinistic*

nistic doctrines, that is so often spoken of as worthy to be greatly rejoiced in by the friends of truth, learning and virtue, as an instance of the great increase of light in the Christian Church; I say, it may be worthy to be considered, whether this be indeed a happy change, owing to any such cause as an increase of true knowledge and understanding in things of religion; or whether there is not reason to fear, that it may be owing to some worse cause.

And I desire it may be considered, whether the boldness of some writers may not be worthy to be reflected on, who have not scrupled to say, that if these and those things are true (which yet appear to be the demonstrable dictates of reason, as well as the cetain dictates of the mouth of the Most High) then God is unjust and cruel, and guilty of manifest deceit and double dealing, and the like. Yea, some have gone so far, as confidently to assert, that if any book which pretends to be Scripture, teaches such doctrines, that alone is sufficient warrant for mankind to reject it, as what cannot be the Word of God. Some, who have not gone so far, have said, that if the Scripture seems to teach any such doctrines, so contrary to reason, we are obliged to find out some other interpretation of those texts, where such doctrines seem to be exhibited. Others express themselves yet more modestly: they express a tenderness and religious fear, least they should receive and teach any thing that should seem to reflect on God's moral character, or be a disparagement to his methods of administration, in his moral government; and therefore express themselves as not daring to embrace some doctrines, though they seem to be delivered in Scripture, according to the more obvious and natural con-

construction of the words. But indeed it would shew a truer modesty and humility, if they would more entirely rely on God's wisdom and discerning, who knows infinitely better than we, what is agreeable to his own perfections, and never intended to leave these matters to the decision of the wisdom and discerning of men; but by his own unerring instruction, to determine for us what the truth is; knowing how little our judgment is to be depended on, and extremely prone, vain and blind men are, to err in such matters.

THE truth of the case is, that if the Scripture plainly taught the opposite doctrines, to those that are so much stumbled at, *viz.* the *Arminian* doctrine of free-will, and others depending thereon, it would be the greatest of all difficulties that attend the Scriptures, incomparably greater than its containing any, even the most mysterious of those doctrines of the first reformers, which our late free thinkers have so superciliously exploded.—Indeed, it is a glorious argument of the divinity of the holy Scriptures, that they teach such doctrines, which in one age and another, through the blindness of men's minds, and strong prejudices of their hearts, are rejected, as most absurd and unreasonable, by the wise and great men of the world; which yet, when they are most carefully and strictly examined, appear to be exactly agreeable to the most demonstrable, certain, and natural dictates of reason. By such things it appears, that the *foolishness of God is wiser than men*, and God does as is said in 1 Cor. i. 19, 20. *For it is written, I will destroy the wisdom of the wise; I will bring to nothing the understanding of the prudent. Where is the wise! Where is the scribe! Where is the disputer of this world! Hath not God made foolish the wisdom of this world?* And as it is used ufed to be in time paft, fo it is probable it will be in time to come, as it is there written, in ver. 27, 28, 29. *But God hath chofen the foolifh things of the world, to confound the wife: and God hath chofen the weak things of the world, to confound the things that are mighty: and bafe things of the world, and things which are defpifed, hath God chofen: yea, and things which are not, to bring to nought things that are; that no flefh fhould glory in his prefence.* Amen.

INDEX.

INDEX.

[N. B. The capital P. signifies the *Part*; Sect. the *Section*; Concl. the *Conclusion*; and the small p. the *Page*; where the things here specified are to be found.]

A.

L.

M.

R.

S.

T.

V.

W.

REMARKS

ON THE

ESSAYS on the PRINCIPLES of MORALITY and NATURAL RELIGION.

In a LETTER to a Minister of the CHURCH of SCOTLAND:

By the Reverend Mr. JONATHAN EDWARDS, President of the College of NEW-JERSEY, and Author of the late INQUIRY into the MODERN NOTIONS of the FREEDOM of WILL.

Rev. SIR,

THE intimations you have given me of the use which has, by some, been made of what I have written on the *Freedom of the Will*, &c. to vindicate what is said on the subject of liberty and necessity, by the Author of the *Essays on the Principles of Morality and Natural Religion*, has occasioned my reading this Author's Essay on that subject, with particular care and attention. And I think it must be evident to every one, that has read both his *Essay* and my *Inquiry*, that our schemes are exceeding reverse from each other. The wide difference appears particularly in the following things.

THIS Author supposes, that such a necessity takes place with respect to all men's actions, as is inconsistent with liberty,* and plainly denies that men have any liberty in acting. Thus in p. 168. after he had been speaking of the necessity of our determinations,

* P. 160, 161, 164, 165, and many other places.

minations, as connected with motives, he concludes with ſaying, "In ſhort, if motives are not under our power or direction, which is confeſſedly the fact, we can at bottom have——NO LIBERTY." Whereas, I have abundantly expreſſed it as my mind, that man, in his moral actions, has true liberty; and that the moral neceſſity, which univerſally takes place, is not in the leaſt inconſiſtent with any thing that is properly called liberty, and with the utmoſt liberty that can be deſired, or that can poſſibly exiſt or be conceived of.*

I FIND that ſome are apt to think, that in that kind of moral neceſſity of men's volitions, which I ſuppoſe to be univerſal, at leaſt ſome degree of liberty is denied; that though it be true I allow a ſort of liberty, yet thoſe who maintain a ſelf-determining power in the will, and a liberty of contingence and indifference, hold an higher ſort of freedom than I do: but I think this is certainly a great miſtake.

LIBERTY, as I have explained it, in p. 38. and other places, is *the power, opportunity, or advantage that any one has to do as he pleaſes, or conducting,* IN ANY RESPECT *according to his pleaſure*; without conſidering how his pleaſure comes to be as it is. It is demonſtrable, and, I think, has been demonſtrated, that no neceſſity of men's volitions that I maintain, is inconſiſtent with this liberty: and I think it is impoſſible for any one to riſe higher in his conceptions of liberty than this: If any imagine they deſire higher, and that they conceive of a higher and greater liberty than this, they are deceived, and delude themſelves with confuſed ambiguous words, inſtead of ideas If any one ſhould here ſay, "Yes, I conceive of a freedom above and beyond the liberty a man has of conducting in any

* *Inquiry*, P. 38—43, 186, 187, 278—288 300, 307, 326, —335.

any respect as he pleases, *viz.* a liberty of *chusing* as he pleases." Such an one, if he reflected, would either blush or laugh at his own instance. For, is not chusing as he pleases, conducting, IN SOME RESPECT, according to his pleasure, and still without determining how he came by that pleasure? If he says, "Yes, I came by that pleasure by my own choice." If he be a man of common sense, by this time he will see his own absurdity: for he must needs see that his notion or conception, even of this liberty, does not contain any judgment or conception how he comes by that choice, which first determines his pleasure, or which originally fixed his own will respecting the affair. Or if any shall say, "That a man exercises liberty in this, even in determining his own choice, but not as he pleases, or not in consequence of any choice, preference, or inclination of his own, but by a determination arising contingently out of a state of absolute indifference;" this is not rising higher in his conception of liberty: as such a determination of the will would not be a voluntary determination of it. Surely he that places liberty in a power of doing something not according to his own choice, or from his choice, has not a higher notion of it, than he that places it in doing as he pleases, or acting from his own election. If there were a power in the mind to determine itself, but not by its choice or according to its pleasure, what advantage would it give? and what liberty, worth contending for, would be exercised in it? Therefore no *Arminian*, *Pelagian*, or *Epicurean*, can rise higher in his conceptions of liberty, than the notions of it which I have explained: which notion is apparently, perfectly consistent with the whole of that necessity of men's actions, which I suppose takes place. And I scruple not to say, it is beyond all their wits to invent a higher notion, or

form

form a higher imagination of liberty; let them talk of *sovereignty of the will, self-determining power, self-motion, self-direction, arbitrary decision, liberty,* ad utrumvis, *power of chusing differently in given cases,* &c. &c. as long as they will. It is apparent that these men, in their strenuous affirmation, and dispute about these things, aim at they know not what, fighting for something they have no conception of, substituting a number of confused unmeaning words, instead of things, and instead of thoughts. They may be challenged clearly to explain what they would have: they never can answer the challenge.

The Author of the *Essays*, through his whole Essay on Liberty and Necessity, goes on that supposition, that, in order to the being of real liberty, a man must have a freedom that is opposed to moral necessity: and yet he supposes, p. 175, that *such a liberty must signify a power in the mind of acting without and against motives, a power of acting without any view, purpose, or design, and even of acting in contradiction to our own desires and aversions, and to all our principles of action; and is an absurdity altogether inconsistent with a rational nature.* Now, who ever imagined such a liberty as this, a higher sort or degree of freedom, than a liberty of following one's own view and purposes, and acting agreeable to his own inclinations and passions? Who will ever reasonably suppose that liberty, which is an absurdity altogether inconsistent with a rational nature, to be a kind of liberty above that which is consistent with the nature of a rational, intelligent, designing agent.

The Author of the *Essays* seems to suppose such a necessity to take place, as is inconsistent with some supposable POWER OF ARBITRARY CHOICE;* or that there is some liberty conceivable, whereby men's

* P. 169.

men's own actions might be more PROPERLY IN THEIR POWER,* and by which events might be more DEPENDENT ON OURSELVES:† contrary to what I suppose to be evident in my *Inquiry*.‡ What way can be imagined, of our actions being more *in our power*, *from ourselves*, or *dependent on ourselves*, than their being from our power to fulfil our own choice, to act from our own inclination, pursue our own views, and execute our own designs? Certainly, to be able to act thus, is as properly having our actions in our power, and dependent on ourselves, as a being liable to be the subjects of acts and events, contingently and fortuitously, *without desire, view, purpose or design, or any principle of action* within ourselves; as we must be, according to this Author's own declared sense, if our actions are performed with that liberty that is opposed to moral necessity.

THIS Author seems every where to suppose, that necessity, most properly so called, attends all men's actions; and that the terms *necessary*, *unavoidable*, *impossible*, &c. are equally applicable to the case of moral and natural necessity. In p. 173, he says, *The idea* of necessary *and* unavoidable *equally agrees, both to moral and physical necessity*. And in p. 184, *All things that fall out in the natural and moral world are alike necessary*. P. 174, *This inclination and choice is* unavoidably *caused or occasioned by the prevailing motive. In this lies the necessity of our actions, that, in such circumstances, it was* impossible *we* could *act otherwise*. He often expresses himself in like manner elsewhere, speaking in strong terms of men's actions as *unavoidable*, what they *cannot* forbear, having *no power* over their own actions, the order of them being *unalterably* fixed, and *inseparably* linked together, &c.||

On

* P. 191, 195, 197, 206. † P. 183. ‡ P. 395, 396.
|| P. 180, 188, 193, 194, 195, 197, 198, 199, 205, 206.

On the contrary, I have largely declared, that the connection between antecedent things and consequent ones, which takes place with regard to the acts of men's wills, which is called moral necessity, is called by the name of *Necessity* improperly; and that all such terms as *must*, *cannot*, *impossible*, *unable*, *irresistible*, *unavoidable*, *invincible*, &c. when applied here, are not applied in their proper signification, and are either used nonsensically, and with perfect insignificance, or in a sense quite diverse from their original and proper meaning, and their use in common speech:* and, that such a necessity as attends the acts of men's wills, is more properly called *certainty*, than *necessity*; it being no other than the certain connection between the subject and predicate of the proposition which affirms their existence.†

Agreable to what is observed in my *Inquiry*,‡ I think it is evidently owing to a strong prejudice in persons minds, arising from an insensible habitual perversion and misapplication of such-like terms, as *necessary*, *impossible*, *unable*, *unavoidable*, *invincible*, &c. that they are ready to think, that to suppose a certain connection of men's volitions, without any foregoing motives or inclinations, or any preceding moral influence whatsoever is truly and properly to suppose such a strong irrefragable chain of causes and effects, as stands in the way of, and makes utterly vain, opposite desires and endeavours, like immovable and impenetrable mountains of brass; and impedes our liberty like walls of adamant, gates of brass, and bars of iron: whereas, all such representations suggest ideas as far from the truth, as the East is from the West. Nothing

* *Inquiry*, P. 18—28, 32, 33, 34, 36, 37, 232, 289—293, 296, 304——308, 397, 398. † *Inquiry*, P. 22—24. ‡ P. 289—293.

Nothing that I maintain, ſuppoſes that men are at all hindered by any fatal neceſſity, from doing, and even willing and chuſing as they pleaſe, with full freedom, yea with the higheſt degree of liberty that ever was thought of, or that ever could poſſibly enter into the heart of any man to conceive. I know it is in vain to endeavour to make ſome perſons believe this, or at leaſt fully and ſteadily to believe it: for if it be demonſtrated to them, ſtill the old prejudice remains, which has been long fixed by the uſe of the terms *neceſſary*, *muſt*, *cannot*, *impoſſible*, &c. the aſſociation with theſe terms of certain ideas inconſiſtent with liberty, is not broken; and the judgment is powerfully warped by it; as a thing that has been long bent and grown ſtiff, if it be ſtraitened, will return to its former curvity again and again.

The Author of the *Eſſays* moſt manifeſtly ſuppoſes, that if men had the truth concerning the real neceſſity of all their actions clearly in view, they would not appear to themſelves, or one another, as at all praiſe-worthy or culpable, or under any moral obligation, or accountable for their actions:* which ſuppoſes, that men are not to be blamed or praiſed for any of their actions, and are not under any obligations, nor are truly accountable for any thing they do, by reaſon of this neceſſity; which is very contrary to what I have endeavoured to prove, throughout the *third part* of my *Inquiry*. I humbly conceive it is there ſhewn, that this is ſo far from the truth, that the moral neceſſity of men's actions, which truly take place, is requiſite to the being of virtue and vice, or any thing praiſe worthy or culpable: that the liberty of indifference and contingence, which is advanced in oppoſition to that neceſſity, is inconſiſtent with the being of theſe;

* P. 207, 209, and other places.

theſe; as it would ſuppoſe that men are not determined in what they do, by any virtuous or vicious principles, nor act from any motives, intentions or aims whatſoever; or have any end, either good or bad, in acting. And is it not remarkable, that this Author ſhould ſuppoſe, that, in order to men's actions truly having any deſert, they muſt be performed *without any view, purpoſe, deſign, or deſire*, or *any principle of action*, or any thing *agreable to a rational nature?* As it will appear that he does, if we compare, p. 206, 207, with p. 175.

THE Author of the *Eſſays* ſuppoſes, that God has deeply implanted in man's nature, a ſtrong and invincible apprehenſion, or feeling, as he calls it, of a liberty, and contingence of his own actions, oppoſite to that neceſſity which truly attends them; and which in truth does not agree with real fact,* is not agreable to ſtrict philoſophic truth,† is contradictory to the truth of things,‡ and which truth contradicts,‖ not tallying with the real plan:§ and that therefore ſuch feelings are deceitful,** are in reality of the deluſive kind.†† He ſpeaks of them as a wiſe deluſion,‡‡ as nice artificial feelings, merely that conſcience may have a commanding power:‖‖ meaning plainly, that theſe feelings are a cunning artifice of the Author of Nature, to make men believe they are free, when they are not.§§ He ſuppoſes that, by theſe feelings, the moral world has a diſguiſed appearance.‡‡‡ And other things of this kind he ſays. He ſuppoſes that all ſelf-approbation, and all remorſe of conſcience, all commendation or condemnation of ourſelves or others, all ſenſe of deſert, and all that is connected with this way of thinking, all the ideas, which at preſent are ſuggeſted by the words

ought,

* P. 200. † P. 152. ‡ *P*. 183. ‖ P. 186. § P. 205. ** P. 203, 204, 211. †† P. 183. ‡‡ P. 209. ‖‖ P. 211. §§ P. 153. ‡‡‡ P. 214.

ought, *ſhould*, ariſe fro[m] th[is] deluſion, and would entirely vaniſh witho[ut] it.*

ALL which is very contrary to what I have abundantly inſiſted on and endeavoured to demonſtrate in my *Inquiry*; where I have largely ſhewn, that it is agreable to the natural ſenſe of mankind, that the moral neceſſity or certainty that attends men's actions, is conſiſtent with praiſe and blame, reward and puniſhment;† and that it is agreable to our natural notions, that moral evil, with its deſert of diſlike and abhorrence, and all its other ill-deſervings, conſiſts in a certain deformity in the nature of the diſpoſitions and acts of the heart, and not in the evil of ſomething elſe, diverſe from theſe, ſuppoſed to be their cauſe or occaſion ‡

I MIGHT well aſk here, whether any one is to be found in the world of mankind, who is conſcious to a ſenſe or feeling, naturally and deeply rooted in his mind, that, in order to a man's p[e]rforming any action that is praiſe or blame-worthy, he muſt exerciſe a liberty that implies and ſignifies a power of acting without any motive, view, deſign, deſire, or principle of action? For ſuch a liberty, this Author ſuppoſes, that muſt be which is oppoſed to moral neceſſity, as I have already obſerved once and again. Suppoſing a man ſhould actually do good, independent of deſire, aim, inducement, principle or end, is it a dictate of invincible natural ſenſe, that his act is more meritorious or praiſe-worthy, than if he had performed it for ſome *good end*, and had been governed in it by *good principles* and *motives?* and ſo I might aſk, on the contrary, with reſpect to evil actions.||

THE

* P. 160, 194. 199. 205, 206, 207, 209. † *Inquiry* Part IV. Sect. 4. throughout. ‡ *Idem* Part IV. Sect. 1. throughout. and P 395—.97. || See this Matter illuſtrated in my *Inquiry*, Part IV. Sect. 4. eſpecially, 302—304.

The Author of the *Essays* supposes that the liberty without necessity, which we have a natural feeling of, implies *contingence:* and, speaking of this contingence, he sometimes calls it by the name of *Chance.* And it is evident that his notion of it, or rather what he says about it, implies things happening *loosely*, *fortuitously*, by *accident*, and *without a cause**. Now I conceive the slightest reflection may be sufficient to satisfy any one, that such a contingence of men's actions, according to our natural sense, is so far from being essential to the mortality or merit of those actions, that it would destroy it; and that, on the contrary, the dependence of our actions on such causes, as inward inclinations, incitements and ends, is essential to the being of it. Natural sense teaches men, when they see any thing done by others of a good or evil tendency, to inquire what their intention was; what principles and views they were moved by, in order to judge how far they are to be justified or condemned; and not to determine, that, in order to their being approved or blamed at all, the action must be performed altogether fortuitously, proceeding from nothing, arising from no cause. Concerning this matter, I have fully expressed my mind in the *Inquiry* †.

If the liberty, which we have a natural sense of as necessary to desert, consists in the mind's self-determination, without being determined by previous inclination or motive, then indifference is essential to it, yea absolute indifference; as is observed in my *Inquiry* ‡. But men naturally have no notion of any such liberty as this, as essential to the morality or demerit of their actions; but, on the contrary, such a liberty, if it were possible, would be inconsistent

* P. 156, 157, 158, 159, 177, 178, 181. 183, 184, 185.

† P. 258--261, 267, 302, 303, and other Places.

‡ P. 89--91.

inconſiſtent with our natural notions of deſert, as is largely ſhown in the *Inquiry* *. If it be agreeable to natural ſenſe, that men muſt be indifferent in determining their own actions; then, according to the ſame, the more they are determined by inclination, either good or bad, the leſs they have of deſert: the more good actions are performed from good diſpoſition, the leſs praiſe worthy; and the more evil deeds are from evil diſpoſitions, the leſs culpable; and, in general, the more men's actions are from their hearts, the leſs they are to be commended or condemned: which all muſt know is very contrary to natural ſenſe.

Moral neceſſity is owing to the power and government of the inclination of the heart, either habitual or occaſional, excited by motive: but, according to natural and common ſenſe, the more a man does any thing with full inclination of heart, the more is it to be charged to his account for his condemnation, if it be an ill action, and the more to be aſcribed to him for his praiſe, if it be good.

If the mind were determined to evil actions by contingence, from a ſtate of indifference, then either there would be no fault in them, or elſe the fault would be in being ſo perfectly indifferent, that the mind was equally liable to a bad or good determination. And, if this indifference be liberty, then the very eſſence of the blame or fault would lie in the liberty itſelf, or the wickedneſs would, primarily and ſummarily, lie in being a free agent. If there were no fault in being indifferent, then there would be no fault in the determination's being agreeable to ſuch a ſtate of indifference: that is, there could no

 fault

* Eſpecially in Part III. Sect. 6, and 7.

fault be reasonably found with this, *viz.* that opposite determinations actually happen to take place *indifferently*, sometimes good and sometimes bad, as contingence governs and decides. And if it be a fault to be indifferent to good and evil, then such indifference is no indifference to good and evil, but is a determination to evil, or to a fault; and such an indifferent disposition would be an evil, faulty disposition, tendency or determination of mind. So inconsistent are these notions of liberty, as essential to praise or blame.

THE Author of the *Essays* supposes men's natural delusive sense of a liberty of contingence, to be, in truth, the foundation of all the labour, care and industry of mankind*; and that if men's *practical ideas had been formed on the plan of universal necessity, the* ignava ratio, *the inactive doctrine of the* Stoics, *would have followed; and that there would have been no* ROOM *for forethought about futurity, or any sort of industry and care* †: plainly implying, that, in this case, men would see and know that all their industry and care signified nothing, was in vain, and to no purpose, or of no benefit; events being fixed in an irrefragable chain, and not at all DEPENDING on their care and endeavour; as he explains himself, particularly, in the instance of men's use of means to prolong life ‡: not only very contrary to what I largely maintain in my *Inquiry* §, but also very inconsistently with his own scheme, in what he supposes of the ends for which God has so deeply implanted this deceitful feeling in man's nature; in which he manifestly supposes men's care

* P. 184. † P. 189. ‡ P. 184, 185. § Especially Part IV. Sect. 5.

care and industry not to be in vain and of no benefit, but of great use, yea of absolute necessity, in order to the obtaining the most important ends and necessary purposes of human life, and to fulfil the ends of action to the BEST ADVANTAGE; as he largely declares *. Now, how shall these things be reconciled? That, if men had *a clear view of real truth*, they would see that there was *no* ROOM for their care and industry, because they would see it to be in vain, and of no benefit; and yet that God, by having a clear view of real truth, sees that their being excited to care and industry, will be of excellent use to mankind, and greatly for the benefit of the world, yea absolutely necessary in order to it: and that therefore the great wisdom and goodness of God to men appears, in artfully contriving to put them on care and industry for their good, which good could not be obtained without them; and yet both these things are maintained at once, and in the same sentences and words by this Author. The very reason he gives, why God has put this deceitful feeling into men, contradicts and destroys itself; that God in his great goodness to men gave them such a deceitful feeling, because it was very useful and necessary for them, and greatly for their benefit, or excites them to care and industry for their own good, which care and industry is useful and necessary to that end: and yet the very thing that this great benefit of care and industry is given as a reason for, is God's deceiving men in this very point, in making them think their care and industry to be of great benefit to them, when indeed it is of none at all; and if they saw the real truth, they would see all their

* P. 188—192. and in many other Places.

endeavours to be wholly uſeleſs, that there was NO ROOM for them, and that the event does not at all DEPEND upon them *.

AND beſides, what this Author ſays, plainly implies (as appears by what has been already obſerved) that it is neceſſary men ſhould be deceived, by being made to believe that future events are contingent, and their own future actions free, with ſuch a freedom, as ſignifies that their actions are not the fruit of their own deſires, or deſigns, but altogether contingent, fortuitous and without a cauſe. But how ſhould a notion of liberty, conſiſting in accident or looſe chance, encourage care and induſtry? I ſhould think it would rather entirely diſcourage every thing of this nature. For ſurely, if our actions do not depend on our deſires and deſigns, then they do not depend on our endeavours, flowing from our deſires and deſigns. This Author himſelf ſeems to ſuppoſe, that if men had, indeed, ſuch a liberty of contingence, it would render all endeavours to determine or move men's future volitions, in vain: he ſays, that, in this caſe, *to exhort to inſtruct, to promiſe, or to threaten*, would be to no purpoſe †. Why? Becauſe (as he himſelf gives the reaſon), *then our will would be capricious and arbitrary, and we ſhould be thrown looſe altogether, and our arbitrary power could do us good or ill only by accident.* But if ſuch a looſe fortuitous ſtate would render vain other endeavours upon us, for the ſame reaſon would it make uſeleſs our endeavours on ourſelves: for events that are truly contingent and accidental, and altogether looſe from, and independent of, all foregoing cauſes, are independent on every foregoing cauſe within ourſelves, as well as in others.

I SUP-

* P. 188, 189, &c. † P. 178, 213, 214.

I suppose that it is ſo far from being true, that our minds are naturally poſſeſſed with a notion of ſuch liberty as this, ſo ſtrongly, that it is impoſſible to root it out, that indeed men have no ſuch notion of liberty at all, and that it is utterly impoſſible, by any means whatſoever to implant or introduce ſuch a notion into the mind. As no ſuch notions as imply ſelf contradiction and ſelf-abolition can ſubſiſt in the mind, as I have ſhewn in my *Inquiry* *; I think a mature ſenſible conſideration of the matter, ſufficient to ſatisfy any one, that even the greateſt and moſt learned advocate themſelves for liberty of indifference and ſelf determination, have no ſuch notion; and that indeed they mean ſomething wholly inconſiſtent with, and directly ſubverſive of, what they ſtrenuouſly affirm, and earneſtly contend for. By a man's having a power of determining his own will, they plainly mean a power of determining his will, as he pleaſes, or as he chuſes; which ſuppoſes that the mind has a choice, prior to its going about to confirm any action or determination to it. And if they mean that they determine even the original or prime choice, by their own pleaſure or choice, as the thing that cauſes and directs it; I ſcruple not moſt boldly to affirm, that they ſpeak they know not what, and that of which they have no manner of idea; becauſe no ſuch contradictory notion can come into, or have a moment's ſubſiſtence in, the mind of any man living, as an original or firſt choice being cauſed, or brought into being, by choice. After all, they ſay, they have no higher or other conception of liberty, than that vulgar notion of it, which I contend for, *viz.* a man's having power or opportunity

* P. 257.–258. See alſo P. 49, 56, 57, 73, 74, 79, 183.—187, 281, 282, 298—301.

nity to do as he chooses: or if they had a notion that every act of choice was determined by choice, yet it would destroy their notion of the contingence of choice; for then no one act of choice would arise contingently, or from a state of indifference, but every individual act, in all the series, would arise from foregoing bias or preference, and from a cause predetermining and fixing its existence, which introduces at once such a chain of causes and effects, each preceding link decisively fixing the following, as they would by all means avoid.

And such kind of delusion and self-contradiction as this, does not arise in men's minds by nature; it is not owing to any natural feeling which God has strongly fixed in the mind and nature of man; but to false philosophy, and strong prejudice, from a deceitful abuse of words. It is *artificial*; not in the sense of the Author of the *Essays*, supposing it to be a deceitful artifice of God; but artificial as opposed to natural, and as owing to an artificial deceitful management of terms, to darken and confound the mind. Men have no such thing when they first begin to exercise reason; but must have a great deal of time to blind themselves, with metaphysical confusion, before they can embrace, and rest in such definitions of liberty as are given, and imagine they understand them.

On the whole, I humbly conceive, that whosoever will give himself the trouble of weighing, what I have offered to consideration in my *Inquiry*, must be sensible, that such a moral necessity of men's actions as I maintain, is not at all inconsistent with any liberty that any creature has, or can have, as a free, accountable, moral agent, and subject of moral government; and that this moral necessity is so far from being inconsistent with praise and blame, and the benefit and use of men's own care

and

and labour, that, on the contrary, it implies the very ground and reason, why men's actions are to be ascribed to them as their own, in that manner as to infer desert, praise and blame, approbation and remorse of conscience, reward and punishment; and that it establishes the moral system of the universe, and God's moral government, in every respect, with the proper use of motives, exhortations, commands, counsels, promises, and threatenings; and the use and benefit of endeavours, care and industry: and that therefore there is no need that the strict philosophic truth should be at all concealed from men; no danger in *contemplation* and *profound discovery* in these things. So far from this, that the truth in this matter is of vast importance, and extremely needful to be known; and that the more clearly and perfectly the real fact is known, and the more constantly it is in view, the better; and particularly, that the clear and full knowledge of that, which is the true system of the universe, in these respects, would greatly establish the doctrines which teach the true Christian scheme of Divine Administration in the city of God, and the Gospel of Jesus Christ, in its most important articles; and that these things never can be well established, and the opposite errors, so subversive of the whole Gospel, which at this day so greatly and generally prevail, be well confuted, or the arguments by which they are maintained, answered, till these points are settled: while this is not done, it is, to me, beyond doubt, that the friends of those great Gospel Truths, will but poorly maintain their controversy with the adversaries of those truths: they will be obliged often to dodge, shuffle, hide, and turn their backs; and the latter will have a strong fort, from whence they never can be driven, and weapons to use, which those whom they oppose will find no shield to ſcreen themſelves from; and they will always puzzle, confound, and keep under the friends of ſound doctrine; and glory, and vaunt themſelves in their advantage over them; and carry their affairs with an high hand, as they have done already for a long time paſt.

I CONCLUDE, Sir, with aſking your pardon for troubling you with ſo much ſaid in vindication of myſelf from the imputation of advancing a ſcheme of neceſſity, of a like nature with that of the Author of the *Eſſays on the principles of Morality and Natural Religion.* Conſidering that what I have ſaid is not only in vindication of myſelf, but, as I think, of the moſt important articles of moral philoſophy and religion; I truſt in what I know of your candour, that you will excuſe,

Your obliged friend and brother,

J. EDWARDS.

STOCKBRIDGE,
July 25, 1757.

F I N I S.

www.ingramcontent.com/pod-product-compliance
Lightning Source LLC
LaVergne TN
LVHW042123070326
832902LV00036B/562

* 9 7 8 3 7 4 2 8 4 0 6 7 7 *